Drug
Dependence

JASON M. WHITE

University of Adelaide

PRENTICE HALL, Englewood Cliffs, New Jersey 07632

Library of Congress Cataloging-in-Publication Data

WHITE, JASON M.
  Drug dependence / Jason M. White.
    p. cm.
  Includes bibliographical references.
  Includes index.
  ISBN 0-13-221607-8
  1. Drug abuse. 2. Drug abuse—Treatment. I. Title.
  [DNLM: 1. Substance Dependence. WM 270 W585d]
  HV5801.W439 1991
  362.29—dc20
  DNLM/DLC
  for Library of Congress   90-7619
                                      CIP

Editorial/production supervision
  and interior design: Rob DeGeorge
Cover design: Ray Lundgren Graphics, Ltd.
Prepress Buyer: Debbie Kesar
Manufacturing buyer: Mary Ann Gloriande

© 1991 by Prentice-Hall, Inc.
A Division of Simon & Schuster
Englewood Cliffs, New Jersey 07632

Printed in the United States of America

10 9 8 7 6 5 4 3 2 1

ISBN 0-13-221607-8

PRENTICE-HALL INTERNATIONAL (UK) LIMITED, *London*
PRENTICE-HALL OF AUSTRALIA PTY. LIMITED, *Sydney*
PRENTICE-HALL CANADA INC., *Toronto*
PRENTICE-HALL HISPANOAMERICANA, S.A., *Mexico*
PRENTICE-HALL OF INDIA PRIVATE LIMITED, *New Delhi*
PRENTICE-HALL OF JAPAN, INC., *Tokyo*
SIMON & SCHUSTER ASIA PTE. LTD., *Singapore*
EDITORA PRENTICE-HALL DO BRASIL, LTDA., *Rio de Janeiro*

Contents

4 SOCIAL ASPECTS   *164*

Preface

The use of drugs that alter our behavior and subjective experience is wide-spread in all modern societies. We take for granted the fact that most of us act under the influence of a drug at one time or another and that considerable resources are devoted to drug production and distribution. These drugs may either be accepted (caffeine, for example) or controlled in some way. Controls vary from complete prohibition (heroin or cocaine to name two) to more moderate restrictions (as is the case with alcohol). Increasingly, it is being recognized that there is a great deal of commonality in the factors determining use of, and dependence on, these differing drugs. Research shows that practices as diverse as cigarette smoking and intravenous heroin usage have much in common.

The above is the basic approach of this book. The first chapter provides an overview of drugs under discussion. It covers origins, effects, medical uses, and the history of each drug in particular. Those discussed range from plants used over thousands of years to modern pharmaceuticals. The main body of the text is contained in the next three chapters. These deal with biological, psychological, and social aspects of drug use, respectively. Each chapter is written at an introductory level so that no particular background is assumed. While examples are given from the different drug classes, emphasis is placed on the general principles that help our understanding of drug use. The final two chapters are concerned with problems that can arise from drug use and how these can be dealt with. The first of these discusses medical consequences, and the final chapter deals with therapy for dependence problems. In both cases, the reader is given a broad overview rather than a description of how to carry out particular treatments.

A limited number of references have been cited in the text. Wherever possible, I have tried to select the best available reviews so that the reader can pursue particular issues of interest. In other cases, original research reports have been cited—either for illustration or as support for some point of controversy.

Research on drug use is producing exciting findings on many fronts. We now understand much about the diverse determinants of drug use and dependence. The reader looking for simple answers to "the drug problem" will not find them here. What I hope they will find is a complex and fascinating picture of this important aspect of human behavior.

There are numerous people who have contributed to this book in some way. First and foremost, there are the many teachers, colleagues, and students whose ideas have influenced me. I hope the synthesis presented here is a worthy one. I also wish to thank those who helped with typing and preparation, particularly Ingrid Portans, Despina Green, Tina Schulze, and Allison Vaughton. Finally, the patience and support shown by my wife and two daughters has been invaluable.

CHAPTER 1

Introduction: Drugs and Dependence

The use of drugs is often considered a problem that needs an effective solution. People are galvanized by the popular media, and governments are forced into action against this "evil" in society. In reality it is almost impossible to separate drug use from any society. Such use is part of our heritage: many customs and rituals involve drug consumption, and the production and distribution of drugs is an important part of most economies.

Within most contemporary societies a great variety of drugs are available. There are always socially acceptable drugs, on which few restrictions are placed. In the West these include caffeine, alcohol, and nicotine. Other drugs are intended to be used for medical purposes, and regulations and delivery systems have been developed to try to ensure use is restricted to these purposes only. Some drugs are totally proscribed by law, however, and in most modern societies heroin and cocaine fall into this category.

Drugs in the first group are unique because we are socialized to use them. Children observe their parents and other adults using these drugs, and as a consequence, are likely to follow in their footsteps. This may result in moderate use of the drug, which allows the person to experience its beneficial effects without the deleterious consequences which can result from over-use. On the other hand, there will always be a certain proportion of people who use these drugs excessively, ultimately causing problems for themselves and others around them.

Social judgments regarding drug acceptability change with time. Acceptable or common patterns of drug use of any given era may be completely altered fifty or one hundred years later. So, what is now penalized heavily by law may become the standard intoxicant in the future. Change happens to be occurring now in the case of tobacco. Smoking has been considered acceptable in many societies, but as evidence of its danger to health accumulates, it is becoming less and less so. Although it is still legal, acceptance of the practice is declining.

Medical uses also change with time. Virtually every drug that is now illegal has been used for medical purposes at some time. Amphetamine for example, was prescribed as an appetite suppressant only a few years ago, but today, its medical uses are few. Instead, it is used outside of medical contexts in an illegal manner. While the medical use of some drugs is curtailed in this way however, new drugs are constantly being introduced — and this seems to be occurring at an ever increasing rate.

This constant change, the differences in drug use between contemporary societies, and the way in which some drugs are used both medically and nonmedically, make it impossible to categorize drugs in terms of their acceptability to society. Thus, while we frequently define a drug as being either legal or illegal, prescription or "street drug," etc., these categories are not well-defined and are subject to frequent change. It will also become clear later in the book that these categories have little logical status. There are simply many reasons why a drug is accepted in society or not. The effects of the drug itself are only one factor determining this.

The remainder of this chapter is devoted in part to a description of a number of drugs that can be used in a voluntary way. That is, drugs which people choose to use outside of any need created by illness or other clear medical or psychological symptoms. Each drug (or drug group) is introduced with an explanation of its origin, and the effects of the drug are described in general terms. Medical uses are mentioned and then a short history of the drug is given.

In doing this, it is necessary to classify the drugs under discussion. There are so many used in this way that it would be both wasteful and inefficient to consider them individually. It should be recognized that any such classification can only be flawed: Any two pharmacology textbooks are likely to classify drugs in different ways. However, the classifications are all based on commonalities in the effects of the drugs and in the way they produce these effects rather than criteria such as legality or societal patterns. The classification employed in this text is as follows:

Opiates—morphine, heroin, codeine, etc.
Sedative—Hypnotic/Antianxiety

  a) Barbiturates—pentobarbital, phenobarbital, etc.
  b) Benzodiazepines—diazepam, chlordiazepoxide, etc.
  c) Alcohol
  d) Others—meprobamate, methaqualone, etc.

Psychomotor Stimulants

  a) Amphetamine group—amphetamine, methylphenidate, etc.
  b) Cocaine
  c) Nicotine
  d) Caffeine

Hallucinogens

  a) LSD group—LSD, mescaline, psilocybin, DOM, MDA, etc.
  b) PCP

Anticholinergics—atropine, scopolamine
Marijuana
Solvents and Aerosols—toluene, nitrous oxide, etc.
Miscellaneous—Betel, Kava-Kava, etc.

The list presented here should not be regarded as comprehensive. There are, of course, other drugs that could have been included. However, most of the major drugs and drug classes used in a voluntary, nonmedical manner are covered. Not included are certain drugs used only in relatively narrow geographical locations (for example, certain stimulants and hallucinogens used in South American countries) and drugs that are only rarely used outside of medical contexts (such as antidepressants).

TERMINOLOGY

Before discussing individual drugs or drug classes, two issues should be covered: drug terminology and the use of such terms as "dependence," "addiction," and "abuse," among others.

Drug Terminology

Several notes need to be made concerning terminology. First, the term *drug* will be used here in a very general sense. It is often suggested that this term should only be employed when the substance is used medically. This seems simple enough, but raises a number of questions. Are vitamins drugs? Is alcohol a drug since it is used as an antiseptic? What if the substance was originally used medically, but is not now? Instead, the usage adopted here is the more common one and includes a variety of substances not employed in medical contexts. The substances to be discussed are those which fall into the categories above.

Another issue concerns the differing names given to each drug. In general, drugs used medically in recent times have three types of names: The *chemical name* is of interest only to certain people involved in drug research. The *generic name* is the more general name given to that particular drug and the *trade name* is used in the marketing of the drug. Where a drug is sold by several different pharmaceutical companies it may have several different trade names. For example, diazepam (generic name) was originally sold only under the trade name Valium, but is now sold under a variety of other names—the patent has expired and it is manufactured by several pharmaceutical companies. Further confusion arises because the same drug may be given different trade names in different countries, even when produced by the same manufacturer. For these reasons, generic names will be used throughout. Examples of generic names and equivalent trade names for Australia, the U.K., and the U.S. are given in Table 1.1.

There are also many *street* or *common* names for drugs. Heroin is sometimes known as "smack" and PCP as "angel dust." But current names change and they also vary from country to country, and within the differing social groups of a given country. Such terms will not be used here unless they are of particular importance.

Common terms for drug classes have been used in the classification. Thus, certain drugs are *sedative-hypnotics* or *psychomotor stimulants*. How-

TABLE 1.1 Generic Names and Examples of Trade Names for Therapeutic Drug Classes

GENERIC NAME	TRADE NAMES		
	U.S.	U.K.	AUSTRALIA
Opiates			
morphine	Duramorph MS Contin	Mundidol	Anamorph Morphalgin
fentanyl	Sublimaze	Sublimaze	Sublimaze
methadone	Althose Dolophine	Physeptone	Physeptone
pentazocine	Talwin Fortral	Fortral	Fortral
buprenorphine	Buprenex	Temgesic	Temgesic
Barbiturates			
pentobarbital/ pentobarbitone (short-acting)	Dorsital Nembutal	Nembutal	Carbrital Nembutal
phenobarbital/ phenobarbitone (long-acting)	Eskibarb Luminal	Luminal	(Phenobarbitone)
amobarbital/ amylobarbitone (intermediate acting)	Amytal	Amytal	Neur-Amyl
Benzodiazepines			
diazepam	Valium Q-pam	Valium Tensium	Valium Pro-pam
oxazepam	Serax	Serenid	Serepax Alepam
flurazepam	Dalmane	Dalmane	Dalmane
chlordiazepoxide	Librium Murcil	Librium Tropium	Librium
Psychomotor Stimulants			
amphetamine	Dexamex Amphate	Benzedrine Dexedrine	Dexamphetamine
methylphenidate	Ritalin	Ritalin	Ritalin
phenmetrazine	Preludin	Preludin	
Anticholinergics			

Atropine, scopolamine, and hyoscine appear in a variety of over-the-counter medications and mixed with a variety of other drugs. Pure drug is used mainly in injectable form.

ever, as will be discussed in Chapter Three, such terms do not always provide good descriptions of the effects of the drugs: In essence, sedatives do not always sedate, and stimulants do not always stimulate. These terms are inappropriate, but for historical reasons the labels have remained.

Dependence, Addiction, and Abuse

While drugs can be and frequently are used casually and infrequently, some people seem to use them to excess. This manifests itself in several ways. For instance, lifestyle can be oriented around obtaining and taking the drug. If the particular drug is affordable, easily available, easily consumed, and does not produce obvious intoxicating effects, then drug use may not interfere with other aspects of their lives to any great extent. Two examples of drugs such as these are caffeine (from tea and coffee) and nicotine (from cigarettes). Both can be used excessively with relatively little immediate impact on the user's life, even though chronic high level use is associated with considerable health risks.

Alcohol is a slightly different case. It is somewhat less affordable, and less readily available (because of restrictions on sale), but is easily consumed. And it does produce an obvious intoxicating effect. A person who uses alcohol excessively cannot carry on their life as if they never used the drug — there are likely to be frequent periods of intoxication that can interfere with other activities. The excessive alcohol user has to dedicate more time and effort to drinking and in experiencing drinking consequences than the smoker or coffee drinker does with regard to his or her drug use.

At the other end of the spectrum are a number of illegal drugs. Because they are illegal they are almost always expensive, somewhat more difficult to obtain, and not always in an easily consumable form. Illegal drugs may vary as to the degree of intoxicating effects they produce. In the doses usually taken, few would have the profound effects of a large dose of alcohol. For example, marijuana intoxication may result in some excitation, talkativeness, etc., followed by a period of sedation, but normal activities are not otherwise impaired. Similarly, an opiate may render the user apparently sleepy, but there is no gross disruption to behavior. Even if they do not produce such intoxication, illegal drug use may dominate a person's life. Very often this is simply because of the difficulty inherent in obtaining the money to buy drugs.

If a person's life seems to be oriented around taking drugs, they are often said to be *dependent* on the drug. Thus, a person who drinks fifteen cups of coffee a day has to arrange his or her life to ensure that the coffee is available throughout the day. The forty-a-day smoker has to have cigarettes available almost all the time and spend several hours a day smoking. The heroin user has to get sufficient money and then obtain enough "fixes" to last through the day, as well as go through the ritual of preparation and administration. In this particular case, there may be little time for anything else.

When such dependence occurs, people often look for causes. Two main types of causes are often proposed: *physical* and *psychological*. Physical dependence is said to occur when the body seems to need the constant presence of the drug; if drug use is suddenly terminated then the person suffers withdrawal. Because the symptoms of withdrawal are unpleasant, drug use may continue in order to alleviate them. This will be discussed in Chapter Two.

Psychological dependence is a little harder to define, but occurs when an individual finds a drug so attractive that he or she seems unable to stop using it. It may be that if the individual finds his or her life to be somewhat bland, those periods under the influence of the drug shine out. Unfortunately, psychological dependence is not so clearly marked by withdrawal symptoms when drug use discontinues. Nevertheless, the phenomenon is real enough and will be discussed further in Chapter Three.

The term addiction is also used when referring to repeated drug use; persons can be addicted to drugs and too, drugs can be highly addictive. For the person, the words "addicted" and "dependent" will be used in the text synonymously. Labelling drugs as addictive or not addictive is another matter. A drug may be more or less likely to be used repeatedly, and a drug may be more or less likely to induce physical dependence in the long-term user. These evaluations can be made and will be discussed. But a simple judgment as to whether a drug is addictive or not is almost impossible. In the right circumstance, any drug can be addictive. As we shall see, the factors influencing drug use are far too complex to simply state that a drug is or is not addictive.

Finally, a term frequently used is *drug abuse*. The difference between use and abuse of a drug is that the latter term implies deleterious effects on the person's own life or on the lives of others around them — effects which are a result of drug use. If a person is using a drug repeatedly, it does not appear to harm either him/her or others who come in contact with that person, then he or she cannot be said to abuse the drug. The differentiation between use and abuse has important implications. Unless one has moral or religious objections, drug use per se does not seem to be a bad thing. After all, everyone seems to do it in one form or another. But if the person is in some way damaging himself or others, then drug use becomes a problem.

It is relatively easy to think of examples of both drug use and drug abuse. Many people use alcohol on an occasional or daily basis. It appears to have a number of desirable effects, including relaxation and promotion of social interaction. Although alcohol has a number of adverse physical effects, they are unlikely to be of great concern if the alcohol is taken in small amounts. In contrast, the heavy drinker or person who goes on occasional binges may be causing physical damage to him- or herself, may endanger other people by driving under the influence, and may cause conflicts with his or her family. Such a pattern of usage may be best categorized as drug abuse.

The problem, of course, is deciding at what stage the behavior can be labelled abusive. Virtually any drug has deleterious physical effects, but it is not always clear what amount is needed to produce them. For example, continual use of cocaine by inhalation through the nose (or "snorting") can damage the tissues of the nasal passages. One result may be a diminished sense of smell. But how much cocaine is needed to produce such damage? Does a small amount result in no damage, in some damage? Such questions are difficult, if not impossible, to answer.

When one comes to deleterious effects which are not so readily specified the problem is even more difficult. Some would say that simply coming to rely on a drug, for instance using alcohol to relax, is bad in and of itself. Others might want stronger evidence of substantive effects on the individual (such as diminished work output) or those around them (such as stress from having to continually care and cover for an intoxicated individual) before using the term abuse. Thus, while the concept is a useful one, the line between drug use and drug abuse is often difficult to draw.

ORIGINS, EFFECTS, MEDICAL USES, AND HISTORY OF INDIVIDUAL DRUGS

Much of the remainder of this chapter is devoted to a description of the various drugs that are widely used for their psychoactive effects, and which can cause problems of dependence. The organization largely follows the categories of drugs described above. In each case the origin of the drug or class of drugs will be noted, its effects described, any medical uses indicated, and a brief history of its use given.

Opiates

Opium is in actuality, the dried sap obtained from the opium poppy. The opium poppy appears to be native to central southern Asia, but cultivation now occurs over a much wider area. At a certain point in the development of the poppy seed pod, relatively high concentrations of morphine and some codeine are present in the sap. This sap is then collected after slicing the seed pod to let it ooze out.

While morphine and codeine are the two naturally occurring opiates, many more have been developed in the laboratory. A number of these have actions very similar to morphine, and can be classified as morphine-like opiates. Most notable among these is heroin. The main variation in this group is the amount or dose of the drug required to produce the characteristic effects and length of time the effects last. The latter can vary from a few hours to a few days.

There is a second group of opiates that have somewhat different properties. Their "high" is less pronounced than that of the morphine-like opiates, and use of these drugs may be less likely to lead to dependence. Many have been laboratory-developed with the goal of producing a medically effective opiate with less potential for dependence and abuse as the scientific focus. Examples of these drugs include pentazocine and buprenorphine.

Effects Following administration of an opiate, the person generally becomes less active and finds it difficult to concentrate. The person will often feel drowsy and may even lapse into sleep for a time. A very pleasant "high" or euphoria also occurs. This particular effect has been much-celebrated in literature; perhaps the most eloquent statement was made by Thomas de Quincey:

> But I took it; and in an hour — oh, heavens! What a revulsion! What an upheaving, from its lowest depths, of the inner spirit! What an apocalypse of the world within me! That my pains had vanished was now a trifle in my eyes; this negative effect was swallowed up in the immensity of those positive effects which had opened before me in the abyss of divine enjoyment thus suddenly revealed. Here was a panacea, a $\phi\alpha\rho\mu\alpha\varkappa o\nu$ $\nu\iota\epsilon\nu\theta\epsilon\delta$ for all human woes; here was the secret of happiness about which philosophers had disputed for so many ages, at once discovered; happiness might now be bought for a penny and carried in the waistcoat pocket; portable ecstasies might be had corked up in a pint bottle; and peace of mind could be sent down in gallons by the mail coach (de Quincey, 1822).

Not everyone experiences the rapturous effects described by de Quincey. For one thing, the experience may be less intense with opiates such as pentazocine. Some people may not experience it at all, even after using morphine or heroin. Rather, they may become anxious or frightened. This may possibly be a reaction to the accompanying effects of the drug, rather than a direct effect of the drug itself. Nausea is another prominent effect which inhibits euphoria, and is particularly common in novice users. Vomiting may occur if the dosage is high.

Heart rate and blood pressure are not affected greatly by opiates. However, the circulatory system is slow to compensate when a person gets up from a supine position. The result may be a short period of dizziness. Opiates have a powerful effect on respiration as well. With large doses breathing simply stops, and this is the main cause of death through overdose.

Opiates are particularly effective pain-killers. Their analgesic action is the most powerful of all drugs and they are used in many situations where strong pain is a problem. It is often said that pain involves two components: the sensation of pain and the reaction to that sensation. The opiates seem to diminish both, but the reaction to pain especially. Patients often report that they are aware of the pain but that it no longer bothers them.

Other, sometimes uncomfortable, symptoms are experienced by regular opiate users. Amongst these are impaired sexual functioning, constipation, and pinpoint pupils. Together with most other drugs, opiates have at various times been labelled aphrodisiacs. It is likely that the only benefit they produce is a longer time to ejaculation in males. While this may be seen as a benefit, regular use may create an impotence problem. Both constipation and pinpoint pupils are characteristic signs of opiate use. Neither disappears with repeated use of the drug.

The other major problem associated with long-term use of opiates is physical dependence. Opiate physical dependence is relatively strong and the withdrawal syndrome can be uncomfortable (see Chapter Two).

Medical use   The primary medical use of opiates is to alleviate pain. While drugs such as aspirin may be effective in relieving mild pain, they are ineffective against severe pain. Opiates are the most effective agents in such cases. The number of people who suffer such pain through illness or injury is enormous, and it is probably the case that doctors relied more on opiates in earlier times than they do now. Without the benefit of antibiotics and other tools of modern medicine, they were less able to treat the underlying problems than they can at present.

A second medical use is for alleviation of diarrhea. Morphine has a severe, constipating effect which will reverse the worst dysentery. Again, in earlier times this was a very common medical use for opiates. Another minor medical effect of opiates is that they relieve coughing. Drugs chemically similar to opiates are today used in cough syrups (for example, dextromethorphan).

More detailed information on the effects and medical uses of opiates can be found in Meyer and Mirin (1979) and Jaffe and Martin (1985).

History   Opium resin has been an item of trade for many thousands of years. Descriptions of opium, its use as a pain-killer and accounts of its pleasurable effects can be found in ancient Egyptian, Greek and Roman writings. The name opium is derived from the Greek *opius,* meaning "little juice" (Latimer and Goldberg, 1981).

The Roman Empire enabled the spread of opium use and cultivation of the poppy, but as the empire declined, so apparently did opium usage. While it diminished in many areas formerly under Roman control, opium use later spread through the Arab world. Arab physicians, like their Roman predecessors, praised its use for a variety of ailments. Opium also took hold because it was an alternative recreational drug to alcohol. The Koran expressly forbade the use of alcohol, so many Arabs chose opium and hashish as alternatives.

The influence of Arab traders was enormous. Opium use spread as far as North Africa in the west and China in the east. It was not immediately popular in China, however. Introduced in about the eighth century, it did not appear to be widely used medically until 400 or 500 years later. In China, the preparation found the form of a beverage made from seeds. A change to resin eating came with the spread of medicinal use and local cultivation in the period from the eleventh to the sixteenth centuries. It is from this time that the first written records of use in India also come. Undoubtedly though, use in this country dated back some hundreds of years to introduction by the Arabs.

Although earliest uses of opium were mainly medicinal, recreational use was quite common. Records suggest that care was advised in the use of opium, but there does not seem to be any notion of problems of addiction or social problems associated with use of the drug. Indeed, the Indian government took over the whole operation of opium cultivation and sales. The revenue from this state monopoly was an important source of government funds.

Medicinal use of opium was common in Europe by the seventeenth century, and probably increased up until the mid-nineteenth century. As in ancient times, it was praised by physicians who used it to treat a large variety of problems. In the United States this widespread medicinal use culminated in the mid- and late-nineteenth century with the huge range of patent medicines that became available. Many of these contained opium and their exaggerated claims of relief from a variety of ailments depended in large part on this particular ingredient.

In nineteenth century Europe, recreational use was enjoyed by a number of famous literary figures (Hayter, 1968). De Quincey (quoted previously) and Coleridge were clearly dependent for long periods of their lives. Others such as Walter Scott, John Keats, Elizabeth Barrett Browning, and Charles Dickens used it only occasionally or for short periods in their lives. For some it was simply an escape or a pleasure. Others used opium to enhance their literary activities. Coleridge is said by some to have devised his famous poem, Kubla Khan, while under the influence of opium, although there is some debate on this issue.

In Britain, recreational use was aided by the ready availability of opium, found in the form of *laudanum* in particular. This preparation was a mixture of opium and distilled alcohol, and being a cheap means of intoxication and an alternative to alcohol, it was used by all classes. While recognition of opium dependence was growing (aided by de Quincey's book), opium use was still not associated with health or social problems (Parssinen, 1983).

The development of major social and economic problems as a result of opium first occurred in China. Tobacco had been introduced to China in the sixteenth and seventeenth centuries. It was popular and use spread rapidly. In the late eighteenth century, however, the practise of smoking tobacco and opium mixtures was introduced from the East Indies. Many people then changed from eating opium to smoking it, though some warned about its dire consequences. Fearing problems with this new habit, the emperor prohibited opium use and merchants were punished by death. Despite this edict, opium smoking continued to gain popularity. There was also a gradual increase in importation of the drug. While it could be grown in China, higher quality opium was available from nearby India. This trade was dominated by British commercial interests.

The problems associated with opium smoking escalated with its use. They included widespread corruption, the outflow of silver reserves to pay for the opium, and increasing dependence on the British. Attempts by China to restrict trade in opium and other goods caused conflict with the British which culminated in the two Opium Wars (dating 1839–1842 and 1856–1860). British victory resulted in legislation and free trade in opium.

The period of the late nineteenth and early twentieth centuries was the time when views on opium began to change markedly. Several developments hastened this. In 1803, pure morphine had been isolated as the main active ingredient in opium. In 1898, *heroin,* a close chemical relation of morphine, was introduced by Bayer laboratories and, interestingly, proposed as a nonaddicting alternative to morphine. Another very important development was the introduction of the *hypodermic needle.* Although intended for medical use, it was soon diverted to administration of the pure chemicals for nonmedical purposes.

Most countries adopted strict regulation of opiates in the early part of this century. The British opium trade with China was stopped and there was some international cooperation in trying to eliminate the opium business. These moves were not without some opposition. Many regarded opium as harmless, and certainly not worse than alcohol.

This latter view was most prevalent in Britain, and was probably responsible for their regulatory system. In 1920, an act was passed enabling doctors to distribute opiates to addicts. In contrast, users in the United States were forced to obtain their supply from illegal dealers who charged very high prices. The British system seems to have been effective until relatively recently. The number of addicts was small until the late '60s and early '70s when it began to match that of other countries. Use of opiates has increased in the United States since the banning. Most users buy heroin and inject it using a syringe and needle. Smoking is also common, but less popular, and eating is virtually unheard of.

Opium use continued at a reasonable level in China, but down considerably from its peak between the opium wars. This changed dramatically with the revolution of 1949, and use since that time has been very low. Indian use too, has declined over this century. Opium was never a major problem in that country as it was in so many others interestingly. Although there was some smoking, eating remained more common. Regulation gradually tightened during this century and trade was controlled by the government.

The use of opiates has now spread to virtually every country in the world. The most common practise is injection of heroin. Other methods of administering the drug include smoking (usually in a tobacco mixture) and inhalation of vapor (called 'chasing the dragon'). Heroin has its origin in a number of regions, particularly the "Golden Triangle" of South East Asia and parts of the Middle East. It is distributed by extensive networks who operate a multi-billion dollar trade. Unfortunately, modern opiate use is associated with major health and social problems in the many countries in which it is now used.

Barbiturates

The barbiturates are not naturally occurring substances, but were one of the early products of the modern pharmaceutical industry. Barbital was introduced to medicine in 1903. Since then, a large number of barbiturates have been synthesized and marketed; some have been listed in Table 1.1. The effects of the different barbiturates are very similar. One way in which they do vary, however, is in their time course. Barbiturates are often divided into short (effects lasting two to three hours), intermediate (five to six hours) and long-acting (six to ten hours or more). Thus, depending on what therapeutic purpose they are to be used for, a drug might be chosen for medical use from one of the three groups. Barbiturates are generally available in tablet form. They can also be injected.

Effects   The most prominent effect of the barbiturates is general sedation and sleepiness. Changes in brain activity reveal a widespread depression. Sleep and even coma occur with high doses. Respiration declines and death may result from a high dose if breathing becomes too infrequent.

The sleep induced by barbiturates is not exactly the same as normal sleep. During a normal night's sleep we pass through a number of different stages, each of which seems to be required if we are to feel satisfied and rested on awakening. With barbiturates there is less REM (rapid eye movement) sleep. REM sleep is frequently associated with dreaming. A person who uses barbiturates on a daily basis will develop tolerance (see Chapter Two) and the amount of REM sleep will gradually return to normal or near-normal levels, usually within two weeks. However, when that person ceases taking the drug there is often a rebound effect for some nights. REM becomes prominent and the person awakes feeling unrested. If use is stopped abruptly in this way and the person is not made aware of these likely effects, he or she may return to the drug rather than wait for the effects to disappear with time.

While sedation is the most prominent effect of barbiturates, it should not be assumed that they will have this effect only. Low doses of these drugs may actually result in stimulation and higher activity levels than normal. This is rarely seen because people usually take a dose high enough to produce sedation. The other type of stimulation comes from the disinhibitory effects of barbiturates, to be discussed in Chapter Three. The release of inhibitions produced by the drug may result in extreme, excessive or even antisocial behavior. Which of the varied effects of barbiturates is most prominent depends on a large number of factors, including the person's susceptibility, the circumstances, and the dose of the drug taken.

Chronic users of barbiturates may develop very strong physical dependence with prominent physiological and psychological withdrawal symptoms (see Chapter Two). Withdrawal can be very unpleasant; in extreme cases death may result. Withdrawal should only be carried out under medical supervision.

Medical use   Medical use of barbiturates has been declining since the 1960s as they have been replaced by the *benzodiazepines*. The uses for the two groups of compounds almost overlap totally, but barbiturates have a lesser margin of safety than benzodiazepines. Nevertheless, they are still used in a number of areas.

Most prescriptions for barbiturates have been for people suffering from anxiety, insomnia, or both. These drugs alleviate the symptoms of anxiety and have been useful in those for whom it has been debilitating. Similarly, sufficient doses of barbiturates induce sleep and have been widely used by those unable to sleep under normal conditions. A related use is as a general sedative where a calming or quieting effect is required. The intermediate-acting barbiturates such as *pentobarbital* are usually employed for this purpose. Another use is in general anesthesia. A short-acting barbiturate such as *thiopental* is often given together with a gaseous anesthetic, most commonly nitrous oxide.

The final, and one of the most valuable medical uses is in the treatment of epilepsy. Before the introduction of phenobarbital early in this century there was little in the way of effective treatment for this disorder. While barbiturates do not cure the disorder, they suppress the symptoms sufficiently to enable the person to lead a more normal life. A number of other drugs have been developed for epilepsy in this century, but long-acting barbiturates are still used. Particular care is needed in adjusting the dosage so as to get the antiepileptic effect without too much sedation. Barbiturates are also effective in the emergency treatment of convulsions arising from epilepsy, tetanus, cerebral hemorrhage, and other causes.

History   The history of barbiturates is a relatively short one. The first barbiturate was introduced into medical practice in 1903. From that time until recently more and more were added to the list (see Dundee and McIlroy, 1982). Barbiturates have always been controlled drugs, available only through prescription. While there has been some illegal trade, the amount is small relative to that obtained by legal means.

Barbiturate use has occurred mainly in Western societies. In these countries barbiturates were at one time amongst the most widely prescribed drugs. Use tends to be highest among women, particularly those in the 40–50 year age group. Most simply obtain regular prescriptions from a single doctor, but others who use a higher dosage may obtain prescriptions from several sources concurrently.

Barbiturates are also used illegally in a variety of ways. School-aged children sometimes use them as an alternative to alcohol. In such cases they are usually drugs taken from parents or other adults who have obtained them legitimately. "Serious" barbiturate users may require large quantities of the drugs, at least some of which they obtain illegally. The drug is taken orally or injected intravenously. Barbiturates may be mixed with heroin to give a stronger effect (although there is little similarity in the effects of the two).

Problems associated with the availability of barbiturates have been recognized for some time. The principle ones are death through overdose and severe withdrawal. Barbiturates used to be a frequent means of suicide, and in some cases death through overdose was thought to be accidental. The severe withdrawal syndrome too was extremely dangerous in and of itself but also helped create a pattern of addiction. Stopping the drugs was so uncomfortable that many people simply could not endure the experience. These types of problems resulted in dramatically decreased use of barbiturates when alternatives such as the benzodiazepines came into being.

Benzodiazepines

The benzodiazepines are products of the modern pharmaceutical industry. Since their introduction in the 1950s a large number have come into the market; some have been listed in Table 1.1. Like the barbiturates the benzodiazepines do not vary much in their effects, but the time course of their action does. Effects may last from a few hours to several days. While they cannot be grouped as clearly as the barbiturates, in a medical context the choice of which is to be used should be based in part on the desirable time-course.

Effects Administration of a series of progressively larger doses of benzodiazepine would create a circumstance similar to that produced by alcohol and barbiturates. Low doses may produce either excitation or less inhibited behavior. The person is likely to report feeling very good at this stage. Any previous anxiety will have been diminished or will disappear.

Sedation will begin to appear at higher doses. The person will slow down, and may become sleepy. The person's reactions to things happening around him or her will become delayed and the person may appear to have little muscle facility. Eventually sleep will predominate. As compared to barbiturates, the lethal dose of a benzodiazepine is very high. The difference between a dose which produces sleep and one which results in death is considerable. Accordingly, the risk of death from overdose of benzodiazepines is extremely small.

Like barbiturates, benzodiazepines alter the pattern of sleep. While both have beneficial effects such as decreasing the time necessary to fall asleep and producing fewer awakenings, benzodiazepines may have less effect on the proportions of the different kinds of sleep. In particular, the amount of REM sleep may be affected less by these drugs. The result may be an easier adjustment after the drug is first taken and in the first few nights after its use is abandoned.

Benzodiazepines alter heart rate and blood pressure only slightly. An increase in heart rate and a decrease in blood pressure are most common. Respiration is reduced, but a significant decrease requires a very large dose. One other interesting result of taking benzodiazepines that can be observed is an increase in weight. This appears to be due to increased food intake (see Chapter Three).

There has been some controversy over the degree of physical dependence which results from taking benzodiazepines on a regular, frequent basis. It is clear that if they are taken in large quantities these drugs can produce very strong physical dependence with severe withdrawal syndromes. However, it also seems that a milder dependence can develop even with more moderate doses such as those sometimes prescribed for treatment of insomnia. The physical symptoms of the syndrome are similar to those associated with barbiturate withdrawal. Psychological symptoms such as increased anxiety and depression have been reported by some people as recurring temporarily or for long periods after they have ceased taking the drug.

Medical use   The medical uses of benzodiazepines are very similar to that of barbiturates. The vast majority of prescriptions are written for people who suffer from anxiety (diazepam, chlordiazepoxide, and oxazepam are commonly prescribed) or insomnia (nitrazepam and flurazepam are common). Although often distinguished on the basis of manufacturers recommended use, there are no major differences in the benzodiazepines used for either anxiety or insomnia (Harvey, 1985).

While these are the most common reasons for taking benzodiazepines, there are a large number of other uses. They are very effective muscle relaxants and can be used where there are problems of muscle spasm. This is common with certain types of spinal damage, for example, and in diseases such as tetanus. This property and the general sedation they produce make them useful as a preanaesthetic medication. They are also used by obstetricians.

Like barbiturates, benzodiazepines play an important role in the control of epilepsy. While barbiturates are still used in some cases, benzodiazepines have replaced them as the drug of choice for treatment of certain types of epilepsy. They offer the advantage of controlling epilepsy while producing lesser sedation.

One final use which is of interest here is the control of withdrawal symptoms. Withdrawal from drugs such as opiates, alcohol, and barbiturates may be severe. In some instances benzodiazepines may be given over the withdrawal period to ease discomfort. There is an inherent danger in substituting one type of drug for another, especially during alcohol and barbiturate withdrawal, but this method can be useful if care is taken.

History   While barbiturates had been in use for many years, the benzodiazepines began to be developed in the 1950s and marketed in the 1960s. The first alternative to the barbiturates was a drug called meprobamate. Originally devised as a muscle relaxant, it was found to have sedative properties similar to that of the barbiturates, but also had a greater margin of safety. Meprobamate was extremely popular for several years, particularly in the United States. This popularity spurred the development of other, similar drugs.

The first benzodiazepine to be released on to the market was chlordiazepoxide. It had similar antianxiety and sleep-inducing properties (as did the barbiturates and meprobamate), but was safer than both. The safety was two-dimensional. First, it was difficult to take a lethal dose of chlordiazepoxide because the amount required was so large. Second, it did not appear to have the same type of withdrawal syndrome. Indeed, it was initially claimed that there was no real physical dependence or withdrawal associated with "normal" benzodiazepine use.

Soon after chlordiazepoxide came a whole range of benzodiazepines. Rival pharmaceutical companies vied for success in this lucrative market. The one which rose to most prominence was *diazepam,* marketed as *Valium* by Roche. Valium became the top-selling pharmaceutical drug in the world, and stayed so for many years. Others were also successful, but less spectacularly so. While Valium was mainly prescribed for anxiety, *nitrazepam (Mogadon)* has been among the most popular benzodiazepines for aiding sleep.

Supplies of benzodiazepines are dependent on the activities of pharmaceutical manufacturers. While they are most widely used in the West, use has spread throughout most of the world. The drugs can only be obtained by prescription, but, because the disorders for which they are used are so common, they are readily available. The majority of users are women (in ratio of about 3:1), and Valium is often stereotyped as a "housewives' drug." Elderly people are also prescribed these drugs frequently. Illegal trade in benzodiazepines is relatively small and localized within communities rather than being international.

For further detail on both barbiturates and benzodiazepines see Rickels, Downing, and Winokur (1978) and Harvey (1985).

Alcohol

Alcohol (ethyl alcohol, ethanol) is a colorless, volatile liquid with an unpleasant taste and odor. It is produced as a result of a fermentation process. Yeasts are able to convert sugar to alcohol and carbon dioxide. The source of the sugar can vary. If grapes are used, the resulting beverage is known as wine; if apples, it is known as cider; if honey, mead. Grains may also be used, but they must first go through a process of malting in which their starch is converted to sugar.

The maximum alcohol content obtainable by fermentation is about fifteen percent. This is because the yeast dies at levels of alcohol above this point. In order to obtain higher alcohol concentrations it is necessary to distill the liquid. Distillation involves heating a solution containing alcohol and condensing the vapors. Because alcohol has a lower boiling point than water, it is simple to heat the solution so that the vapors have a very high alcohol concentration.

A list of alcoholic beverages, their origins and alcoholic content is shown in Table 1.2.

Effects The effects of alcohol are very similar to that of the other sedative drugs including the barbiturates and benzodiazepines. They vary from

TABLE 1.2   Origins and Alcohol Contents of Various Alcoholic Drinks

BEVERAGE	AVERAGE OR TYPICAL ALCOHOL CONCENTRATION	SOURCE
Beer	4%	Fermentation of malted barley
Cider	7%	Fermentation of apples
Wine	11%	Fermentation of grapes
Fortified wine (e.g. sherry, port)	20%	Distilled alcohol (e.g. brandy) added to wine
Whisky	37.5%	Distillate of fermented malted barley
Brandy/cognac	37.5%	Distillate of fermented grapes
Rum	37.5%	Distillate of fermented molasses or sugar cane juice
Gin	37.5%	Distillate of fermented malted grains (various) filtered through juniper berries
Vodka	37.5%	Distillate of fermented malted wheat mash

increased activity and disinhibition at low dose levels, to sedation and sleep at higher doses. Table 1.3 shows several levels of intoxication as measured by the BAC (blood alcohol concentration), together with some of the characteristic changes in behavior which occur at these levels.

The table clearly illustrates the change from relatively pleasurable symptoms at lower dose levels to marked impairment at higher dose levels, leading ultimately to death. This range of effects is, of course, not unique to alcohol. Almost any drug will produce death if taken in large enough doses and all the drugs being discussed here are capable of producing desirable effects. It should be noted that the table is meant as a rough guide only. The effects of alcohol will be determined by factors in addition to BAC, including the person's prior experience with the drug (see Chapter Two) and the environment in which it is taken (see Chapter Three).

Alcohol also affects a number of bodily functions, depending on the dose. There are variable effects on respiration at lower alcohol doses, and definite respiratory depression following ingestion of higher doses. Body temperature is lowered by alcohol. This is due to both dilation of blood vessels in the skin, resulting in a warm, flushed feeling, but also greater heat loss and increased sweating. At higher doses there is also a direct effect on temperature regulating mechanisms in the brain. Gastric acid secretion is enhanced by alcohol and there is increased urine production as a result of altered hormone activity. (See Wallgren and Barry, 1970, and Ritchie, 1985 for a more detailed description of these effects.)

Long-term alcohol use can produce marked physical dependence. As

TABLE 1.3 Gross Behavioral Effects at Different Blood Alcohol Concentrations

PEAK BAC (g/100 ml) (%)	EFFECTS AT PEAK
.02–.03	Slight increase in talkativeness; relaxation
.05	Relaxation, talkativeness, and some lowering of inhibitions. Impairment in some tasks requiring skill
.06–.10	Very talkative; speech is louder, acts and feels self-confident. Less cautious and inhibited than usual
.20	Sedated rather than active, may be sleepy. Impairment now includes slurred speech, clumsiness, reduced responsiveness, and marked intellectual impairment
.30–.40	Semiconsious or unconscious. Body functions are beginning to break down
.50–.70	Dead

with barbiturates, the withdrawal symptoms are very severe. There are also a number of other problems associated with chronic alcohol use, including degeneration in the brain and liver. These will be discussed more fully in Chapter Six.

Medical use There are few remaining medical uses for alcohol, none of which involve its effects on the brain. These include application as a disinfectant and antiseptic, as a means of cooling the skin in case of fever and for prevention of bed-sores. However, this was not always the case. At certain periods in history, alcohol was used as a cure for a variety of disorders. Perhaps this was not without foundation: illness brought on or made worse by anxiety and insomnia may well have been alleviated by the alcohol.

History The only requirement for alcohol production is some form of sugar and the appropriate conditions for fermentation. This process occurs naturally without human intervention. Because no special material is needed, alcohol seems to have developed concurrently in a number of places. The discovery predates historical records, but the drug certainly has a rich and colorful history. Much of this is documented in Austin (1985).

Alcohol use was common in the ancient civilizations of Mesopotamia, Egypt, Greece, and Rome. One difference from drugs such as opium was that the dangers of alcohol use and the problems caused by it were recognized at this time. In the records of all Mediterranean civilizations there are descriptions of alcohol's disabling effects and the various measures adopted to limit public drunkenness. The same sorts of descriptions are lacking for other drugs, suggesting that excessive alcohol use may have been the only recognized dependence problem in the ancient world (Blum, 1969).

Alcohol use was an integral part of ancient society just as it is in many modern societies. There were public bars, but people also drank privately in their own homes. Alcohol was used at celebrations, at public entertainments, and as part of religious ceremonies. There was hardly an aspect of ancient life which was not affected in some way by use of the drug.

One of the most significant changes in alcohol use came with distillation. Discovered by the Arabs around the ninth or tenth century, it was introduced to Europe in the thirteenth century. Up until that time, alcoholic drinks had been in the form of beer, mead, or wine made from various fruits. The effects of distillation were not immediate, however, in that the products of distillation were used initially as medicines only. The first of these was brandy. Because such a large amount of wine had to be used to produce the distilled liquor, it was found to be relatively expensive. However, the wealthy were prepared to pay for it because of its purported medicinal value.

The problems associated with use of these distilled spirits were first made clear following the development of gin in seventeenth century Holland. Spirits had been expensive because they were made from wine. However, gin was cheap to produce and affordable to everyone. In England this was aided by government encouragement of the local distilling industry to compete with the imported French brandy. The result was London's infamous gin epidemic.

Various social changes in eighteenth century England encouraged the epidemic. Gin use was most common amongst the London poor, who alternated between suffering unemployment and enduring very harsh working conditions for low wages. The squalor and degradation of the mass of poor people provided the opportunity for the spread of cheap, readily available gin. Consumption was so high that birth rates actually declined in London over the period, despite increases in the rest of the country. Birth defects caused by alcohol (see Chapter Five) also became more common.

Eventually the gin epidemic was halted by legislation that imposed duties and restricted sale. The harsher duties made it less affordable, particularly to the poor. Restrictions clearly separated distillation from sale: only licensed businesses could sell spirits, and distillers were prevented from assuming that role as they previously had. Within a few years, production of gin declined to about one fifth of its peak as a result of this legislation.

Controls were also introduced gradually in the American colonies. Beer was the most common alcoholic drink in the colonies; wine was also available, but relatively expensive. Rum was the most readily available and widely consumed spirit. By the end of the eighteenth century, prior to the revolution, trade in rum and whisky became an important part of the colonial economy. Sale of alcoholic beverages was gradually limited to licensed premises and control of individual intake was regulated by laws concerning public drunkenness.

In the period of 1800–1830 there was a massive rise in alcohol consumption in the American colonies. A number of factors may have contributed to this, including general social disruption, a lessening of social controls with the westward migration, and low whisky price due to abundant grain. Though not as bad as the London gin epidemic, the increase was a large one and ended quite rapidly.

Whether as a reaction to this increase or not, a temperance movement began as a genuine social force around this time. This movement was to become very influential in the United States and would eventually spread its message through many parts of the world. The original temperance movement supported moderation in drinking, but was gradually taken over by those who favored prohibition. Throughout its history it was strongly aided by the churches.

There were three major attempts to enforce prohibition in the United States. The first, in the middle nineteenth century, involved legislation in a number of states to prohibit sale of alcohol. These efforts were a failure in all cases and by 1865 the various pieces of legislation were repealed. The second, beginning in the 1880s, also involved a wave of state prohibition, but again these efforts were not successful. All were repealed by 1904. Success for the prohibition movement came on the third attempt, which began with state prohibitions in 1907. The difference however, was that legislation in individual states was now backed up by federal legislation which came into force in 1920.

Prohibition certainly reduced alcohol consumption in the United States. Nevertheless, there were a number of sources which were exploited. These included the production from illicit stills, doctors' prescriptions (the only legal source of drinking alcohol), and alcohol smuggled across the borders. The repeal of prohibition in 1933 came about partly as a result of the inability of authorities to stop these illegal sources. The other main reason was the loss of tax revenue previously gained through the legal alcohol industry.

The United States was not the only country to try prohibition. A strong temperance movement grew in Finland, beginning in the 1830s. It was inspired in part by United States groups that had similar ideals. The Finnish movement had some early influence in limiting alcohol use, mainly through restrictions on sale and the imposition of taxes and duties. Full scale prohibition began in 1919 and ended in 1932. Again, the main reason it was repealed was that such legislation was nearly impossible to enforce. Alcohol was still consumed and the problem of drunkenness continued.

In contrast to the United States, prohibition laws were not simply repealed in Finland. Instead, control was vested in the *State Alcohol Monopoly.* As well as governing all aspects of alcohol production and sales it worked to minimize consumption. The principal methods employed were limiting availability, especially in rural areas, and structuring prices in a manner that favored beverages with lower alcohol content. However, many of the controls were lifted with further liberalization in 1969. The result was a massive increase in alcohol consumption to nearly fifty percent higher in one year's time.

Prohibition can clearly be seen as a failure in Western countries. Alcohol use decreased, but only through repressive state action. Still, illegal trade and legal medical supplies prospered. In contrast, prohibition has been successful in a number of Arab countries for many hundreds of years. This is associated with strict religious prohibition of alcohol use. In many of these countries the penalties for alcohol sale or consumption are severe by Western standards.

One country that had a bad alcohol abuse problem but reacted with more moderate forms of control was Sweden. In the first half of the nineteenth century, alcohol problems were common. A spirit made from the potato was the most common drink, and it was not unusual for people to produce it in their own homes. Two systems of government control were introduced. The first, the *Gothenburg system*, eliminated private financial interests in the retailing of potato spirits and replaced them with governmentally-controlled outlets. This had some success in decreasing alcohol use. The stricter Bratt system was introduced in 1919, partly in response to pressure from the temperance movement. Under this system each person kept a book in which purchases of spirits were recorded. An individual was given a set allowance per month and purchases beyond that allowance were forbidden. The Bratt system used this, and other means such as higher taxes and duties on high alcohol content beverages to encourage moderate rather than excessive alcohol use. Interestingly, the Bratt system was abandoned in 1955 and an increase in alcohol consumption and alcoholic problems occurred as a result.

In China and Japan, drinking appears to have been a problem for some hundreds of years. Evidence indicates the same range of views about alcohol as in the West — everything from the highest praise to total condemnation. Prohibitions against drinking were enforced from time to time, but none lasted for very long. Buddhism was somewhat influential in curbing drinking, although its originally strong strictures against alcohol were eventually relaxed.

Perhaps the people who have suffered most from the effects of alcohol are those groups to whom it has been suddenly introduced. While this has occurred in a number of parts of the world, the most striking examples are the North American Indians and the Australian Aborigines. Their respective societies began to disintegrate under the influence of the European invaders. One important factor in this change was alcohol. With no prior history of use, there was little social control or regulation and drunkenness soon became rampant practice. Uncontrolled alcohol use may well have been both a cause of, and a reaction to, the social disintegration. For both groups of peoples the problem remains. They have made some efforts to arrest it, usually by total prohibition in certain defined areas over which they have control. This seems to be at least partly successful.

Cocaine

Cocaine is the main active ingredient of the plant *Erythroxylon coca,* native to South America. It grows in mountainous regions of Columbia, Peru, Bolivia, and Argentina at altitudes many other plants will not withstand. A shrub or small tree which grows to 6 or 8 feet, it is usually kept smaller when cultivated. The extracted cocaine takes the form of a white powder.

Effects   Administration of moderate cocaine doses produces pronounced stimulatory effects (Van Dyke and Byck, 1977). The user feels and acts very alert. It is most obvious when the person takes the drug when in a tired, relaxed state. Fatigue is almost totally eliminated for the period of time the person is influenced by the drug.

Users also report great feelings of self-confidence. Doubts about themselves seem to disappear and they feel capable of great things. Subjective impressions also include euphoria—a very strong feeling of happiness. If the drug is injected, this euphoria comes suddenly in the form of a "rush"—an intense feeling lasting only a few seconds.

The bodily changes accompanying cocaine administration include increased heart rate and blood pressure. Body temperature is elevated, often giving the person a feeling of chills for a short time. Breathing also tends to be faster and more shallow than normal. Deaths from cocaine overdose are usually a result of respiratory failure.

Cocaine has a local anesthetic action. If administered to a part of the body, pain in that region will be eliminated for a period of time. Some sensation still remains: the person may feel tissue damage being done, but will not experience it as painful. There may be some numbness and tingling sensations in the area. These effects are noticeable if cocaine is administered via the nose or mouth.

Cocaine also prevents the onset of hunger. Users under the influence of the drug may not eat at all, even if the drug is taken repeatedly over a considerable period of time. Cocaine may also stave off feelings of hunger which had begun before the drug was ingested.

In vary large doses cocaine may produce a psychotic effect. The person experiences a paranoid psychosis not unlike that of certain schizophrenics. The effect is most unpleasant and any such reaction should be attended to medically. Other adverse effects are associated with the physiological reactions to cocaine administration. For example, the increased heart rate may be dangerous in certain individuals.

While it had been thought that there was little physical dependence associated with cocaine use, this now appears to be incorrect (Gawin and Kleber, 1986). The principal withdrawal symptoms appear to be directly opposite to the effects of the drug itself. They include tiredness, hunger, and depression. While not as severe as withdrawal after sedative-hypnotic use, for example, the symptoms may be distinctly uncomfortable and last for some days or weeks. They can only be resolved by further drug use. Psychological dependence on cocaine can be quite marked and may or may not be associated with any signs of physical dependence.

Medical use   The only remaining medical use for cocaine is as a local anesthetic. While many other synthetic derivatives of cocaine are available, some doctors and dentists prefer to use the original. This practice is declining with time.

History   Cocaine has been used in Peru for many hundreds of years. The exact time of first use is not known, although it probably predates 500 A.D. The South American Indians do not extract the actual drug, but simply chew the coca leaves. Usually a ball of leaves is kept in the mouth, and occasionally chewed. This practice maintains the effects over an extended period of time.

The Incas incorporated the coca leaf as part of their religious ceremonies. At this time use was probably controlled very tightly. However, these sanctions appear to have gradually broken down, so that by the time of the Spanish invasion in the sixteenth century, use was much more widespread. Coca leaves were even used as a form of money.

The people of Peru used coca for a number of reasons (Mortimer, 1974). It was employed extensively to combat hunger and fatigue. Along well-travelled routes, messengers and troops could obtain the leaves from storehouses placed at appropriate intervals. Undoubtedly, coca was valuable at high altitudes, where lack of oxygen, cold, and poor food supply can all contribute to the rapid onset of fatigue. These functional reasons were not the only ones for use of coca: there is evidence that the pleasurable subjective effects were also clearly recognized. Such use continues amongst Indian communities in a number of South American countries, although some are endeavoring to restrict use of the plant.

Introduction of cocaine to Europe was slow, but not for want of trying. Coca was transported to Europe, but, unlike tobacco, it never became popular. Some Europeans even believed that the Peruvian Indians imagined the effects coca was said to produce. One reason that has been suggested to explain this lack of acceptance was the failure of the coca leaves to maintain their potency in the long sea voyage across the Atlantic (Ashley, 1975). By the time they reached Europe their cocaine content was so low as to make them worthless. It is interesting to speculate on how contemporary patterns of drug use would have been different if coca leaves did maintain their potency for long time periods.

Widespread use outside of South America came only with the isolation of the active ingredient, cocaine. There is some doubt as to who was the first person to do this, but the discovery was made in the late 1850s. Once cocaine was isolated, storage and transport were easy—unlike the coca leaves, the powder does not deteriorate. Use spread rapidly in the second half of the nineteenth century after this discovery.

Medical use came after the demonstration of its local anesthetic properties in 1873. This was a great breakthrough—it was the first such local anesthetic. The other main medical uses were as a general tonic and a cure for addiction. Cocaine was used to help those trying to give up use of drugs such as morphine. This was promoted by Sigmund Freud (Byck, 1974).

A second major use came in the form of drinks. These included the famous *Vin Mariani,* a mixture of wine and cocaine which was a favorite of the Pope at the time. Another was Coca-cola, containing cocaine from coca leaves and caffeine from the Kola nut. Now only the caffeine remains. There were many other such drinks and the line became fuzzy as to which were simply taken for pleasure and which were intended to have medicinal value as tonics.

Administration of cocaine by other routes also began in the second half of the nineteenth century. Both intranasal administration and injection became popular. Injection was probably more common among "serious," regular users of the drug. Other, more occasional users probably preferred intranasal administration, since it did not leave any tell-tale marks.

Distribution of cocaine in powder form was practiced mainly through physicians. This occurred in the United States, England, the countries of Europe, and Egypt. Many physicians—Freud as an example—actively promoted its use and encouraged friends to use it. As a result, use of cocaine was more common amongst those who mixed socially with the physicians, usually those in higher socio-economic groups.

For a period of time in the United States, use was also frequent amongst lower-paid workers. In states where alcohol was banned it served as an alternative to that drug; elsewhere it was added to whisky to make a potent drink. Many whites expressed fears that it would incite violence and rebellion amongst the black laborers who used it. There is much conflicting evidence about the frequency of use amongst blacks. Popular accounts suggested a high proportion, while other, perhaps more realistic estimates suggested a lower rate of use comparable to the rate of the white population (Kennedy, 1985).

Towards the end of the nineteenth century physicians discovered more and more problems with cocaine. Reports of adverse effects from overdose and dependence convinced many of the dangers of its use. As a result, use diminished and many countries legislated against it. The variety of tonics containing cocaine also disappeared gradually. Coca-cola lost its cocaine around 1903. Use continued in certain social circles and there was something of a rise in popularity during the 1920s. Most users at this time were again amongst the higher socioeconomic groups.

With the realization of dangers associated with cocaine came attempts to find alternative drugs. The problem was that it was still needed as a local anesthetic, and as long as this use continued physicians would still have access to it and new people would be exposed to it even if only in a medical context. Research was carried out to develop drugs which had the local anesthetic properties of cocaine, but not those properties which made it attractive for recreational use. The first alternative was *procaine,* synthesized in 1905. Many others have since followed.

Cocaine use went into something of a hiatus from the 1930s through the 1970s, but has now increased dramatically again. This resurgence began in the United States and continues at a high level. Initially, intranasal use was the most preferred method of administering the drug, and partly because of price it was confined mainly to upper socioeconomic groups in American society. However, in the 1980s smoking of cocaine in the form of "crack" became popular. The relative efficiency of this method of administration, together with an increase in supply, meant that the price for a single "hit" decreased considerably. One consequence has been increased use among lower socio-economic groups.

Although strongest in the United States, cocaine use is spreading to many other countries. It has become more and more popular in many parts of the world, including Europe and South America. At present, the trend still seems to be in an upward direction, with ever-increasing use and ever-increasing profit by the producers and smugglers. The cocaine trade has had an enormous effect on the economics and politics of many South American countries (see, for example, Massing, 1988).

Amphetamine and Related Compounds

Amphetamine is available in three forms: *amphetamine, dextroampheta-mine (d-amphetamine)* and *methamphetamine.* The three have almost identical effects, but there are slight differences in the dose required to produce their characteristic effects. They are all products of the pharmaceutical industry. Amphetamine was synthesized in the late nineteenth century. Its properties were not well recognized and general use did not begin until the 1930s. A white powder, it has been taken as an inhalant, swallowed in tablet form, and injected.

Since the development of amphetamine a number of other compounds with similar properties have been introduced into the pharmaceutical market. These include *phenmetrazine, diethylpropion,* and *methylphenidate.* Although the effects of each differ somewhat from those of amphetamine, they are very similar. The differences are matters of degree: they have much the same set of effects, but may produce any one effect to a greater or lesser extent. These are mostly taken in tablet form.

More recently, a number of so-called "designer drugs" have been developed from modifications of the amphetamine molecule. A number of these have clear hallucinogenic effects and will be discussed below. However, some are much more like the parent compound. The best known of these is *ecstasy* or *MDMA.* It is primarily an amphetamine-like stimulant, but may produce hallucinations in some users.

Finally, the plant *Khat* contains compounds which have effects very similar to those of amphetamine. The most important of these is *cathinone.* Khat is most commonly found in Arabia and in East Africa where it has a long history of use. It is taken by chewing the leaves of the Khat plant (Nencini and Ahmed, 1989).

Effects The effects of amphetamine are very similar to that of cocaine (Angvist and Sudilovsky 1978). One of the main differences is the length of time over which these effects occur. Whereas a cocaine high may last only thirty minutes, the duration may be several hours with an amphetamine. Users report feelings of self-confidence, greater alertness, and loss of fatigue over this period. Performance may be improved in situations involving physical activity or where boredom or fatigue is a problem. On the other hand, performance in intellectual tasks may be worsened. Users also report euphoria which is most apparent when the drug is injected intravenously. Amphetamine delays the onset of sleep and suppresses appetite. Users who go on an amphetamine "binge" for several days may barely eat or sleep at all during that time.

The range of bodily effects produced by amphetamine includes increased blood pressures and a relaxation of the bronchial tubes of the lung. Others are variable and may be experienced on some occasions but not others. In this group are increased rate and depth of respiration, slowing of heart rate, and difficulty in urination. High doses of amphetamine cause a psychotic-like state: patients have symptoms such as paranoia, delusions, and hallucinations. The symptoms are very similar to those of the paranoid schizophrenic. They usually last for only a day or two, but may result in the user being admitted to a psychiatric clinic before the cause is discovered.

Chronic use of amphetamines can cause severe problems. Users may administer the drug in "runs" to get a continuous amphetamine effect for several days. Paranoid psychosis may become severe during this time. Bizarre behavior, often repetitive and stereotyped, may occur. Hallucinations may be experienced. A run is usually followed by a period of recovery—and sleep, voracious eating, and depression are noticeable symptoms. Like cocaine, there has been some controversy over whether this is a true withdrawal syndrome. However, it is now generally accepted that amphetamine can produce physical dependence and that withdrawal can occur on termination of use. Death from overdose is reported occasionally, usually as a result of cerebral hemorrhage.

Medical uses Medical uses for amphetamine and amphetamine-related compounds have been extensive. However, these uses have varied over the period that these compounds have been available. The drug's original use was in the treatment of asthma and other disorders involving breathing difficulties. Its ability to act as a bronchodilator was soon exploited and the drug was sold in the form of an inhalant under the brand name *Benzedrine.*

Use of amphetamine as a stimulant and an appetite suppressant sprang from observations of effects produced when the amphetamine inhalant was used. For people unable to lose weight by other means, amphetamine became a method for controlling eating. The stimulant properties led to its use as a general treatment for depression and fatigue—a high-powered "pick-me-up." However, there was also a group of people for whom this property was very useful. *Narcolepsy* is a disorder characterized by very frequent sleeping. Sufferers may have twenty or more sleeping bouts each day and they begin at unpredictable times. Use of amphetamine through the day can help control this sleeping.

The final use of amphetamine is in the treatment of *hyperkinetic disorder*. A childhood problem, it has been referred to in a variety of ways at different times, including *hyperactivity, minimal brain damage,* and *attention deficit disorder.* It is characterised by restlessness, impulsiveness, short attention span, and disruptive behavior. *Methylphenidate* (better known under its trade name *Ritalin*) is the most commonly prescribed drug for this disorder. It is often said to be paradoxical that a stimulant is prescribed for treatment of overactivity. However, as will be discussed in Chapter Three, this is not necessarily the case. The paradox may come only because of the assumption that drugs labelled stimulants only have "stimulant" properties.

Of all these uses, many countries now permit amphetamine or related compounds to be prescribed for narcolepsy or hyperkinetic disorder only. Their use for other purposes has been found to be either inappropriate (for example, bronchodilation—there are other, better bronchodilators available) or controversial (in the issues of control of appetite, reversal of fatigue, or depression).

History   Amphetamine use began in the 1930s when it was marketed as an inhalant. By the mid 1930s its stimulant properties were well recognized and it began to be used for the treatment of narcolepsy. Its ability to suppress appetite was recognized a few years later and amphetamine prescriptions were written for those who wanted to lose weight.

Use as a stimulant increased dramatically with the onset of the Second World War. Armies used amphetamine to prevent fatigue. It was of particular help when it was necessary for the soldiers to keep awake for extended periods of fighting or travelling. It is difficult to gauge how widespread this practise was, although British service personnel were given over seventy-two million tablets in the war (Bett, Howells and McDonald, 1955).

Widespread problems of abuse began in a number of countries after the war (Ellinwood, 1974). Perhaps the most severe problems arose in Japan (Tamura, 1989). Stockpiles of amphetamine that remained at the end of the war were dumped onto the market by the drug companies. No prescription was needed for the drug, and in this time of social upheaval, it was readily accepted by many. Amphetamine was widely advertised for its antifatigue and energizing properties. Although oral use was most common at first, intravenous injection of the drug became more frequent. Use was concentrated among economically and socially disadvantaged urban males.

Although use was restricted through legislation both in 1948 and further in 1951, the controls were relatively ineffective. Use eventually reached a plateau, and began to decline in the period between 1954–1956. This seems to have been brought about by a very active campaign carried out by Japanese authorities. The campaign involved very tight controls over the drug and the raw materials required for its manufacture, a public education program, and expanded treatment facilities.

While amphetamine use was reduced dramatically, there was some rise in the use of other illicit drugs in the 1960s. The problem of amphetamine abuse resurfaced in the 1970s as well, and is still present today. While the Japanese did not eradicate amphetamine use they were remarkably successful as compared to efforts to control drug use in other countries.

Sweden also experienced widespread problems associated with amphetamine use. Amphetamine had been widely prescribed during the war, but use had declined in the period immediately after. However, abuse problems began to be noticed in the early 1950s. Intravenous administration was popular among the frequent users. As amphetamine became more difficult to get, users turned to substitutes such as phenmetrazine and methylphenidate. The problem reached its height around 1967. Estimates suggest that there were around 10,000 intravenous users in Stockholm at the time. With stricter controls and a public education campaign, use of the drug decreased and stabilized in the 1970s. By that time amphetamine was competing with a range of other illegal drugs.

Although the patterns in Sweden and Japan could be regarded as extreme, they were repeated elsewhere. Legal amphetamine use during, and soon after the war was followed by problems of abuse leading to tighter controls and other measures to curb the drug. Use was most common amongst the youth and marginal groups of society. Another important change was from oral to intravenous administration, the latter method being more often associated with abuse problems than the former. Contemporary amphetamine use and abuse is very widespread. It is common in both developed and third-world countries and shows no signs of abating.

In contrast to amphetamine and the other compounds produced by pharmaceutical manufacturers, khat has a long history dating back many hundreds of years. Unfortunately, there is little information on its origins. While early use may have been for mystic or intellectual purposes, contemporary use is widespread and designed to counter fatigue and produce the other benefits of this group of drugs. It is frequently used in traditional social gatherings that center on khat chewing. Very few drugs have reached the level of popularity of khat. Recently, governments have become interested in curbing its use, claiming that much valuable agricultural land is set aside for its production, that the poor spend money on khat instead of food, and that it causes a number of physical and psychological problems in users (Kalix, 1987).

Nicotine

Nicotine is the main active ingredient in tobacco. There are actually over sixty species of tobacco plant, but the large leafed *nicotiana tobacum* is the main one under cultivation and it is native to the Americas. Tobacco is now processed in several stages. After harvesting the tobacco is cured. The leaves dry out as a result of natural moisture loss (called air-curing) or because of added heat (flue-curing). It is then aged, usually for one to two years. Proper curing and ageing are necessary for the development of desirable taste and odor in the tobacco. Depending on the subspecies of tobacco plant, the way it is grown, and the nature of the curing and aging processes, the tobacco may be one of a number of kinds. Common ones include bright, Burley, and Turkish tobacco. Most cigarettes contain a mixture of several types. Cigar and pipe tobacco are grown and processed somewhat differently than cigarette tobacco. Pipe tobacco may also have flavorings such as licorice added to it.

Effects   Many effects of nicotine are similar to those of other stimulants, but there are important differences. There is a general alerting effect, a loss of fatigue, and improved performance on certain tasks, but the degree of change may be less than that which occurs with the more powerful stimulants. There is also evidence that nicotine can have a calming effect under certain conditions (Gilbert, 1979). The feelings of self-confidence and euphoria associated with cocaine and amphetamine may not be as strong in the case of nicotine, although the effects are clearly reported as pleasant by smokers.

The circulatory system is also stimulated after nicotine. Heart rate increases, blood pressure rises, and there is increased cardiac output. Respiration is also increased. Dizziness, nausea, and vomiting are prominent effects associated with nicotine, particularly in the novice user. Nicotine can also act as a mild appetite suppressant.

Nicotine is a highly toxic compound if taken in sufficient doses. One of its uses is as an insecticide, and people who handle large quantities sometimes experience symptoms of actual poisoning. These include salivation, sweating, vomiting, disorientation, difficulty in breathing, and weak pulse rates. Death usually results from respiratory failure due to paralysis of the muscles.

The symptoms of chronic use of low levels of nicotine are difficult to determine. This is because chronic nicotine users obtain the drug in tobacco, which has many other constituents. Indeed, most of the major problems associated with smoking (lung cancer, heart disease, and emphysema) are due mainly to other constituents of tobacco smoke. Carbon monoxide, for example, is responsible for the shortness of breath experienced by smokers, and may be involved in heart disease (see Chapter Six for a more complete discussion of these issues).

Nicotine appears to be able to induce mild physical dependence. The withdrawal symptoms include headache, sleep disturbance, difficulty in concentrating, irritability, and anxiety. Increased food intake with associated weight gain has been known to occur in those who stop smoking.

History   The early history of tobacco use among American Indians is not well known. Archaeological work has shown that tobacco smoking was practiced in 200 A.D. Records also suggest that it spread from west to east in North America. While pipe smoking appears to have been the dominant method of administration among the Indians, they also used it as snuff. Early tobacco use by them was controlled and ritualized. It was employed for ceremonial purposes but also for the prevention of hunger and as a medicine. Many early explorers, including Columbus, described its use.

Although brought to Europe by several explorers and traders in the early and middle sixteenth century, use at this time was mainly medicinal. The widespread popularity it was to enjoy eventually probably began when Sir Francis Drake returned to England with it in 1586 (Robert, 1967). The suddenness with which tobacco use was adopted is difficult to explain, but may have depended on several factors.

First, through the influence of Drake and Sir Walter Raleigh, tobacco smoking became fashionable amongst the aristocrats of the time. A man who aspired to be successful in this social group felt compelled to adopt the habit of pipe smoking. Those who did not smoke were considered to be at a serious social disadvantage.

The second important factor was the belief that tobacco smoke had powerful medicinal properties. The list of ailments said to be cured or helped by tobacco was enormous. Among these were illnesses leading to nasal congestion. This belief in medicinal properties was common to just about every group who adopted the habit, beginning with the Indians of America. While it is understandable in the case of a substance like opium, it is difficult to see how it could have arisen with tobacco. Although the belief received a boost in the plague of 1614 when people became convinced that smokers were less likely to catch the disease, it seemed to have died out in England about fifty years after the introduction of tobacco.

Several attempts were made to control its use in England. One group who wanted greater regulation was the medical profession. Tobacco was a substance which was assumed to have great curative powers, but was out of their control. However, the speed at which its use spread and its great popularity gave them little chance of exercising this control. The other main attempt was by King James I, who acceded to the throne in 1604. He was one of the most outspoken critics of smoking. He raised the duty on imported tobacco some forty-fold. This had the effect of increasing local production and smuggling rather than reducing consumption. In order to maintain revenue by reducing smuggling he was forced to reduce the duty significantly. Eventually, James forbade local production and made importation a royal monopoly. The only allowable source was the English colony of Virginia.

While this was occurring, tobacco use was spreading throughout Europe and Asia. By the early sixteenth century it had reached China and Japan. It is fair to say that no other drug has been adopted so widely in such a short space of time. Its spread across the two continents required only a few decades at a time when transport was relatively slow and many trade routes insecure.

Smoking was the main method of tobacco use. However, there were some variations in how this was done. While the common technique was to smoke a pipe in the same manner as is done today, the Russians adopted a different practice. They inhaled very deeply, producing rapid intoxication and unconsciousness for a period of time. This practise was also adopted elsewhere, including parts of Africa. Besides smoking, tobacco was chewed, taken in the nose as snuff, or drunk as a tincture.

The main conduits for the spread of tobacco were the soldiers, sailors, merchants, and ambassadors who travelled widely. In many countries the pattern of adoption was similar. It was first introduced by travellers from a country already using tobacco. The first peoples to use it would come from the wealthy and powerful groups in the country. If for no other reason this would have occurred because of the expense of the drug. Then, gradually, as it became more abundant, use would spread to the general population.

Playing an important role in this spreading of the drug were various commercial interests. They helped introduce the drug by selling and encouraging the use of tobacco. They also sold the various implements used to administer it. A second important role was in the setting up of growing, processing, and distribution in a country once the habit had been adopted. Tobacco offered the possibility of great returns for those commercially involved from the beginning. In addition, governments frequently obtained great revenue from taxes and duties on tobacco. As a result, there were powerful vested interests with a strong financial stake in the adoption and spread of tobacco.

It should not be thought that tobacco use spread without any opposition, however (Corti, 1931). It is true that European countries such as France and Italy accepted it with relatively little opposition. In France it had been introduced by the French ambassador to Portugal, Jean Nicot. When the active ingredient in tobacco was isolated by French chemists it was named after him. Ready acceptance in France resulted from the need for extra government revenue. In Italy it spread through the nobility and the clergy and eventually to the rest of the population. The Pope attempted to prohibit its use in churches through a papal bull, but this was eventually repealed.

Opposition was considerably more forceful in countries such as Turkey and Russia. Tobacco was first introduced to Turkey around the end of the sixteenth century. Its use spread rapidly, but not without considerable resistance from many quarters. Religious leaders suggested that it was forbidden by the Koran, and many also had a fear of fire. At a time when most houses were made of wood, this was an important consideration. Local merchants also opposed it in the beginning. As was the case elsewhere, tobacco was first traded by foreigners and was therefore outside the control of the local merchants. There was also considerable fear amongst these people that tobacco may reduce sales of other goods, particularly coffee. Finally, tobacco houses were seen as places of sedition by the Sultan. People went there to smoke, but also had the opportunity to discuss affairs of the day. The Sultan did not want to foster an atmosphere of discontent. Rather than simply eliminating the tobacco houses where seditious discussions could occur, the Sultan banned smoking completely.

The first penalty for smoking in Turkey was to have the smoker parade through the streets with a pipe stem stuck through the nose. Later this penalty was increased to death. Despite the harshness of these penalties, smoking continued. Many people were executed until 1648, when a Sultan came to the throne who was himself a smoker. Turkey then changed to a country that profited through trade of the tobacco, spreading the drug throughout the Ottoman empire.

Tobacco use was introduced to Russia in the early seventeenth century. This period was a watershed in Russian history. Outside influences were becoming stronger and stronger, but were met with opposition from conservative forces inside the country. Chief among these were the clergy. The conservatives saw tobacco as one more aspect of Western influence, and through their actions incited prohibition in 1634. The initial penalty was whipping or torture, usually in public, repeat offenders being exiled to Siberia. When these measures were found to be unsuccessful, the death penalty was imposed. Use continued despite the harshness of these penalties.

Peter the Great was strong in his opposition to conservatives and willing to adopt many Western ways. From the time he became Tsar in 1689, use and trade in tobacco was liberalized. In his court smoking became a symbol of modernism, and this use by the aristocracy was an important influence in the spread of smoking after the penalties were removed.

Turkey and Russia were not the only countries in which smoking was met with harsh opposition. Similar penalties were imposed in Japan and China, but again, found to be ineffective. In Berlin there was a successful people's revolt against the ban on smoking, and it would seem that, with this as a good indicator, tobacco use can be seen as never truly being controlled successfully despite the penalties. Authorities have been forced to accept use of the drug, but then take advantages of this use through taxes and duties.

After its initial acceptance, fashions changed as to the way tobacco was used. Snuff became particularly common in eighteenth century Europe. Its use was popularized by the French and then spread to England and other countries. Pipe smoking declined as a result. In the United States, chewing tobacco was very popular in the nineteenth and early twentieth centuries, while cigars were widely used in the latter part of that period.

By far the biggest change in smoking habits came with the introduction of the modern cigarette. Much milder than anything else available, the smoke is easier to inhale deeply. People found the practice of smoking cigarettes easier to adopt and there was a massive increase in the number of tobacco users throughout many countries. Cigarette manufacture actually began in Europe in the middle of the nineteenth century, but the more popular, milder cigarettes date from the early twentieth century.

With the introduction of the cigarette came a change in the pattern of use. Whereas most pipe and cigar smokers had been men, women quickly adopted cigarette smoking. The tobacco companies also launched huge advertising campaigns, with much of the material directed towards women and younger people.

In most countries use of tobacco has increased through this century. Nicotine has become one of the most widely used drugs, perhaps second only to caffeine. However, in many Western countries usage has started to decline in recent years. This follows the accumulation of evidence that smoking is an important risk factor in many diseases, including lung cancer, heart disease, and emphysema. These dangers have been widely advertised and, at the same time, advertising by tobacco companies has been restricted in many countries. Some bans on smoking in certain places (elevators, hospitals, theaters, etc.) have also been introduced and are becoming more widespread, making public use increasingly difficult. In contrast, tobacco use is still growing in many third-world countries where the old pattern is repeating itself — in other words, smoking is seen as a symbol of modernization and is pushed by commercial interests while the government comes to view it as an important source of revenue.

Caffeine

Caffeine is one of a group of compounds called *methylxanthines.* The other major members of this group are *theophylline,* which is found in tea leaves, and *theobromine,* found in the cacao bean. Caffeine itself is found in a number of plants including coffee beans, tea leaves, and in the cacao bean. While all the methylxanthines have similar effects on the body, caffeine appears to have the strongest effect on the brain, and theobromine the weakest.

Caffeine is ingested mostly as a beverage. Coffee is produced from beans of the plant *Coffee arabica.* The beans are first roasted, cooled rapidly, and then ground to a fine powder. Hot water is used to extract caffeine and other soluble compounds to make the coffee drink. Instant coffee is made from soluble parts of the ground coffee, and has a different flavor and a lower caffeine content.

Tea comprises the new, tiny leaves of *Thea chinensis.* The leaves are picked and dried, and the dried leaves are then rolled and crushed. They may then be mixed with hot water to extract the caffeine and flavorings to make green tea. The leaves may also be left in a moist atmosphere to oxidize and form black tea before being mixed with water.

Chocolate was originally a drink made by grinding the dried roasted kernels of the cacao bean. Chocolate powder (cocoa) is produced by removing most of the fat (cocoa butter) from this thick liquid. Cocoa butter mixed with both chocolate powder and sugar produces the familiar type of solid chocolate we know today.

The relative amounts of caffeine obtained from the different sources are shown below in Table 1.4. These estimates are based on figures from a number of sources (see Barone and Roberts, 1984).

Effects   The effects of caffeine are similar to that of other stimulants already described (Dews, 1984). While some stimulation may be felt at relatively low doses (after, say, one cup of coffee), higher doses such as two hundred to four hundred grams can result in quite marked stimulation. Alertness may be increased, and performance of simple manual tasks improved. Sleep onset may be delayed and the pattern of sleep disturbed. Such effects may be less obvious to regular users who may report feelings of relaxation and calmness instead. The difference may be due to the development of tolerance in regular users (see Chapter Two).

The effects of caffeine on bodily functions are complex. Low doses may produce a slight increase or even a slight decrease in heart rate. Higher doses produce a definite increase in heart rate, even to the point of cardiac irregularities appearing. The effects on blood vessels are varied. Blood vessels in the brain are constricted, decreasing blood flow. In the body they are dilated. The net result from this and from changes in the performance of the heart creates an increase in rate of blood flow. This action, together with the increase in metabolic rate and the facilitation of muscular work that the methylxanthines produce, may help alleviate fatigue. Other effects of caffeine and the methylxanthines include increased secretion of gastric acid, increased urine production and relaxation of smooth muscle, including the lungs.

Regular users of high doses of caffeine report a number of adverse effects. These include irritability, insomnia, anxiety, and headache. Such symptoms may appear with doses around eight hundred milligrams per day.

TABLE 1.4   Caffeine Content of Various Beverages and Chocolate

SOURCE	AMOUNT	AVERAGE CAFFEINE CONTENT (mg)
Roasted and ground coffee	200 ml cup	110
Percolated drip coffee	200 ml cup	150
Instant coffee	200 ml cup	80
Tea	200 ml cup	50
Cola drink	150 ml	15
Chocolate	30 g	20

Other problems which may be associated with high caffeine intake include peptic ulcer and cardiac arrhythmias. Very high doses, unlikely to be taken by a normal user, can result in convulsions and even death. Discontinuing high caffeine use results in a withdrawal syndrome, the most prominent symptom of which is headache.

Medical uses   The methylxanthines have a number of therapeutic uses (Rall, 1985). Their effects on the heart make them useful in treatment of heart failure. Their ability to relax the smooth muscle of the lungs makes them of value in the treatment of asthma, both in emergency situations and as preventive measure. Caffeine is used as part of the treatment for severe headache, particularly migraine headache. This beneficial effect is probably due to its ability to constrict blood vessels in the brain. The stimulant actions of caffeine are sometimes of use as well in treating patients suffering from barbiturate overdose.

History   The origins of coffee are obscure. It appears to be native to Ethiopia and to have been used at first in the acts of either chewing the beans or making an infusion with the leaves. Up until the fourteenth century it was used mainly as a medicine though at about that time the pattern of use was altered: the practice of making a drink from ground, roasted beans began and cultivation of the plant commenced in Arabia.

One of the plant's early uses was in religious observances. People spending entire nights in prayer used the coffee to maintain their alertness. Eventually, this became so common that coffee became an integral part of almost all religious festivals. However, some Arab religious leaders opposed this development.

Coffee use spread into other areas of life and from country to country in the Arab world. The first coffee houses appeared in the fifteenth century. People would visit them to drink coffee, but also to talk and be entertained. Perhaps because of the opportunity of discussion the houses were often seen as places of sedition. Rulers believed that coffee drinkers were plotting against them. For this reason, and because of religious objections, coffee use was banned from time to time in parts of the Arab world. Although penalties were very harsh in some cases, coffee drinking continued. The houses sometimes disappeared for a time as coffee drinking went underground, but would reappear as soon as bans were revoked. (See Hattox, 1985, for descriptions of the coffee houses and the legal debates over coffee in these countries.)

The first European accounts of coffee appeared in the late sixteenth century, but use did not begin until the early seventeenth century. The practices of the Europeans were copied from the Arabs. Initially there were claims of medical and religious virtues, although medical opinion on the new drug was divided. However, spread of coffee drinking was mediated mainly through coffee houses. Modeled on those in Arab countries, they began in

England in the early seventeenth century spreading through Europe and the United States by the early eighteenth century (Wellman, 1961).

The coffee houses of seventeenth and early eighteenth century England were colorful places. That period of English history was a turbulent one, witnessing great public debates over democracy and the nature of government. Much of the argument about the role of the monarchy and of parliament was carried on in the coffee houses. It was said that if one couldn't argue for one side or the other then there was little point in frequenting a coffee house. These houses also played a role in other aspects of intellectual life, and literary figures often met to discuss their work and ideas.

European opposition to coffee use came from two main sources. The first was one already encountered in the Arab world: the monarchy was afraid of the sedition they believed to be fomenting at these establishments. As a result, Charles II banned all coffee houses in England. The protest that resulted was so overwhelming that he shifted the dictate and instead imposed a heavy tax on coffee.

The second source of opposition came from those with a financial interest in the production and sale of alcohol. In many European countries, coffee use actually replaced alcohol use. People reduced their alcoholic consumption as they began to use the new drug. Various commercial interests, such as the breweries, were threatened by this change. They petitioned strongly for restrictions on coffee use, or at least for heavy taxes on the new drug. Governments of some countries also had a financial interest in the sale of alcohol. They obtained substantial revenues that were threatened by the change in drug use. The Prussian government was one such example and, working with the breweries, endeavoured to encourage alcohol drinking and discourage coffee drinking. Their methods included taxation and restrictions on coffee availability. Although these may have had some effect, there was relatively little change in the popularity of coffee and the desire of people to associate in the coffee houses.

A decline of the coffee houses came in the eighteenth century. A number of factors contributed to this. One was a change in clientele, as the upper class gradually replaced the ordinary working people who had been the primary customers. The houses also began to sell a wider range of drinks and many became indistinguishable from clubs and taverns. Consumption of coffee in the home also began to increase in the eighteenth century. Another, perhaps, final factor for many countries was the rising popularity of tea.

Tea use began in China, probably several thousand years B.C. The first verifiable use of tea was in the fourth century A.D. By the eighth century it was sufficiently widespread for taxation to be imposed.

Tea was first introduced to Europe in the early seventeenth century. Dutch traders brought with them the leaves and the practice of making an infusion. Tea was imported from both China and India. While the Dutch continued to trade in tea, it was the English and, in particular the British East

India Company, that came to dominate the tea trade. Revenues generated by the Indian tea trade, both through private interests and through government taxes, helped fund the British Empire.

In eighteenth century Britain tea gradually came to replace coffee as the major source of caffeine. This change was due in part to an advertising campaign by the East India Company—perhaps the first such campaign. Tea use also received official encouragement as an alternative to coffee. This was because profits from tea stayed within the British Empire, whereas coffee beans had to be imported from outside. Because of the various pressures, tea drinking assumed greater popularity, although coffee was still widely used.

An opposite pattern developed in the United States. There had been much unhappiness in American colonies over taxes on tea levied by the British government. Eventually, the government was forced to lift the taxes, but also allowed the East India Company to bypass the colonial merchants and sell directly. The Boston Tea Party and other acts of rebellion were led by merchants who stood to lose an enormous amount by the implementing of this change. It then became American patriotic duty to refrain from drinking tea. The result: an increase in the popularity of coffee. Although patterns are slowly changing, today these historical differences (greater popularity of tea in Britain and of coffee in the United States) still remain.

Coffee and tea are now almost universally available throughout the world. Tea is still grown mainly in China and India, but coffee is now very widely distributed, the South American countries being amongst the largest producers. Recent changes have included faster and simpler methods of preparing the beverages; these being both "instant" coffee and the "tea bag."

In addition to tea and coffee, there are other sources of caffeine. One is cola drinks, made with the caffeine of the kola nut. Chocolate and cocoa are also minor sources of caffeine and other methylxanthines. In some countries caffeine is sold over-the-counter in tablet form as a stimulant or an antifatigue compound. Finally, some South Americans make a drink called *maté* that is produced from the plant *Ilex paraguensis* containing caffeine. Use seems traditional but the origins of this custom are obscure.

Hallucinogens

The hallucinogens are a diverse group of compounds, most of which are of plant origin though some are produced by chemical synthesis. For many years there has been debate as to how to classify these compounds, and indeed, which drugs should or should not be called hallucinogens (Brimblecombe and Pinder, 1975).

One problem is that many drugs produce hallucinations if a sufficient dose is taken. Marijuana is such a drug. The user who takes a large dose of this substance may experience vivid hallucinations. However, the effect does not usually occur in the range of doses commonly taken. Many long-standing marijuana users would have never experienced hallucinations while under the influence of the drug.

Another group of compounds capable of producing hallucinations, but discussed under a separate heading, are the *anticholinergics*. Again, while they may produce hallucinations, they do not necessarily do so. These drugs are not discussed here both for this reason and because they produce their effects in a different manner from that of the major group of hallucinogens. Similarly, drugs such as amphetamine are capable of hallucinatory action, however not at the usual dose and through implementation of a different brain mechanism.

The main group of hallucinogens share a number of properties. In particular, the hallucinations they produce have similar characteristics and their pharmacological effects are much the same. This group includes the naturally occurring compounds *mescaline* (the main active ingredient in the *peyote cactus*), *psilocybin* (the active ingredient in certain *hallucinogenic mushrooms*), *ergot alkaloids* (components of certain *fungi* and other *plants*) and *muscimole* (a component of the mushroom, *fly agaric*).

The best known synthetic compound in this group is *LSD* (*d*-lysergic acid diethylamide). Others are chemically similar to amphetamine but produce effects like mescaline and LSD. Among this group are *DOM* or *STP* (2, 5-dimethoxy-4-methylamphetamine), *MDA* (3, 4-methylenedioxyamphetamine) and *MMDA* (3-methoxy-4,5-MDA). These compounds all require relatively sophisticated chemical techniques for their manufacture. They are often known as "designer drugs."

Effects   The physiological changes produced by the hallucinogens are most prominent in the first few hours after the drug is taken. They include dilated pupils, lack of muscular coordination, muscular weakness, and tremors. Heart rate and blood pressure may rise, but the effects are small and variable. The user may also experience dizziness, nausea, and even vomiting in this early part of the drug experience (Hollister, 1981).

There are a number of perceptual changes that are characteristic of the hallucinogens. The first type are *simple distortions*. For example, colors may be brighter and more intense, and objects around the person may change shape. The second type are experiences of *synesthesia*. This term refers to the translation of experiences from one sensory modality into another: sounds may be "seen," tastes "heard," etc. Finally, there are the frank hallucinations. These are mainly visions of objects and patterns that are usually in a constant state of change. Other senses may be involved, but visual hallucinations predominate (see Siegel, 1977, for examples of these).

Associated with the perceptual changes are feelings of depersonalization or of being "external to the self," almost as if one is looking at oneself from the outside. This may provoke anxiety in some users, particularly those who are inexperienced. Users also report feelings of insightfulness, as though discovering great truths about the world. This belief may continue beyond the drug experience. Great emotional changes may accompany the experience. These can vary from ecstasy to despair, possibly even in the same "trip."

This pattern of effects can be altered in one of two ways, both of which result in "bad trips." First, the individual may panic. This is frequently associated with a feeling of loss of control. Experiences may seem all too real, rather than being drug-induced phenomena. Panic may also result simply from unpleasant experiences — for instance, in the common hallucination that spiders are crawling over the body. The second type of "bad trip" may involve psychotic reactions. Symptoms such as paranoia and delusions are common, but other schizophrenic-like symptoms may also result. In such cases bizarre behavior, even suicide, can occur. Sometimes the psychosis may persist long after other symptoms of drug use have disappeared.

Another effect of hallucinogens that can happen after the drug-taking episode is the recurrence of the drug-induced experience days, weeks, or even months later. The person may have an emotional or perceptual experience similar to one that had occurred under the influence of the drug, seemingly without any provocation or inducement. These "flashbacks" are usually brief. Their cause is unknown.

Medical uses   There are no apparent medical uses for the hallucinogens. Some exploratory work has been conducted by psychiatrists with LSD, but without clear or validated success.

History   The various hallucinogens have very diverse histories. Indeed, one of the interesting aspects is that they are found almost all over the world and have been noted to be used at least at some stage by a wide range of peoples. It has been suggested that man may have begun using hallucinogens after noting their effects on animals (Siegel, 1981). The evidence for this comes mainly from the folklore of different countries. Whatever the origins, people appear to have used hallucinogens as medicines, in magicoreligious ceremonies and for simple recreational purposes (Furst, 1976).

Fly agaric (amanita muscaria) is an hallucinogenic mushroom common to many parts of Europe and Asia. Its use dates back hundreds, perhaps thousands of years. Unfortunately, early evidence of its use has been more legend than established fact. One such legend is that it was used by certain Viking warriors prior to battle. The drug was supposed to increase their ferocity. Certainly, the Norse warriors were famous for their ferocity; whether it was due to fly agaric, alcohol, or some other means is not clear. It has also been argued that fly agaric was the drug known as *soma* in poetry from ancient India (Wasson, 1968). Soma was much celebrated, but the description has made it difficult to positively identify the drug, or even to be sure that it was a real drug.

One interesting characteristic of fly agaric is that the active ingredient, probably muscimole, is excreted unchanged in the urine. Because of this, and the relatively scarcity of the mushrooms, people often saved their drug-containing urine and reused it. Such practises have been reported amongst people in Siberia and elsewhere.

Mushrooms were also used in Central America. Called *teonacatl,* the most potent contained psilocybin. Stone carvings found in the region suggest that use dates back to at least 1000 B.C. The Spanish reported that use was for both social and religious reasons. The mushrooms may also have been employed as medicines. In their efforts to westernize the Indians and convert them to Christianity, the Spanish attempted to suppress teonacatl use. Partly as a result of these efforts and partly due to the profound social changes that occurred amongst the Central American Indians, hallucinogenic mushroom use was thought to have died out by this century. However, its continued use by certain Indian tribes was rediscovered in the 1950s.

Contemporary mushroom use also occurs in Western societies. After the upsurge of interest in hallucinogens in the 1960s and 1970s, people began seeking out the so-called magic mushrooms. Unfortunately, these people were not always good botanists and many poisonings and even deaths occurred. This use continues today, but is not so common.

Another hallucinogen described by the Spanish was peyote. A cactus native to Central America, the Aztecs used it in a similar manner to teonacatl. It is harvested in November and December of each year, then sliced and dried. Each piece is known as a *mescal button.* Peyote use has also continued to present day Central America. Again, this is despite the efforts by the early Spanish conquerors to eliminate it. Characteristic patterns of peyote use have not changed in those tribes who have kept their traditional ways.

Peyote use spread to the North American Indians in the nineteenth century. It has now become a sacrament of the Native American Church, an amalgamation of Christianity that espouses traditional beliefs and practices. Peyote use is an important part of the church's activities, and the cactus is believed to be a gift of God to man. The United States government has allowed sacramental use of peyote by members of the church.

Another hallucinogen used by the Aztecs was *Ololiuqui* – or seeds of the morning glory plant. These seeds contain *ergot alkaloids* with hallucinogenic properties. Ergot alkaloids were also known in the West, mainly through the fungus *Claviceps purpurea* which grows on grain. Ingestion of the grain on which the fungus had grown resulted in an illness known as *ergotism* or *St. Anthony's fire.* The varied effects of the ergot alkaloids produced many unpleasant symptoms in those who ingested large quantities of the grain. It has been suggested that a related fungus (*Claviceps paspali*) was used in Ancient Greece to produce hallucinations. In particular, it has been claimed that the Mysteries of Eleusis, a secretive religious ceremony, famous in the ancient world, which only initiates could attend, were based on ingestion of ergot alkaloids in this fungus (Wasson, Ruck and Hoffman, 1978).

Various specific ergot alkaloids became important to medicine for the treatment of a diverse range of disorders, but often created problems by their severe side-effects. In fact, in the late 1930s and early 1940s, a Dr. Albert Hoffman was working in the Sandoz Laboratories in Switzerland on the development of compounds derived from ergot alkaloids. On one occasion he left his laboratory because of feelings of dizziness. After arriving home he had strong hallucinogenic experiences and was convinced that these resulted from accidental ingestion of one of the compounds on which he was working. After further investigation, this turned out to be the compound now known as LSD.

Initial scientific interest in LSD centered on the belief that it may help reveal the key to schizophrenia. There is a degree of similarity between some schizophrenic symptoms and certain effects of LSD. Unfortunately, this line of research has not, as yet, been fruitful.

Illegal use of LSD became very popular in the late 1960s and early 1970s. Mainly centered in the United States, it also spread to other Western countries. Most users were in their late teen years or early twenties. While many users simply took the drug for recreational purposes alone, there were also "serious" users. These people took the drug for the insight it gave them, for the experience of self-discovery it provided or for other spiritual reasons. Drug use was often associated with a variety of mystical beliefs. Users also felt themselves alienated in modern Western society. The "guru" of this movement was Timothy Leary (see, for example, Leary, 1965).

While recreational use of LSD has continued in the West, "serious" use has declined. LSD no longer attracts the attention it once did. In part this may have been because claims for its spiritual value had been perceived by most to be exaggerated somewhat.

Phencyclidine

Phencyclidine (PCP) is an hallucinogenic drug which differs from the LSD group, from the anticholinergics and from marijuana. Introduced through medical use, it was quickly adopted as a recreational drug, particularly in the United States. While some of the PCP available on the street might divert from legal sources, it is also relatively easy to manufacture using readily available raw materials. PCP usually comes in the form of a white powder that is either ingested, taken through the nose, possibly mixed with tobacco, parsley, or marijuana, or smoked in a cigarette.

Effects   PCP is a relatively long-acting drug. Depending on the dose, the period of intoxication may last from a few hours to several days. Users of the drug generally report a feeling of dissociation or "unreality." Their use of the drug seems to allow them to "cut off" from the world, allowing an escape from usual, day-to-day existence. While this is true of many drugs, the effect appears to be a particularly powerful one in the case of PCP. Hallucinations also occur, but these are different from the LSD type. In particular, they are very frequently auditory, whereas LSD hallucinations are almost solely visual.

Many people report that the PCP hallucinations are unpleasant; they may evoke feelings of anxiety and paranoia.

Activity levels can be very low or very high under the influence of PCP. If very low, the person is in a catatonic-like state; unmoving, often with eyes closed. At other times the person may move constantly in a relatively uncoordinated fashion. This can make it difficult to control someone using PCP. Physiological effects include increased heart rate, blood pressure, sweating, lack of muscular coordination, and vomiting. Sensitivity to pain is also decreased.

High doses of the drug can induce anesthesia: the person appears to go into a coma and can remain unresponsive for an extended period of time. If severe enough, respiration may stop and the person may die. High doses may also induce a psychotic state requiring hospital admission. While some of the symptoms resemble those of schizophrenia, the drug effects are not an exact model of that disorder. The psychotic state may last many days.

A number of deaths have been reported as a direct or indirect result of PCP usage. For example, in one United States study (Burns and Lerner, 1978), a total of nineteen deaths were recorded over a seven year period in two counties. Of these, twelve were accidental (eight from drowning), five resulted from suicide, and two were homicides. In addition to fatalities, PCP intoxication can result in bizarre or damaging behavior.

Medical uses Phencyclidine and the chemically-related *ketamine* are effective anesthetics. Their effectiveness is contingent on their ability to produce analgesia and a dissociated state. The state makes the patient relatively unaware of what is going on during surgery, producing little recall of the events after recovery. The major advantage of PCP and ketamine is that the anesthetic effects occur at doses that do not depress respiration to as great a degree as other anesthetics. These properties make them particularly useful for minor surgery where light anesthesia is required. While many countries have now prohibited use of PCP for this purpose, ketamine is still widely used.

History Phencyclidine was developed by the Parke Davis Company, and marketed as *Sernyl* in the United States in the late 1950s. Very soon it was noted that patients reported bizarre and unpleasant effects from the drug. Symptoms such as hallucinations, agitation, and anxiety were not uncommon. Although it had a number of advantages, these side effects forced its removal from the market. It continues to be used as an anesthetic in veterinary medicine where it is particularly valuable for minor surgery.

Recreational use of the drug was first noted in 1967. Like many other drugs it was associated with the "hippie" movement and was used at a time when people seemed willing to try almost anything. After a brief period of use its popularity declined simply because people did not seem to like its effects. Use may have then been confined to adulteration of other drugs.

Following this period of decline, it reemerged in the late 1970s in the United States. Known commonly as *angel dust,* its use has escalated rapidly. Some have suggested that there is a PCP "epidemic" in the United States, but estimates of use may be inflated because of the high frequency with which it produces severe problems. Some PCP use has also been reported in other countries. Feldman, Agar, and Beschner (1979) provide a very interesting account of the street use of PCP.

Marijuana

The hemp plant *Cannabis sativa* is the source of marijuana. Hemp has been used for a variety of purposes, including using its fiber for the making of rope. It is also a producer of oil seeds, in addition to being a potent drug source. For these reasons it has been extensively cultivated, and in some areas, selectively bred for different purposes. Because of its great economic value, cultivation of *Cannabis sativa* has spread all over the world. Its native habitat is not clearly known but is most likely Central Asia.

The hemp plant exists in both male and female forms. Both contain the main active ingredient, $\triangle^9$–THC ($\triangle^9$–tetrahydrocannabinol). However, the female plant secretes a sticky resin which covers the flowers and upper leaves of the plant. (Depending on conditions it can grow to be about fifteen feet tall). The highest concentration of the active ingredient is found in this resin.

Marijuana is used in several forms. The simplest and least potent form consists of dried stalks and leaves. More highly prized is a mixture of dried upper portions of the plant, particularly the flowers. These contain a larger amount of the resin. Finally, there is the resin itself, which is scraped or chemically extracted from the plant. This is usually known as *hashish,* although this term is sometimes applied to any potent form of marijuana.

Marijuana is usually taken in one of two ways. It is commonly smoked, either in the form of a cigarette or in a pipe. The other way is to ingest it — either by itself or in some prepared food. Because the active ingredient is viscous and insoluble in water it cannot readily be injected.

While $\triangle^9$–THC is thought to be the main active ingredient in marijuana, there are a number of other potentially active compounds. Many of these could contribute in some way to the effects of the drug. They are currently the subject of much research, both to help unravel the effects of marijuana and because this group of compounds, the cannabinoids, may be a useful source of pharmaceuticals.

Effects   Marijuana produces a wide range of biological and psychological changes that have been well-documented (Jones, 1978). The marijuana user typically feels a sense of well-being or euphoria and will probably be very relaxed. If a group of people use the drug together there may be a great deal of social interaction and spontaneous laughter. Users also report a sense of unreality and claim great insightfulness that they would not, under usual circumstances, have had otherwise. This effect is shared with hallucinogens such as LSD.

Some perceptual effects of marijuana are similar to, but much less intense, than those of the hallucinogens. Users often report greater acuity: sights, tastes, and smells seem very clear and intense. The sense of touch may be affected similarly. On the other hand, vision may be blurred and things may appear hazy. Discrimination of time is also often distorted such that time seems to pass very slowly. Higher doses may produce effects similar to those of the hallucinogens: perceptual distortions, synesthesia, and at very high doses, hallucinations.

While an initial excitation and increase in activity often accompanies the early part of marijuana intoxication, this may be replaced by sedation after a period of time. The user may feel tired, and may even drift into sleep. Marijuana does not appear to influence the different stages of sleep consistently, although some individuals may be affected.

The most prominent physiological change is an increase in heart rate, often of the order of twenty to fifty beats per minute. Another characteristic change is a reddening of the eyes. Blood pressure and respiration are not altered in any predictable manner, but there may be a slight lowering of body temperature. There is usually some decrease in muscular strength and coordination. Users also report increased appetite and a dry mouth and throat.

Depending on factors such as experience, the setting in which the drug is taken, and the dosage, the user may experience a "bad trip." This is not as severe as the "bad trip" associated with use of hallucinogens. Rather, a state of confusion and feelings of loss of control are induced. The user may become paranoid unless convinced that his or her experience is due to the drug alone and will disappear when the drug effect wears off.

Various adverse effects associated with long-term use of marijuana have been proposed. These include the induction of schizophrenia, an amotivational syndrome, release of inhibition leading to criminal behavior, organic brain dysfunction, and teratogenic effects. For some of these (for example, criminal behavior) the evidence is weak; for most, the problem is that there is no convincing evidence one way or the other. In general, the data are suggestive, but need further confirmation or additional support. These issues are considered in more detail in Chapter Five.

Both tolerance and physical dependence can develop with long-term marijuana use, but it is unusual for either to be a major problem. Indeed, experienced users sometimes report needing less of the drug to get a "high" as a result of their experience. There is some experimental support for this (for example, Weil, Zinberg and Nelson, 1968), but additional evidence is needed. While physical dependence can develop, the withdrawal symptoms after terminating even frequent marijuana use are relatively mild (see Chapter Two).

Medical use In earlier times, marijuana was used for a variety of ailments, but the practise of prescribing this drug died out, at least in Western societies. However, the drug has begun to find new uses, and in some areas (as in some states of the United States for example) it is legal to use it for treatment of glaucoma and to help alleviate the nausea associated with use of anticancer drugs. In each case there is some evidence for its efficacy, but more research is being conducted on its varied effects.

History   Despite widespread use, the history of marijuana is somewhat fragmentary (Blum, 1969). There are claims of very early use (c. 2000–1000 B.C.) in China and India, but there is no strong evidence supporting them. It is clear that the drug was used by various central Asian groups, including the Scythians, Persians, and Assyrians around 700–500 B.C. The nature of this use is not known, but in at least some cases it appears to have been ceremonial. Marijuana has had a long association with religion and spiritualism in India, although the origin of its use as well, are unknown. There are also Indian manuscripts from the twelfth century describing its use for medical purposes.

Elsewhere, the spreading of the drug occurred mainly through Arab influence. By the tenth century the intoxicant effects of marijuana were known through most of the Arab world. In many of these countries the plant itself was already growing, so that it was the actual practice of marijuana ingestion that was passed on. Use may have also spread to Europe during this time, but there are few details. In any case it does not seem to have become particularly popular in that continent. It is likely that people in most countries used marijuana for both medical and recreational reasons; in some areas there may have been an association with religion or spiritualism.

European use was clearly recorded in the nineteenth century, particularly by writers such as Gautier, Dumas, and Baudelaire. They, along with other French literary and artistic figures of the time, were members of the *Club des Haschischins,* and met regularly to consume hashish together. It was amongst such elite members of society that marijuana was most popular at the time.

A major change in marijuana use occurred when it began to be smoked. The technique of smoking originated with the American Indians and their consumption of tobacco. However, as tobacco smoking spread, it was quickly realized that the same method could be used with marijuana. Smoking has a number of advantages, including rapidity of effect and greater control over dose (see Chapter Two). For these reasons smoking of the drug virtually replaced its eaten and beverage forms.

With the advent of smoking came a greater spread of marijuana use over the world and a greater frequency of use in the many countries in which it was established. However, while use increased in Europe and the United States, the drug was not as popular in those areas as it was in countries where it had been used for hundreds of years, including India and countries to its north as well as central Asia and North Africa.

One area where high levels of marijuana use have become common is

Jamaica. Marijuana was probably introduced by Indian migrants to the West Indies. It became very popular amongst poor blacks in the population and use has continued despite attempts beginning in the last century to stamp it out. To one particular group, the Rastafarians, religious significance has been attributed to the use of marijuana. Their particular religion is a variant of Christianity that regards Hailie Selassie, the former emperor of Ethiopia, as a messiah, and marijuana as a holy plant. It is most common among the poor black people of Jamaica. (See Rubin, 1975, for a description of marijuana use in Jamaica and in other societies.)

Coinciding with the increase in hallucinogen use in the West in the 1960s was an upsurge in the use of marijuana as well. During that period it became a symbol of rebellion and a means for rejecting old values and gaining new insights. Safer and milder than the hallucinogens, it was used by many more young people. Recently, the social and mystical significance of marijuana use has become less important.

Together with increased popularity have come moves to repeal laws forbidding marijuana use. These have been at least partially successful in some places, such as certain states of Australia and the United States where use incurs a fine. However, in some countries it is regarded as a social and medical evil, and heavy penalties are imposed. While such measures keep usage rates low in some places, they are relatively ineffective in others.

Solvents and Aerosols

A wide range of chemical solvents have been used as drugs. Amongst these are *toluene, acetone, naptha,* and *trichloro-ethylene.* Sources for these solvents include glue and plastic cements, petrol, thinners, and cleaning solutions. Propellants found in aerosols are used in a similar manner. Not all are psychoactive, but nitrous oxide, the chlorofluorocarbons, and others are used recreationally. Reviews of their use are given in Nagle (1968) and Barnes (1979).

All of these compounds are inhaled. Glue is usually placed in a paper or plastic bag which is held tight with the person inhaling from the opening. A pure solvent may be placed on a piece of cloth which is then held over the nose and mouth, or placed in a bag and sniffed. Aerosol users generally try to separate the propellant from the other material in the can. This may be done in a number of ways, including spraying the contents onto the inside of a closed plastic bag and inhaling the gas trapped in the bag.

Effects Many of the compounds used in this way have properties similar to those of general anesthetics. Indeed, two of them, trichloroethylene (a solvent) and nitrous oxide (a propellant) are also used for this purpose. The user may have feelings of light-headedness and drunkenness. At low doses this may be very pleasant, and associated with euphoria and self-confidence. Speech may be slurred and movement uncoordinated. In some cases the user may become impulsive, reckless, and uninhibited about his or her actions; in others there may be a quietness and even sleep. In the latter case users often report feelings of "nothingness." Although rare, some people experience visual and auditory hallucinations. More common are distortions of perception.

A number of adverse effects may be experienced by the user. These include nausea, muscular weakness, confusion, and disorientation. Respiration may be depressed, particularly at high doses, and palpitations of the heart may occur. As the effects wear off a "hangover" may develop, with symptoms such as headache, nausea, and pain.

Use of these substances has potentially fatal consequences. Death may result from cardiac arrhythmias or from respiratory arrest. Fatalities have been found amongst both novice and experienced users. In Australia deaths have been most commonly associated with aerosol use (Senate Select Committee on Volatile Substance Fumes, 1985).

Chronic use may produce a number of adverse effects, the exact nature of which depends on the particular chemical or chemicals being used. Kidney and liver damage are relatively common, while others include bone marrow toxicity, anemia, and nervous system degeneration. The latter effect is somewhat controversial, and will be discussed in more detail in Chapter Five. While some toxic effects may disappear once the individual ceases to use the substance, others are more permanent. Some toxic effects also result from other substances present in the solvent. For example, lead in petrol may cause major toxic effects to a chronic petrol sniffer. Physical dependence does not appear to be a major problem with the use of solvents and aerosols.

Medical uses   As mentioned, the solvent trichloroethylene and the propellant nitrous oxide are also used as general anesthetics. Other propellants are used in sprays which enable inhalation of drugs involved in the treatment of asthma and other disorders.

History   The earliest reported recreational use of a solvent or anesthetic occurred in the last century. *Ether* had been introduced in the eighteenth century and marketed as both an industrial solvent and as medicine. By that time, it had become popular as an alternative to alcohol. A few drops, inhaled or drunk, were sufficient to produce intoxication. The first users were members of the upper class of Europe and America, but use gradually spread to those in lower socioeconomic groups.

One important factor in the spread of ether was its price. Because of taxation and other reasons, alcohol was very expensive for many peasant people. If one compared the two drugs in terms of cost per intoxicating episode, then ether could be considered to be cheaper than spirits. One country where ether use became widespread was Ireland. While restrictions on sale eventually curtailed use early in this century, at one time ether was being used by up to one-eighth of the population of certain areas of Ireland.

Most other solvents and propellants are of much more recent origin. Although reports of recreational use appeared in the United States during the 1950s, it was not until a decade later that the extent of the problem became known. By that time the practise had spread throughout the United States and to many other countries of the world. Estimates of use are very difficult to make, but it is clear that users are almost entirely teenagers. While surveys suggest approximately equal numbers from both sexes, fatalities are predominantly male. Sniffing of the solvents and propellants can be a solitary activity, but is often done in groups as well. Users may have a preference for one substance over another (often based on factors such as volatility and smell as well as availability), although there is some degree of interchange. Most people who try sniffing do so on an experimental basis only; still fewer become regular users, and only a small percentage actually show any form of dependence.

Anticholinergics

Atropine and *scopolamine* are the two major, naturally occurring anticholinergics (see Chapter Two for an explanation of the term). They are found in a number of plants, but four in particular have been ingested in order to obtain the effects produced by these drugs. *Datura* (also known as Jimson weed or thorn apple) and *mandrake (Mandragona othicinarum)* contain both substances, *henbane (Hyoxyamus niger)* contains scopolamine, and *deadly nightshade (Atropa belladonna)* contains atropine.

With the exception of datura, these plants are mainly of European origin. There are a number of different species of datura, and they can be found over many parts of the world. All of the plants containing anticholinergics are ingested, either eaten, or made into an infusion. The practice of smoking them, usually with some other leaf such as tobacco, is also common in Asia.

More recently, anticholinergics such as atropine and scopolamine, as well as newer compounds in this class have been produced by pharmaceutical manufacturers. They are administered in the form of tablets or by injection.

Effects   The effects of anticholinergics depend very much on the dose taken. With low doses the user may simply become drowsy, confused and disoriented, and may lapse into a dreamless sleep. Higher doses may cause restlessness and excitement, marked disorientation, hallucinations, and delirium. The user who takes a high dose may experience these excitatory effects first, followed by drowsiness and sleep. To the outside observer, the user appears uncoordinated and confused, his or her movement appearing to be aimless. Users are often disinterested in what is going on around them.

Anticholinergics produce a number of bodily changes. Administration of low doses results in a small decrease in heart rate, but larger doses cause an increase. Respiration is stimulated and body temperature is increased. Muscle tone is depressed, making coordinated movement difficult. Pupils are dilated. A number of secretions are inhibited by anticholinergics, both in the respiratory tract (nose, throat, and lungs) and the alimentary tract (mouth and stomach). Gut motility is diminished.

Problems that arise with anticholinergics occur mainly due to overdosing. The result is usually a psychotic episode that requires hospitalisation. The person may lapse into a coma and death may occur from respiratory failure. The drugs are not usually taken repeatedly, so that physical dependence and withdrawal are not a problem.

Medical uses   Anticholinergics, either the naturally occurring atropine and scopolamine, or other synthetic compounds with similar action, are used in a number of medical contexts (Weiner, 1985). Their drying effects are employed both in cold remedies and in the treatment of disorders where congestion is a problem. They are also used in general anesthesia to counter the excess salivation and respiratory tract secretion produced by certain anesthetics.

The ability of these drugs to dilate pupils is frequently exploited in eye examinations. Atropine and the other compounds are also antidotes to poisoning caused by anticholinesterase agents, which are used as pesticides in agriculture and in chemical warfare.

Anticholinergics have also been used in treating parkinsonism. Previously the only effective drugs, they are now generally used together with *l*-dopa. Another early use of the drugs was in treatment of peptic ulcers, but they have now been replaced by other drugs. Certain heart attacks can be treated effectively with anticholinergics. The drugs also prevent motion sickness.

History   Plants containing anticholinergics have been used for various purposes dating back to ancient times (see, for example, Furst, 1976). Egyptian women were known to use deadly nightshade to enlarge their pupils, making them more attractive (hence the alternative name for this plant, *belladonna,* meaning beautiful woman). This same plant has been used as a poison (hence the term "deadly" and the name atropine, from Atropa of the Three Fates of Greek mythology — the one who cut the thread of each person's life at the appropriate time), as have other plants containing anticholinergics.

Anticholinergics have also been used as aphrodisiacs throughout history. It has been suggested that they were used in combination with wine in the Bacchanalian feasts and orgies of ancient Greece (De Repp, 1957). Similarly, the witches of Medieval times used them in the Black Mass, both as an aphrodisiac and to help produce the "flying" sensation. There is no real evidence that they do have aphrodisiac qualities, but in both cases they may have increased excitement and aided the spirit of wild abandon.

The magical and religious importance of datura was most apparent in the Americas. Different species of the plant were used by the Aztecs and the Indians of North America. Priests or *shamans* ingested relatively high doses of anticholinergics. The dreams and hallucinations they experienced were thought to be communication with the gods and visions of the future. Datura was also used in ceremonies such as funerals and rites of initiation. A further use was as medicine; this too was controlled by the priests.

Anticholinergics are probably less popular than they once were. Certainly, there is relatively little use in contemporary Europe and use among the Indians of America may have declined. The demise of traditional Indian religious practise has contributed to this change. In contrast to many other compounds, the ready availability of anticholinergics for medical purposes has not resulted in extensive use of these drugs. While some of the prescription and over-the-counter anticholinergics have been diverted for recreational use, the number of users is very small. Similarly, use of plants containing anticholinergics certainly occurs (for example, Hall, Popkin, and McHenry, 1977), but is not widespread. As a result, control and regulation of these drugs has not been a major problem.

Betel

Betel is the common name for a chew based on the areca nut (*Areca catechu*). The areca nut is chewed and held between the teeth and the lining of the mouth. It is then pressed with the tongue and sucked. Two other ingredients are sometimes added: the betel fruit or pepper (*Piper betle*) and lime (calcium hydroxide). The essential ingredients of the areca nut are *arecoline* and *arecaidine*.

The practise of chewing betel extends from the West coast of Africa to the South Pacific region. Although native to a number of these areas, cultivated areca nut is usually preferred. One current estimate puts the number of users worldwide at two hundred million (Burton-Bradley, 1979).

Effects   The betel chew has an immediate effect which is somewhat uncomfortable to the novice user: a powerful astringency that dries the mouth instantly. This is something to which the user must become accustomed, and in those experienced in use of the drug, saliva flows almost constantly to keep the mouth moist. Other effects felt by inexperienced users include dizziness, nausea, vomiting, and sweating. The act of mixing the lime and areca nut produces red stain in the saliva.

While inexperienced users may appear to be highly intoxicated, most betel chewers engage in the habit during their normal activities. In this sense it resembles cigarette smoking. Users report a relaxed, happy feeling, with increased alertness rather than sedation. It is sometimes used in the same way as stimulants, to postpone sleep or increase concentration (see Arjungi, 1976, and Burton-Bradley, 1980, for a more detailed description of these effects).

Medical uses   There are no current medical uses for betel.

History   The origin of betel chewing is unclear. In countries such as Papua New Guinea, for example, it is not known whether the practise was developed by the local people or introduced by traders some time ago. Its use was first documented several hundred years B.C. and by 600 A.D. it was extremely popular in Persia. As with many other drugs, Arab traders may have been instrumental in spreading the drug widely. In some countries use seems to have declined, while in others (such as Papua New Guinea) it is still very strong.

OVERVIEW

This brief survey has revealed a considerable degree of diversity amongst the drugs used for nonmedical purposes. No single common factor emerges which might distinguish this group from other available psychoactive chemicals not taken on a recreational basis (for example, antipsychotic drugs). It is also clear that the drugs now regarded as acceptable are difficult to distinguish on any rational basis from those which are banned.

The sources of drugs are quite diverse. Many are of plant origin. In some cases the entirety of the plant is used, though sometimes only a part of the plant and sometimes just an extract from it. The plant material may be modified by drying, heating, or mixing with another ingredient. More modern drugs are mainly synthetic pharmaceuticals. Some are based on naturally occurring chemicals, others are not. Finally, some drugs are industrial chemicals used for a range of purposes.

Methods of administration also vary. Originally, most drugs were probably ingested: eaten or taken in some form of drink. The technique of smoking was brought from the Indians of the Americas and became popular with a number of drugs. Administration via the nose was also developed initially by these people and, at different times, has been proven to be a popular way of taking certain drugs. And from late in the last century, drugs began to be administered via a hypodermic syringe. With certain drugs this has become the standard method of administration, particularly amongst those who use the drug frequently.

The effects of the different drugs are quite diverse. While some produce perceptual distortions and hallucinations, most do not. Some produce euphoria or a "high," others do not. Most, if not all drugs also vary in the effects they produce, depending on the conditions prevailing at the time of administration (an issue to be taken up in Chapter Three). The physiological effects can be quite diverse, but it is interesting to note that so many drugs have adverse effects (such as nausea) which make them unpleasant to the novice user.

There is also considerable variation in the histories of the drugs. Their origins are spread over almost all the world. Some are ancient and we have little idea of when use started, while use of others began only in the last few decades. Popular views relating to drug use have also changed through history. Tobacco is now known for instance to contain highly toxic substances in addition to nicotine, making its use undesirable. Perhaps of more interest is that opium use seemed to cause few problems in the "older" societies. This stands in marked contrast to the contemporary views of heroin, despite the similarity in the effects of the two.

Perhaps one thing common to all the drugs is that at one time they were thought to have valuable medicinal properties. Medicine was and is still instrumental in the introduction and spread of drug use. In some cases we can see the benefits of the drug. Opium can be seen as an example of this. However, many of the medical benefits ascribed to tobacco and others (both in Europe and America) are hard to understand from a contemporary perspective. Many currently used drugs also have legitimate medical uses. The benzodiazepines are a good example. Very often an individual may begin use for valid medical reasons, but continue even when those reasons are no longer valid.

Clearly then, a cursory examination of these drugs reveals little about why people use them, and why in one way and not another. To do this it is necessary to look at the issue from a range of perspectives, trying to find the factors which determine drug use. The following three chapters attempt to do this. The first looks at biological aspects: the principles of drug action in the body. The second examines drug use from a psychological perspective, while the third examines social aspects. Many of the themes which have emerged from the brief historical analyses above will be covered in more detail in this latter chapter.

REFERENCES

ANGVIST, B. & SUDILOVSKY, A. (1978).   Central nervous system stimulants; Historical aspects and clinical effects. In L.L. Iversen, S.D. Iversen & S.H. Snyder (Eds.), *Handbook of psychopharmacology*. (Vol. 16, pp. 389–424). New York: Plenum Press.

ARJUNGI, V.K.N. (1976).   Areca nut: A review. *Arzneimittel-Forschung, 26,* 951–956.

ASHLEY, R. (1975).   *Cocaine: Its history, uses and effects.* New York: St. Martin.

AUSTIN, G.A. (1985).   *Alcohol in Western society from antiquity to 1800.* Santa Barbara, California: ABC - Clio Inc.

BARNES, G.E. (1979).   Solvent abuse: A review. *International Journal of the Addictions, 14,* 1–26.

BARONE, J.J. & ROBERTS, H. (1984).   Human consumption of caffeine. In P.B. Dews (Ed.), *Caffeine.* (pp. 59–73) Berlin: Springer-Verlag.

BETT, W., HOWELLS, L. & MCDONALD, A. (1975).   Amphetamine in clinical medicine. A survey of the literature. *Postgraduate Medical Journal, 2,* 205–222.

BLUM, R.H. (1969).   A history of alcohol. In R.H. Blum and Associates, *Society and drugs.* (pp. 25–44) San Francisco: Jossey Bass.

BLUM, R.H. (1969).   A history of cannabis. In R.H. Blum and Associates, *Society and drugs.* (pp. 61–86) San Francisco: Jossey Bass.

BRIMBLECOMBE, R.W. & PINDER, R.M. (1975).   *Hallucinogenic agents.* Bristol: Wright-scientechnica.

BURNS, R.S. & LERNER, S.E. (1978).   Causes of phencyclidine related deaths. *Clinical Toxicology, 12,* 463–481.

BURTON - BRADLEY, B.G. (1980).   Psychosomatics of arecaidinism. *Papua New Guinea Medical Journal, 23,* 3–7.

BURTON - BRADLEY, B.G. (1980).   Arecaidinism: Betel chewing in transcultural perspective. *Canadian Journal of Psychiatry, 24,* 481–8.

BYCK, R. (1974).   *Cocaine Papers: Sigmund Freud.* New York: Stonehill.

CORTI, COUNT (1931).   *A history of smoking.* London: George G. Harrop.

DE ROPP, S. (1957).   *Drugs and the mind.* New York: Grove Press.

DE QUINCEY, T. (1822).   Confessions of an English opium eater. Reprinted in De Quincey, T. (1966).   *Confessions of an English opium eater and other writings.* A. Ward (Ed.) New York: Signet.

DEWS, P.B. (1984).   Behavioral effects of caffeine. In P.B. Dews (Ed.) *Caffeine.* (pp. 59–73) Berlin: Springer-Verlag.

DUNDEE, J.W. & MCILROY, P.D.A. (1982).   A history of the barbiturates. *Anaesthesia, 37,* 726–734.

ELLINWOOD, E.H. (1974).   The epidemiology of stimulant abuse. In E. Josephson & E.E. Carroll (Eds.), *Drug use: Epidemiological and sociological approaches.* (pp. 303–332) Washington: Hemisphere.

FELDMAN, H.W., AGAR, M.H. & BESCHNER, G.M. (1979).   *Angel Dust.* Lexington, Mass.: D.C. Heath.

FURST, P.T. (1976).   *Hallucinogens and culture.* San Francisco: Chandler and Sharp.

GAWIN, F.H. & KLEBER, H.D. (1986).   Abstinence symptomology and psychiatric diagnosis. *Archives of General Psychiatry, 43,* 107–113.

GILBERT, O.G. (1979).   Paradoxical tranquilizing and emotion reducing effects of nicotine. *Psychological Bulletin, 86,* 643–661.

HALL, R.C.W., POPKIN, M.K. & MCHENRY, L.E. (1977).   Angel's trumpet psychosis: A central nervous system anticholinergic syndrome. *American Journal of Psychiatry, 134,* 312–314.

HARVEY, S.C. (1985).   Hypnotics and sedatives. In A.G. Gilman, L.S. Goodman, T.W. Rall & F. Murad (Eds.) *The pharmacological basis of therapeutics* (7th ed., pp. 339–371.) New York: Macmillan.

HATTOX, R.S. (1985).   *Coffee and Coffee Houses.* Seattle: University of Washington Press.

HAYTER, A. (1968).   *Opium and the romantic imagination.* London: Faber and Faber.

HOLLISTER, L.E. (1981).   Effects of hallucinogens in humans. In B.L. Jacobs (Ed.), *Hallucinogens: Neurochemical, behavioral and clinical perspectives.* (pp. 1–18) New York: Raven Press.

JAFFE, J.H. & MARTIN, W.R. (1985).   Opioid analgesics and antagonists. In A.G. Gilman, L.S. Goodman, T.W. Rall & F. Murad (Eds.) *The pharmacological basis of therapeutics* (7th ed., pp. 491–531.) New York: Macmillan.

JONES, R.T. (1978).   Marijuana: Human effects. In L.L. Iversen, S.D. Iversen & S.H. Snyder (Eds.), *Handbook of Psychopharmacology.* (Vol. 12, pp. 95–185.) New York: Plenum Press.

KALIX, P. (1987).   Khat: Scientific knowledge and policy issues. *British Journal of Addiction, 82,* 47–53.

KENNEDY, J. (1985).   *Coca Exotica.* Cranbury: Associated Universities Presses.

LATIMER, D. & GOLDBERG, J. (1981).   *Flowers in the blood: The story of opium.* New York: Franklin Watts.

LEARY, T. (1965).   *The politics of ecstasy.* New York: G.P. Putnam's Sons.

MASSING, M. (1988).   The war on cocaine. *The New York Review of Books, 35* (Dec.), 61–67.

MEYER, R.E. & MIRIN, S.M. (1979).   *The heroin stimulus.* New York: Plenum.

MORTIMER, W.G. (1974).   *History of coca.* San Francisco: And/Or Press.

NAGLE, D.R. (1968).   Anesthetic addiction and drunkenness: A contemporary and historical survey. *International Journal of the Addictions, 39,* 25–39.

NENCINI, P. & ASHMED, A.M. (1989). Khat consumption: A pharmacological review. *Drug and Alcohol Dependence, 23,* 19–29.

PARSSINEN, T.M. (1983). *Secret passions, secret remedies: Narcotic drugs in British society 1820–1930.* Philadelphia: Institute for the Study of Human Issues.

RALL, T.W. (1985). Central nervous system stimulants: The methylxanthines. In A.G. Gilman, L.S. Goodman, T.W. Rall & F. Murad (Eds.) *The pharmacological basis of therapeutics* (7th ed., pp. 589–603). New York: Macmillan.

RICKELS, K., DOWNING, R.W. & WINOKUR, A. (1978). Antianxiety drugs: Clinical use in psychiatry. In L.L. Iversen, S.D. Iversen & S.H. Snyder (Eds.), *Handbook of psychopharmacology.* (Vol. 13, pp. 395–430). New York: Plenum Press.

RITCHIE, J.M. (1985). The aliphatic alcohols. In A.G. Gilman, L.S. Goodman, T.W. Rall & F. Murad (Eds.), *The pharmacological basis of therapeutics* (7th ed., pp. 372–386). New York: Macmillan.

ROBERT, J.C. (1967). *The story of tobacco in America.* Chapel Hill: University of North Carolina Press.

RUBIN, V. (Ed.) (1975). *Cannabis and culture.* The Hague: Moulton.

SENATE SELECT COMMITTEE ON VOLATILE SUBSTANCE FUMES. (1985). *Volatile substance abuse in Australia.* Canberra: Australian Government Publishing Service.

SIEGEL, R.K. (1977). Hallucinations. *Scientific American,* 1977 (October), 132–144.

SIEGEL, R.K. (1981). The natural history of hallucinogens. In B.L. Jacobs (Ed.), *Hallucinogens: Neurochemical, behavioral and clinical perspectives.* (pp. 19–33). New York: Raven Press.

TAMURA, M. (1989). Japan: Stimulant epidemics past and present. *Bulletin on Narcotics,* XLI, 83–93.

VAN DYKE, C. & BYCK, R. (1977). Cocaine 1884–1974. In E.H. Ellinwood Jr. & M.M. Killey (Eds.), *Cocaine and other stimulants.* (pp. 1–30). New York: Plenum Press.

WALLGREN, H. & BARRY, J. III. (1970). *Actions of alcohol.* (Vols. 1 and 2.) New York: American Elsevier.

WASSON, R.G. (1968). *Soma: Divine mushroom of immortality.* New York: Harcourt.

WASSON, R.G., RUCK, C.A.P. & HOFFMAN, A. (1978). *The road to Eleusis.* New York: Harcourt Brace Jovanovich.

WEIL, A.T., ZINBERG, N.E. & NELSON, J.M. (1968). Clinical and psychological effects of marijuana in man. *Science, 162,* 1234–1242.

WEINER, N. (1985). Atropine, scopolamine and related antimuscarimic drugs. In A.G. Gilman, L.S. Goodman, T.W. Rall & F. Murad (Eds.) *The pharmacological basis of therapeutics* (7th ed, pp. 105–129) New York: Macmillan.

WELLMAN, F.L. (1961). *Coffee.* London: Leonard Hill.

CHAPTER 2

Biological Aspects

Humans are complex biological organisms, and in order to understand the changes drugs produce, it is essential to understand how they affect us biologically. The drugs of interest here all have their primary effects on the brain. Through these effects they alter physiological functions within the body (for example, heart rate), subjective experience, and behavior. Most will have effects in other parts of the body, but the brain is the most important site of action.

The first area of concern that must be focused on is the fate of the drug in the body. How does it get to the brain to produce its effects, and how do the levels of drug change in the body over time? One important determinant is the way in which the drug is taken (for example, smoking marijuana vs. ingesting it). The chemical characteristics of the drug used are also important. Through knowledge of the various processes which ensue when a drug is administered we can better understand why drugs vary in the speed with which they produce their effect, their duration of action, and their strength. These are all factors that influence patterns of drug use.

A second important issue is how the drugs actually produce their effects once they reach the brain. It has long been thought that all drugs of dependence may share some common action in the brain. There is much support for such a notion, but it is still very much a hypothesis. Understanding brain mechanisms is important for two other reasons: it can help explain the variability in the effects of different drugs (for example, hallucinogens vs. benzodiazepines) and also then, enable prediction of the effects of new drugs. Drugs that produce similar activity in the brain also tend to have similar effects on biological functions, subjective experience, and behavior. It may also be necessary to evaluate whether a drug has adverse effects on brain function, an issue to be addressed further in Chapter Five.

The final matters to be addressed are tolerance and physical dependence. Tolerance is important in the initial stages of drug use and both are central to an understanding of long-term maintenance of drug use. In this chapter the biological aspects of tolerance will be considered; in the next chapter the psychological aspects which influence tolerance will be discussed. Likewise, physical dependence will be considered in this chapter, and psychological dependence in the next. One other biological factor, genetic predisposition to drug use, will be considered in the overall context of predisposing factors (Chapter Four).

MOVEMENT OF DRUG IN THE BODY

Routes of administration

In order for a drug to produce its effects it must reach the brain. This can be a long, complex process taking some time, or it may be very quick and simple. The first step is for the drug to be deposited inside the body. The method used for depositing the drug is termed the *route of administration*. The following routes are all in common use:

Oral
Injection

   Intravenous
   Intramuscular
   Subcutaneous

Inhalation
Application to mucous membranes

   Mouth
   Nose (intranasal)

What route is chosen depends on several factors. One is the physical form of the drug itself. Some drugs come in plant form and are relatively unprocessed. Examples include tobacco and marijuana. Obviously, drugs in this form cannot be injected. They may be applied to mucous membranes (for example chewing tobacco, snuff), taken orally (marijuana mixed with foods) or burnt, and the smoke inhaled (the most common method for both). Other drugs are in the form of a gas (for example, nitrous oxide) or a highly volatile liquid (solvents). In these forms the only possible route is through inhalation.

A very large number of drugs come as soluble powders. If this is the case, the user can choose just about any of the methods listed. The powder may be placed in the mouth (relatively uncommon) or nose (for example, cocaine), it may be swallowed, heat can be applied, and the smoke then inhaled (sometimes used with heroin — "chasing the dragon"), or the drug may be dissolved and injected.

Problems can arise when attempting to smoke certain drugs. In some cases the heat is actually destructive and there is relatively little effect. This is the case with the normal form of cocaine, *cocaine hydrochloride.* However, with the hydrochloride removed the cocaine free base can be smoked without this problem. The drug known as "crack" is simply cocaine free base produced by one particular method. It has the same effects as cocaine but can be smoked with little loss of the drug (Siegel, 1982).

Injection may be dangerous if there are insoluble substances mixed with the drug. These may be other powders used to "cut" the drug in the process of it being bought and sold. Such problems also arise when tablets are crushed, mixed with water, and injected. Tablets contain many compounds other than the drug itself and a number of these are insoluble. Although not apparent immediately after injection, lesions may develop on the skin. Lesions may also occur after injection of a highly acidic or highly basic drug. Thus, some drugs are simply not in a suitable form for injection.

The second major consideration in choice of route is the speed with which the person wants the drug to act. Effects occur most rapidly after intravenous injection and inhalation. Application to mucous membranes and the other two routes using injection are somewhat slower, while the oral route is the slowest of all. The variation is from a few seconds to a number of minutes. In general, the slower the onset of action, the more gradual the build-up in effect: for instance, swallowing heroin will produce similar effects to injecting it, but there will be no "rush." The reasons for this type of variation will be discussed in the next section.

A third factor, and one which is frequently overlooked, is control of the dose. Assume, for example, that someone wishes to take marijuana. A friend may suggest that he or she mixes it in with some food and swallows it. After doing so they find that this batch turned out weak and the effect minimal. By this time they have wasted several hours. Alternatively, they might find the batch to be strong and the effects more extreme than they can enjoy. They may then regard the whole experience as unpleasant. On the other hand, if they smoke the marijuana, they can experience the effects while they are still in the process of administering the drug. They have the opportunity to alter their pattern of administration accordingly. If it is strong, they may inhale fewer times and less deeply, or they may hold the smoke in their lungs for a shorter time; if it is weak they can adjust their actions in the opposite manner.

Having control of the dose is an important factor, in that many drugs have unpleasant side-effects when taken in large doses. This is the case with nicotine. Tobacco smokers adjust their dose in the manner described for marijuana. Consciously or, more likely, unconsciously, a smoker will take more puffs and may inhale more deeply and hold the smoke in longer if he or she has just shifted from a high to low nicotine cigarette (Russell, 1987). In general, smoking is the route that allows most precise control over the level experienced by the user.

One final factor in choosing a route of administration is concern over health issues. Most importantly, use of second-hand needles can result in transmission of a number of diseases, including *hepatitis* and *acquired immune deficiency syndrome* (AIDS). Other methods may have long term adverse effects as well. For example, repeated use of cocaine by application to the mucous membranes of the nose can lead to rhinitis, a damaged nasal septum and other disorders (Chitwood, 1985). The symptoms may include loss of sense of smell and a continual nasal discharge.

Absorption

The drugs we are discussing all produce their most important effects by altering brain function in some way. Since they are not administered directly into the brain they must move from where they are deposited in the body to the brain. Most of the movement is achieved via the circulatory system. However, the first step is for the drug molecules to actually reach the bloodstream. This process is known as absorption. Differences in the time taken for various drugs to produce their effects and differences resulting from changing the route of administration can be explained in large part by the variation in their rates of absorption.

One route where absorption rate is not a factor can be found in intravenous administration. The needle is placed in a vein (most commonly in the arm) and the drug is deposited directly into the bloodstream. From there it travels throughout the body via the heart and lungs. In all other methods the drug molecules must at least cross one cellular membrane to reach the bloodstream. The number and nature of such barriers depend on the route of administration — however, the four factors determining the rate at which a drug crosses a membrane are the same in each case. These need to be considered for a proper understanding of the processes of absorption and distribution.

The first factor is the degree to which the drug is soluble in *lipids* (fats). The membrane itself is made up largely of lipid. Thus, movement through the membrane is aided if the drug is dissolved in the membrane lipids. Most drugs that are in gaseous form, the solvents and the anesthetics, are highly lipid soluble. As a result, the membrane is virtually no barrier at all to them and they pass across it very rapidly. Alcohol is another drug that is highly lipid soluble.

A second factor is the degree of ionization. In solution, a certain proportion of the molecules ionize and become charged particles. What is most important is that the ionized form of the drug is much less likely to cross the membrane than the unionized form. Thus, the greater the proportion of ionized molecules, the slower the rate of movement of the drug across the membrane. This proportion is, in turn, affected by the relationship between the acidity/alkalinity of the fluids adjacent to the membrane surface and the acidity or alkalinity of the drug itself. If there is a match, there will be little ionization, and therefore rapid movement across the membrane. If one is acidic and the other alkaline, then there will be a high proportion of ionized molecules and a slow absorption.

A third factor is molecular size. Some drugs of small molecular size pass through membranes faster than would be expected on the basis of their lipid solubility. One theory put forward to explain this phenomenon: that tiny, water-filled holes in the membrane allow small molecules to cross the membrane via these holes, but do not allow larger molecules to pass through.

Finally, the rate of movement across the membrane is determined by the difference in concentration of the drug on the two sides of the membrane. The greater that concentration difference, the more rapid the movement. This means that if drug molecules were not taken away from the other side, then the rate of movement across the membrane would be very fast in the beginning and then slower over time. However, the bloodstream actually removes the drug after it crosses the membrane so that concentration cannot build up. It also means that the drug will cross a membrane more rapidly if a greater concentration reaches the membrane in the first instance.

Having considered these factors, we can now turn to the different routes of administration. Inhalation is the method that produces the most rapid effect after intravenous administration. Drugs which are inhaled enter the lung either as a gas (for example solvents, nitrous oxide) or in the form of tiny smoke particles. The lung is an organ specialized for absorption; it has a very large surface area and blood passes through the lungs at a very rapid rate. At each point in this area a single membrane separates the air-space in the lung from the capillary. This specialization is, of course, for the absorption of oxygen, but it works equally well for the absorption of drugs.

Absorption is aided particularly by the rapid flow of blood. This prevents a build-up in the concentration of the drug as it is absorbed. Such a build-up would reduce the concentration difference between the moisture-laden air of the lung and the blood. The absorption of gaseous drugs is aided by their high lipid solubility and small molecular size. With drugs that enter as part of smoke particles, absorption is a little slower, but still very fast compared with most other routes. In this case there will also be some variation due to the solubility of the drug. Highly soluble drugs will separate from the smoke particles rapidly, whereas less soluble ones will do so more slowly.

The mucous membranes of the inside of the mouth and nose are composed of several layers of cells. Although thin compared to external skin layers, these membranes still create a much greater barrier than the single membrane in the lung. Blood supply to the nose and mouth is very rich and this aids in rapid absorption. When drugs are taken via this route the problem is in maintaining the drug in its contact with the surface for a long enough period of time. This can be something of a well-practiced art, especially in the case of snuff-taking.

There is an interesting difference between cigar and pipe smoking on the one hand, and cigarette smoking on the other. In the former, absorption of nicotine and other compounds in the smoke is mostly routed via the mouth — and these smokers do not usually inhale deeply. In the latter, absorption occurs almost totally in the lungs and very little is absorbed through the mouth. This difference can be explained by the different curing processes. Curing of either pipe or cigar tobacco results in smoke that is more alkaline in nature; this alkaline nature is also characteristic of the inside of the mouth. Thus, there is relatively little ionization and good absorption through the mouth's mucous membranes. Curing of cigarette tobacco results in a smoke which is quite the opposite in character. Its higher acidity means that there is a much greater degree of ionization and, as a result, poor absorption through the mouth. Cigarette smoke must then be inhaled into the lungs for any significant absorption to occur. (See Mangan and Golding, 1984, for a more detailed discussion of this issue.)

Injection via intramuscular or subcutaneous routes is very rarely used outside of medical contexts. Perhaps the most common time is when intravenous drug users find that their veins have collapsed and they are unable to inject by the normal route. Either of these routes may then be used as a last resort. Absorption is fairly rapid from subcutaneous sites. The main limiting factor is the rate of blood flow. Generally, the drug molecules have only to pass through capillary walls into circulation. However, at most sites there is not the same blood flow as can be found in the lung, or even in the nose and mouth. Because of this, absorption via the subcutaneous route is somewhat slower than absorption via the other routes.

Much of the same principles apply to intramuscular injections. Again, the drug is deposited under the skin, but instead in muscular tissue. Muscles usually have a higher density of capillaries than most subcutaneous sites, thus, the rate of absorption may be slightly faster. This may be augmented by exercising the muscle, thereby increasing bloodflow.

The final route is perhaps the most commonly used. It is certainly the most common for drugs used medically, such as the various antianxiety compounds. Oral administration is also favored for many of the drugs acceptable in modern Western society, such as caffeine and alcohol. However, absorption is slowest and least predictable when a drug is administered orally.

Many drugs are administered orally in a solid form — tablet, capsule or powder. Before absorption can take place the drug must dissolve in the contents of either the stomach or the small intestine. The faster the drug dissolves the more rapidly it will be available for absorption. This will be influenced by the chemical character of the drug itself, but also by the other chemicals combined with it in the tablet or capsule. The same amount of drug in one tablet form may dissolve and be absorbed several times faster than if combined in a different tablet form. Unfortunately, this is often not predictable without the benefit of complex laboratory testing.

After the mouth, the stomach is the first part of the gastrointestinal tract where absorption may occur. The lining of the stomach consists of a number of folds, providing a large surface area for absorption. However, the contents of the stomach are highly acidic. This results in a high degree of ionization and slow absorption of alkaline drugs. In contrast, drugs which are themselves acids will be ionized to a lesser degree and will therefore be more likely to be absorbed.

Unfortunately, there is one overriding factor that makes the process of absorption through the stomach wall highly variable. That factor is the amount of time the drug spends in the stomach. If the drug is taken on an empty stomach with a glass of water, it will almost certainly pass quickly into the small intestine, stopping in the stomach for a very short time only. If the drug is taken with a heavy meal, however, the opposite may occur and much of it may stay in the stomach for 40 minutes or more. Even the drug itself may alter the time taken for the stomach to empty its contents. For example, alcohol can slow and even completely stop gastric emptying for periods of hours (Hunt and Pathak, 1960). If this has occurred then there is more time before it reaches the small intestine. During this period the drug may be absorbed through the stomach lining.

Although some absorption may occur through the stomach, in the case of virtually every drug much more absorption occurs in the small intestine. The main reason for this is that this particular area is specialized for food absorption and much the same factors govern the absorption of drugs as would govern the absorption of food. The small intestine provides a very large surface area which has many more folds than the stomach. The cells are also specialized for the absorption process and a high density of blood vessels allows for the rapid removal of drugs or food. Finally, the environment inside the small intestine ranges from the weakly acidic at one end, to the weakly alkaline at the other. For just about any drug there will be ideal conditions for absorption along some part of the small intestine.

Some absorption may occur further down the gastrointestinal tract in the large intestine, but it will be small relative to the amount of drug absorbed higher in the tract. In fact, much of the drug which still remains after passing through the small intestine is likely to be excreted in the feces.

Clearly, absorption via the oral route is a complex process. There are a large number of factors involved and they can all interact. As a result, the time taken for a drug to produce its effect and the amount of effect it will have are very difficult to predict. A person may ingest a drug in the same way on two consecutive days and find a much faster, more intense effect on one of the days. Despite this variability, the popularity of the oral route is probably due to both its relative simplicity, and the perception that it is safer than other methods.

Distribution

Once a drug is deposited in the body and enters the bloodstream it can move to the site of action. The drugs under consideration here need to move through the bloodstream and into the brain. However, the process is not an active one; the drug molecules do not selectively seek out the brain in order to produce their effect. Rather, the drug is distributed through the body and the effects come as a result of that portion which has reached the brain.

Having entered the bloodstream, the drug rapidly courses through the body. As this occurs, the drug gradually dilutes. If no drug at all were to leave the blood vessels then the drug molecules would be distributed evenly over a volume equal to plasma volume, the fluid component of the blood. In a person of average weight this would be about three liters and distribution would occur in a matter of minutes.

However, the blood vessel walls are simply composed of cells whose membranes have the properties described earlier. Thus, the principles governing passive diffusion into the bloodstream are the same as those governing passive diffusion out from the bloodstream. In addition, the pressure caused by the blood flow provides some force on the drug molecules, encouraging their exit.

The rate at which the drug leaves the circulating blood for the body tissue will depend on how lipid soluble it is, what the size of the molecules and the proportion of ionized molecules are, and what the existing concentration of the drug in the plasma is. A drug that crosses membranes rapidly and easily will eventually be distributed throughout the entire body. Instead of a volume of three liters, it will be about forty liters — which is the total water content of the body. Drugs that cross membranes less readily may be less evenly and less widely distributed. In any case, there is an enormous dilution factor. As a result, a relatively small proportion of drug molecules are actually in a position to modify brain function. The greatest proportion will be distributed to tissue where they have little or no effect.

One factor that can modify the process is the binding of drug molecules to certain tissues in the body. There is a natural chemical affinity between certain drug molecules and tissues or parts of tissues. For example, barbiturates bind to albumin, a component of blood plasma. This binding reduces the amount of barbiturate which can leave circulation. Thus, the process of distribution is slowed down by binding. However, once the concentration in the blood drops, the drug molecules will gradually become unbound and are freed to be distributed through the body.

The other main consequence of binding is that a drug may not be evenly distributed throughout the body but instead concentrated in one area. The drug may remain bound in that area for only short periods or for relatively long periods (days, or perhaps weeks). For example, $\triangle^9$–THC, the main active compound in marijuana, binds to fat tissue (Garrett, 1979). The drug molecules can become unbound, but this occurs very slowly. As a result of this process a regular marijuana user may have relatively large stores of $\triangle^9$–THC in the fatty tissues of his or her body. Because of gradual unbinding the amount released from these stores at any one time is probably too small to have any notable effect. However, this small, slow release of $\triangle^9$–THC may diminish any withdrawal symptoms if the user discontinues marijuana use.

The passage of drug molecules from the blood to the brain is limited by what is known as the blood-brain barrier. This barrier is actually the *endothelium* or lining of the brain capillaries. The main difference between the capillary endothelium here and elsewhere in the body appears to be the very tight junctions between endothelial cells. The small water-filled gaps or pores described earlier appear to be absent (Bradbury, 1979; Crone, 1986). As a result, it is considerably harder for certain molecules to enter the brain. In particular, molecules of large size, those that are ionized and those that are not lipid soluble have difficulty crossing the blood-brain barrier. This appears to have evolved as a means of protecting brain tissue against certain chemicals.

However, the existence of this structure has considerable implication for the distribution of a range of drugs of much more recent use.

One interesting ramification to follow from the existence of the blood-brain barrier concerns the conversion of morphine into heroin for the illegal drug trade. Morphine is the main, active constituent of opium. It is a very effective painkiller and is still widely used in medicine. However, because of their structure, morphine molecules have difficulty penetrating the blood-brain barrier. Some morphine does get across, but the amount is much less than would be the case in the absence of the barrier.

A relatively simple chemical process converts morphine into heroin. The alteration in the chemical structure makes crossing the blood-brain barrier that much easier. In fact, if the same amount of heroin and morphine were injected into the body, about four times as many heroin molecules would reach the brain. Thus, heroin can be seen as a stronger drug only because it crosses the blood-brain barrier that much more readily. As far as is known at present, there are no important differences in the type of effects produced by the two drugs — their subjective, behavioral, as well as other effects appear to be identical. An interesting quirk: chemical processes in the body convert a certain proportion of heroin molecules back into morphine.

Elimination

The processes of absorption and distribution allow the drug to enter the body and eventually reach the site of action. Exactly what happens at that site of action will be discussed below. One more process must be considered first — the means by which the drug is eliminated from the body. Until now, the body has been seen as relatively passive, accepting and distributing the drug. In contrast, active bodily processes work to rid the body of the drug. If it weren't for these processes the effect of the drug would be indefinite. What occurs instead, is that all drugs have only a limited time-course of action.

Elimination comprises two main processes. *Biotransformation* (or metabolism) is the chemical transformation of a drug into a different compound within the body. *Excretion* is the removal of a drug from the body to the outside world. The actions of a drug may be terminated by one or both of these processes.

There are a number of routes by which excretion can occur. In the case of drugs which are gases at normal temperatures (for example, nitrous oxide) excretion occurs almost totally via the lungs. This is true to a lesser extent for the volatile liquids (solvents, alcohol) as well. The processes by which a drug is excreted through the lungs are exactly the same as the processes by which it is absorbed via this route. The same membrane barriers need to be crossed, but in the reverse direction — from the blood to the lung-space. In fact, an equilibrium is established so that the concentration of the drug in the lung matches blood concentration. However, some of the drug present in the lung is being lost through expiration and, therefore, more drug has to move from the bloodstream into the lung to maintain that equilibrium. The result is a decrease in blood concentration.

That assumption of an equilibrium in drug concentration between drug and lung-space is the basis for determination of alcohol intoxication by a breathalyzer. This instrument uses a chemical process to measure the concentration of alcohol in expired air. Because of the equilibrium that occurs, the concentration should match the concentration of alcohol in the blood. Thus, blood alcohol levels can be determined without it being necessary to take blood samples.

Drugs which are not gaseous at bodily temperatures cannot be eliminated in this manner. Instead, they have to be excreted via some fluid. Note that they are already in a soluble form in the body. A number of such fluids are available. These include sweat, tears, saliva, mucous secreted through the nose, urine, bile, and, in the case of lactating mothers, human milk. The last is clearly very important. It means that an infant can receive drugs taken by the mother simply through its natural feeding. Thus, a mother dependent on a particular drug may induce dependence in her child simply by breast-feeding him or her.

The amount of drug excreted via each of these different bodily fluids will be in direct proportion to the amount of such fluid lost from the body each day. The greatest volume of lost fluid is urine. Approximately one liter per day is excreted by the average adult. By comparison, all other means of fluid loss are relatively minor. The volume of tears and mucous secreted through the nose is very small. Sweat volume is also small under all but the most exceptional of circumstances. Saliva and bile are two fluids that are eventually eliminated via the feces. Of these, bile is the most important. Approximately half to one liter of bile is deposited into the small intestine each day, but most of this is recovered and recirculated. A drug secreted through bile may later be reabsorbed in the small intestine and distributed through the body. Thus, while bile turnover is relatively high, in most cases it is much less important than urine as a mode of drug excretion. For these reasons only urinary excretion will be considered in detail below.

The kidney has a number of functions, but perhaps the main one is in acting as a filtering device. In a constant, ongoing process the blood enters the kidney and is then reabsorbed back into circulation. What is not reabsorbed forms urine. The barrier to reabsorption comes in the form of a membrane having properties similar to those discussed earlier. Thus, nonionized, lipid soluble drugs easily reenter circulation, whereas those with molecules that are ionized or nonlipid soluble have some difficulty. Excretion will also depend on the acidity of the urine. It is normally more acidic than plasma, but this is highly variable.

Other specialized processes in the kidney may alter the rate of excretion of certain drugs. These processes maintain the appropriate chemical balance in the blood. The number of drugs affected by these processes is relatively small.

If a drug undergoes biotransformation or is metabolized, it is subject to one of a number of possible chemical processes that transform the drug into a new compound. If that new compound is an inactive one then the action of the drug will be terminated by that process. In some cases however, the product of biotransformation itself becomes an active drug which may have more or less effect than the original drug.

Some of the best examples of biotransformation to active compounds are to be found in the group of antianxiety drugs, the *benzodiazepines* (see Kaplan and Jack, 1981). Certain members of this group have very long time-courses — up to several days. This is partly because they are excreted poorly and also partly because the products of their biotransformation are very frequently active benzodiazepines themselves. For example, one of the metabolites of diazepam is *oxazepam*. This compound is active and has a very similar effect to diazepam. It is also manufactured for commercial sale as a benzodiazepine which has a shorter time-course.

Another example is the biotransformation of codeine into morphine. Both are natural constituents of opium and are still widely used for pain relief. The metabolic product of the demethylation of codeine is morphine. Indeed, it seems likely that much of the effect of codeine is due to its conversion to morphine. Codeine itself may have only weak opiate activity (see Misra, 1978).

Biotransformation can take place in a number of organs of the body, but most of the chemical reactions occur in the liver. The reason for this is that each chemical reaction requires the presence of a specific enzyme. The enzyme facilitates or enables the transformation of the drug into some other molecular form. Because the liver has the highest concentration of enzymes in the body it is the place where biotransformation is most likely to occur.

One result of biotransformation in the liver is that some drugs become much less effective when taken orally. Blood from the major sites of absorption in the gastrointestinal tract proceeds first to the liver and then to the rest of the body. If there is a high rate of liver biotransformation, then relatively little of a drug may be available to produce an effect. This can be compensated for by increasing the dose, but this makes oral administration relatively inefficient.

Interestingly, there is a belief that this is the case with cocaine. It is widely believed and even reported in texts that the drug is ineffective when taken orally. Research has shown, however, that while absorption is slow it is virtually complete (Van Dyke et al., 1978). Thus, efficiency or effectiveness is not a reason for using cocaine intranasally rather than orally.

The chemical reactions that can occur are of two types. The first are the *synthetic reactions*. In these reactions the drug molecule combines with some other, usually larger molecule (for example, an amino acid) in the presence of the appropriate enzyme. The drug then becomes pharmacologically inactive. The result of this process most commonly takes the form of a molecule with low lipid solubility, that is more highly ionized. The resultant compound then, is less likely to be reabsorbed and is usually excreted at a greater rate than the original drug.

The *nonsynthetic reactions* comprise the second type. Included in this category are the common chemical reactions of oxidation, reduction, and hydrolysis. It is only by means of nonsynthetic reactions that drugs can be changed into other active forms. An example is the oxidation of codeine into morphine. Whether a drug will undergo such transformation will depend on its chemical structure and the presence of the appropriate enzymes. As mentioned, such enzymes are most commonly found in the liver.

Very frequently drugs actually undergo both types of biotransformation before being excreted. A drug may undergo some nonsynthetic reaction at first and then this product may join with some larger molecule in a synthetic reaction. The final product may then be excreted. Phenobarbital can be metabolized in this way: The drug is oxidized and the resultant compound undergoes one of two possible synthetic reactions.

Time- and Dose-Effect Relationships

From the foregoing discussion it is clear that the amount of drug at the site of action will vary over time. It may first increase as the drug is absorbed and distributed, but then decline as it is eliminated. These effects can be represented graphically to give a better understanding of how drug effects change with time.

The first process is absorption—the time taken for a drug to cross some biologic barrier (for example in lungs, the small intestine) and enter the bloodstream. This process could be evaluated by depositing a single, fixed amount of drug and then measuring changes in the concentration of the drug in the bloodstream. Such an experiment would yield results similar to those in Figure 2.1. Note that no units have been included in this graph, as the exact concentration would depend on the amount of drug deposited. The time would also depend on the actual biologic barrier. In the lungs the process may take only seconds, but in the small intestine it would take many minutes.

What is important here is the shape of the line. A straight line would indicate that a constant amount of drug is absorbed in each time period. Instead, the drug is absorbed rapidly at first when there is a lot to be absorbed, and slowly at the end when there is only a little. The reason for this is that passive diffusion across a membrane is dependent on concentration: the higher the concentration, the greater the diffusion rate. With a fixed amount of drug deposited in the beginning, concentration will only decline with time. Thus, rate of diffusion into the bloodstream will also decrease. In the absence of processes of elimination, a final equilibrium point will be reached when concentration is equal on both sides of the membrane. This is because passive diffusion is a two-way process: drugs can diffuse out of, as well as into the blood. These types of results show that when concentration in the intestine or

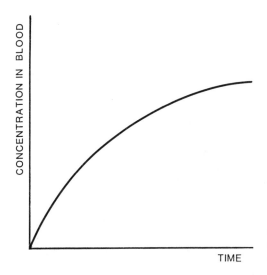

FIGURE 2.1
Drug absorption: increase in concentration over time following administration of a fixed amount of drug

CONCENTRATION IN BLOOD

TIME

lung is high, blood concentration will build up rapidly; concordantly, lower concentrations will result in a gradual build up of blood levels.

Two main processes are involved in elimination: *biotransformation* and *excretion*. Both processes are going to occur at a greater rate when the concentration of the drug in the body is higher. Biotransformation will be faster simply because there are more drug molecules that can be rendered inactive; excretion will be faster for the same reasons as absorption. In order to show this, it is best to measure the concentration of a drug in the blood after intravenous administration. This obviates any role of absorption. Allowing a short time for distribution, the result would be something like that shown in Figure 2.2. Again, units are not included as they would depend on the particular drug and dose administered.

This graph clearly illustrates how concentration drops off very rapidly at first. The rate of elimination then declines slowly until there is very little change in concentration over time. Like absorption, excretion reaches an equilibrium point where concentration of the drug in urine (or other fluid) matches concentration in the blood. Such results indicate that elimination is considerably faster when blood levels of a drug are higher.

There are some exceptions to the elimination pattern depicted above. Recall that biotransformation requires the presence of specific enzymes. Sometimes the enzyme is in relatively short supply and its availability determines the rate of elimination. In such cases the same experiment would yield a change in concentration over time like that in Figure 2.3. Here the drug is eliminated at a constant rate, irrespective of the concentration in the blood.

In practice, this difference can be very important. Normally, if we take a drug, the greater the dose, the greater the rate of elimination. As a result, while the time-course may be longer for a large dose, it won't be very much longer.

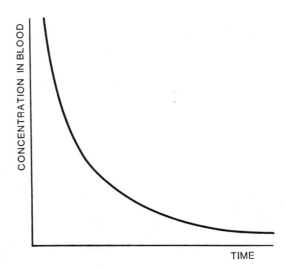

FIGURE 2.2
Drug elimination: decrease in
concentration over time
following distribution of a fixed
amount of drug

If, however, the drug is eliminated at a constant rate irrespective of concentration, then it will take very much longer to get rid of a large dose. The time-course will then be highly dependent on dosage. Relatively few drugs fall into this category, but there is one which does in particular – alcohol. Above a certain small amount (probably less than one drink) the body must eliminate alcohol at a constant rate (Kalant, 1971). The consequences are all too obvious: if someone gets very drunk the intoxication may persist for many hours. If a sufficient quantity is drunk a person may wake up the morning after a night of heavy drinking in an intoxicated state. If alcohol elimination was faster at higher concentrations such prolonged intoxication could not occur.

FIGURE 2.3
Drug elimination: change in
concentration over time when
the rate of elimination is
independent of concentration

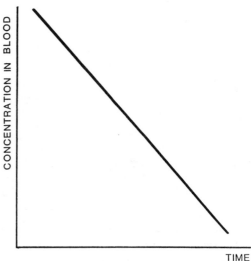

The processes of absorption, distribution (which is really absorption across different biologic barriers), and elimination do not occur independently. Once a drug is administered, all processes begin within a very short time and continue to occur concurrently. The result is constant change in the concentration of the drug at the site of action. This time-course will depend on the route of administration, but the curves in Figure 2.4 indicate the type of time-courses which might be expected from several different routes. With intravenous administration there is very rapid absorption leading to a high concentration and then a rapid fall-off. The maximum concentration is less with the other routes, but the concentration stays at a reasonably high level for a longer period of time. The time-course for inhalation would be similar to that for intravenous administration. If administration is to the tissues of the nose or mouth, the time-course may be similar to the subcutaneous route.

It is worth indicating that the time-course is measured in terms of the concentration at the site of action, the brain. Although the effect of the drug is dependent on the concentration at the site of action, there are numerous other factors that determine the magnitude of the drug effect. These will be discussed later in this and in the ensuing chapters. It is sufficient to note here that although the concentration of the drug which gets to the brain may be the primary factor, other biological factors as well as psychological and social factors all play a role.

The dose of the drug administered will have a profound effect on the concentration at the site of action. The primary result of an increase in dose will be an increase in the maximum concentration reached at the site of action. However, there will also be a lengthening of the time-course. Thus, if two different doses of the same drug are administered in the same way then the changes in concentration over time may be as depicted by the curves in Figure 2.5. This difference in time-course becomes important if a person is trying to

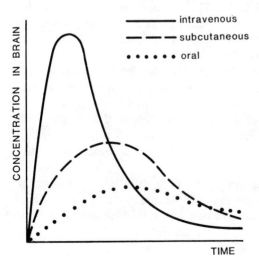

—————— intravenous
— — — subcutaneous
• • • • • • oral

FIGURE 2.4
Change in concentration over time following administration of the same fixed amount of drug by three different routes of administration

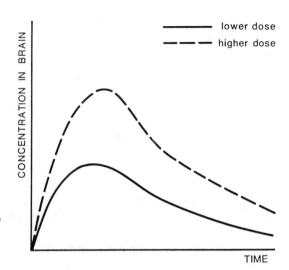

FIGURE 2.5
Change in concentration over time following administration of two different doses of a drug via the same route of administration

maintain a relatively constant level of drug in their body. This may occur in people physically dependent on certain types of drugs. Keeping a relatively constant level means that the person has to readminister the drug when the level becomes too low. To some extent, the period between administrations can be lengthened if a higher dosage is used. This is limited with most drugs, in that elimination occurs at a faster rate with higher concentrations. With drugs such as alcohol this is not the case; a large dose will ensure that a reasonable concentration of alcohol will remain in the brain for long periods of time.

Along with the route of administration and the dose, the time-course is dependent on the drug itself. If a drug crosses membranes readily for example, it will be quickly absorbed and distributed. The time it takes to peak concentration in the brain will then be short. This is the case with short-acting barbiturates. All are highly lipid soluble and produce a very rapid effect. In contrast, the longer-acting ones have low lipid solubility and are slow to reach the brain to produce their effect (Curry, 1977).

As mentioned, the maximum concentration achieved also increases with the dose. If a number of different doses of the same drug were administered (the route is irrelevant here) then we would find a relation between maximum or peak concentration and dose like that depicted in Figure 2.6. At the lower end of the dose scale, a small increase in dose produces a big increase in concentration, but at the upper end of the scale the same increase in dose produces a smaller increase in concentration.

Remember that the chemical properties of a drug will determine the absolute value of the concentration that will be reached. For example, a concentration of heroin in the brain will be much greater than that of morphine if the same dose of the two drugs is administered.

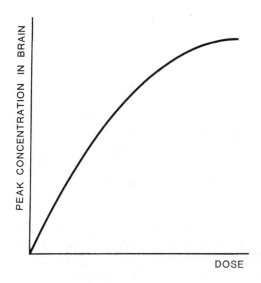

FIGURE 2.6
Effects of dose on the peak concentration of drug achieved in the brain

Individual Variability

Up until now we have been considering the general processes by which a drug is deposited in the body, reaches its site of action, and is eliminated. While these processes are common to everyone, there are quantitative and, occasionally, qualitative differences in the way different people react to these drugs. There are certain obvious factors that influence these processes, including body weight, sex, and age. There are also idiosyncratic responses — a certain individual could, for instance, react in quite a different way from the majority of the population. Such a response is thought to be due to genetic differences.

As discussed above, a drug is distributed throughout the body, irrespective of its site of action. The concentration of the drug in the body (and, therefore, at the site of action) depends on the total fluid volume in the body: the larger the fluid volume, the lower the concentration. This means that the same dose administered to two people will result in a higher concentration at the site of action in the smaller person.

For this reason, if the intention is to produce a certain drug effect, as is the case in medical contexts, then the dose should be adjusted to allow for variation in size. The most convenient measure of size is body weight. A standard body weight is often taken to be seventy kilograms. Someone weighing only forty-five kilograms should receive then only two–thirds of the usual dose, whereas someone weighing one hundred five kilograms should receive one and one–half times the usual dose.

When drugs are administered in nonmedical contexts, such adjustments are not usually made. For example, a group of friends drinking in a bar do not drink at a rate proportional to their weight. If they are all drinking at the same rate, then the smallest one in the group will, all things being equal, have the highest concentration of alcohol in his or her body. This person is receiving what is in effect a larger dose than the others. Conversely, the heaviest individual will then be receiving what is in effect a smaller dose. This factor is not very important when the amount of drug taken is relatively small, but may become so with higher doses. It is possible, for example, that the smaller person may experience adverse effects which the larger person does not.

Although there can be considerable overlap in weights, women characteristically weigh less than men. Though some women could actually be heavier than a number of men, on average, they are smaller. Thus, we might expect women to be perhaps more affected by the same dose of a drug than most men.

Women also have a different body composition than men; a smaller proportion is water and a higher percentage is fat. Again, these are averages only and there is considerable overlap. However, the smaller proportion of water may also mean a higher concentration (and, therefore, more effect) following administration of the same dose. This appears to be the case with alcohol. Even accounting for body weight, on the average women have slightly higher blood alcohol concentrations after a fixed dose of alcohol. But again, a large degree of overlap between the two groups remains. This is reflected in the fact that not all researchers have found such differences. For example Jones and Jones (1976) and Graham (1983) report higher BACs in women, though Taberner (1980) does not. It should also be noted that men and women may differ in other relevant respects, such as experience with alcohol, which may influence blood alcohol concentration. (Sex differences in susceptibility to alcohol-induced disease is covered in Chapter Five.)

One factor that can be highly significant is age. Even when taking into account differences in body weight, the very young and the very old frequently can react in a more extreme way to drugs, particularly those drugs whose site of action is the brain. One factor is similar in both age groups however; this being a reduced ability to excrete and biotransform drugs, resulting in a higher concentration of drug in the brain for longer periods of time.

In the young, excretion is slowed because of high blood volume relative to body size. This lowers the concentration of the drug at the kidney where it is absorbed as part of urine. Rate of blood flow is also lower in an infant. In older people, kidney function frequently becomes impaired, resulting in less effective excretion of a wide range of compounds, including drugs. The impaired ability to eliminate drugs through biotransformation results from underdeveloped enzyme systems in the infant, and from generally impaired functioning in the elderly (Curry, 1977).

Genetic differences play an important role in determining the effects of drugs. In particular, differences in the concentration of a drug reaching its site of action may be due to genetically determined factors (Goldstein, Aronow and Kalman, 1974). This has not always been well understood. It has however, usually been evident that certain people had highly unusual reactions to certain drugs. For example, they might act as if the administered dose was actually ten times the dose given. A number of these idiosyncratic reactions have been found to be genetically determined and it is not inconceivable that in time all could be found to be.

Several different types of abnormalities may result from genetic factors. For example, an enzyme responsible for biotransformation of a drug may not be present in certain individuals. This may result in a considerably lower rate of elimination of the drug. Alternatively, if the effect of the drug actually depends on the product of metabolism then there might be a lesser effect or no effect at all.

Alcohol is eliminated from the body in several ways. One is through biotransformation, first to *acetaldehyde* and then to other, inactive compounds. Acetaldehyde itself causes a number of effects, one of which is the flushing of the face. A relatively high proportion of Asians and low proportion of Caucasians are deficient in the normal enzyme responsible for biotransformation of acetaldehyde (Chan, 1986). In such individuals the ingestion of alcohol results in an accumulation of acetaldehyde, followed by a magnification of its effects. Whereas facial flushing is usually not noticeable in experienced individuals, it can be very pronounced in this particular group.

DRUGS AND THE NERVOUS SYSTEM

Principles of Neurotransmission

To date we have discussed how drugs reach their site of action, which factors determine how much of the drug reaches this site, and how and why the drugs stay there for any length of time. For the drugs of interest, the brain is the most important site of action. This is not to say that it is the only site at which bodily function is altered. As will be noted, there are always sites of action outside the brain. However, it is action in the brain that facilitates their use. In order to understand this process it is necessary to understand a little bit about brain functioning.

The brain is composed of a number of different types of cells. The most important of these are the nerve cells or *neurons.* They are specialized cells which perform two main functions: First, they receive input from a number of other cells (in some cases only a few, in other cases, thousands) and modify their own activity accordingly. Second, their own activity is communicated to other neurons (again, from a few to many thousands). Their activity consists of changes in potential or voltage caused by movement of charged particles into and out of the cell. Communication between cells is via chemical means: the cell sends out chemical "messengers" that influence the activity of the target cells. It is this process of chemical communication which most drugs influence.

In order to examine this more closely it is helpful to look at what is involved when one cell communicates directly with an adjacent cell. This is known as *neurotransmission,* and the chemical that does the communicating is known as the *neurotransmitter.*

Figure 2.7 illustrates the basic processes that can occur at the points where adjacent cells communicate. These junctions are known as *synapses.* The first process that must occur is the synthesis of the neurotransmitter. In most cases this is done using raw materials drawn from outside the neuron and enzymes which originate from other parts of the cell. The newly synthesized transmitter is then stored, awaiting release. Storage prevents the neuro-transmitter from being biotransformed.

When the cell is electrically activated to a sufficient degree, a fixed amount of the stored neurotransmitter is released into the fluid-filled space between the cells. From there, a number of things can happen to each of the molecules. A molecule may fulfill its role and activate the cell on the other side of the space or cleft via the receptor. This process will be discussed in detail below. Also it may be biotransformed by enzymes present in the cleft or simply move from the region, and will be excreted eventually. It may be taken back up into the cell, where it may then undergo biotransformation or be stored, to be used again. It should be noted that occupation of a receptor is not permanent, and within a very short space of time (milliseconds) a molecule may once again be back in the cleft.

Views of the process of neurotransmission have changed radically in the last twenty years or so, and are still changing at a great pace (Dismukes, 1979, Bloom, 1985). Consequently, it is difficult to give a very precise picture of the

FIGURE 2.7   Processes of neurotransmission occurring at a synapse

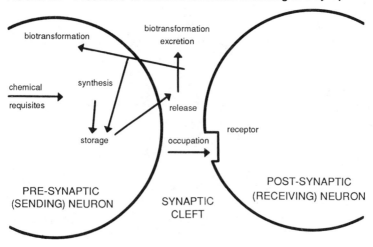

whole process. For example, a textbook twenty (or perhaps less) years ago would probably have listed the following as the neurotransmitters: *acetylcholine, noradrenaline (norepinephrine), dopamine, serotonin* and *GABA (gamma aminobutyric acid)*. Give or take one or two, this list would have been regarded as definitive. More recently, at least thirty substances are considered to be likely chemical messengers in the central nervous system (Barchas et al., 1978), and some researchers have predicted that the list may extend into the hundreds. A partial list is shown in Table 2.1.

Unfortunately, it is difficult to show that a chemical has a messenger function and satisfies the criteria for being a neurotransmitter (Bloom, 1985). It is one thing to note the presence of the chemical in the brain and to see that it affects brain function, but another to show that it is a neurotransmitter. The research and debate as to which substances should or should not be included in the list is likely to continue for many years.

A second change that has occurred in recent years is that we have broadened our view as to how chemical messengers can act. It used to be thought that all neurotransmission followed the model given above — that a neurotransmitter simply crosses the tiny gap between two adjacent cells. It now seems that many chemical messengers are released into the general fluid medium of the brain to influence surrounding neurons, often at some distance. These types of messengers seem to act like hormones and, indeed, the term *neurohormone* is sometimes used to delineate a second category of messengers in the brain.

A third, and related, change has concerned the time-course over which the chemical messengers act. Earlier views presented the brain as a series of interconnected telegraph lines (the neurons) with relays (synapses) at each junction. The effect of the neurotransmitter was instantaneous and lasted only

TABLE 2.1   Potential Neurotransmitters or Neurohormones

Acetylcholine	Serotonin
Histamine	Tryptamine
Glutamate	5–Methoxytryptamine
Aspartate	
δ-aminobutyric acid (GABA)	Substance P
Glycine	Enkephalins and Endorphins
Taurine	Somatostatin
Adenosine	Angiotensin II
	Luteinizing hormone releasing hormone (LHRH)
Dopamine	
Noradrenaline/Norepinephrine	Adrenocorticotrophic hormone (ACTH)
Adrenaline/Epinephrine	
Octopamine	
Tyramine	

milliseconds—just long enough to activate the cell on the other side. It now seems as though some neurotransmitters or neurohormones may alter activity in the target cell for more than milliseconds—perhaps seconds, minutes, or even hours. If this is linked to the idea of a neurohormone, we can start to imagine chemical messengers which can alter a great deal of brain activity for long periods. The result may be increased sleepiness, feelings of anxiety, "good moods," etc. Unfortunately, this remains only speculative at present (Barchas et al., 1978).

One final change is the abandonment of a long-held pharmacological principle. Dale's principle states that each neuron releases only one type of neurotransmitter. There is now evidence that cells exist in which there are two types of neurotransmitter substances (Gilbert and Emson, 1983). It is possible that one may be the main neurotransmitter and act over a short time-course, while the other over a long time-course, which serves only to modulate the activity of the first. Naturally, this added complexity only increases the possible ways in which drugs can alter brain functioning.

Considerable advances have also been made in our understanding of how chemical messengers and exogenously administered drugs interact with receptors. Because of these developments and because this is perhaps the most important way in which drugs influence brain function, it is worth spending some time understanding the process by which molecules and receptors interact.

Receptors

The membrane surface of each neuron has a number of large molecules embedded in it. Coupled with each of these is a biochemical mechanism for influencing the activity of that neuron. This effector mechanism may alter cellular activity in a small localized manner or in a more gross, overall manner.

Neurotransmitter or neurohormone molecules activate the effector mechanisms by chemically bonding or attaching themselves to the receptor. The chemical bonds are relatively weak and the bonding is not permanent. However, by means not yet completely understood, the chemical bonding can result in the effector mechanism going into action, even though bonding may occur only for a very short period of time.

The neurotransmitter or neurohormone may not be the only type of molecule that can bond to the receptor. Other types of chemical messengers and drugs may also have this effect. While evolutionary forces may have resulted in receptors designed to accommodate the natural chemicals, they cannot prevent their exploitation by the "unnatural" chemicals we administer.

Most compounds that bond to the receptor also activate the effector mechanism, but there are some that do not. The former are known as *agonists* at the receptor, and the latter are known as *antagonists*. An antagonist occupies the receptor, preventing any agonists from doing so, but not producing any effect itself. The analogy most commonly used is that of a lock and key—the receptor being the lock and the molecules of neurotransmitter, neurohormone, or drug being the various keys. Many keys will not fit the lock at all and therefore have no effect. Some keys will fit the lock, but will not turn it. These are the antagonists. The keys that can both fit the lock and turn it are the agonists.

Just to complicate matters, there are compounds that are not quite agonists and not quite antagonists. It is as if they turn the key half-way only. These compounds are known as partial agonists or mixed agonist-antagonists. Indeed, for certain types of receptors we could compile a list of substances that act as agonists, antagonists, and mixed agonist-antagonists at those receptors. While there is always at least one compound that acts as an agonist (the natural chemical messenger for which the receptor has evolved), in many cases we may know of no other compounds that bind to that receptor—either natural or introduced.

Having a range of such compounds which can bind to a receptor can be very useful. First, it aids pharmacologists in understanding the properties of that type of receptor and the effects produced by the agonist. Second, antagonists are useful in blocking the effects of a drug. For example, if someone is admitted to a hospital emergency room as a result of a heroin overdose the person can be administered an antagonist of the receptor where heroin is an agonist. If enough of the antagonist compound is administered, the antagonist molecules will prevent the heroin molecules from occupying the receptors and producing their effects. By this means the effects of heroin can be blocked almost immediately (with intravenous administration), perhaps saving the person's life. However, it is usually better to do this slowly and carefully as too much of an antagonist compound may precipitate withdrawal in an individual who is physically dependent (see below).

The amount of effect produced by a drug will depend on the number of receptors occupied by the drug. At the same concentration, those drugs which bind easily to the receptor will occupy a larger number of receptors than those that bind with greater difficulty. Drugs which bind readily are said to have a greater affinity for the receptor (Kenakin, 1987). As a result, fewer drug molecules are required to produce the same effect compared to a drug with a lower affinity.

The amount of drug which must be administered in order to produce a fixed level of effect will be determined both by the ease with which the drug reaches the brain from its site of administration and its affinity for the receptor to which it binds. These two factors determine the potency of a drug. One drug is more potent than another if the same effect is produced by a lower dose, or equivalently, if the same dose produces a greater effect. Table 2.2 shows a comparison in potencies amongst some benzodiazepines (data were obtained from Harvey, 1985). For each drug, the approximate dose required to induce sleep in humans is indicated. Thus, the effect is the same in each case, but the dose required to produce it varies enormously from drug to drug.

TABLE 2.2 Comparison of Hypnotic Doses of Four Different Benzodiazepines Used for This Purpose

BENZODIAZEPINE	MINIMUM DOSE TO INDUCE SLEEP IN ADULTS (mg)
Triazolam	0.25
Lorazepam	2
Flurazepam	15
Temazepam	15

It is worth noting that potency is not always of great practical importance. In the case of drugs produced by pharmaceutical companies the amount of drug is usually tiny and a doubling or tripling of that amount makes little difference. The cost of manufacture of the drug itself is often very small so that whether two milligrams or four milligrams goes into a tablet makes little difference. However, in the case of some illegal drugs it is very important. The conversion of morphine to heroin in order to increase potency has already been mentioned.

One other important consideration is the subtypes of receptors at which a drug acts. Studies of chemical transmission in the brain has shown that many neurotransmitters and neurohormones act at several different subtypes of receptors. Structurally, the receptors are all very similar, yet may produce quite different, even opposite effects. Drugs may act at one, or at two or more subtypes.

One of the earliest known examples of multiple receptor subtypes concerned the receptors for the neurotransmitter *acetylcholine* (McGeer, Eccles and McGeer, 1978). The receptors were actually determined from activity in the peripheral nervous system rather than in the brain, but the same subtypes have since been found in the brain. The two subtypes were named *nicotinic* and *muscarinic* after compounds which activated each. The characteristic effects produced by activation of the nicotinic receptor are those seen after administration of nicotine. They include increased arousal and alertness, elevated heart rate and blood pressure, and decreased hunger and nausea. On the other hand, muscarinic agonists produce salivation, sweating, diarrhea, confusion, and weakness. The effects resulting from blockade of muscarinic receptors (drowsiness, impaired psychomotor performance, and hallucinations) are produced by drugs such as atropine and scopolamine.

While activation of different receptor subtypes sometimes produces quite varied effects, it is not necessarily the case. For example, the analgesic or pain-killing properties of opiate drugs which have made them so valuable in medicine can result from activation of at least two different subtypes of opiate receptor (Martin, 1983). The actual number of opiate-receptor subtypes is still a matter for research and debate, however.

Finally, it should be noted that receptors (and the chemical messengers which activate them) are not dispersed evenly throughout the brain. Each receptor subtype will be located in some areas of the brain, but not in others. Even in those areas where receptors are to be found, the density may vary from low to high. Since each region of the central nervous system is associated with certain functions, the distribution of receptors obviously limits the potential actions of the neurotransmitter or neurohormone that activates the receptor, as well as any drug which may exert its influence via the receptor.

Drug Effects

Having examined some of the complexities of chemical transmission in the brain we can look at the effects of specific drugs. It is important to note that virtually any drug can affect several different neurotransmitter systems. However, the influence on some of these systems may be minor. The actions that are included below are those which are thought to result in the major effects of the drugs. Where there is evidence of activity but little effect, the nature of that activity has not been described. Table 2.3 summarizes some of the known effects of the major drug types.

Recent years have brought about considerable research directed toward understanding the natural opiate substances in our brain — the *enkephalins* and *endorphins*. It now seems that there are a large number of such substances that have a variety of functions (Akil et al., 1984); these include involvement in food and water intake, and modulation of pain. These opiate chemical messengers act at several different types of opiate receptors. Opiates of the "classical" type such as morphine and heroin act mainly at one type of opiate receptor. Others, particularly the mixed agonist-antagonists act at other types of receptors. These include different opiate receptors and a type of nonopiate receptor where PCP also appears to act (the *sigma receptor*). Thus, certain opiates may produce their effects as a result of activity at both opiate and nonopiate receptors.

Many of the drugs in the sedative-hypnotic, antianxiety group produce effects which seem to be due to enhancement of the activity of the neurotransmitter GABA (Haefely, 1985). Again, this is a very active area of research where the picture constantly changes. At present, it seems that GABA receptors are associated frequently with a second type of receptor — the *benzodiazepine receptor*. When a benzodiazepine drug activates this receptor it potentiates activity at the GABA receptor. The chemical messengers which activate the so-called benzodiazepine receptors are as yet unknown. Barbiturates also enhance the effects of GABA.

The actions of alcohol which result in its characteristic effects are not well understood. It is not that there are no known actions of alcohol, but, rather, that they are nonspecific. In particular, alcohol alters the properties of neuronal membranes. One neurotransmitter system that is affected is GABA. This is the basis for the commonalities between alcohol and other sedative-

TABLE 2.3

DRUG CLASS	MAIN NEUROTRANSMITTER OR NEUROHORMONE SYSTEM AFFECTED	ACTION
Opiates		
morphine, heroin, etc.	opioids	agonists
pentazocine etc.	opioids	agonists and mixed agonist/antagonists
	?	agonist (at sigma receptor)
Sedative-Hypnotic/Antianxiety		
barbiturates	GABA	potentiates GABA
benzodiazepines	GABA	agonists at benzodiazepine receptor associated with GABA
alcohol	GABA and ?	potentiates GABA
Stimulants		
amphetamine and cocaine	dopamine, noradrenaline	block re-uptake and cause release
nicotine	acetylcholine	agonist at nicotinic receptors
caffeine	adenosine	antagonist
Hallucinogens		
LSD, mescaline, etc.	serotonin	agonists at 5–HT$_2$ receptor
PCP	l-glutamate	antagonist at PCP receptor
	?	sigma receptor activity
Marijuana	?	?
Anticholinergics	acetylcholine	antagonists at muscarinic receptors
Betel	acetylcholine	?
Solvents and Aerosols	?	?

hypnotic drugs. However, alcohol also influences other neurotransmitter systems, particularly at higher doses.

The two stimulants that produce the most prominent behavioral and subjective effects, amphetamine and cocaine, have very similar actions in the brain (Pitts & Marwah, 1988). Both block the re-uptake of the neurotransmitters *noradrenaline* and *dopamine*. The effects of a re-uptake blocker cause more of the neurotransmitter substance to remain in the synaptic cleft where it can activate the receptors (or be metabolized). Amphetamine causes release of dopamine and noradrenaline from the nerve terminals; cocaine may have similar actions.

The other two stimulants in common use have quite different actions. As mentioned, nicotine is an agonist at nicotinic cholinergic receptors. Directly or indirectly, it is also known to cause release of dopamine and noradrenaline (Pomerleau and Pomerleau, 1984). Caffeine, on the other hand, is an antagonist at receptors activated by the neurotransmitter/neurohormone adenosine. Little is known of the role of adenosine in the brain.

Hallucinogens also vary in their effects. LSD is thought to produce its major effects as an agonist at one type of *serotonin receptor* — the *$5-HT_2$ receptor*. Other hallucinogens are also believed to modulate serotonin activity in this way. However, the hallucinogens also act at other sites which may play a role in their effects (Pierce and Peroutka, 1989). PCP, which produces hallucinations of a different type, appears to act at two different kinds of receptors. One is the sigma receptor mentioned above. The other is associated with a subtype of receptor for the neurotransmitter glutamate (the NMDA receptor). At this latter site PCP is an antagonist.

Of the drugs in the final category, only the anticholinergics are understood. These are antagonists at muscarinic cholinergic receptors. Marijuana, and its main active ingredient $\triangle^9$-THC in particular, affects a number of neurotransmitter systems. These include histamine and serotonin systems. Which, if any, is responsible for the major effects of marijuana is not known at this time.

Explaining Drug Use

There are three main types of theories relating the use of drugs to the chemical changes they produce in the brain. The first, which we could label the deficiency theory, suggests that an individual deficient in a particular neurotransmitter or neurohormone will use the drug as a replacement for it. The second suggests that there is a group of neurons in the brain which, if activated, produce a rewarding or pleasurable feeling. Drugs that can activate this pathway will produce the rewarding effects which people seek. The third suggests that each drug produces a constellation of effects in the brain, any or all of which may alter our behavior and experience in a way that contributes to their use.

The deficiency theory has been argued for most strongly in the case of opiate addiction (for example, Dole and Nyswander, 1967). It suggests that in certain individuals there is a deficiency in the opiate systems of the brain. This deficiency is presumably present from birth or results from inappropriate brain development. People with such a deficiency suffer in certain ways. One of these is a lack of pleasurable experience — a blunting of affect. Another may be an inability to cope with stress. However, because opiates such as heroin mimic the effects of the natural brain opiates they are able to restore balance in the brain. The opiate-deficient person can then experience normal pleasure and cope better with stress.

From this argument we could consider a heroin addict as someone with an inborn deficiency for which he or she compensates by using heroin on a regular basis. It is a model of drug dependence which views the cause as an underlying abnormality or disease. The "cure" that most people use is an illegal drug. However, it is possible to provide a "cure" in the form of a medically supplied opiate as an alternative. Methadone is the opiate most commonly used for this purpose (see Chapter Six).

Although attractive in its simplicity, the deficiency model suffers due to lack of evidence. While it has been bolstered by the discovery of extensive, complex opiate systems in the brain, there is no direct evidence that any individuals (or heroin addicts in particular) have underactive opiate systems. The only real evidence is very indirect — that people who become heroin addicts tend to have a low level of pleasure in their lives (see Chapters Three and Four). However, it is a very big step to say that this is caused by a deficiency in opiate systems.

There are several other criticisms that could be levelled at this theory. The evidence reviewed in Chapter Three, which shows that animals such as rats and monkeys will actually administer drugs such as opiates to themselves, is one such criticism. Virtually every animal given the opportunity will administer the drugs, and, if allowed, will eventually become physically dependent. Are all these animals deficient in the same way as the human heroin addicts are said to be? It could hardly be called a deficiency if this were the case, since a deficiency is a deviation from the norm.

Although the argument has been made most strongly with respect to opiate addiction, the question of other drugs arises. Are there deficiencies in neurotransmitter/neurohormone systems that give rise to the use of nicotine, caffeine, alcohol, etc.? While this is possible there is no more convincing evidence for any of these drugs than there is for heroin.

The second primary theory concerns brain reward mechanisms. There is considerable evidence suggesting that certain neurons produce a pleasurable or rewarding effect when activated; dopamine is the neurotransmitter for these neurons (Wise, 1981; Bozarth, 1986). They can be activated by the administration of certain drugs, particularly the stimulants amphetamine and cocaine. If, however, the activity of these dopamine neurons is blocked, amphetamine and cocaine no longer produce their rewarding effects. Indeed, all drugs which produce pleasure may stimulate these reward neurons. In many cases this stimulation may be indirect. For example, nicotine may stimulate certain neurons with nicotinic cholinergic receptors, which in turn stimulate the dopamine reward neurons.

Much research has centered on opiate reward: for instance, do opiates produce their rewarding effects by (direct or indirect) activation of these same dopamine-containing cells or by some independent means? To date the evidence is equivocal (see Koob et al., 1987). There seem to be opiate receptors in the vicinity of the dopamine neurons mediating amphetamine and cocaine reward, but opiates may also be able to produce rewarding effects via other neuronal systems.

The theory that drugs of dependence share the property of activating a central reward system has some plausibility. However, the evidence now more strongly suggests the existence of multiple neuronal systems mediating reward. There are many drugs too, which simply do not produce a classical euphoric effect like cocaine and heroin (see discussion of subjective effects in the following chapter). The hallucinogens and the benzodiazepines are obvious examples of this. It is not clear that their use could be ascribed to activation of the same reward pathways as the psychomotor stimulants and opiates.

The third view is a more general one, suggesting that effects on a variety of neural systems are likely to be involved in mediating the effects of drugs. No one simple effect (such as "pleasure") is likely to be responsible for drug use. Instead a range of drug effects may be responsible for its use. This range of effects comes about because any neurotransmitter-receptor system affected by a drug is likely to be found in a number of brain regions involved in a variety of actions, and because any drug will affect several systems, either directly or indirectly.

We can take nicotine as an example of a drug which has a variety of effects. Pomerleau and Pomerleau (1984) have summarized these effects and the brain systems responsible for them. The first is a rewarding or pleasurable effect. This is likely to be mediated by certain dopaminergic or opiate systems, as mentioned above. Unfortunately, there is not yet any strong evidence of nicotine influencing either of these systems. A second effect is the increased alertness after smoking which users report, along with certain objective improvements in the speed and accuracy engendered during certain tasks (Wesnes, 1987). This may be due to direct modulation of cholinergic activity or activation of dopamine or noradrenaline systems, all of which activate circuits involved in arousal. Smokers also report relaxation associated with reduction in anxiety or tension. This type of effect may be mediated by opiate systems in the brain, indirectly activated by nicotine.

Other possible effects, such as improvement of memory, have also been suggested, but the evidence is even less secure for these. The point is clear, however: nicotine has a variety of effects, all of which may contribute to its use. A small dose may be sufficient to increase alertness and produce a pleasurable effect, while a larger one may lead to longer-term anxiety reduction and a stronger pleasurable effect. Each different effect may be mediated at different anatomical sites and perhaps through different neurotransmitter/neurohormone systems activated as a result of the agonist activity of nicotine at nicotinic cholinergic receptors.

The same argument could apply equally well to other drugs. For the full constellation of effects, any or all of which may be reasons for its use, we need to look at systems indirectly as well as directly affected by the drug. At present our understanding of the brain is far too poor to make any real progress in evaluating this view, or in even understanding how it would work. It is also important to determine whether one type of effect, the activation of reward circuits, is in some way critical, or at least more important than the other drug actions.

TOLERANCE

Tolerance after Repeated Administration

When a drug is administered repeatedly the effects of that drug very frequently diminish with each administration. Such a change is an example of the development of tolerance — decreased responsiveness to a drug after continued exposure. Tolerance is often associated with physical dependence, to be discussed in the next section.

Tolerance occurs with repeated administration of all the major drugs under discussion here. There is some variation in the rate at which it develops and the maximum degree of tolerance observed. Opiates are often said to be the class of drugs that exhibits the greatest degree of tolerance. Certainly, there can be very large decreases in the effects resulting from opiate administration if repeated often, but comparison between drug classes in this way is difficult.

If a particular drug is administered on a number of occasions, then it will not only be the effect of that particular drug which is reduced. Administration of any drug in the same pharmacological class will result in a smaller effect than would have otherwise occurred. For example, if a heroin user tries an alternative opiate such as morphine or one of the newer, synthetic compounds, then they will be as tolerant to that alternative as they would be to heroin. This phenomenon is known as *cross-tolerance*. It also extends to drugs that are quite dissimilar, but belong to the same pharmacological class. For example, someone who used alcohol extensively would show a cross-tolerance to drugs in the barbiturate and benzodiazepine group as well. In the stimulant group there is some cross-tolerance between cocaine and amphetamine, but none between these and nicotine or caffeine.

The phenomenon of cross-tolerance provides strong evidence that the drugs in question share a common mechanism of action. However, because drugs do not usually have exactly the same mechanisms of action, cross-tolerance can often be incomplete. For example, alcohol has some actions which differ from the benzodiazepines and barbiturates. While there is considerable cross-tolerance between these groups, a barbiturate user may not be tolerant to all the effects of alcohol, particularly those not mediated by GABA systems.

It is possible that a person will use a drug repeatedly and find that rather than a diminution of the effect of the drug, there is an increase. For example, repeated cups of coffee in a short period of time may eventually result in a heightened state of excitement and anxiety, a much greater effect than the mild stimulation produced by the first cup. What may be happening in such cases is that the drug doses are being added to one another so that the quantity of drug in the body after the final administration is much more than was actually administered in that final dose. A graph showing change in drug effect as a result of this type of administration pattern is given in Figure 2.8. Tolerance may still occur, but it is counteracted by the addition of doses.

One of the unusual aspects of tolerance is that it does not develop at equal pace with all effects of a drug. There may be rapid diminution of some effects, but slower or even no change in other effects. Opiates such as morphine and heroin provide a very good example of this (Jaffe, 1985). While tolerance to the effects of these drugs is said to be quite pronounced, it is not universally so. Strong tolerance to the many behavioral effects of opiates develops, both to their subjective effects and to the inducement of nausea and vomiting. In contrast, little or no tolerance develops to the slowing of gastrointestinal motility which results in constipation. Chronic heroin users, or those who have changed to methadone, will report that the problem of constipation does not disappear or even diminish with repeated use. Similarly, the constriction in pupil size produced by opiates does not appear to diminish significantly. Why there are such differences in the degree of tolerance development is not well understood. Unfortunately, research on the mechanisms of tolerance, to be discussed below, does not indicate why there is a diminution in some effects, but not others.

Tolerance itself, and the differences in the rates of tolerance development, have very important implications for drug use (see Cappell and LeBlanc, 1987, for an extended discussion of this). One of the obvious implications of tolerance is that a user has to keep increasing the dose of a drug in order to maintain a constant effect. A dose that produces a desirable effect when the person first starts using the drug may no longer produce an effect of nearly that magnitude when it is administered for the fiftieth time. It would stand to reason then, that a user who starts off with a relatively small dose would eventually come to administer the high doses of more experienced users.

Groups of heroin users often assign a higher status to those with more expensive "habits." The user who needs $500 per day to maintain their habit assumes a higher social rank than the person who spends only $200 per day. This difference is due to different degrees of tolerance. Those with more expensive habits will have acquired them through more frequent use and through use of higher doses. Once a high level has been "achieved," it is very difficult to come back down. A very experienced user who reduces the amount

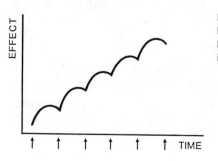

FIGURE 2.8
Increasing magnitude of drug effect with a high frequency of repeated dosing. Arrows indicate drug administrations

of drug administered may find very little or no effect from administration of this smaller quantity. Without tolerance, reduction in dose and a gradual weaning off the drug would be considerably easier.

The rate at which tolerance develops changes with continued use of a drug. Data from animal studies (see for example Kalant, 1977) and reports of drug users indicate that tolerance develops rapidly in the inexperienced, but much more slowly in those who are experienced in use of the drug. A person who for years has used a drug such as caffeine in a very regular manner, drinking the same number of cups of tea and coffee every day, is unlikely to continue to develop tolerance to any noticeable extent. Such an individual is only likely to develop further tolerance if they increase the amount they take, either through binges, more frequent usage, or greater doses.

In contrast, the inexperienced individual is likely to develop tolerance very rapidly. With their first few uses the effects will be relatively strong, but this will diminish quickly. Furthermore, it seems that tolerance develops more rapidly to the adverse or unpleasant effects of drugs than to their desirable or pleasant effects. This is particularly true in the initial stages of drug use. Many drugs have quite unpleasant effects which would normally prevent people from using them regularly. To the extent that tolerance develops more rapidly to these effects compared to the pleasant ones, the latter become more prominent relative to the former.

A very good example of this is the use of nicotine. The inexperienced user who inhales smoke for the first time will experience a number of adverse effects including nausea, even vomiting, raised heart rate and blood pressure, and sweating. If these effects remained it would be unlikely that anyone would continue smoking. Instead, tolerance develops to these effects and the experienced user begins to comfortably inhale nicotine doses that had been very unpleasant when the person had first tried smoking.

The same principle applies with many, if not all, drugs being considered here. Initially, their pleasant or desirable effects may be masked partly by quite unpleasant effects. The user has to withstand this until tolerance develops and the desirable effects become prominent. For the first-time heroin user, the most obvious effect may be nausea. This can be lessened somewhat by lying down, but in some cases it may be quite unpleasant. The other way for a beginning user to avoid these effects is to reduce the dose to the point that is tolerable. Thus a smoker may inhale less, a heroin user inject only a small quantity, or a young coffee drinker mix relatively weak coffee with a lot of milk. Eventually, tolerance develops and they can increase the dose without experiencing the unpleasant effects.

Acute Tolerance

While we commonly think of tolerance occurring with repeated use or administration of a drug (most research has been done in this area), tolerance also develops within the time-course of a single drug administration. Thus, if concentrations are the same, the effect toward the end of the period the drug is in the body is somewhat less than it was at the beginning. This phenomenon is known as acute tolerance. It is best illustrated diagrammatically. Figure 2.9 shows a hypothetical time-course of concentration and its effect plotted on the same axes. On the upward part of the curve which depicts a rising concentration, little tolerance can be shown since the drug has only been in the body for a short time. However, on the downward part of the curve, tolerance has begun to develop and the same concentration now produces a lesser effect. Compare times a and b. The concentration is the same at both times, the difference being that a is on the upward and b is on the downward part of the concentration curve. The effect produced at b is considerably less than it is at a. Some phenomena have changed during that time period to make the system less responsive to the concentration.

This acute tolerance has been reported for a variety of drug effects. Even something as simple as reporting how drunk a person feels after the ingestion of a fixed amount of alcohol shows acute tolerance (Radlow and Hurst, 1985; Portans, White, and Staiger, 1989). Estimates of drunkenness relative to blood alcohol concentration show a pattern similar to the one in Figure 2.9. Thus, at a concentration of 0.05% a person might report being more drunk—as reflected by the upward rather than the downward part of the curve. Indeed, people are often surprised at how high their blood alcohol readings are some time after they have stopped drinking. The feelings of inebriation may have diminished, but the concentration of the drug in the body is still high.

Acute tolerance is actually poorly understood. There are a number of questions still to be answered. We do not know the relation between acute tolerance and the tolerance that can develop with repeated administration.

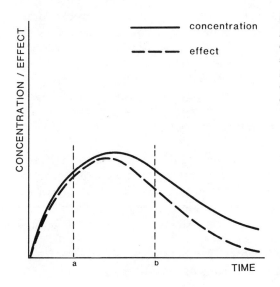

——— concentration

— — — effect

FIGURE 2.9
Acute tolerance. Drug concentration and drug effect are scaled to be plotted on the same axis. Effect is diminished on the descending portion of the concentration curve

Presumably both reflect the actions of the same mechanisms, but while mechanisms of long-term tolerance have received some attention (see below), those of acute tolerance have received relatively little. Another interesting dynamic is whether or not acute tolerance changes with each administration. Also, what is the interplay between acute tolerance and acute withdrawal?

Mechanisms of Tolerance Development

The effect of a drug is determined both by the amount of drug that reaches the brain and by its action once it gets there. Tolerance can arise as a result of changes within either or both of these processes. If the change is in the amount that reaches the brain, the terms *pharmacokinetic, drug-disposition,* or *metabolic tolerance* are used.

Drug-disposition tolerance is a relatively rare phenomenon. It involves alteration of one of the processes involved in the drug reaching its site of action. The drug has to reduce its own absorption and distribution, or increase its own elimination. Alcohol is perhaps the best example of this type of tolerance.

Alcohol changes its own disposition in two main ways. First, alcohol may slow down absorption (Hunt and Pathak, 1960). This occurs because it slows the rate at which stomach contents are emptied into the duodenum. Food stays in the stomach longer if a person has been drinking beforehand. While some alcohol is absorbed in the stomach, it is absorbed at a much greater rate in the duodenum. Thus, any alcohol already in the bloodstream will result in a slower rate of absorption of recently ingested alcohol by increasing the time it takes to get to the duodenum.

In addition to slowing its own rate of absorption, alcohol increases the rate of its own elimination. The mechanism in this case is the stimulation of one of the two enzyme systems in the liver which are responsible for its oxidation (Chrusciel, 1982). The enzymes increase their activity in the presence of alcohol. Naturally, if the rate of elimination is increased there will be a lower concentration of alcohol at the site of action.

As mentioned above, there are relatively few drugs whose effects are subject to dispositional tolerance. Where it does occur, dispositional tolerance is likely to be relatively minor. The greatest degree of tolerance appears to be due to changes at the site of action rather than due to changes of concentration that reach the site of action.

There are a number of theories concerning the development of tolerance at the site where the drug has its effect (*pharmacodynamic tolerance*). In the case of drugs that are receptor agonists, it has been suggested that tolerance is due to a decrease in the number of receptors in the brain, a decrease in their sensitivity and a decrease in the responsiveness of the target nerve cell on which the receptor is located.

All these mechanisms could account for the development of tolerance. It is known, for example, that drug receptors are not fixed permanently. Old receptors disappear and new ones appear so that there is a constant turnover. In addition, the total number of receptors seems to fluctuate. And for some types of receptors, there is evidence that this number decreases when there is a high concentration of agonist in the vicinity for a prolonged period of time (Overstreet and Yamamura, 1979). This certainly suggests that there is a means for adjusting the system according to prevailing conditions.

There is also evidence for the other proposed mechanisms of pharmacodynamic tolerance, but at this stage there is no single definitive mechanism. It is quite likely that pharmacodynamic tolerance is the net result of the action of a number of different mechanisms. The number of receptors, their sensitivity and the responsiveness of the cell, may all change as a result of continued drug presence. What is common to each is that the system is acting *homeostatically*—continually adjusting in an attempt to return toward the normal state.

PHYSICAL DEPENDENCE

When a person takes a drug repeatedly for a long period of time, he or she may not simply be able to stop and carry on with their lives normally, even if he or she has stopped ingestion of the drug for the time-being. Instead, a number of physiological functions may be disrupted for a period of time (days, weeks, or even months) before the body gradually returns to normal. This disruption of physiological function is known as the *withdrawal* or *abstinence syndrome.* A person who suffers withdrawal if drug use is terminated abruptly is said to be physically dependent on the drug. Physical dependence is of great importance here, as it provides an important motivation for continued use of the drug (Cappell and LeBlanc, 1981). If the consequences of discontinuing usage are discomfort and ill feelings, then a person may find it much easier to continue to use the drug.

With many drugs both psychological and physical dependence can develop. Thus, a person may find the drug so pleasurable that they are compelled to continue to use it, and the consequences of stopping so unpleasant that he or she feels unable to discontinue its use. However, the two are not necessarily associated. There are drugs that can induce strong physical dependence without inducing psychological dependence. Certain opiate mixed agonist-antagonists fall into this category (Martin, 1967). Drugs used in the treatment of schizophrenia (the antipsychotics) also induce some physical but no psychological dependence. People have no desire to use such drugs per se, but do suffer various symptoms when their use (for medical purposes) is stopped for any reason (Baldessarini, 1985). Problems of illicit use or abuse are extremely rare with these drugs.

Physical dependence is not an inducement to begin drug use, as it develops only after use has begun. Nor does it seem to be a sufficient reason by itself to cause drug use. Nevertheless, it can be a particularly important contributing factor in the maintenance of a pattern of high level drug use once usage has begun. For most of the drugs under consideration here, physical dependence is likely to be preceded by psychological dependence.

A number of factors determine the severity of the withdrawal syndrome. One is the pattern of drug use. Full-blown physical dependence requires that the person have a sufficient level of drug in his or her body consistently for a long period of time. If the duration of action of a drug is about six hours, then a person will have to take it about four to five times a day at fairly regular intervals in order to maintain a high level of physical dependence. Such is the case with heroin. With some drugs, their short time-course means that they have to be used very frequently if physical dependence is to develop. Nicotine and cocaine are examples of such drugs. A second factor is the dose of the drug taken by the person. The higher the dose, the greater the degree of physical dependence. Indeed, some withdrawal symptoms may not appear in an individual who takes only a low dose regularly, but may in others who use higher doses. For example, *delirium tremens* is the name given to severe alcohol withdrawal. Symptoms such as seizures and hallucinations are characteristic, but do not occur in people who drink more moderate doses of alcohol and develop correspondingly lower level physical dependence. Progression to use of high doses is usually a gradual process that is accompanied by the development of tolerance.

A third factor determining the severity of the withdrawal syndrome is the amount of time a person has been using the drug. All things being equal, the longer a person has taken a drug, the more severe the withdrawal syndrome. For example, a brief period (say, one month) of barbiturate use can be terminated more readily than long-term levels of use, maintained over a period of years.

So, an individual in this situation is likely to experience a severe withdrawal syndrome if frequent and regular usage of high drug dose occurs over a long period of time. If any one factor is not present in a particular user's case, then the syndrome will be correspondingly less severe.

One other important consideration concerns the time-course of the drug itself. This can affect both the timing and the severity of the withdrawal syndrome. Withdrawal will appear much sooner and may be more severe after terminating use of a short-acting drug; a long-acting drug will remain in the body for some period of time. This will postpone the beginning of withdrawal, though small remaining traces of the drug may prevent some of the early symptoms from appearing, or diminish their severity. The other consequence of more gradual elimination is a more prolonged period of withdrawal.

One example of how this can be used is in treatment of heroin withdrawal (see Chapter Six). Another opiate, methadone, has similar effects to heroin but is much longer-acting. If methadone is substituted for heroin for a short period before withdrawal, then the symptoms will be less severe than withdrawal after heroin use. Although the person may have to tolerate them for a little longer, the diminished severity may make withdrawal easier to accept.

Types of Physical Dependence

The exact withdrawal syndrome depends on the drug taken. The symptoms of withdrawal are quite different following termination of alcohol than following the termination of heroin, for example. However, each drug is not completely unique. Rather, the type of physical dependence and the withdrawal syndrome are common to all drugs with similar pharmacological actions. Thus, the withdrawal syndrome is similar for both heroin and morphine. Most other opiates also share very similar withdrawal symptoms, although the severity of each symptom and the timing of withdrawal vary from drug to drug.

Just as there is cross-tolerance between drugs of similar effects, there is also *cross-dependence.* Someone who is physically dependent on heroin can stop using that drug and begin using an equivalent amount of morphine without suffering withdrawal. There is cross-dependence amongst all the morphine-like opiates, but only partial cross-dependence between these and the mixed agonist-antagonists. Cross-dependence also occurs amongst the sedative-hypnotic group of drugs. The characteristic withdrawal symptoms for a number of individual drugs or drug classes are described below. For more detail on these, the reader is referred to Jaffe (1985).

Opiates A high degree of tolerance develops to almost all effects of opiates – two exceptions are constipation and the constriction of pupils. Physical dependence develops with regular frequent dosing. Withdrawal is uncomfortable, but not dangerous. The timing of withdrawal depends on the specific opiate used, but usually begins around the time of the next scheduled dose and peaks thirty-six to seventy-two hours later.

The first symptoms are a craving for the drug and continual demands or requests for it. A little later the person may begin to sweat, their eyes may tear and their nose run; yawning may become frequent. Approaching the peak intensity a number of other symptoms develop, including restlessness, chills, goose-bumps, muscle twitches, aches and pains, insomnia, and loss of appetite. Both vomiting and diarrhea are common. Weight loss may be significant due to these symptoms, and spontaneous ejaculation or orgasm may occur.

The symptoms begin to subside after several days and most will have disappeared after a week. This time-course and the precise symptoms may vary across the different opiates. In general, the longer-acting opiates produce a milder, more delayed and longer-lasting withdrawal syndrome.

Barbiturates Tolerance to the barbiturates develops readily, particularly to the behavioral effects of these drugs. Thus, a regular user will not appear intoxicated at a dose that would cause a novice to appear drunk. However, tolerance to the lethal effects of these drugs is not pronounced, so that there is always a danger of overdose. The usual therapeutic dose will result in mild physical dependence; much greater doses are needed to produce the stronger dependence associated with the full-blown withdrawal syndrome.

The characteristic symptoms of barbiturate withdrawal include restlessness, insomnia, anxiety, tremulousness, weakness, nausea, and vomiting. The circulatory system has trouble adjusting when the person stands up, and fainting may result. The symptoms first appear twelve hours or so after the last dose, but this can vary considerably, depending on the time-course of the barbiturate used. A worse stage is reached if the person experiences convulsions. Convulsions can vary in number, and are usually followed by a psychotic-like state. The person may experience hallucinations and delusions which are usually very frightening and are associated with agitated behavior. This is very similar to delirium tremens after alcohol withdrawal (see below). Withdrawal usually ends a week to ten days after the last dose taken.

Barbiturate withdrawal can be dangerous: deaths during the convulsion stage are not uncommon if the person is not receiving any help. Under medical supervision withdrawal is usually preceded by a change to a long-acting barbiturate (for example, phenobartibal). Withdrawal is then gradual, sometimes with a slow reduction in dosage over weeks. Even if termination is abrupt, withdrawal is less severe after the use of these long-acting barbiturates.

Other Sedative-Hypnotic/Antianxiety Drugs   The characteristics of withdrawal are similar for all drugs in this class. However, withdrawal is usually less severe after terminating usage of benzodiazepines. Usually only the milder symptoms, such as insomnia and anxiety, are reported. However, more severe symptoms, including seizures, will occur if very high doses of benzodiazepines are taken.

Withdrawal from alcohol is very similar to barbiturate withdrawal. Most alcoholics will experience the initial symptoms, some will then have convulsions, and a few will enter the final phase of hallucinations and agitation known as delirium tremens.

Amphetamine   For a long time it was believed that there was little or no physical dependence associated with amphetamine use. However, this has been proven otherwise. Amongst those who consume large amounts of the drug a common pattern of use is to administer it at frequent intervals over several days. The concentration of the drug in the body may be relatively constant or the dose and/or frequency may be escalated gradually to counteract the development of tolerance. Use then stops abruptly and the person may sleep for a long period of time. Hunger may also be very strong. Many people interpreted this behavior not as withdrawal, but simply as compensation. Anyone who didn't eat or sleep for several days would be tired and hungry, whether taking amphetamine or not. However, there is more to this than simple compensation. Tiredness, lethargy, and hunger have all been shown to persist beyond the period required to make up for lost food and sleep. The lethargy may be quite marked and is sometimes associated with depression. For these reasons, it is now thought that the syndrome associated with discontinuation of high level amphetamine use is withdrawal, and therefore amphetamine is capable of producing physical dependence.

Cocaine   Cocaine is similar to amphetamine in many respects. Although there are differences, the two have similar actions in the brain and similar general effects. Tolerance develops to most effects of cocaine and there is cross-tolerance between cocaine and amphetamine. Also, results of terminating chronic cocaine use are similar to those for amphetamine. However, strong physical dependence is less likely to develop with cocaine, simply because of its short time-course, in that maintaining reasonable blood levels for a period of time requires more frequent administration. There is no real verifiable information concerning cross-dependence between cocaine and amphetamine at present.

Caffeine   Some tolerance develops to the effects of caffeine, but this is usually relatively minor—the dose required to produce a certain effect in a regular user may be only double that required in a nontolerant individual. Thus, there is no massive increase in the dose taken, as is seen with some other drugs. However, there is a mild withdrawal syndrome. Symptoms include headache, tiredness, anxiety, irritability, and nausea. Headache is probably the most characteristic symptom.

Nicotine   Tolerance develops quite rapidly to many effects of nicotine, and as a result, the experienced smoker does not suffer unpleasant symptoms such as nausea. The experienced individual also appears to inhale more deeply than the novice, thereby taking in a greater dose of nicotine. Abrupt cessation of smoking results in a withdrawal syndrome that peaks several days later. The symptoms include behavioral and subjective changes such as increased irritability, hostility, and difficulty in concentration. Bodily changes include decreased heart rate and blood pressure, and body weight may increase. The syndrome can be relatively mild, and in some cases may not be apparent to others.

LSD   Tolerance can develop to the effects of LSD with repeated usage, but disappears after a short period of abstinence. There is cross-tolerance between all other hallucinogens with similar pharmacological actions, but no evidence of physical dependence with this group. Use of hallucinogens is virtually always intermittent so that the conditions for physical dependence do not usually arise. However, it does not seem that withdrawal symptoms occur even when high level hallucinogen use stops.

PCP   Use of PCP tends to be occasional as well, but some individuals take it very frequently. Tolerance develops to the effects and a withdrawal syndrome may be experienced if a pattern of chronic use is terminated. Symptoms include nervousness, anxiety, and depression. There are also reports of difficulties in speech, thinking, and recall lasting for many months after PCP use has ceased.

Marijuana   Tolerance develops to many effects of marijuana. However, there is some evidence that chronic users may experience a "high" after using actually very little of the drug. The extent to which this may be due to the development of *placebo responding* (see Chapter Three) is unclear. The very large amounts taken by individuals in some societies indicate that tolerance must have developed in those individuals. However the level of physical dependence associated even with these patterns of use is relatively low. Withdrawal symptoms may include nausea, diarrhea, and irritability. These are only sometimes observed and tend to be mild. As mentioned above, it is possible that marijuana withdrawal is masked by the slow release of the drug stored in fat tissue. There is no definite evidence on this point, however. If confirmed, it would suggest that marijuana use results in a higher level of physical dependence than was previously thought.

Solvents and Aerosols   There is relatively little information available on the development of tolerance to, and physical dependence on these substances. In part, the problem is simply that there are so many of them. Tolerance certainly develops to a number of these substances, but the degree of cross-tolerance is not as yet known. There is no consistent evidence of a withdrawal syndrome following cessation of use. It may be that there is little or no physical dependence associated with use of the drugs, but to date there is not enough information to make a definitive statement.

Anticholinergics   Repeated use of anticholinergics results in the development of a limited degree of tolerance, and there is some evidence of physical dependence. In patients given high doses of these drugs as part of medical treatment, abrupt cessation sometimes results in sweating, salivation, and vomiting. Thus, physical dependence and withdrawal may be associated with high doses of anticholinergics. When taken outside such medical contexts, doses tend to be smaller and are taken irregularly. As a result, physical dependence is unlikely to develop.

Betel   While some tolerance clearly develops to the effects of betel, there is insufficient evidence on which to judge the degree of physical dependence.

Mechanisms of Physical Dependence

What is obvious when one looks at the withdrawal symptoms that follow from discontinuance of drug use is that they are frequently opposed to the actual effects produced by the drug. For example, opiates are analgesics, but people suffering from withdrawal experience considerable pain without any obvious cause. Stimulants alleviate fatigue, but one of the characteristics of withdrawal from these drugs is a prolonged feeling of lethargy. Anticholinergics have a drying action, reducing a number of bodily secretions. During anticholinergic withdrawal however, excess salivation occurs.

It would be easy to list many more examples, but a more interesting issue is whether or not all withdrawal symptoms can be characterized in this way. Another issue is whether there is a drug withdrawal symptom of the same kind corresponding to each effect of a drug, but instead in an opposing manner. Unfortunately these issues are often difficult to evaluate. For example, moderate doses of alcohol have been shown to increase heart rate (Wallgren and Barry, 1970). Elevated heart rate is also characteristic of alcohol withdrawal. However, the elevation may simply be a result of general autonomic arousal and may mask an underlying tendency to a decrease in heart rate.

Most theories of physical dependence and withdrawal suggest that during continued exposure to a drug the system regulates itself in one or more of the ways described earlier — change in number of receptors, change in receptor sensitivity, or a change in sensitivity of the target cell. Initially then, the drug produces an effect which may be above the normal resting value of the system (for example, an increase in sweating above the normal level). Over time the system will become less responsive to the drug as tolerance develops and the effect is reduced in magnitude. If the drug is suddenly stopped, the result is a drop below the normal resting value (for example, a decrease in sweating below normal). During this period the individual experiences withdrawal. Eventually the system returns to normal sensitivity and withdrawal ceases.

At present, this is only theory. It is certainly a simple and elegant one that explains the relationship between tolerance and physical dependence. The problem is that too many questions remain unanswered: Can all withdrawal symptoms be explained in this way? What mechanism or mechanisms are responsible for decreased sensitivity? And what about the drugs that fail to produce physical dependence?

Acute and Protracted Withdrawal

Typically, physical dependence is thought of as something that develops only after repeated administrations of a drug and results in a withdrawal syndrome that lasts for days or, in a few cases, weeks. It now appears that both these assumptions may be incorrect. Recent evidence indicates that dependence may develop within the time-course of a single administration and that withdrawal symptoms sometimes persist for very long periods of time.

The process of physical dependence may begin from the time a drug enters the body and starts to produce its effect. After some hours the drug effect wears off and mild withdrawal symptoms may appear. Regular users are usually familiar with such rebound effects. In some cases they may not be true withdrawal symptoms (for example, being tired after several hours of increased alertness following stimulant use), but in other cases they almost certainly are. Laboratory experimentation has confirmed the existence of very mild withdrawal after single experiences of a drug (see Boisse et al., 1986).

Such acute dependence may be very important to understanding the way in which people come to adopt a pattern of repeated drug taking. Two things are clear about withdrawal: it is unpleasant, and can only be relieved by taking more of the drug (or another drug which has similar actions). Some people respond to these unpleasant symptoms by taking the drug rather than simply enduring them. Once a person begins this pattern of use it is impossible to get off without experiencing withdrawal, and the longer the pattern is continued, the worse withdrawal can be.

Many of us will have experienced this type of withdrawal in the form of a hangover. Not all hangover symptoms are due to acute withdrawal—many come from dehydration caused by alcohol, the disturbance of normal sleep patterns it produces, and the effects of its metabolite acetaldehyde. However, it would seem that some symptoms must indeed be withdrawal, given that the most common hangover cure is "the hair of the dog that bit you." More alcohol will relieve withdrawal but not the other after-effects of a high dose of alcohol.

Why some people respond to withdrawal by reingesting the drug is not clear. It is possible that they may suffer worse withdrawal symptoms than others. Alternatively, the variation may be due to social factors (see Chapter Four) and to differences in their reaction to the drug experience. Physical dependence provides motivation for continued drug taking, but is only one factor amongst many which play a role in determining patterns of drug use.

At the other end of the time-scale is *protracted withdrawal.* It is generally assumed that a person recovers from withdrawal after days or weeks. However, it seems that in some cases the symptoms may persist in a mild form for a considerably longer period of time. Physiological and psychological changes have been observed to continue for many months after opiate withdrawal (Martin et al., 1973). It may be that many psychological problems experienced by former addicts are also a manifestation of this protracted abstinence. Unfortunately, there is little research in this area.

Protracted withdrawal may help to explain the high relapse of former addicts. While many experience some success and stop taking the drug, a very large proportion return to using it some time later (see Chapter Six). It would stand to reason that the person should have gone through withdrawal earlier.

However, if withdrawal persists for very long periods of time then relapsing into drug usage becomes much easier to understand. The individual may be doing the only thing he or she can to alleviate the unpleasant state.

CONCLUSION: BIOLOGICAL DETERMINANTS OF DRUG USE

Biological factors play a critical role as determinants of drug use. They need to be considered if we are to understand why drugs are used via particular routes, and why some drugs are preferred over others with similar actions. Biological factors also help explain the reaction following early use of a drug and the maintenance of long-term patterns of high level use.

It is clear that different drugs are used through different routes of administration. One factor here is simply the physical form of the drug — marijuana can't be injected, for example. A second is speed of effect. In general, users prefer to have a more rapid onset of action. This is borne out by historical trends and individual preferences. Thus, routes like smoking and intravenous injection that allow rapid absorption and distribution are preferred over oral consumption, which tends to result in a slower, more irregular pattern of onset.

The ability of a drug to penetrate biological barriers may also be an important determinant of its use. The clearest example is the preference for heroin over morphine. This appears to be due entirely to the greater ease with which the former accesses the central nervous system. A related reason for drug preference may be time-course of action. Drugs which are rapidly eliminated will have a shorter time-course. For many users this may be preferable (it causes less disruption to their lives), while in other circumstances a longer time-course may be preferred (for example, if a person is physically dependent).

The effects that follow the first use of a drug have a profound influence on later use. One of the major determinants of these effects is the dose administered. Because they have had no opportunities to develop tolerance, novice users need only a small dose to produce a large effect. Too much, and the adverse effects would be overwhelming. The importance of this is hard to overestimate. Many people simply refuse to take a drug for the rest of their lives after an initial unpleasant experience, whereas others may immediately begin to seek the same experience again, should it be a pleasurable experience. Compare the rapturous description of the effects of opium in Chapter One written by de Quincey, with the following account of a boy growing up in Harlem in the 1950s and having his first experience with heroin:

> Everything was so slo-o-ow. And then my head started. My head seemed to stretch, and I thought my brain was going to burst. It was like a headache taking place all over the head at once and trying to break its way out. And then it seemed to get hot and hot and hot. And I was so slow; I was trying to grab my head, but I couldn't feel it. I tried to get up, but my legs were like weights. I got scared. I'd

never felt this way in my life before. I wanted to fall down on my knees and say, "Oh, Mama, Mama, help me."

I couldn't seem to talk to Tito. I couldn't seem to talk to Dunny. They were right there in front of me, but they seemed to be so far away that I couldn't reach them. I fell down on my knees and crawled over to them. They were down there scrambling for some horse (heroin); they seemed to be talking and hollering about horse and horse and horse, and they couldn't hear me. They couldn't feel me. They didn't know if I was here dying or if something had a hold on me.

My guts felt like they were going to come out. Everything was bursting out all at once, and there was nothing I could do. It was my stomach and my brain. My stomach was pulling my brain down into it, and my brain was going to pull my guts out and into my head. And I said, "O Lawd, if you'll just give me one more chance, one more chance, I'll never get high again."

And then it seemed like everything in me all of a sudden just came out, and I vomited. I vomited on Tito, and he didn't even feel it. He didn't even know it. The cats were still getting high. I was so scared. I thought we'd just killed ourselves. I wanted to pray. I wanted to tell these guys to pray. And they were so wrapped up in this thing; they were still snorting and snorting and talking about nodding and nodding. And it seemed like this went on for years . . . I couldn't talk to them. I tried to touch them, but I couldn't reach them. I was trying to say something. I was trying to yell, and all these cats could do was nod, nod, nod, nod. I was dying, I was dying. I seemed to roll over fifty times, and every time I rolled over, I thought my guts were going to pour out on the floor.

I threw up and I threw up. It seemed like I threw up a million times. I felt that if I threw up one more time, my stomach was just going to break all open; and still I threw up. I prayed and I prayed and I prayed. After a while, I was too sick to care (Brown, 1965).

Interestingly, the author never used heroin again while his companions both became dependent.

Other initial effects of the drug will be important in determining further use. One theory suggests that those who develop high frequency patterns of use have some kind of central nervous system chemical deficiency. The drug brings the person back to equilibrium by making up for the deficit in the endogenous chemical. Another suggests that the activation of reward neurons in the brain is the critical event. While drugs have clear rewarding effects, what may be critical is whether there are other rewarding events in an individual's life (see Chapter Three). Other accounts suggest that we have to look at the whole range of CNS effects to understand why people continue drug use. Exactly what these are depends on the drug and the individual. The drug may improve the ability of a person to keep up a high-pressure job, or relax at the end of a day. It may increase their enjoyment of sex or provide a stimulus to artistic activities. Any drug can affect behavior and experience in a multitude of ways. Some of these may be beneficial to the individual, others may not. If the circumstances are appropriate, use may continue because of the beneficial effects.

With repeated drug use tolerance will develop. This will mean that the adverse effects will become less severe, but also that the dose has to increase so that the person can again experience the beneficial aspects of the drug. With certain drugs avoidance of withdrawal may become a major motivating factor once use becomes sufficiently frequent, and particularly if the dose has escalated to a considerable extent. Even relatively mild withdrawal (for example, withdrawal from nicotine) may be perceived as very unpleasant by users.

Clearly, biological factors play central roles at all stages of drug use — from choice of the drug and route of administration, to the outcome of initial use, and finally to the maintenance of high level patterns of use.

REFERENCES

AKIL, H., WATSON, S.J., YOUNG, E., LEWIS, M.E., KHACHATURIEN, H. & WALKER, J.M. (1984). Endogenous opioids: Biology and function. *Annual Review of Neuroscience, 7,* 223–255.

BALDESSARINI, R.J. (1985). Drugs and the treatment of psychiatric disorders. In A.G. Gilman, L.S. Goodman, T.W. Rall, & F. Murad, (Eds.) *The pharmacological basis of therapeutics.* (pp. 387–445). New York: Macmillan, 1985.

BARCHAS, J.D., AKIL, H., ELLIOT, G.R., HOLMAN, R.B. & WATSON, S.J. (1978). Behavioral neurochemistry: Neuroregulators and behavioral states. *Science, 200,* 964–973.

BLOOM, F.E. (1985). Neurohormonal transmission and the central nervous system. In A.G. Gilman, L.S. Goodman, T.W. Rall, & F. Murad, (Eds.) *The pharmacological basis of therapeutics.* (pp. 236–259). New York: Macmillan, 1985.

BOISSE, N.R., PERIANA, R.M., GUARINO, J.J., KRUGER, H.S. & SAMORISKI, G.M. (1986). Pharmacologic characterization of acute chlordiazepoxide dependence in the rat. *Journal of Pharmacology and Experimental Therapeutics, 239,* 775–783.

BOZARTH, M.A. (1986). Neural basis of psychomotor stimulant and opiate reward: Evidence suggesting the involvement of a common dopaminergic system. *Behavioral Brain Research, 22,* 107–116.

BRADBURY, M. (1979). *The concept of a blood-brain barrier.* Chichester: John Wiley and Sons.

BROWN, C. (1965). *Man-child in the promised land.* New York: Macmillan.

CAPPELL, H. & LEBLANC, A.E. (1981). Tolerance and physical dependence; Do they play a role in alcohol and drug self-administration? In Y. Israel, F.B. Glaser, H. Kalant, R.E. Popham, W. Schmidt & R.G. Smart (Eds.), *Research advances in alcohol and drug problems.* (Vol. 6, pp. 159–196). New York: Plenum Press.

CHEN, A.W.K. (1986). Racial differences in alcohol sensitivity. *Alcohol and Alcoholism, 21,* 93–104.

CHITWOOD, D.D. (1985). Patterns and consequences of cocaine abuse. In N.J. Kozel & E.H. Adams (Eds.), *Cocaine use in America: Epidemiologic and clinical perspectives.* Bethesda, MD: National Institute on Drug Abuse.

CHRUSCIEL, T.L. (1982). General pharmacology and toxicology of alcohol. In F. Hoffmeister & G. Stille (Eds.), *Handbook of experimental pharmacology* (Vol. 55/III, pp. 161–176). Psychotropic agents. Berlin: Springer-Verlag.

CRONE, C. (1986). The blood-brain barrier: A modified tight epithelium. In A.J. Suckling, M.G. Rumsby & M.W.B. Bradbury (Eds.), *The blood-brain barrier in health and disease.* (pp. 17–40). Chichester, Ellis Horwood.

CURRY, S.H. (1977). *Drug disposition and pharmacokinetics.* Oxford: Blackwell.

DISMUKES, R.K. (1979). New concepts of molecular communication among neurons. *The Behavioral and Brain Sciences, 23,* 409–448.

DOLE, V.E. & NYSWANDER, M. (1967). Heroin addiction — a metabolic disease. *Archives of Internal Medicine, 120,* 19–24.

GARRETT, E.R. (1977). Pharmacokinetics and disposition of $\triangle^9$-tetrahydrocannabinol and its metabolites. In G.G. Nahas & W.D.M. Paton (Eds.), *Marijuana: Biological effects.* (pp. 105–121). Oxford: Pergamon Press.

GILBERT, R.F.T. & EMSON, P.C. (1983).   Neuronal coexistence of peptides with other puta-
tive transmitters. In L.L. Iversen, S.D. Iversen & S.H. Snyder (Eds.), *Handbook of
psychopharmacology.* (Vol. 16, pp. 519–556). New York: Plenum Press.

GLENNON, R.A. (1985).   Involvement of serotonin in the action of hallucinogenic drugs. In
A.R. Green (Ed.), *Neuropharmacology of serotonin.* (pp. 253–280). Oxford: Oxford
University Press.

GOLDSTEIN, A., ARONOW, L. & KALMAN, S.M. (1974).   *Principles of drug action* (2nd
ed.) New York: John Wiley and Sons.

GRAHAM, T.E. (1983).   Alcohol ingestion and sex differences on the thermal responses to mild
exercise in a cold environment. *Human Biology, 55,* 463–476.

HAEFELY, W. (1985).   The biological basis of benzodiazepine actions. In D.E. Smith & D.R.
Wesson (Eds.), *The benzodiazepines: Current standards for medical practice.* (pp. 7–41).
Lancaster: MTP Press.

HARVEY, S.C. (1985).   Hypnotics and sedatives. In A.G. Gilman, L.S. Goodman, T.W. Rall &
F. Murad, (Eds.), *The pharmacological basis of therapeutics.* (pp. 339–371). New York:
Macmillan, 1985.

HUNT, N.J. & PATHAK, J.D. (1960).   The osmotic effects of some simple molecules and ions
on gastric emptying. *Journal of Physiology, 154,* 254–269.

JAFFE, J.H. (1985).   Drug addiction and drug abuse. In A.G. Gilman, L.S. Goodman, T.W.
Rall & F. Murad (Eds.), *The pharmacological basis of therapeutics.* (pp. 532–581). New
York: Macmillan, 1985.

JONES, B.M. & JONES, M.K. (1976).   Alcohol effects in women during the menstrual cycle.
Annals of the New York Academy of Sciences, 273, 576–587.

KALANT, H. (1971).   Absorption diffusion, distribution, and elimination of ethanol: Effects on
biological membranes. In B. Kissin & H. Begleiter (Eds.), *The biology of alcoholism.* (Vol.
1, pp. 1–62). Biochemistry. New York: Plenum Press.

KALANT, H. (1977).   Comparative aspects of tolerance to, and dependence on alcohol, barbiturates, and opiates. In M.M. Cross (Ed.), *Alcohol intoxication and withdrawal* – IIIb. (pp.
169–186). New York: Plenum Press.

KAPHAN, S.A. & JACK, M.L. (1981).   Pharmacokinetics and metabolism of anxiolytics. In F.
Hoffmeister & G. Stille (Eds.). *Handbook of experimental pharmacology.* (Vol. 55/II, pp.
321–358). Psychotropic agents. Berlin: Springer-Verlag.

KENAKIN, T.P. (1987).   *Pharmacologic analysis of drug-receptor interactions.* New York:
Raven Press.

KOOB, G.F., VACCARINO, F.J., AMALRIC, M. & SWERDLOW, N.R. (1987).   Neural
substrates for cocaine and opiate reinforcement. In S. Fisher, A. Raskin & E.H. Uhlenhuth
(Eds.), *Cocaine: Clinical and biobehavioral aspects.* (pp. 80–107). New York: Oxford
University Press.

MCGEER, P.L., ECCLES, J.C. & MCGEER, E. (1978).   *Molecular neurobiology of the mam-
malian brain.* New York: Plenum Press.

MANGAN, G.L. & GOLDING, J.F. (1984).   *The psychopharmacology of smoking.* Cambridge:
Cambridge University Press.

MARTIN, W.R. (1967).   Opioid antagonists. *Pharmacological Reviews, 19,* 463–521.

MARTIN, W.R. (1983).   Pharmacology of opioids. *Pharmacological Reviews, 35,* 283–323.

MARTIN, W.R., JASINSKI, D.R., HAERTZEN, C.A., KAY, D.C., JONES, B.E., MANSKY,
P.A. & CARPENTER, R.W. (1973).   Methadone – a reevaluation. *Archives of General
Psychiatry, 28,* 286–295.

MISRA, A.L. (1978).   Metabolism of opiates. In M.L. Adler, L. Manara & R. Samanin (Eds.),
Factors affecting the action of narcotics. (pp. 297–343). New York: Raven Press.

OVERSTREET, D.J. & YAMAMURA, H.I. (1978).   Receptor alterations and drug tolerance.
Life Sciences, 25, 1865–1877.

PIERCE, P.A. & PEROUTKA, S.J. (1989).   Hallucinogenic drug interactions with neurotransmitter receptor binding sites in human cortex. *Psychopharmacology, 97,* 118–122.

PITTS, D.K. & MARWAH, J. (1988).   Cocaine and central monoaminergic neurotransmission:
A review of electrophysiological studies and comparison to amphetamine and antidepressants. *Life Sciences, 42,* 949–968.

POMERLEAU, O.F. & POMERLEAU, C.S. (1984).   Neuro-regulators and the reinforcement
of smoking: Towards a bio-behavioral explanation. *Neuroscience and Biobehavioral Reviews, 84,* 503–513.

PORTANS, I., WHITE, J.M. & STAIGER, P.K. (1989).   Acute tolerance to the subjective effects of alcohol in human social drinkers. *Psychopharmacology, 97,* 365-369.

RADLOW, R. & HURST, P.M. (1985).   Temporal relations between blood alcohol concentration and alcohol effect: An experiment with human subjects. *Psychopharmacology, 85,* 260-266.

RUSSELL, M.A.H. (1987).   Nicotine intake and its regulation by smokers. In W.R. Martin, G.R. Van Loon, E.T. Iwamato & L. Davis (Eds.), *Tobacco smoking and nicotine: A neurobiological approach.* (pp. 25-50). New York: Plenum Press.

SIEGEL, R.K. (1982).   Cocaine smoking. *Journal of Psychoactive Drugs, 141,* 277-359.

TABERNER, P.V. (1980).   Sex differences in the effects of low doses of ethanol on human reaction time. *Psychopharmacology, 70,* 283-286.

VAN DYKE, C., JATLOW, P., UNGENER, J., BARASH, P.G. & BYCK, R. (1978).   Oral cocaine: Plasma concentrations and central effects. *Science, 200,* 211-213.

WALLGREN, H. & BARRY, H. III (1970).   *Actions of alcohol.* (Vols. I & II). New York: American Elsevier.

WESNES, K., (1982).   Nicotine increases mental efficiency: But how? In W.R. Martin, G.R. Van Loon, E.T. Iwamoto & L. Davis (Eds.), *Tobacco smoking and nicotine: A neurobiological approach.* (pp. 63-79). New York: Plenum Press, 1987.

WISE, R.A. (1981).   Brain dopamine and reward. In S.J. Cooper (Ed.), *Theory in psychopharmacology.* (Vol. 1, pp. 103-122). London: Academic Press.

CHAPTER 3

Psychological Aspects

The previous chapter was concerned with both how a drug comes to affect brain tissue, and also the factors that determine the magnitude of the effect. The aim of the present chapter is to characterize the results of that activity. In the best of all worlds it might be possible to do this by carefully analyzing the way in which drugs act in different areas of the brain, under varying conditions. However, our knowledge of brain function is extremely limited, making such an approach impossible. Instead, we need to adopt the methods and perspectives of psychology.

The first section covers research that is concerned most directly with drug self-administration and factors affecting that behavior. The results presented here suggest that drugs vary in their ability to maintain drug-seeking and drug administration. With some drugs, there is a greater likelihood of dependence. Users of those drugs are obviously at a much greater risk.

In the following sections, two types of drug effects are examined: *subjective* and *behavioral*. These effects are of interest both because we need to understand them in order to properly characterize what a drug does, and because such effects may help in understanding the reasons for drug use. Both these types of effects are likely to contribute to the maintenance and cessation of drug use.

The next section examines how effects which mimic those of a drug can occur in the absence of any drug (placebo effects), and how withdrawal-like symptoms can occur in the absence of physical dependence. Despite their unusual nature, such phenomena can be observed readily, can be explained reasonably, and may be very important to the maintenance of drug use.

Finally, our ability to predict a person's drug use from an understanding of her personality will be considered. A number of theories have been put forward concerning the type of person who develops drug problems. Many people cite personality as the main determinant of drug use patterns rather than any of the factors described above. Evidence on the importance of personality will be considered here.

Aspects of social psychology relevant to drug use will be discussed in the next chapter, and drug-induced impairment of psychomotor function will be discussed in Chapter Five.

DRUG SELF-ADMINISTRATION

What is obvious about drug-taking is that many people go to considerable effort to obtain and administer the drug or drugs of their choice. They may grow and process the drug themselves, or in order to obtain sufficient funds to purchase it, they may work at a job or engage in illegal activities. Considerable effort may be spent in the absence of any real physical dependence. For example, recreational alcohol, cocaine, and marijuana users may all spend considerable time, effort, and money in obtaining their drugs.

Not only do people go to some lengths to be able to use their drug, but, in doing so, they sacrifice other pleasures in their lives. The money spent on cigarettes could be used for entertainment or to purchase goods. Time devoted to the cultivation of drugs may be used for other recreational purposes. An extreme example concerns the cultivation of khat in a number of African countries. Governments have tried to restrict this activity because it limits production of badly needed food supplies (Kalix, 1987).

In the case of any individual drug user, a certain part of his or her behavior is directed toward obtaining and administering the drug. The effect of the drug is the final consequence of what may be a very long sequence of behavior. That behavior is said to be maintained or reinforced by the effect of the drug, and the drug is a reinforcer for the behavior.

People's behavior can be analyzed in a similar way with respect to other reinforcers. We spend time and effort in obtaining food, for example. For some people the sequence of behavior may begin with cultivation of the soil and in tending crops, while for most of us it involves working to obtain money in order to purchase the food. Because of taste preferences and other factors, considerable work also goes into preparation of the food.

The behavior of any individual will be motivated by a number of different reinforcers. In addition to food, there will be other basic requirements such as warmth and shelter, things that other people do to reinforce us (give us approval, sexual reinforcement, etc.) and many more. The exact list will depend on the individuals themselves — in that we all have clearly differing tastes.

If, as this analysis suggests, a drug is simply another type of reinforcer, does it have the properties of other reinforcers? For example, does the quantity of drug used depend on its cost, and on the amount of work required to obtain it? Does the pattern of drug use change when the size of each dose changes (for example, in changing the nicotine content of cigarettes or the strength of street heroin)? The answers to such questions have important consequences for understanding and dealing with drug use.

In researching these questions, investigators have endeavored to simplify the situation. Rather than researching a long chain of complex behavior leading to purchase and administration of a drug, a simple task may be presented to a male or female subject in an experiment. A certain amount of work at this task is reinforced by the quantity of the drug used. To minimize the possibility of human error, the procedure is very often an automatic one. For example, after one hundred presses on a button a quantity of whisky may be dispensed into a cup for the subject to drink. Alternatively in the experiment, the subject may simply be allowed to use the drug at certain times.

Unfortunately, there are complex legal and ethical problems associated with such research, particularly when dealing with drugs like cocaine and heroin. As a result, much of the experimental work in this area has been carried out using as subjects people hospitalized for treatment of drug problems who are willing to volunteer their participation. Using volunteer subjects from the general population in this way is simply not feasible for many studies.

Another strategy has been to use animals and give them the opportunity to self-administer the drugs we use (Johanson and Schuster, 1981; Young and Herling, 1986). This has enabled comparison of their drug-taking to ours. What is interesting is that the drugs they will administer themselves are much the same as the drugs humans self-administer (Griffiths, Bigelow, and Henningfield, 1980). They include nicotine, amphetamine, cocaine, alcohol, and representatives from most of the major classes. The one exception is the group comprising LSD, mescaline, and similar hallucinogens. While these are taken by at least some humans, they are rejected by animals. In contrast, the main active component of marijuana, $\triangle^9$-THC is taken by animals under at least some conditions (Takahashi and Singer, 1979). Table 3.1 shows the range of drugs that animals will voluntarily administer, together with examples of drugs that do not function as reinforcers. With the exception of mescaline, most members of this latter group are not usually taken by humans outside a medical context.

Drug-taking then, is not uniquely human. Given the opportunity, animals show a similar propensity to administer drugs, and will even overdose unless protected from doing so. Over an extended period of time they will become physically dependent. Such behavior may be only natural: As noted in Chapter One, animals in the wild are frequently observed to seek out and ingest plants containing drugs.

**TABLE 3.1   Drugs Which Either Are or Are Not Self-Administered
by Laboratory Animals**

Drugs self-administered by laboratory animals

    Sedative-hypnotic/antianxiety
    —including barbiturates, benzodiazepines, and alcohol

    Psychomotor stimulants
    —including cocaine, amphetamine, nicotine, and caffeine

    Hallucinogens
    —PCP and ketamine

    Marijuana ($\triangle^9$-THC)

    Solvents and aerosols
    —including ether and lacquer thinner

Drugs *not* self-administered by laboratory animals

    Antipsychotics

    Antidepressants

    Aspirin and other similar analgesics

    Mescaline

In the following discussion of results from self-administration research, human and animal studies will not be differentiated clearly. In virtually all cases where similar experiments have been performed in humans and animals, the same pattern of results emerges. Before beginning this discussion however, some of the methods used in these studies will be discussed briefly.

Methods

A variety of techniques have been used to allow self-administration of drugs (Krasnegor, 1978a). With animals, the drug may simply be placed in a water bottle and measures taken of the amount of drug solution consumed. Or, the animals may instead work at a simple repetitive task in order to obtain access to the solution. For example, the animal may be required to make a fixed number of presses on a lever to earn the opportunity to drink several milliliters of a drug solution.

Using ingested solutions too, creates several problems. One is that taste factors become important, and most drug solutions have an unpleasant taste. Second, and more importantly, many of the drugs of interest are not ingested by human users. In order to better mimic the human situation the same route of administration is to be used wherever possible. This may mean the intravenous route, for example. In such cases, rather than give individual injections, researchers usually fit the animals with permanent catheters that allow the drug to pass straight into the vein. Methods for drug delivery via inhalation have also been developed. This route is used by humans for solvents and aerosols as well as drugs that are a constituent of smoke. A final method is intragastric. This involves depositing the drug directly into the stomach. The pattern of drug absorption will be much the same as with oral administration, but it eliminates any taste factors.

Where human subjects are used, they are given the opportunity to take the drug in its usual form. For example, when studying drinking, a reinforcer may consist of a fixed quantity of spirit. Smoking behavior may be studied by counting the number of puffs people take on a cigarette. Many drugs are simply taken in tablet or capsule form. Use has also been made of the intravenous route of administration.

Depending on the purpose of the study, human subjects may be required to work in order to obtain each dose. Again, the task is usually a simple and repetitive one—pushing a button or pulling a lever a fixed number of times, or perhaps a certain amount of riding on an exercise bike. More complex, intellectual tasks have sometimes been used, but the problem is that the drug may directly affect the individual's ability to carry out that task. Thus, self-administration may cease because the person is unable to complete the requirements for reinforcement. This adds a confounding factor to experiments examining determinants of self-administration.

Drug Dose

Changes in the amount or dose of the drug available have a remarkably uniform effect on the pattern of intake, under a wide range of conditions. As the dose is increased from a relatively low level, the individual increases work rate and the frequency of obtaining the dose is also increased. In this range, a larger dose is a more powerful reinforcer than a smaller one. For example, Griffiths, Bigelow, and Liebson (1976) studied patterns of alcohol intake in people being treated for problem drinking. Subjects were given a task to obtain alcohol, and the dose was varied from 1.9 to 11.1 grams per ingestion. (Ten grams is the approximate alcohol content of a standard drink.) They found that the larger the dose subjects could obtain, the more they obtained. High levels of consumption occurred only when the dose was in the normal range for a drink; not when it was lower.

However, a point can be reached where higher doses result in a drop in intake frequency. The drug is taken less often, and correspondingly less work is done to obtain it. While this might indicate that in the higher range, larger drug doses are less reinforcing than smaller ones, an examination of intake patterns suggests otherwise. If we actually measure the total amount of drug taken we can see that this increases with dose across the whole range. A hypothetical example is presented in Fig. 3.1. These data have come mainly from animal studies.

Findings like this suggest a pattern of increased intake with greater doses of drug, but with an adjustment so that there is a limit on the amount of drug taken. If the frequency of intake remained the same irrespective of the unit dose, total intake would increase much faster along with increases in the unit dose.

One consequence of increased total consumption is greater changes in the behavior of the individual. Such changes may limit the amount of drug that can be taken. If that dose of the drug causes extreme intoxication, the individual is unlikely to be able to work in order to obtain more. Only once the level of intoxication has decreased is it likely that he or she will begin again the sequence of behavior which leads to drug administration. With lower unit doses, the level of intoxication will be correspondingly lower and there will be less impairment of drug-seeking behavior.

These behavioral effects may in some cases explain the decreased frequency of intake with higher unit doses. However, they may not be the sole reason. In studies of human cigarette smoking, increasing the concentration of the tobacco products in the smoke over a given range results in a decrease in the rate of puffing (see for example, Henningfield and Griffiths, 1980). This is despite any clear inability to puff at the high dose levels. At very low dose ranges, puff rate would presumably be close to zero. Thus, with smoking we are likely to find the same inverted-U shaped curve in the absence of obvious

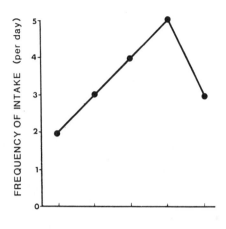

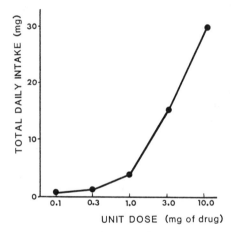

FIGURE 3.1
A hypothetical example of changes in frequency of drug intake and total daily intake when the dose available for self-administration is increased

intoxication. In a study of caffeine, Griffiths and Woodson (1988) found a decrease in reinforcing effects over the range 100–600mg. Doses lower than this (in other words, in the range for a cup of tea or instant coffee) were not tested.

In summary, higher doses of a drug tend to be more reinforcing than lower doses, but only to a certain limit. After that, the adverse effects may make high doses less effective reinforcers. Across a range of doses, total intake tends to increase with unit dose. This change may involve an increase, a decrease, or no alteration in the amount of work expended to obtain the drug. These points can be illustrated by the following: If the quality of street heroin were to suddenly rise for instance, (with no change in price or availability) then we would expect to see an increase in the average intake of users. There may be a number of adverse results, including deaths through overdose. Those users currently taking relatively small amounts of the drug may increase their rate of usage, while heavier users may use the drug as often or even less often.

The opposite change, a decrease in unit dose through diminished quality, would have the opposite effect on total intake. It would be likely to decrease. However, many users would increase the frequency with which they administer the drug. Some lighter users, on the other hand, may diminish their frequency of drug use. The example illustrates how changes in the pattern of drug use produced by alterations in unit dose cannot be specified simply, but are dependent on the prior pattern of use.

Drug Cost

One factor related to unit dose is the amount of work required (or cost) to obtain each dose. What happens if a person has to work harder or pay more for his or her drug? In the case of illegal drugs, large price fluctuations are both common and frequent. The prices of legal drugs tend to change more slowly, but as will be outlined in Chapter Four, there have been marked changes in the relative cost of drugs such as alcohol over the last twenty years.

One common view is that demand for drugs like heroin and alcohol stays much the same, irrespective of cost. In particular, it is claimed that those dependent on the drug need to obtain it and will do so irrespective of what is required. Stories of the various criminal activities engaged in by users and the lengths to which they go to obtain sufficient quantities of the drug tend to support this position.

According to this view, demand for drugs, at least amongst regular users, does not vary much with cost. This puts drugs in the same category as the essential commodities such as basic foodstuffs. In economic terms, the demand for these items is said to be *price inelastic*. This is in contrast to goods for which demand changes considerably with price. These are termed *price elastic* and tend to be luxury rather than essential items.

Research which uses the drug self-administration paradigm as its basis suggests that this view may be incorrect. As the cost of drugs increases, use of them declines. This has been observed with people diagnosed and hospitalized as sedative abusers who work to obtain barbiturates (Griffiths, Bigelow, and Liebson, 1976) and diagnosed alcoholics who work to obtain alcohol (Bigelow and Liebson, 1972). If the cost (in work requirement) for each drink is increased, then the amount of alcohol ingested will decline. And with a large increase in cost, the decline in consumption can be quite marked.

If we look at work output, we find that this will increase if the cost per unit dose is increased, but only up to a certain level. Eventually, higher costs result in a lower work output. Thus, if more work is required to obtain the drug, people will do so, but only to a certain limit; from that point on their output declines. These two relations—between work output and unit-cost, and frequency of intake and unit cost — are illustrated by a hypothetical example in Fig. 3.2. Note that since unit dose is constant, frequency of intake is equivalent to total intake.

Increasing the cost of a drug may be an effective way of reducing its use. If the cost is relatively low then in response to a price increase people may pay more and partially compensate. However, once a certain limit is reached, consumption will decline with an elevation in price. Of course, in a normal population the relative cost is going to vary enormously amongst the different individuals. If cost is solely in monetary terms then relative cost will be greater for the poor. Cost may also vary if some people have easier access to the drug than others. Thus, while a change in cost may have an overall effect on use within a population, it will not immediately affect every user in the same way.

The elasticity of demand for drugs has been exploited by governments throughout history (see Chapter One). Price increases have been and still are

FIGURE 3.2
A hypothetical example of changes in total daily expenditure and frequency of intake when the cost per unit dose self-administered (in units of work required) is increased

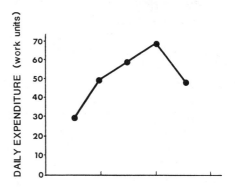

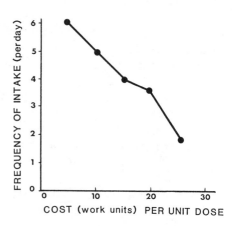

used to decrease demand, as well as to increase revenue. Their effectiveness will be discussed further in Chapter Four.

Drug Type and Pattern of Intake

Of the range of drugs that humans and animals self-administer the pattern of intake varies considerably. For example, the pattern of the administration of alcohol contrasts markedly with the pattern seen with other sedative-hypnotic/antianxiety drugs such as barbiturates and benzodiazepines. Given free access, alcohol tends to be taken in an irregular pattern, with occasional periods of abstinence lasting one or more days (Mello and Mendelson, 1972). On the other hand, there is a much more stable pattern of barbiturate and benzodiazepine intake: Variation in rate of intake is relatively small, and extended abstinence periods are much less likely (see for example, Griffiths, Bigelow, and Liebson, 1979).

A relatively stable intake pattern is also observed with opiates such as morphine and heroin, although with free access there may be a gradually increasing intake over a period of months (for example, Schuster, 1970). This may stabilize so that intake remains at a fairly constant level from that point on. Apart from nighttime, voluntary periods of abstinence are not usually observed with opiates.

In contrast, the pattern of use with stimulants tends to be cyclic. Each cycle begins with high intake rate and continues for a number of days. Relatively little sleeping or eating occurs during this time and toxic effects of the drug may appear. The high intake rate is then followed by abstinence for one or more days, perhaps even several weeks. Eating and sleeping may be more frequent than the norm during this time. The cycle then begins again with reinitiation of intake. In animals, stimulant intake frequently has to be regulated in order to prevent overdose during the 'binge' times (Johanson, Balster, and Bonese, 1976).

What is interesting about these results is that the patterns of intake observed in highly controlled but somewhat artificial laboratory settings are very similar to those observed in real life. Those familiar with use of the various types of drugs will recognize the irregular intake pattern of many dependent alcohol users, the relatively constant need of opiate users (although there are exceptions — see for instance Chapter Four), and the cyclic pattern of amphetamine users. The fact that these patterns occur even though the users are laboratory animals suggests that they are due to specific effects of the drug and not social or other factors. In some cases we can speculate about these effects. For example, amphetamine users do not usually sleep or eat very much because both types of behavior are directly suppressed by the drug. However, one cannot continue to do without eating and sleeping and, eventually, drug use must stop to allow for some "catching up." Once recovered, drug use may begin again and the pattern continue.

While we can construct a plausible hypothesis concerning the intake pattern of amphetamine users, it is a little more difficult to do so in the case of high level alcohol users. Why do they allow for periods of abstinence in which they must experience withdrawal? Again, the pattern has been observed under laboratory conditions in which there has been a constant availability of drugs and no outside factors intervening to prevent intake. One answer is that the toxic effects of the drug (on the gastrointestinal system, for example) become so great that the person is simply unable to continue.

Prior Conditions

Some of the factors which determine the ability of a drug to act as a reinforcer are specific to the individual. They include the person's genetic history, previous experience with drugs, and current circumstances. Those factors relating to earlier events will be discussed here and the effects of current circumstances discussed in the next section.

Hereditary influences are very difficult to determine. However, there is some animal research indicating that they have an effect. Animals from different strains within a species have different genetic characteristics. Experiments have shown that this variation can influence the rate at which the animals self-administer certain drugs. For example, certain mouse strains show a much stronger preference for alcohol than do other strains (Erwin and McClearn, 1981). Other effects of drugs also vary across different strains.

The possible importance of this factor is borne out by human genetic research which shows that, on average, a close biological relationship to an alcoholic makes it more likely that an individual will develop an alcohol abuse problem (Dietrich and Spuhler, 1984; see also Chapter Four). The mechanism is as yet unknown. It may be any of a number of factors which alter the reinforcing or some other effect of the drug. Unfortunately, we have little information on the role genetic factors may play in the use of other types of drugs.

A second factor is the prior drug history of the individual. Having prior drug experiences seems to make it more likely that a person will self-administer a drug when given the opportunity to do so, and experience with the particular drug in question is likely to have the greatest effect. That is, individuals with a history of using a drug are more likely to reinitiate use than individuals with no experience. If the evidence for this had come solely from human studies we might question its worth. Someone who had previously used amphetamine is quite likely to use it again. They may have the genetic background, personality, and lifestyle that make amphetamine particularly reinforcing. Many of these factors would not have changed from the earlier to the later period of use. And some might argue that a person who used one type of drug (for example, amphetamine) may simply have the propensity to engage in drug use in general.

However, much of the evidence comes from animal studies. In these experiments the animals are not selecting the drugs from a wide range. Furthermore, virtually all animals will self-administer many of the drugs commonly used in these experiments, including amphetamine, cocaine, and morphine. Thus, it is not simply a small minority who mark themselves different by their willingness to seek out and use various drugs. While this may be important, it is also more generally the case that voluntary or involuntary prior exposure to a drug makes that and other drugs more powerful reinforcers.

Prior exposure becomes even more important immediately after termination of drug use. In the case of some drugs (see Chapter Two) such termination leads to withdrawal. Research has shown that a drug will be a more powerful reinforcer if the individual is suffering withdrawal from the drug (Schuster, 1970; Woods and Schuster, 1971). Thus, physical dependence on a drug increases its reinforcing efficacy, but is not necessary for a drug to act as a reinforcer.

Current Conditions

The current situation or environment of individuals is also an important determinant of whether they will self-administer a drug or not. Unfortunately, there is relatively little research on self-administration under varying environmental conditions. However, the little data available suggest some interesting relations. In studies where animals have been exposed to mild electric shocks, drug intake was shown to be higher when the shocks were present than in their absence. In one study, the drug used was alcohol, and the shocks were to be avoided by engaging in a specified behavior (Cicero, Myers, and Black, 1968). In the second, a barbiturate was made available and the shocks were to be unavoidable (Davis and Miller, 1961).

These results are consistent with both the commonly-held view that alcohol functions to reduce stress and the clinical evidence available on the antianxiety properties of sedative-hypnotics. One corollary is that stress-reduction is one of the main reasons for alcohol use. While there is some evidence supporting such views, alcohol does not reduce stress under all circumstances and stress reduction is not the sole reason for alcohol use (Pohorecky and Brick, 1983). Nevertheless, these results suggest that an environment which could be described as stressful may increase the likelihood of self-administration of certain drugs.

A second aspect of the current conditions is the availability of other reinforcers. It was suggested earlier that drugs could be viewed as just another set of reinforcers, certainly with some unique aspects, but with many properties similar to other reinforcers. Several experiments have suggested that drugs are self-administered less frequently if other reinforcers are concurrently available. For example, people may have the opportunity to work for tokens which can be exchanged for either money or a quantity of drug. Increasing the money value but not the drug value of each token will reduce the frequency with which subjects choose the drug alternative (Stitzer, McCaul, Bigelow, and Liebson, 1983). Thus, to some extent drugs are interchangeable with other reinforcers.

A related area of research has examined rates of drug self-administration as a function of the way other reinforcers in the individual's environment are scheduled. It has been found that some apparently irrelevant behaviors can occur excessively when there are distinct periods in which reinforcement is not available. These are known as *schedule-induced* or *adjunctive behaviors,* and drug self-administration is one such behavior (see Sanger, 1986, for a review). Drugs may be consumed at a greater rate when the individual experiences periods of no reinforcement between periods of reinforcement availability.

These results demonstrate that drugs must be seen in the context of other types of reinforcers an individual has available. If there are few alternative reinforcers or distinct periods when alternative reinforcers are not available then a drug may be very powerful. On the other hand, if many highly-valued reinforcers are almost always available, the reinforcing efficacy of a drug may be low. This suggests that one factor predisposing people to drug use may be the lack of a range of reinforcers in their lives. With relatively few reinforcers a drug may shine out. At least some types of therapy attempt to redress such imbalances (see Chapter Six). Other aspects of current circumstances are concerned more directly with the social environment. These will be covered in Chapter Four.

Elimination of Self-Administration

Of particular interest to those concerned with helping people who would like to reduce their drug intake are environmental changes which decrease self-administration. As we have noted already, the ability of a drug to act as a reinforcer is not fixed, but depends on factors such as the availability of other reinforcers in the individual's life.

Reduction of drug-seeking behavior can be effected most simply by somehow making the drug inert. Thus, if a benign substance is substituted for the drug, the behavior involved in obtaining the drug will eventually disappear. If the person is told that is the case then the change will be fairly rapid; if not, the process will be somewhat slower. Indeed, attempts to seek the drug from that source may temporarily increase before eventually diminishing.

As an example, consider what might happen if the market were flooded with heroin so weak as to make it virtually inert. There may be an initial flurry of drug buying and administration in a vain effort to get a 'hit.' After a while this would disappear. From time to time users would buy and administer the drug, but as long as it was still ineffective the behavior would slowly diminish. The same pattern might be observed if one could substitute decaffeinated coffee for the real thing. A high-rate coffee drinker may initially increase her consumption rate before it gradually diminishes. In either case, if one single administration produced the desired effect, drug-seeking and drug administration would be reinstated.

A second way in which a drug can be made ineffective is by administration of an antagonist that blocks the effect of that drug. As long as sufficient levels of the antagonist are in the body the drug will have no reinforcing effect. The pattern of drug-seeking behavior will change in the manner described above. The therapeutic use of this means of eliminating drug-seeking behavior will be discussed in Chapter Six.

Drug-seeking behavior can also be decreased by *preloading* – simply giving the individual a sufficient quantity of the drug beforehand. People (and animals) are very sensitive to the concentration of drugs in their bodies. They do not simply continue drug seeking and administration in a fixed pattern, but respond to changing body levels. Accordingly, if there is already a sufficiently high level then self-administration will diminish until that level drops enough. (See for example, Jones and Prada, 1975; Griffiths, Wurster, and Brady, 1975.)

These findings have been exploited therapeutically by allowing people to use a drug in a less harmful form in order to reduce their normal drug administration practices. For example, nicotine chewing gum may be given to smokers to raise body levels of nicotine and thereby reduce smoking behavior. Methadone may be given to heroin users so that they can maintain a reasonably high level of opiate in their bodies and therefore make heroin seeking and administration less likely. These approaches will be discussed in more detail in Chapter Six.

Finally, drug seeking and drug administration are sensitive to consequences other than those produced by the drug itself. Much of the relevant research has been done with animals (Poling and Appel, 1979), but the findings mesh with general observations which can be made when dealing with clinical populations of drug users. For example, drug-seeking behavior will decline if it is subject to adverse consequences that are sufficiently severe. These may be penalties imposed by society, reactions of friends and family, or the interference to normal lifestyle which may result from drug use. Or it may decline because other, more powerful reinforcers are available for not using drugs. Such a situation may arise if an individual is forced to choose between keeping a job and continued drug use. The reinforcing effects of money, workmates, job satisfaction, etc., are pitted against the reinforcing effect of the drug. Whichever is stronger will come to be more important in the person's life.

These factors are all of importance in the therapeutic situation and will be discussed more in Chapter Six. It is sufficient to note here that drug-taking is determined by all its consequences. The behavior does not continue in a blind, irrational manner once begun, but is modified continually by current circumstances.

Conclusions

One point to emerge from this research is that certain drugs have very strong reinforcing properties. That is, a great deal of behavior may be maintained simply because it enables an individual to use the drug. The fact that at least some drugs have been shown to be reinforcers in animals (often several species), in addict or postaddict humans, and in normal human volunteers suggests that such reinforcing properties are inherent to the drug.

The implication is that any individual exposed to such a drug may be at risk of developing behavior devoted to obtaining and administering the drug. The properties of the drug itself make it possible for anyone to become a frequent, and perhaps dependent, user. Why we do not all use every drug to which we are exposed then becomes an important question. Two possible solutions may be given.

One is that only under certain conditions are the drugs *sufficiently* reinforcing for extensive drug use to develop. It may be that certain past histories or personalities make a drug more or less reinforcing. This proposal is discussed later in the chapter. As discussed earlier, genetic factors may also play a role. Alternatively, the right conditions may have to be present at the time of use. For example, when people are anxious or under stress certain drugs may be more reinforcing. Or, if they have few other sources of reinforcement, the effect of the drug may be magnified.

The second solution is that the reinforcing effects of the drug are counteracted by its unpleasant consequences. While increased drug use may have reinforcing effects due to the inherent biological properties of the drug, it may also have unpleasant consequences. Work may suffer, normal social activity may diminish, and people may disapprove of the large amounts of time spent in obtaining or being intoxicated by a drug.

An example of how such factors can affect self-administration comes from a study conducted by Johanson and Uhlenhuth (1981). Subjects were volunteer university students with no specific history of drug dependence. They were required to come in three times a week and choose a moderate dose of amphetamine or placebo (without a knowledge of which was which). Over the course of the study, preference for amphetamine declined from eighty percent to under fifty percent. When questioned, subjects indicated that the disruption to normal life caused by the amphetamine made it unattractive to take on a regular basis. Study and other activities suffered as a result of drug use. While the subjects reported pleasant immediate effects, the longer-term effects made continued use undesirable.

It should be noted that the two explanations are, of course, quite compatible. There will always be variation in the strength of a drug reinforcer, depending on prior conditions, and the range of adverse consequences produced by a drug will act to diminish use of that drug.

A further point to emerge from these studies is that drug-taking, even amongst those classified as addicts, is not some fixed, automatic pattern of behavior. Drugs do not compel people to take them. Whether an individual takes a drug or not will depend on a whole host of facts including its cost, the amount of drug available, and the alternative sources of reinforcement available to them. A change in any one of these factors can drastically alter the likelihood of further drug-taking. These results strongly argue against a view of drug taking which sees the user as victim to the drug.

SUBJECTIVE EFFECTS

Often, the most compelling effects of drugs are the subjective changes they engender. We may be aware of some physiological changes, but most remain unnoticed. Similarly, a number of behavioral changes may occur without our being aware of them. However, changes in sensations, feelings, and mood are impossible to ignore. For this reason we often tend to characterize drugs in terms of these types of changes rather than in terms of any alterations to behavior or physiology.

Subjective changes are also thought to be of central importance because of their role in maintaining drug-taking behavior. Most people would attribute the reinforcing effects of drugs to the subjective changes they induce. For example, the idea that drugs which are abused are those which produce euphoria is a common notion. It will be examined in more detail later in this section.

Three aspects of the subjective effects of drugs will be considered here. The first concerns changes in sensation and perception. How do drugs influence the way we see, hear, smell, taste, and feel the world? The second aspect is concerned with changes in feelings and moods produced by drugs. The third concerns the notion that drugs induce states different from our normal state and that the particular state induced depends on the exact pharmacological activity of the drug.

Unfortunately, there is in each case a relative paucity of information. Subjective effects of drugs are the least understood of the changes they produce. This may seem strange because of their apparent importance, but the reason is clearly their inaccessibility. Subjective effects are by nature private and not public. They cannot be directly observed, making any attempt to record or evaluate them considerably less than perfect.

Sensory and Perceptual Changes

While objective methods for assessment of these changes have been developed, there has been relatively little research on the effects of drugs. Perhaps because of this, the findings do not present a clear, coherent picture. Further results are necessary before more than a simple catalogue of changes can be given. For more detail, the reader is referred to Robinson and Sabat (1975) and Hindmarch (1980).

Vision   A number of drugs impair our visual acuity. In tests of ability to discriminate similar visual patterns, performance is worsened by administration of drugs such as alcohol, amphetamine, opiates, and tobacco. It should be noted that since cigarettes were smoked in these studies, the effects must be attributed to tobacco rather than nicotine. A number of compounds in the tobacco smoke may have influenced performance.

One test that has been used extensively is the *critical flicker fusion threshold.* Each subject is shown a flickering light and the frequency at which the subject reports the flicker disappearing is recorded. In general, the higher the frequency, the better the performance. Stimulants have been found to improve performance on this test while sedatives have been shown to impair performance (Smith and Misiak, 1976).

The most prominent changes in vision have been reported following administration of LSD and similar hallucinogens. Visual acuity seems to be worsened by these drugs. For example, they decrease performance in discrimination tasks, slow adaptation to brightness, and reduce accuracy of color vision. But much more compelling are the distortions, synesthesia, and hallucinations described briefly in Chapter One (see also Siegel, 1977). Despite worsened performance, however, users generally report a more vivid sense of color.

What is interesting about the LSD-induced hallucinations is that they appear to involve a modification of normal sensory input. For instance, blind people do not experience the usual visual effect of LSD. Sighted people who are blindfolded or are placed in a completely darkened room do not report them either. Moreover, on emerging from the dark, sighted people begin to experience the distortions, synesthesia, and hallucinations.

Marijuana has similar, but much milder, effects than members of the LSD group. Subjects may experience synesthesia and distortions, but hallucinations are rare. Like LSD users, marijuana users often report greater visual experiences and improved acuity. However, these reports have also been made when objective tests have shown no change or even a worsening of visual acuity. For example, Caldwell (1969) tested the ability of experienced marijuana users to match the brightness of a variable light with that of a second, standard light. Marijuana ingestion produced a decrease in the subjects' ability to do this task, but they reported that their performance had improved.

Hearing   An auditory task has been developed which is an analogue of the visual critical flicker fusion. Stimulants such as amphetamine facilitate performance on the task (that is, the frequency at which fusion occurs is higher), while sedatives such as alcohol diminish performance. However, interpretation of such data is not easy. For example, while amphetamine facilitates performance on the fusion task, the threshold for detection of sounds is increased. As in studies of vision, the flicker fusion test is not a measure of general acuity.

In contrast to their effects on vision, hallucinogens such as LSD have relatively little effect on hearing. Auditory hallucinations are rare, but interestingly, are more likely to occur in blind people who use these drugs. At one time it was thought that the effects of LSD may mimic the symptoms of schizophrenia. Any argument against this proposition can find basis in the predominance of visual hallucinations incurred with LSD and the auditory hallucinations exhibited in schizophrenia.

Greater appreciation of auditory stimuli is often reported by marijuana users. In particular, music appreciation is said to be greatly enhanced. People also report that they have improved auditory perceptual abilities under the influence of the drug, but again, this is more apparent than real. Marijuana produces little or no change in objective tests.

Taste and smell   The two chemical senses, taste and smell, are closely connected. Indeed, much of what we interpret as taste is actually the effects of volatile components of our food and drink reaching the nose. The effects of drugs on the two senses are similar.

There is evidence that alcohol decreases taste sensitivity. The component of taste that appears to be most affected is bitter (Hellekant, 1967). Other components (salt, sweet, sour) may also be affected, but to a lesser degree. Decreases in sensitivity to odors have also been observed. However, there have also been reports of increased sensitivity, and the difference is yet to be resolved.

When it was first noted that amphetamine and related stimulants reduced food intake, one suggestion was that they made food less appealing by inhibiting taste and smell. Subsequent investigation has shown this not to be the case. There is no evidence of diminished acuity — if anything, acuity may be enhanced by these drugs. Some enhancement has also been found with caffeine.

While cocaine has similar actions to amphetamine, its effects on taste and smell are quite different. This appears to be due to its local anesthetic properties. Like all local anesthetics, it depresses taste, bitter taste being most affected. When applied via the nose, cocaine also has a direct effect on olfactory acuity. The decrease is usually short-lasting, but repeated use can lead to permanently diminished sensitivity. This comes about through destruction of the mucous membranes.

Because of the variety of compounds in tobacco smoke it is difficult to evaluate the effects of nicotine on taste and smell. There is some evidence that smokers are less sensitive to certain components of taste. Also of interest is the fact that smokers have, on the average, slightly different eating habits. They seem to eat fewer sweet foods than nonsmokers. In contrast, craving for sweet foods is often a characteristic of withdrawal following cessation of smoking.

Users of hallucinogens and marijuana often report a greater richness of taste and smell. Familiar tastes and smells appear different, their sensory qualities enhanced by the drug. Unfortunately, there is little evidence to determine whether acuity is actually changed or whether it is simply a change in the appreciation of the stimuli.

Changes in Mood and Feelings

Two main questions have been asked concerning changes in mood and feelings induced by drugs. One is whether there is a common subjective effect produced by all drugs that have strong reinforcing properties. (This is obviously related to the notion discussed in Chapter Two, that these drugs activate specific reward circuits in the brain.) The second is whether different types of drugs can be distinguished on the basis of their mood-altering effects. Tentatively, the answer to both questions is "yes."

Early interest in measurement of the subjective effects of drugs stemmed from the need to identify which of the pharmaceutical products being tested prior to release had a high potential for abuse. In the United States it was thought that detection of such drugs before they were released commercially would reduce at least some drug problems (see for example, Eddy and May, 1973).

Extensive testing was carried out with simple yes/no questions concerning feelings, moods, and perceived bodily changes in order to find out which changes were produced by the various types of drugs. A question might be concerned with whether the subjects feel light-headed, whether they have a metallic taste in their mouth, whether they find it hard to move around, or even whether they have a sentimental feeling. By testing hundreds of such questions in subjects affected by a variety of drugs, and in the nondrugged state, it was found that a number of different types of subjective drug effects could be distinguished.

The result of this work was the Addiction Research Center Inventory (ARCI) described in a series of papers published in the 1960s (Haertzen, Hill, and Belleville, 1963; Haertzen, 1965; Haertzen, 1966). It consists of five hundred and fifty questions of the type described above. An individual under the influence of a drug is likely to answer questions such as these in a characteristic way. The pattern of such answers differs across the various drug types. Thus, if a drug of unknown effects is given, then ARCI results can be used to categorize the drug on the basis of its subjective effects. Results have shown that the classification of drugs according to their responses on the inventory is much the same as one would expect on the basis of their pharmacological activity. The pattern of subjective effects across different drug classes then, matches the patterns of other types of effects.

One scale of the ARCI is sometimes referred to as the euphoria scale. It has questions relating to feelings of satisfaction, absence of worry, feelings of popularity, and general well-being. Drugs which score high on this scale are those that produce the pleasant subjective effects we might expect from a powerful reinforcer. A variety of drugs have been found to modify scores in this manner, including opiates, barbiturates, and stimulants. Drugs that score low include certain opiate mixed agonist-antagonists, pure opiate antagonists, appetite suppressant drugs which are not amphetamine-like, and anti-psychotics.

Clearly, the results from the euphoria scale of the ARCI show a good correlation to the reinforcing effects of the various drugs tested. Those drugs which are reinforcing in laboratory studies and are extensively used and abused are euphoria-producing. In contrast, a number of drugs which are not reinforcers and are not taken voluntarily outside of a medical context fail to produce euphoria.

There are several pieces of evidence which suggest that reinforcing and euphoria-producing properties are not identical. The first comes from use of the ARCI. It has been found that the pattern of subjective effects is different in long-term opiate users compared to those whose use has begun more recently (Haertzen and Hooks, 1969). It seems that the ability of opiates to induce euphoria declines with repeated use, and in the long-term addict the opiates may even induce dysphoria. Despite this, the person will continue to take the drug. These results suggest that there are reasons for drug use other than a desire for euphoria.

The other evidence comes from a series of experiments by Johanson and Uhlenhuth (1980a, 1980b, 1981). These scientists studied the results from a second test used to evaluate the subjective effects of drugs, or the *Profile of Mood States* (POMS). The POMS test consists of seventy-two adjectives commonly used to describe moods and feelings. Following drug or placebo administration subjects are asked to indicate on a scale from zero to four whether that adjective accurately describes how they feel. From these answers, levels can be derived of anxiety, depression, anger, vigor, fatigue, friendliness, elation, arousal, and positive mood.

The data show that compared to a placebo, diazepam increased fatigue and confusion, but decreased vigor and arousal. Amphetamine had quite different effects, increasing vigor, arousal, elation, friendliness, and positive mood and decreasing confusion. (More recent studies have used the POMS with other drugs. See for example, Chait, Uhlenhuth, and Johanson, 1987; Chait et al., 1988; Griffiths and Woodson, 1988.)

In a later part of these studies, subjects were given a choice between taking either a drug or a placebo. The drugs were not labelled so that subjects had to choose solely on the basis of experience with each. Their choices were consistent with the reported subjective effects: Relatively few subjects showed a preference for diazepam over placebo, and most subjects preferred amphetamine to placebo. However, the POMS scores of those subjects who did not choose amphetamine were no different from those who did. Willingness of individuals to self-administer amphetamine could not be predicted from its effects on mood.

In another study briefly discussed earlier, POMS scores were measured over a period of time and the people were given the opportunity to self-administer amphetamine. While self-administration declined with time, POMS scores did not indicate any change in the subjective effects of the drug. Other factors obviously contributed to the change in self-administration.

Together with results from studies using the ARCI, these findings show that while a drug that has positive subjective effects is likely to function as a reinforcer, the two cannot be regarded as identical. A drug may still function as a reinforcer in the absence of positive subjective effects (at least in those dependent on it) and a drug with positive subjective effects may not necessarily function as a reinforcer.

Drug States

Drugs are sometimes said to induce different subjective states in the individual who takes them—not simply a change in mood or feelings, but qualitatively different experiences. The anecdotal reports of users suggest that such a change of state may be an important reason for their use of the drug. People say that they want to "escape from reality" or "forget their troubles." Changing one's state by using a drug is one means of effecting this escape.

Research has shown that the ability to recall learned material is diminished by being in a different state from that in which learning has taken place (Overton, 1982). For example, Rickles, Cohen, Whitaker, and McIntyre (1973) asked subjects to learn a set of nonsense syllable-word pairs. In later recall tests they were given the nonsense syllable and asked for the word. There were four groups of subjects: One group smoked marijuana prior to learning and prior to recall, one group smoked it prior to learning only, and one group prior to recall only. A final group did not have marijuana prior to learning or recall. The results showed that recall was superior in two groups: the group that had marijuana in both situations and the group that had no drug in both situations. The groups who experienced a different state in recall had greater trouble with recall. Thus, whether the information was learned in the drug or nondrug state, it was harder to recall when in the opposite state. This phenomenon is known as *state-dependent learning*. It has been observed in studies with humans and animals, and with a range of drugs and different learning tasks.

A phenomenon related to state-dependent learning is drug discrimination (Overton, 1984). In a number of studies animals and humans have been taught to report whether or not they are in a specified drug state. For example, they may be given a fixed dose of amphetamine or placebo. After time is allowed for a drug to be absorbed and distributed, they report whether the effects are amphetamine-like or not. Most research of this type has been done with animals. A wider range of drugs has been used on animals than has been used on humans, and the animals also have had no prior drug experience which can bias their results. This makes them better test subjects.

One of the interesting aspects of drug discrimination is that those drugs that are self-administered by humans also produce readily discriminable effects or states. Representative drugs from all the major classes described above have been shown to have clear discriminative effects. In contrast, a number of drugs that are not self-administered have no or very weak discriminative effects. These include aspirin and other drugs which produce a negligible effect on the brain, as well as pure opiate antagonists, antidepressants, lithium, and antipsychotics. However, it should also be noted that there are some drugs that have clear discriminative effects, but are not self-administered. They include certain opiate mixed agonist-antagonists and several convulsants (for example, *pentylenetetrazol*). These results suggest that having clear discriminative effects is a necessary condition for self-administration, but is not a sufficient one. Some drugs induce a strong subjective state, but one that is unpleasant.

Research on the opiate group of drugs in particular has shown strong parallels between the subjective effects of drugs as measured by the ARCI and their discriminative effects in animals (Holtzman, Shannon, and Schaeffer, 1977). This suggests that the discriminative effects or drug states are reflecting the same type of drug activity as the subjective effects. It is also interesting to note that the discriminative effects resemble other physiological and behavioral effects in many important respects. There is the same increase in the magnitude of effect with each dose, similarity of effect within each drug class, change in effect over the time-course, and tolerance development (see for example, Shannon and Holtzman, 1976, 1977). These findings show that subjective drug states are not different in principle from other drug effects. With appropriate measurement techniques they can be shown to change in a manner similar to any other effect, behavioral or physiological.

An important role for drug states in the maintenance of drug use has already been mentioned. They provide a means of 'escaping' from or forgetting the normal environment. The person whose life is troubled can get away from those troubles under the influence of a drug. In such cases the type of drug really doesn't matter too much — all that is required is that a strong state be induced. While a person motivated in this way may have a preferred drug, he may also experience the same relief if any of a large range of other drugs were used.

There is also a second implication that can be drawn from this work. It is that people may develop distinct patterns of behavior under the influence of a drug. An individual might behave one way in the normal state and another way in the drug state. In such a situation we might say that the individual undergoes a 'personality change' when under the influence of the drug. The drug discrimination research suggests that such different behavior patterns may develop when the consequences of behavior are different for a person under the influence of a drug. For example, people may be more tolerant and less punishing of aberrant behavior when an individual is intoxicated. The result may be that the individual begins to develop a mode of behavior which only appears in the drug state. In cases such as these, the change that comes over a person when he takes a drug may not be due solely to the direct effects of the drug, but because it allows a degree of dissociation from normality.

BEHAVIORAL EFFECTS OF DRUGS

An earlier section was concerned with one way in which drugs affect our behavior: They provide the motivation for the procurement and administration of the drug. However, drugs affect behavior in a more general manner. A person who is drunk is clearly behaving quite differently from normal. Just about any aspect of his or her behavior can be observed to have changed as a result of taking the drug. Such changes may not be quite so apparent if the person had consumed only three or four drinks, for instance. In this case, the person would appear to walk and talk normally, and most observers would not be able to detect any drug effects. Nevertheless, even at this dose clear behavioral effects could be found if more sophisticated means of measuring behavior were used.

There are several reasons for wanting to investigate the behavioral effects of drugs. One is that behavioral effects may be part of the reason for use of a drug. That is, the behavioral effects may contribute to the reinforcing effects. For example, people often find social interaction difficult in contrived situations such as parties. However, this difficulty appears to diminish when alcohol is taken. Similarly, concentration on boring or repetitive work is often difficult, but may be improved by taking a cup of coffee or a more powerful stimulant.

In both examples the behavioral effects of the drug have beneficial consequences for the individual. One could well imagine a type of drug which does not have the subjective effects of alcohol, but only the ability to increase social interaction in certain settings. Such a drug may well be used even though it had no clear subjective effects. Similarly, coffee would still have some value if it did nothing but improve our ability to work when we are bored or suffering fatigue.

Thus, the behavioral effects of drugs contribute to their reinforcing effects in an indirect manner. They change our behavior in such a way that it brings some benefit (social interaction, the ability to finish work quicker, etc.) to the user. This benefit may then be important in maintaining future drug-taking.

A second reason for examining the behavioral effects of drugs is to try and understand the behavior of the drug user. Much is said about users of illegal drugs in particular. They may be described as being sex-crazed, violent, unmotivated, etc. Looking through history one can find many examples of such descriptions for just about any drug. Of course, as the drug becomes more accepted in a society, such descriptions are abandoned or applied to only the heaviest users.

Unfortunately, the situation is not as simple as these labels might suggest. Drug administration affects a very wide range of behavior and not just specific categories. Indeed, one could argue that all behavior is affected in some way by a drug, given that a reasonable dose is used. In addition, a wide range of factors will determine the direction and magnitude of the behavioral change. These will be discussed below. At this stage it is sufficient to note that while behavior is certainly different under the influence of a drug, being able to predict the change is a difficult problem which has no simple solution.

The third and related reason for studying behavioral changes is that these changes may be part of the toxic or adverse effects of the drug. If behavior is altered in such a way that normal life is disrupted or there is some danger to the individual, then the drug is having clear adverse behavioral effects. These toxic effects of drugs will be discussed in more detail in Chapter Five. However, in order to consider that issue it is necessary to understand something about the more general behavioral changes that drugs can induce.

Behavior Analysis

There are a number of possible approaches to the study of behavior, and unfortunately, no single approach is agreed upon by all those whose business is to do exactly that. The approach to be adopted here is sometimes known as *behavior analysis* (for example, Ferster and Culbertson, 1982). It has been particularly influential in trying to understand how drugs affect behavior (Pickens, 1977).

One of the advantages of behavior analysis is that the methods and techniques can be used with both humans and animals. This is important because many experiments on drug effects require the use of animals. This is the case particularly in studying toxic effects and the induction of dependence. Although human behavior is clearly more complex, it is still possible, with appropriate caution, to extrapolate the results from animal studies, to provide some insight into the behavioral effects of drugs in humans.

Similar techniques are used across a wide range of behavior analytic research. Rather than administer a drug and simply observe the change in the whole range of behavior the human or animal engages in, the focus is narrowed somewhat in this research. A particular behavior is chosen and the changes in that behavior observed under different conditions following drug administration. The behavior itself is simple, so as to ensure that there is minimal disruption due to any impaired ability to perform the behavior. The generality would be limited for example, if we used a behavior that required great physical or intellectual achievement for its execution.

Behavioral research has sometimes been criticized because the experimental arrangement is too "artificial." Critics might say for example that little of what we do is as simple as button pressing. However, this process of simplification and abstraction of the essential, important elements is common to all areas of science. It is only once the simple process is understood that one attempts to explain the complexities of the real world. Most of the research described below has been done with animals in relatively simple situations. However, the work done to date with humans suggests that the results will generalize to the types of situations that are of most interest.

Most of the human behavior we wish to understand is what is sometimes termed voluntary behavior—that is, it is not automatic or reflexive. The principal characteristic of such behavior is that it becomes more or less likely because of its consequences. With certain consequences (usually those we would term pleasant or beneficial) the behavior that produced them becomes more likely. Such consequences are termed reinforcers. One class of reinforcer, drugs, has already been considered. With other consequences (usually those we would term unpleasant or deleterious) the behavior that produces them becomes less likely. These are termed *punishers*. Such consequences may also induce attempts to escape or avoid punishers.

Behavior may also be more likely to occur under certain circumstances. This phenomenon is known as *stimulus control*. Such differential probability arises because the consequences vary, depending on the circumstances. For example, a ribald joke that gets a great laugh from one's friends may not get the same reception from one's grandmother. An important part of our normal functioning is learning to adapt to the different consequences in the various situations we move through.

A third factor of importance in determining our behavior is the way in which the consequence follows behavior. Some reinforcers follow virtually every instance of the behavior. For example, putting money in a coin-operated machine is reinforced by the goods you wish to purchase. In other cases, relatively large amounts of behavior are required for reinforcement. For example, payment for work is given from time to time, either on the basis of units of work done, or more commonly, for having spent a certain amount of time at a job. The term *schedule* is used to denote the way in which consequences follow behavior.

This is a very basic framework for understanding research on the behavioral effects of drugs. Using it, the various factors determining how a drug affects behavior will be discussed. The emphasis here will be on general principles that can be used no matter what type of behavior is under consideration. Following this, we will examine specific types of behavior that are of particular interest: aggressive behavior, sexual behavior, and sleeping and eating behaviors. The general behavioral effects of each major drug type have been described briefly in Chapter One.

Determinants of the Behavioral Effects of Drugs

Types of consequences Early attempts to understand the effects of drugs on behavior focused on emotional states which were said to be induced by important events in the individual's life. Pleasant events were said to induce one type of emotional state which led to behavior aimed at seeking that event out again. Unpleasant events induced fear or anxiety which suppressed the behavior that produced it, and increased attempts to escape or avoid the event.

These are similar to the descriptions of reinforcement and punishment above, but include the hypothesized emotional states. The latter are critically important as the drugs were said to directly affect the emotional state and only indirectly affect behavior through this change. All one had to know was how a drug changed the various emotional states. It would then be possible to take any behavior, decide on the motivation for that behavior, and then predict how it would change with drug administration.

While this is a conveniently simple analysis and is intuitively appealing, it has little basis in fact. A number of experiments have shown that drugs very frequently have similar effects whether the behavior is reinforced (for example, in the case of food) or is motivated by avoidance of a punisher. As long as the schedule and pattern of responding are the same, we can find quite similar changes in behavior as a result of drug administration. On the other hand, slight differences in the way a reinforcer is scheduled can have quite marked changes on the effects of a drug on that behavior (see discussion of the role of schedules, below).

These types of results refute a simple motivational hypothesis of drug effects. However, it is not true that the type of consequence maintaining behavior is of no importance. There is evidence showing that the effects of at least some drugs are dependent on the consequence (Barrett and Katz, 1981). For example, as one would expect from an anorectic drug, amphetamine decreases behavior maintained by food reinforcement. The same dose of amphetamine may have no effect or even increase behavior maintained by other reinforcers (Poschel, 1963).

In a slightly more complex situation, two sets of consequences may be arranged so that behavior is maintained by reinforcement but suppressed to a relatively low level by punishment. Much of our behavior is controlled in this way through the normal social environment. There may be advantages in breaking social rules (for example, obtaining material goods more quickly than by working for the money) but such behavior has also been suppressed (perhaps by the strictures of parents and others).

When examining the effects of drugs on punished behavior, a remarkably consistent pattern emerges. Those drugs usually classed as sedative-hypnotic or antianxiety compounds (alcohol, barbiturates, benzodiazepines, etc.) increase behavior previously suppressed by punishment. At doses which have little effect on ordinary reinforced behavior, suppressed behavior becomes more probable (Seppinwall and Cook, 1978).

Other drugs do not have this effect. Even morphine, which reduces the ability of aversive events to induce escape or avoidance behavior, does not. This rules out any motivational interpretation such as making the punishing stimulus less effective.

It may be that this specific antipunishment effect underlies the clinical usefulness of these drugs in the treatment of anxiety. People suffering from this problem may be overly sensitive to consequences which tend to suppress behavior (or may be in an environment where there are a lot of such consequences). Accordingly, they may benefit from a drug which reduces the suppressive and other effects of aversive events in their environment.

This may also explain certain behavior observed under the influence of alcohol and, occasionally, observed under the influence of other sedative-hypnotics. People sometimes behave in a bizarre or uninhibited manner following use of such drugs. It is possible that previously suppressed behavior simply reappears as a result of the drug. Sometimes, this may be useful. The Latin phrase *'in vino veritas'* (literally, 'the truth in wine') expresses the notion that it is only once this normal suppression has been removed by alcohol that one can truly believe what a person says.

The schedule   As mentioned, reinforcers may be arranged in very different ways. Each reinforcer may follow a given amount of behavior, or a given time period in which the behavior has occurred. Reinforcement may follow only if the behavior occurs sufficiently infrequently. Reinforcement may also be available only at certain times; behavior at other times may have no consequences. Not only can schedules differ in kind, but the schedule value can also vary. For example, if reinforcement follows a fixed amount of behavior, that amount may vary from very small to very great. In one case the schedule is a fairly generous one, in the other quite lean.

The effects of drugs have been found to be very dependent on the schedule maintaining the behavior (Kelleher and Morse, 1968; McKearney and Barrett, 1978). A particular behavior may become more likely as a result of drug administration if it is maintained by reinforcement on one type of schedule, but less likely if the reinforcer is scheduled differently. For example, in an early experiment on the effects of pentobarbital it was shown that a behavior will increase in rate if reinforcement comes occasionally on the basis of time, but decrease if it is dependent on the frequency of the behavior (Dews, 1955). This seems to contradict our usual notions of how drugs act, and introduces a complicating factor. Making it even more difficult is the fact that in real life schedules are hard to define precisely—they are not always as regular as is found in the laboratory.

In addition to the type of schedule, the schedule value is an important determinant. For example, consider the effects of amphetamine on behavior maintained by a schedule which specifies that a fixed number of instances of the behavior is required for reinforcement. If that number is low (that is, only a little work is required for reinforcement) the effect of amphetamine is likely to be a decrease in the frequency of the behavior. On the other hand, if the number is high (that is, a large amount of work is required for each reinforcement) amphetamine is likely to increase the rate of the behavior (Dews, 1958).

This example raises an interesting point which has emerged from the study of the role of schedules. Even though amphetamine is classed as a stimulant, it does not always have the effect of increasing behavior. Depending on the conditions prior to drug administration, it may make behavior more or less likely to occur. In the case of amphetamine, the observation that it increases the relatively low frequency of behavior produced under conditions where a large amount of behavior is required for reinforcement is consistent with observations that it alleviates fatigue in repetitive tasks.

Research in this area has shown that it is difficult to make generalizations about drug effects without knowing the schedule controlling the behavior. Stimulants increase behavior under some conditions only and sedatives decrease behavior under others. This clearly indicates that our labels are over-simplistic. While this seems to add only greater complexity, in the following section we consider one factor that may help predict what the effects of a drug will be.

Rate of behavior.   Different schedules of reinforcement produce different rates or probabilities of behavior. The rate may be varied by altering the type and value of the schedule. An early suggestion then, was that one determinant of the effects of a drug was the rate of behavior prior to drug administration. That is, it is not so much the different schedules, as the different rates produced by these schedules.

Consider a situation in which an individual works for the same reinforcer in two sets of circumstances. In one, such a large amount of work is required that work rate is relatively slow (the person may be 'unmotivated'). In the other, the reinforcer follows smaller amounts of work and work rate is high (the individual now appears to be 'motivated' for the task). If the person were to be given a drug such as amphetamine then the effect would probably be a dramatic increase in the slow work rate. Moreover, the high work rate would be affected to a much smaller degree. Depending on how large it was, it may be slightly increased, it may not change at all, or there may even be a decrease in the rate of the behavior.

The same type of finding can be observed in a single situation. If reinforcement is available only periodically a person may be unlikely to work for it at certain times, but highly likely at others. In this case the effect of amphetamine may be to increase the probability at times when the behavior is unlikely and increase it to a lesser extent, or decrease it, when it is most likely.

In this and the case above, the effect of the drug depends on the rate or probability of the behavior prior to drug administration. This is known as the rate-dependency principle (Robbins, 1981).

Several points need to be made about this principle. First, while it is important and can help predict a lot of behavioral changes produced by drugs, it does not explain all factors. For example, if rate-dependency extended to behavior suppressed by punishment, then amphetamine should dramatically increase the low rate punished behavior. In fact, it is likely to do the opposite: increase higher rate unpunished behavior more than punished behavior. The schedule, the type of consequences, and other factors described below all play a part. However, even by itself rate-dependency is a principle with great predictive value.

A second point is that rate-dependency seems to be general across a wide range of drugs. We have discussed amphetamine because it has been the drug for which most evidence has been collected (see Dews and Wenger, 1977), but rate-dependency has also been found with hallucinogens, opiates, sedative-hypnotics, and other drugs. Indeed, some have argued that rate-dependency reflects nothing more than a general property of drugs to disrupt behavior (McKim, 1981). While the different rates or probabilities of behavior reflect our adaptation to the prevailing circumstances, the effect of the drug is to diminish this differentiation. We are simply less responsive to the circumstances. Whether this interpretation is a valid one or not remains to be seen.

One final note is that rate-dependency has been suggested as a basis for the therapeutic use of amphetamine-like drugs for the treatment of hyperactivity. It is often said that the calming effect of stimulants on hyperactive children is a 'paradoxical' one. A better understanding of the behavioral effects of amphetamines reveals that reduction of high-rate behavior is a characteristic of these drugs (see Robbins and Sahakian, 1979, for a more detailed discussion of this issue).

Stimulus control of behavior.   As mentioned earlier, we learn to respond to aspects of our environment which tell us of changed conditions. For example, we learn to act in a manner appropriate to the company we are in. Acting the same way irrespective of the company would not be very adaptive.

The degree to which our behavior is determined by various aspects of our environment varies considerably. An extreme case may be operation of a machine in which the behavior of the operator is closely linked to gauges, lights, and other signals. Similarly, the behavior of a realist painter is tied to the subject matter. In contrast, the behavior of some free-form artists is not tied to any particular aspect of the environment.

This factor — the degree to which our behavior is controlled by aspects of our environment — is an important determinant of the effects of drugs. In particular, behavior that is under strict control is less affected by drugs than behavior that is not so tightly controlled.

One might predict then, that the drug-influenced product of a realist painter would be little different from normal, but that the abstract painter's work may be greatly influenced by the drug. Unfortunately, there are no data available to support such a prediction. However, informal evidence leads one to believe that artists of many kinds whose work involves free form or free association sometimes use drugs to enhance or in some way modify this work. One may find a jazz pianist using a drug in this way, for example, but a classical pianist who responds more to printed information or at least his or her recall of that information may be much less likely to do so.

In more mundane situations it has been found that the effects of drugs on behavior can be much smaller, even minimal, when the behavior is tied to events in the environment. The same behavior reinforced according to the same schedule may be markedly disrupted if the individual does not respond directly to information in the environment (Laties, 1975).

Consider the example described earlier of behavior that varies over time due to the fact that reinforcement is periodic. If the individual is provided with a clock then this behavior changes somewhat. The person can now tell when the reinforcement is available and adjust his or her behavior accordingly. If we gave amphetamine under these circumstances we would not observe the same sized increases in low rates of behavior that were observed without the clock. The behavior is under the control of the clock and is less disrupted by the drug.

Learning and performance. Conditions in our lives change frequently. As they do so, our behavior adapts until the conditions are once again constant. The process of adaptation during such periods of change is sometimes referred to as learning. The term performance, on the other hand, may be used to denote the stable patterns of behavior that result from relatively constant conditions. Learning may occur when we develop new forms of behavior. This is perhaps the most common and familiar use of the term. It may also refer to the changes that occur when the conditions for an 'old' behavior change.

Some research has been concerned with the effects of drugs on learning. The question is whether there is any difference in the effects of a drug on behavior in changing conditions compared to behavior in steady-state. Across a wide range of situations and with all drugs studied, it seems that learning is disrupted to a greater extent than performance (Thompson and Moerschbaecher, 1979). For example, in complex tasks requiring considerable skill, drugs will generally increase errors. If the task is one already learned the increase may be relatively small. However, if the task is a new one (or a new variant of an old task) the error will be increased to a greater degree.

Interestingly, the degree of disruption can be reduced if the transition is made as error-free as possible. Procedures designed to teach which have the capability of engendering only a minimum number of errors can be used to ensure a smooth, gradual learning period. If these procedures are employed, the drug-induced increase in errors can be much smaller.

These results suggest that the behavior of a person in a relatively constant, unchanging environment will be much less affected by drug use than an individual in an environment constantly in a state of flux. There will be much less disruption to the normal patterns of behavior in the former case than in the latter. Accordingly, the first individual may be able to maintain a relatively normal lifestyle while using drugs, whereas the latter may find the disruptive effects of drugs much more severe.

One group whose behavior is constantly in a state of change is children. Maturation results in changes in their capacities and is affected by the way they are treated by those around them. One might speculate that it is this group whose behavior may be most disrupted by drug use. While there are obviously many factors involved, this suggests that the behavioral effects of drugs may be very prominent in children and adolescents.

These results also suggest that drugs should be used with caution when inexperienced people engage in skilled behavior. One group likely to still be at the learning stage are younger car drivers. The complex nature of this behavior results in a very long period of learning. Driving behavior during this time may be more influenced by alcohol and other drugs than the driving of the experienced person. This does not, however, suggest that a so-called 'experienced' person is not at risk.

Behavioral history.   In a later section we will discuss how one's prior experience or personality influences drug use. Here we wish to note simply that the behavioral effects of drugs are determined, in part, by the individual's behavioral history.

There are two ways in which this can occur. One is that prior experience can influence the way we behave in a given situation. And, since the pattern of behavior in the absence of the drug is an important determinant of the effect of the drug, prior experience will be a factor in determining the drug effect. For example, an individual may have a characteristically rapid, or perhaps easy-going pace of working. In beginning a new job the person may continue this same pattern unless there are demands to work faster or slower. Use of a drug in the work situation (for example, caffeine) may lead to a slowing of pace in the person who works rapidly and a quickening of pace in one who works slowly. The drug effect then, is strongly influenced by the person's prior history in work situations.

Past experience may influence drug effects more directly. This has been illustrated experimentally with several different drugs and different behavioral situations (Barrett and Witkin, 1986). For example, in normal circumstances amphetamine does not increase punished behavior in the manner that sedative-hypnotics do. However, in an animal with prior experience of avoiding that same event which suppresses behavior, amphetamine has been shown to increase the rate of the punished response (Barrett, 1977).

The mechanism for this type of change is not clear. For one thing, the experience with avoidance influences the physical form of the behavior suppressed by punishment. Since the same behavior was required in both situations this could be an important factor. A more likely explanation lies in neurochemical changes resulting from the experience of avoidance. Any behavioral experience induces chemical changes in the brain. Since the actions of drugs are determined by their interaction with brain chemistry, there is a clear possibility for influence by past experience.

A second example also concerns amphetamine. If an individual is in a situation where there is no reinforcement, the effect of amphetamine can often engender distinctive behavior patterns. These are patterns which were previously reinforced in the same situation, but are no longer (Weissman, 1959). Clearly, in such situations the behavior patterns which emerge under the influence of amphetamine will be determined by past experience.

Relatively little research has been done on the role of behavioral history in determining the effects of drugs. However, there is already considerable evidence that it is a very important factor. There are several ways in which it can act, but the underlying mechanisms are still to be elucidated. What is important is that in the very same circumstances a drug may have quite different effects on two individuals, simply because of their respective histories. History may also play a role through prior drug-behavior interactions. This will be discussed separately under "Behavioral Tolerance," below.

Behavioral context.   Other events occurring at the same time in an individual's life are going to influence the effects of drugs on her behavior. Again, this may occur through indirect means, simply because concurrent events will influence behavior, and this is in turn will modify the effects of any drugs used. An example of this is the way in which the rate or probability of behavior is influenced by alternative sources of reinforcement (Catania, 1976). If an individual has many sources of a given type of reinforcement she may not work hard to obtain it from any one source. However, if she were to lose some of these sources of reinforcement, then the rate of work for the remaining sources is likely to increase. It may be a person with a large quantity of money who would put little effort into obtaining a given amount, but would put much more effort in if her other sources were smaller. Clearly then, concurrent conditions influence the rate of behavior, and since the effect of a drug is determined in part by the rate prior to drug use, concurrent conditions are able to influence the behavioral effect of the drug.

The second manner is more direct. Just as prior experience with avoidance can influence the effect of amphetamine on punished behavior, concurrent avoidance experience can have the same effect (McKearney and Barrett, 1975). The mechanism is likely to be the same in both cases.

Thus, another way in which individual variability in the behavioral effects of drugs comes about is through different current circumstances. These circumstances can influence the type and magnitude of behavioral effec

Conclusions.   The discussion in this section has focused on the various factors which will determine in what way a drug influences any one type of behavior. These factors include the reinforcement which maintains the behavior, whether it is a stable pattern of behavior or one just learned, the prior history of that behavior and so forth. In some cases research has enabled clear predictions to be made (for example, stable behavior will be less affected than behavior being learned or in a state of change), while in other cases only general statements emerge (for instance, the effects of the drug depend on the history of that behavior). This situation can be shown to be compounded when we consider that a person has a wide range of behavior patterns in her repertoire, not simply one. Hopefully, future research will allow more precise predictions about the role of the various determinants in modifying the behavioral effects of drugs.

Behavioral Tolerance

The phenomenon of tolerance was discussed in Chapter Two. Tolerance refers to the decreased effect of a drug with repeated administration. Two main mechanisms were considered in that chapter. One was a decrease in concentration of drug which reaches the brain, and the other decreased responsiveness of the neural tissue to the drug.

However, when we come to look specifically at the development of tolerance to the behavioral effects of a drug, these factors (and a further one which will be described in the next section) do not seem to be sufficient to account for the degree of tolerance which develops. There seems to be an extra factor that contributes to tolerance over and above that contributed by the other mechanisms.

This phenomenon can be illustrated by experimental evidence. Consider a situation in which an animal is required to engage in certain behavior in order to obtain reinforcement. The schedule is such that a decrease in the amount of work will lead to decreased reinforcement. Once a stable pattern of behavior has developed, a drug is administered prior to each occasion on which the animal is exposed to the schedule. The drug acts to diminish the rate of the behavior. However, if the drug is administered on a number of different occasions, this disruption becomes smaller and smaller. Eventually, the pattern of behavior under the influence of the drug is almost the same as it was before the drug was administered. Tolerance has developed.

Suppose that at the same time we had other animals who received the drug after each occasion on which they were exposed to the schedule. The dose, number of injections, etc., are the same, but this group does not get the opportunity to engage in the behavior under the influence of the drug. The result is that tolerance development is much slower in this group than in the first. Even though changes in drug concentration and neural response should be the same in both groups, the results from experiments of this kind show marked variation in the rate of tolerance development (Corfield-Sumner and Stolerman, 1978).

One point to note is that this behavioral tolerance is relatively specific. Dispositional and pharmacodynamic factors should influence all effects of a drug equally. Whether it is one type of behavior or another, heart rates or some other physiological change, all should be influenced in the same way. (Although, as noted above, this is not completely true — tolerance develops at different rates to different effects.) With behavioral tolerance this is not the case. If heart rate had been measured, for example, the development of tolerance would have proceeded at the same pace in the two groups. Likewise, behavior other than that engaged in while under the influence of the drug would have changed in a similar manner in the two groups.

Research in this area suggests that the critical factor for the development of behavioral tolerance may be the opportunity to practice or engage in the behavior under the influence of the drug. However, while this is necessary, it is not sufficient for behavioral tolerance to occur. The critical variable appears to be the change in consequences that comes about because of the behavioral effect of the drug. If the drug causes a net loss of reinforcement, then behavioral tolerance will develop very rapidly; if not, there will be little or no behavioral tolerance (Schuster, 1978). In the latter case, normal dispositional and pharmacodynamic factors will account for tolerance development.

Consider a situation in which two conditions prevail. In one, a slow, carefully timed pattern of behavior is required for reinforcement; in the other, reinforcement comes occasionally as long as the behavior occurs at some minimal rate. After a period of adaptation to the situation, the appropriate behavior patterns develop in each condition. If a drug is then administered that increases the rate of behavior in both conditions, we would expect a net loss of reinforcement in the first condition, but little change in the second. With repeated administration we would find rapid tolerance development in the first situation but much slower development in the second. The important factor seems to be the change in rate of reinforcement that results from drug administration.

Behavioral tolerance has been found in a wide range of experimental situations (see Krasnegor, 1978b). Experiments have involved different species (including humans) and different types of behavior. Both learning and performance change in a similar manner. One factor that has received some attention is the type of reinforcer. While most experiments have used positive reinforcers such as food or money, in others the reinforcer has been the opportunity to avoid something aversive. In this case tolerance occurs more rapidly if the effect of the drug is to increase the rate of the aversive event. The critical variable then is that the effect of the drug is to make things worse, rather than make any increase or decrease in the consequence. In the case of positive reinforcement it is a decrease in rate, while for avoidance it is an increase which leads to more rapid tolerance development.

Finally, there is evidence from research with humans that sensitization (reverse tolerance) as well as tolerance may be observed in the appropriate circumstances (Rumbold and White, 1987). If the effect of the drug is to increase reinforcement rate, then the drug-induced behavior change which caused this may be larger on subsequent administrations. For example, suppose that in a certain situation reinforcement rate is proportional to work rate. If the effect of a drug is to increase work rate then reinforcement rate should increase, too. What we will find is that on subsequent occasions on which the drug is administered the drug effect can be even greater than on the first occasion. Up to some limit the drug effect will increase with each administration.

These findings may explain some reports of increases in drug effect with repeated use. Such reports are common in the case of marijuana, despite laboratory findings of tolerance to the effects of the drug. While factors such as improved smoking technique may account for some of these reports, behavioral sensitization may also have a role. If the effects of the drug are beneficial (for example, in producing more social reinforcement) then they may increase on subsequent use. At present this can only be speculative.

Drug Effects on Specific Types of Behavior

Up until now we have been discussing the various factors which determine the effect of a drug on any one behavior. That behavior may be a social one, may be concerned with leisure activity, or may be a part of the repertoire at work. The principles that govern them are much the same.

Another way of analyzing the behavioral effects of drugs has been to determine the changes that occur in specific types of behavior following drug administration. In particular, what are the changes in behaviors such as aggression, sexual behavior, sleeping, or eating? Such changes are of interest to us all, and considerable research has gone into investigating them. While we have some answers, they are far from complete.

One problem with this type of research is that the various factors already discussed are going to influence the type of behavior change induced by a drug. Blanket statements of the form 'drug x affects behavior y in such-and-such a manner' are almost impossible to make. It will depend on the various consequences, prior experience of the individual, etc. Nevertheless, attempts have been made to examine drug effects on these behaviors across a range of conditions, and brief summaries of the major findings will be given below. As before, most of the studies have been done with animals, particularly in areas such as sexual and aggressive behavior.

Eating   In lab experiments, eating is usually measured by depriving an animal of food for a short period of time and then noting how much is eaten when it is given a meal. Spontaneous (nondeprived) eating may be measured by giving quantities of a preferred food. More recently, there has been increased attention paid to changes in meal patterns and in preference for different food types. Such research may be particularly valuable, but is in its very early stages at present.

When we come to look at drug effects it is immediately apparent that there is a vast array of drugs which diminish food intake (Blundell, 1987). This may be looked at in two ways. One is that the neural circuitry underlying food intake and energy balance is very complex, with a number of different neurotransmitter systems involved. Accordingly, it can be disrupted by a variety of drugs (Hoebel, 1977). Until we completely analyze this circuitry, this argument is difficult to justify.

The second explanation is simply that many of these effects are non-specific. That is, while eating may decrease, so may many other behaviors. In an extreme case, a drug which causes sleep will decrease every behavior except that one. For a drug to specifically affect eating it must be shown that it does so at doses which do not markedly affect other behavior. For many drugs that have been shown to alter eating this is not so. When studies are done with humans, the problems are compounded as there is a large placebo effect in experiments on weight loss. People often reduce their food intake even in anticipation of taking a drug which may cause them to lose weight.

The most well-known anorectic (food-intake decreasing) drug is amphetamine. Administration of this drug can produce large decreases in eating, leading to diminished body weight. The effect is more pronounced when higher doses are given. As mentioned in Chapter One, amphetamine used to be prescribed widely for treatment of weight reduction. Abuse problems have curtailed this use.

A second difficulty with use of amphetamine for this purpose is that marked tolerance develops within two to three weeks of commencing treatment. Continued inhibition of food intake requires that the dose be increased markedly. Any increase in the dose used will, of course, magnify problems of abuse.

Other amphetamine-like drugs have similar effects on food intake. Some of these are used commercially for this purpose. All seem to have a lower abuse liability, but may also be less effective anorectics. One drug that has been found to be effective is *fenfluramine*. It has somewhat different actions from amphetamine, with more effect on serotonergic systems in the brain. Interestingly, it has little or no associated problem of abuse and is not self-administered by laboratory animals (Schuster and Johanson, 1986).

Amphetamine and fenfluramine can also be differentiated behaviorally. Amphetamine decreases eating time by increasing the latency to eat, but also increases eating rate. Fenfluramine decreases eating rate, but with little change in eating time. The net result in both cases is reduced food intake.

One group of drugs that has recently been found to reduce food intake are the *opiate antagonists*. Pure antagonists such as *naloxone* and *naltrexone* reduce food intake considerably. This appears to result from their blockade of opiate receptors in the brain. Consistent with this is the finding that opiate agonists may increase food intake. In the case of drugs such as morphine and heroin, such effects may be masked by a general sedating action.

Benzodiazepines have also been shown to increase food intake. However, long-term use does not result in significantly increased body weight. This suggests that tolerance develops relatively rapidly, or that there are some compensatory mechanisms which prevent weight increases.

Sleeping   Superficially, sleeping appears to be a relatively simple phenomenon. However, observation of a sleeping individual suggests that there are changes in the behavior of the sleeper over the course of a sleeping bout. At different times a sleeper may move about and become restless, move his or her eyes to a marked degree, and become more easily awakened. The invention of the *electro-encephalograph* (EEG) enabled more detailed evaluation of these changes.

As mentioned in Chapter One, sleep can be divided up into a number of stages or levels on the basis of EEG patterns and the behavior of the sleeper. This can be done in several ways, but a simple characterization is light sleep, deep or slow-wave sleep, and REM (rapid eye movement) sleep. REM sleep is sometimes, but not always, associated with dreaming. Sleep patterns are cyclic over the course of a night so that we experience each of these levels a number of times.

Results from EEG studies have shown that a wide variety of drugs disturb sleep patterns to some degree (Williams and Karacen, 1976; Wheatley, 1981). However, the two groups of drugs with the clearest effects on sleeping are the sedative-hypnotics and the stimulants. These are also the two groups used therapeutically for treatment of sleep disorders.

The effects of the various sedative-hypnotic drugs are very similar. They include decreased deep sleep and REM sleep, and increased light sleep. One result is less eye movement during the sleep period. In addition, the time until sleep begins is reduced, and during sleep, the number of body movements and awakenings is decreased. While these drugs may be prescribed for treatment of insomnia, there are a number of problems with their use. One is that the changes just described may not always be beneficial. If the sleep pattern is disturbed, sleep may seem very unsatisfying. Anyone who has fallen asleep under the influence of alcohol will have experienced this difference. However, with repeated use this problem may diminish and sleep patterns should return to normal. Another problem is the rebound effects which occur when use is discontinued. These can also make a night's sleep very unsatisfying.

Rebound effects that follow termination of sleeping-pill usage may be the genesis of a drug dependence problem. Stopping use of these drugs results in withdrawal effects for several nights, and the only way to escape this situation often appears to be to simply start using them again. A vicious cycle is created from which the individual finds it difficult to escape. The problem will be compounded if a relatively large dose is being used, in that the withdrawal effects are likely to be more severe.

While sleep disorders are most often related to lack of or the delayed onset of sleep, one particular disorder involves an excess of sleep. *Narcolepsy* is characterized by uncontrollable bouts of sleeping that occur throughout the day. Amphetamine is used for treatment of this problem. This drug is also used illegally to delay the onset of sleep. Long-distance truck drivers have exploited this effect for many years. In addition, many people use milder stimulants such as caffeine to delay onset of sleep and alleviate fatigue. Unfortunately, there is no real evidence on which to judge the importance of this particular behavioral effect for the maintenance of stimulant use.

There are many other drugs that affect sleep in a less dramatic manner than these two groups. For example, LSD increases the proportion of time spent in REM sleep; this is reversed in the case of marijuana. Tolerance tends to develop rapidly to most effects of these drugs: Deviations from normal sleep patterns may be relatively small after only a few nights.

Sexual behavior   Changes in sexual behavior as a result of drug administration have been of interest at least as far back as recorded history attests. Many substances have been presumed aphrodisiacs in different cultures over time. However, the evidence suggests that much of this is due simply to placebo effects rather than to any real change in sexual performance. Research in this area has been reviewed by Sandler and Gessa (1975) and Rubin and Henson (1979).

The effects of drugs have been evaluated in two main ways. First, objective measures of sexual arousal and sexual performance after drug administration have been compared to results obtained under control conditions. Most such studies use male subjects because measurement of penile erection is relatively simple to gage. Female sexual arousal may be more difficult to detect as readily. Animals are usually used in studies of sexual performance. Measures are taken of the frequency of erection, and latencies to mounting and ejaculation.

The second approach has been concerned more with the subjective aspects of sexual desire and performance. People are questioned on their experiences with one or more drugs. The problem with this is that myths can be self-perpetuating. An individual may have at some time been told that a certain drug enhances sexual pleasure. As a result they may indeed find a more pleasurable experience, but the same would have happened if they had used a placebo. If one questioned the users of a variety of ineffective aphrodisiacs, there would almost certainly be considerable evidence of enhanced sexual experience. Accordingly, results of this type should be treated with caution.

Most reports from opiate users indicate decreased sexual performance. Amongst males physically dependent on an opiate, there is a high rate of impotence, although not all are affected to the same degree. These reports have been confirmed in animal studies where a general depression of sexual behavior is observed consistently. In contrast, during opiate withdrawal, ejaculations often occur spontaneously or in response to minimal stimulation.

While opiate agonists have a negative effect on sexual behavior, there is some evidence, mainly from animal studies, of enhanced sexual performance following opiate antagonist administration (for example Gessa, Paglietti, and Pellegrini—Quarantotti, 1979). Whether this is associated with greater sexual pleasure or not is unknown.

Amongst the sedative-hypnotic group, most interest has centered on alcohol. Reference is often made to Shakespeare's famous judgment that it "provoketh the desire, but taketh away the performance." This certainly seems to fit many people's experience. Subjective reports concerning the effects of alcohol emphasize the disinhibitory and antianxiety properties of the drug (which may be the same thing—see above). This decrease in anxiety may be beneficial in cases where sexual performance might otherwise be diminished.

While most people report no change or an increase in sexual pleasure under the influence of alcohol, objective measures of sexual arousal in humans indicate a reduction (see Rubin and Henson, 1976). Penile size and vaginal blood flow are diminished by alcohol administration. In animals, alcohol increases the latency to ejaculation in the male. It is also worth noting that excessive alcohol consumption is a major cause of impotence in human males.

Relatively few reports have been obtained on the effects of other sedative-hypnotics. Most of these show diminished sexual functioning. In animals, diazepam increases the frequency of attempts at copulation but also increases the failure rate.

Amphetamine has been reported to markedly enhance sexual experience. Users indicate that it increases sexual drive and sexual aggression. Confidence in matters sexual, as in other areas, seems to be improved under the influence of amphetamine. Similar reports have also been obtained concerning the effects of cocaine. Indeed, many users indicate that greater sexual pleasure is a principal reason for using stimulants. On the negative side, orgasm may be more difficult to achieve.

These results are consistent with findings from animal studies, which indicate that drugs that enhance the activity of dopamine systems have a positive effect on sexual performance (see for example, Bignami, 1966). Drugs like amphetamine, which have this action, appear to have aphrodisiac properties. However, the effects are critically dependent on dose. The beneficial effects are found only at low doses; higher doses diminish sexual performance. It should also be noted that these drugs do not enhance the desire for sex.

Some enhancement of sexual experience and performance has also been noted with LSD and other similar hallucinogens. Many users report greater sensory awareness under the influence of LSD and in the context of sexual behavior this has a positive effect. Some facilitation of sexual performance in animals has also been reported after the administration of low doses of LSD (Bignami, 1966). Again, high doses can have a negative effect.

Other subjective reports indicate enhancement of sensory awareness during sex when under the influence of marijuana. Users also indicate that the slowing of time produced by the drug increases their pleasure. Some disinhibition has been noted. In contrast, studies of sexual performance in animals have generally shown diminished behavior, although tolerance appears to develop to this change.

Aggression   For obvious ethical and practical reasons it is impossible to study the effects of drugs on aggressive behavior in humans directly. Information is often confined to anecdotal evidence and surveys, although some laboratory studies have been conducted.

Well-controlled research is feasible when animals are used. The various components of aggression such as threat, attack, and escape from the encounter can all be analyzed separately. The most common type of aggressive behavior studied involves the fighting between male mice which occurs in the process of establishing dominance. Aggression also occurs in response to painful stimulation. This animal research has been extensively reviewed by Miczek (1987).

There is little evidence concerning the effects of opiates on aggressive behavior. While addicts are frequently involved in crime, this is usually for the purpose of obtaining money to purchase the drugs (see Chapter Four). There is some indication that an addict's rate of participation in violent crime may actually be lower than average.

The popular view is that alcohol increases violent activity, and this seems to be borne out by experience and by statistics on crime rates. A high proportion of violent crime is committed by people under the influence of alcohol (Pernanen, 1976). Several explanations can be given for this. First, there is the disinhibiting effect of alcohol. Violence carries both reinforcing and punishing consequences. If the punishing consequences are made less effective as a result of alcohol ingestion then violence becomes more likely. Secondly, alcohol may be used simply as an excuse for the exhibition of violent behavior. Society is more accepting of violence when an individual is inebriated. This is an issue that will be taken up in the next chapter. Thirdly, alcohol may just have a very direct, enhancing effect on aggression.

The results from animal studies are relevant to this issue. They show that low doses of alcohol actually increase aggressive behavior, much like other sedative-hypnotics. On the other hand, high doses lead to a decrease in aggression. These findings certainly suggest that social factors cannot be the sole reason for the increase in aggression following alcohol. Disinhibition or some direct effect must be responsible.

The effects of amphetamine, cocaine, and other related stimulants appear to be highly dose-dependent. There is little effect or even a calming when low to moderate doses are taken. This is confirmed by animal studies in which amphetamine decreases both attack and threatening behavior. Flight from the aggressive encounter is enhanced, although this may simply be a by-product of the greater levels of activity. However, high doses of amphetamine and cocaine have been observed to lead to threatening, violent behavior in humans (Asnis and Smith, 1979). It is likely that this occurs as a result of the paranoia induced by such doses of these drugs. The aggression is directed toward that which the user fears — whether this be another individual, an inanimate object, or something imagined.

There is no evidence of marked changes in aggressive behavior under the influence of LSD and related hallucinogens. In contrast, considerable anecdotal evidence suggests that a number of violent crimes, including murder, may be at least partially attributable to the effects of PCP. Unfortunately, there is little indication of the factors determining such occurrences. Certainly, they are not an automatic result of PCP use.

One group of drugs which appear to markedly reduce aggressive behavior are the anticholinergics. Evidence from animal studies indicates that they are effective in reducing all forms of aggressive behavior. Unfortunately, it is difficult to get evidence on their effects in humans because of their relatively low usage rates in contemporary Western society.

Marijuana is also able to reduce aggressive behavior. Both anecdotal evidence from humans and laboratory studies with a wide range of species indicate that this drug causes a general diminution of aggressive activity. This certainly contrasts with some earlier pictures of the marijuana user as a violent, dangerous criminal.

ASSOCIATIVE FACTORS AND PLACEBOS

If a person has been using a drug consistently for a long period of time, termination of self-administration can be a long and painful process. While many succeed eventually, it is often after a number of failed attempts. Along the way there can be considerable discomfort and unhappiness.

On the other hand, there can be occasions when the 'giving up' of a drug is relatively easy, at least for a time. Often this occurs when the person leaves the environment in which he or she used the drug. For example, some problem drug users find that hospital detoxification is not too difficult. Others may go on holiday and discover that their drug use is much easier to control or even eliminate while away from the usual drug environment.

One frequently noted example of this phenomenon concerns the United States soldiers returning from Vietnam (O'Brien et al., 1980). Many had used heroin and become physically dependent on quantities that were large by United States standards. However, relatively few of these soldiers continued their heroin use once back home. It was as if they left their heroin dependence in Vietnam. This evidence suggests that discontinuing use of a drug is likely to be more successful if it occurs in an environment not previously associated with drug use. Simply moving away from such an environment may result in an immediate drop in drug use.

Conversely, a return to the drug-taking environment may lead to an increase or reinstatement of drug use. For example, a person hospitalized for treatment of drug dependence may have ceased drug use for a period of weeks and feel quite capable of continuing abstinence. However, on returning home, meeting up with old friends, and returning to old haunts he or she may find the urge to take the drug irresistible. Similarly, the person whose drug use diminished or disappeared while on holiday may find that the old pattern of use returns as soon as he resumes normal life.

What is clear from these observations is that the tendency to use a drug varies according to the particular situation or environment in which the person finds himself. In the case of someone physically dependent on a drug, the person does not simply react to the change in concentration of drug in the body over time since the last administration. Biological factors such as these, discussed in Chapter Two, are important, but there are other psychological factors that are also important. An individual can have the same history of physical dependence and blood concentration in two different situations and be unlikely to use the drug in one, but extremely likely to do so in the other.

The various situations that can provoke drug use may be characterized in a number of different ways. It may simply be a physical environment—the place where drug use habitually occurred. Another type of situation may be the company of certain people, particularly if these people frequently discuss or engage in drug use. Finally, there is the psychological situation. People often find their greatest need for a drug is in times of stress—they may be depressed, worried, anxious, or in some other way made unhappy. This may have been the circumstance in which they used the drug in the past. Having tried to stop their use, they then find that it is exactly these situations which provoke a desire for the drug.

Clearly, these phenomena are of great importance. If we are to understand drug use it is necessary to know how the environment in which a person finds him or herself can alter the likelihood of further drug use. The following section will review research which indicates how previous drug use in a particular environment can make further drug use in that environment more likely.

Conditioned Withdrawal

Observations concerning the role of the environment were made many years ago, most notably by Abraham Wikler in his treatment of opiate dependence in the United States (see for example Wikler, 1965). Wikler also observed that many of the situations which were likely to lead to further drug use also produced withdrawal-like reactions in the drug users.

The symptoms of these reactions are real enough. In a person who uses opiates for example, symptoms may include yawning, changes in body temperature, and feelings of sickness. The individual also reports a strong craving for the drug. The exact symptoms will, of course, vary according to the drug that has been used and generally resemble the normal withdrawal symptoms characteristic of the particular drug.

Returning to earlier examples, it is suggested that when a person leaves treatment and returns to normal life he or she may experience further withdrawal-like symptoms. This occurs even after having undergone the withdrawal syndrome associated with termination of use of that drug. The reason is that the 'normal life' will involve a number of situations previously associated with drug use. In the absence of any drug-taking, simply being in those situations may elicit withdrawal-like symptoms. Similarly, the person on holiday has few situations which give rise to the withdrawal-like symptoms, but, on returning home, is confronted with a number of these. These may make it more likely that drug use will continue or be reinstated.

If this scenario is correct, how do these situations come to elicit the withdrawal-like reactions? The mechanism that has been proposed is classical conditioning (sometimes known as Pavlovian conditioning or associative learning). The basic requirement for classical conditioning is one or more pairings of a stimulus or situation with an established reflex. In the well-known example from Pavlov's laboratory, the stimulus of the bell was paired or associated with the salivation reflex elicited by food. After a sufficient number of pairings the bell itself elicited salivation in the absence of food. However, the salivation elicited by the bell was characteristically found to be less than that elicited by the food.

One early suggestion was that environments in which withdrawal had been previously experienced could themselves elicit withdrawal symptoms (Wikler, 1965). As a result of the association, these environments would come to produce a minor version of the automatic, reflexive withdrawal reaction to absence of a drug. Certainly, it is true that the normal life of most people physically dependent on a drug involves frequent experiences of withdrawal, at least for short periods of time. For example, a heroin addict who relies on street supplies may frequently undergo withdrawal while engaged in trying to obtain more drugs. As a result, the places he or she visits, the friends he or she meets along the way, and various other aspects of these situations are all associated with withdrawal.

While this explanation can account for some aspects of the phenomena described earlier, it is by no means complete. It is difficult to account for withdrawal-like symptoms induced by certain psychological states, for example. A more recent explanation, complementary to the one above, also involves classical conditioning (Siegel, 1979). It is suggested that conditioning occurs each time a drug is taken. What is conditioned is the body's reaction to the drug.

As an example, suppose that a drug increases heart rate. In reaction to this the nervous system will attempt to reduce the rate so as to bring it back toward the normal level. It is this reduction in rate which is conditioned and will be elicited by stimuli associated with drug administration.

If a drug is taken repeatedly in similar circumstances, these same adaptive changes will be elicited by the circumstances alone. The response is no longer adaptive, but occurs because of the repeated pairing. In that the drug is not present on such occasions, the change in bodily functions will be in the opposite direction to that produced by the drug. However, as many symptoms of withdrawal are opposed to the direct effects of the drug, these conditioned changes will seem withdrawal-like.

Such an explanation fits better with the observation made earlier in this section. It follows that the situations in which withdrawal-like reactions will be experienced are exactly those situations in which the drug is usually taken. They may be particular physical, social, or psychological situations. The user, when confronted with such situations, will experience discomfort which can only be alleviated by his or her administration of the drug.

Conditioning of both types has been demonstrated in the laboratory. (O'Brien, Ehrman, and Ternes, 1986; Stewart and Eikelboom, 1987). A number of studies have been conducted with animals and some with humans. In animals, an environment in which withdrawal is experienced may, by itself, come to elicit withdrawal symptoms. This has been demonstrated when the withdrawal is a natural one, from termination of drug use, and also demonstrated as when induced by administration of an antagonist. A range of withdrawal symptoms are experienced, depending on the particular drug. They are usually milder than the symptoms of the full-blown withdrawal syndrome. In several studies (O'Brien, O'Brien, Mintz, and Brady, 1975; O'Brien, Testa, O'Brien, Brady, and Wells, 1977) human volunteers who were physically dependent on the opiate methadone (for therapeutic reasons—see Chapter Five) were given injections of the antagonist naloxone in association with particular stimuli. After a number of such injections they began to experience mild withdrawal symptoms on exposure to these stimuli.

The second type of conditioning process has been examined in much more detail, using both human and animal subjects, and several different drugs. It has been shown in a number of studies that animals experience mild opiate withdrawal symptoms (for example, diarrhea and increased respiration rate) if simply placed in a cage where they had been previously injected with morphine. Very few such injections are required to produce these reactions. However, it should be noted that up to some limit, the more the drug is a part of the environment, the stronger the withdrawal reaction will be. Alcohol withdrawal effects have been conditioned with human subjects. In a study from the author's laboratory (Staiger and White, 1988) subjects were given an alcoholic drink in one room and a differently-flavored nonalcoholic drink in a second room. The drink flavors were such that subjects could not tell which contained alcohol on the basis of taste alone. The rooms were decorated differently. After attending four sessions each, subjects were tested for their reaction when no alcohol was given. With the combined drink and room previously associated with alcohol, the subjects showed a decrease in heart rate. This reaction was opposed to the effect produced by alcohol in the earlier sessions.

A number of studies have examined whether conditioned reactions do occur in people who once used opiates extensively, but who no longer do so. As mentioned earlier, informal evidence obtained in interviews with such people indicates that these withdrawal reactions and cravings are reliably produced in some situations—even by the interview conversation itself. The results of presenting material designed to elicit withdrawal reactions have confirmed these observations. Slides of drug-related scenes and written material related to drug use elicit physiological and subjective changes that are similar to the symptoms of opiate withdrawal (see for example, Sideroff and Jarvik, 1980). These occur even though the subject may not have used opiates for some considerable period of time. Similarly, mild withdrawal symptoms can be produced in exalcoholics by the act of simply showing them their favorite brand of drink.

Clearly, these withdrawal-like reactions can be elicited in people who have considerable experience with drug use. The question then becomes whether they occur frequently in situations outside the laboratory and whether they are important in the initiation of drug use. This is of course, a very difficult question to answer. We cannot follow individuals everywhere they go, noting what they see and hear and measuring physiological and subjective changes. However, there is some preliminary evidence indicating that conditioned withdrawal-like reactions do occur.

In several studies (O'Brien, 1975) people who had returned to opiate use after a period of abstinence were interviewed to determine the reasons for this change in behavior. Close to one half of the people interviewed were able to identify situations which made them feel a need for the drug. In such situations they experienced illness and anxiety for no apparent reason. Most such situations were closely associated with obtaining drugs, but others included certain moods.

Tolerance and Conditioned Withdrawal

The conditioned reactions, which are opposed to the drug's direction, may also contribute to the development of tolerance. In Chapter Two, tolerance was described as a reduction in magnitude of a drug effect with repeated administration (although it may also occur within the time-course of a single administration). Several different mechanisms were suggested to contribute to the development of tolerance. Conditioned drug-opposing reactions may be another such mechanism.

Through conditioning processes, responses develop which are, in most cases, opposed to the effects of the drug itself. These responses can be observed by putting the person (or animal) in the situation in which a drug is administered without the stimulus of the actual drug. However, when the drug is administered in that same situation the conditioned response should reduce the drug effect. The final observed result will then be a combination of the action of the drug and the conditioned response elicited by the environment. As the conditioned response develops it will gradually diminish the effect of the drug and tolerance will be observed.

If this view is correct, then such tolerance should disappear if the individual is placed in an environment not previously associated with the drug. This is exactly what has been observed in a number of studies (Siegel, 1983). Greater tolerance is found in environments previously associated with drug administration than in new environments. These observations have been confirmed in experiments using a variety of drugs (alcohol, morphine, etc.) and in measuring a range of drug effects (body temperature, activity level, etc.).

This type of tolerance has very important practical as well as theoretical implications. One is that danger from drug overdose may be greater when the person is in a novel environment — one where they have not experienced the drug before. Tolerance may have gradually developed in the usual drug-taking situation and, to compensate for this, the dose may have been slowly increased. If the person then goes to a new situation they will not have the same degree of tolerance and the high dose may prove dangerous.

Some anecdotal evidence supports this prediction. In one study (Siegel, Hinson, Krank, and McCully, 1982) heroin overdose survivors were interviewed concerning the occasion on which they took their near-fatal dose. A majority reported atypical circumstances. That is, they injected themselves in an environment where they had never administered the drug before.

Many questions still remain about this environmentally-specific tolerance. For example, some studies suggest that relative to other factors (drug-disposition and pharmacodynamic) it is particularly important, but the degree of tolerance attributable to the different mechanisms and how they interact have not been determined precisely in any one situation.

There is also some controversy concerning the basis for this type of tolerance. Some investigators have found evidence for environmentally-specific tolerance, but no evidence for conditioned responses. They have concluded that such tolerance does not arise by the means described above. However, it is possible that with improved measurement techniques conditioned responses will be observed which can account for these instances. Certainly, there are a number of studies in which conditioned responses have been measured that can account for the development of environmentally-specific tolerance.

Clinical Importance

The work here has obvious implications for therapy designed to reduce drug use. This will be discussed in Chapter Six, but a brief summary is appropriate here. The research conducted to date has demonstrated the existence of conditioned withdrawal, shown how these reactions contribute to tolerance, and demonstrated that it is part of the experience of drug users.

What is difficult to tell is how important these conditioned withdrawal effects are likely to be in maintaining self-administration and reinstating it after a drug-free period. Two lines of evidence suggest that it is important. One is simply the anecdotal evidence obtained from drug users. Many can report situations which cause withdrawal-like reactions which, in turn, seem to compel them to drug use. The second is from research with animals. It has been shown that self-administration is more likely to be reinstated if the animal is placed in the environment where self-administration has occurred previously rather than a novel environment (Thompson and Ostlund, 1965). This may arise because the old environment elicits withdrawal-like reactions whereas a novel one does not.

Although there is only a little evidence at this stage, it suggests that reduction in the strength of conditioned withdrawal responses may be an important part of any treatment designed to reduce drug-taking and, particularly, treatment designed to prevent relapse to drug use after an initial drug-free period. It also suggests problems with many approaches which do not account for conditioned withdrawal reactions. Since these reactions persist for some considerable length of time it is not sufficient to simply eliminate drug use for a short period, especially if the person is taken out of the normal environment to do so. Returning the individual to her home, friends, and the stresses of normal life may result in conditioned withdrawal reactions which are difficult to tolerate and can only be alleviated by drug use.

Drug-Like Reactions

As mentioned earlier, many of the conditioned responses that have been observed are opposed to the effect of the drug. It is suggested that what is conditioned is the body's reaction to the drug, rather than the drug effect itself. However, opposite effects are not always observed. Sometimes the conditioned response is in the same direction as the observed drug effect. For example, experiments with animals have shown that some opiate-like responses are evoked in situations where such drugs had been administered previously (for example, Miksic, Smith, Numan, and Lal, 1975).

Another example concerns the "needle freak" phenomenon observed amongst opiate addicts (Levine, 1974). In situations where the drug is unavailable, some addicts will go through the whole ritual of "cooking up" and administration, but with an inert substance rather than the drug itself. They report a mild "high"—not as good as the drug, but better than nothing.

This type of effect is not restricted to a few "needle freaks." In studies with heroin users in the presence of detoxification (O'Brien, Ehrman, and Ternes, 1986), injection of saline that subjects expected to be opiate were reported as producing mild opiate-like effects. However, if saline continued to be substituted for the opiate on a number of occasions the effect reversed: The injections produced mild withdrawal-like reactions. Subjects have also injected heroin, but in addition, received an antagonist that blocked its effects. Some subjects were observed to show physical opiate-like changes (for example, constriction of the pupil, increase in heart rate, etc.) in response to the blocked heroin. These changes disappeared after a few injections. This occurred about the time the subjects decided to stop self-administering the heroin.

One attempt to account for the existence of drug-like and drug-opposite reactions suggests that what is important is the response mediated by the central nervous system (Eikelboom and Stewart, 1982). With some drug effects the drug acts through the CNS. In such cases the conditioned response will be the same as the drug effect. However, other drug effects are not mediated via the CNS, and indeed, the CNS acts to oppose or neutralize the effect. In these cases this drug-opposite CNS response is the one which is conditioned.

The other evidence for drug-like reactions in the absence of any drug has come from research designed to investigate the role of expectancy in mediating the effects of drugs (Marlatt and Rohsenhow, 1980). Most experiments have used alcohol in human subjects. It is argued that much of the behavior change that occurs following alcohol administration is due to our expectancies about the effects of the drug rather than due to a direct effect of the drug itself.

Expectancy is manipulated by convincing some subjects that they have had alcohol when they have not, and others that they have not had the drug when they did indeed have it. The methods include pouring the placebo from an alcohol bottle and giving it the odor of alcohol. Although experimenters have gone to considerable trouble to effect such deception, one of the problems with this research is that their efforts are not always successful (Bradlyn and Young, 1983).

A number of different types of behavior have been examined in studies of expectancy. The results suggest that sexual arousal, mood, and aggression may all be influenced by expectancy factors. In contrast, simple motor skill or learning tasks may not be. However, there are a large number of additional factors which influence these results. For example, effects on sexual arousal are different for males and females. In some cases mood has been influenced by expectancy but in others not. And effects opposed to those of alcohol have also been observed.

Despite these problems, there are at least some results showing that, if the appropriate conditions are arranged, alcohol-like effects can be observed without administration of the drug itself. Together with the results of animal studies and those from opiate users, it is clear that conditions associated with drug use can produce drug-like effects.

The question of whether drug-like or drug-opposite effects will occur in any situation is still to be answered. While it is clear that the nature of the drug effect and the body's reaction to it are important, there are other factors as well. For example, in several experiments it has been shown that one can produce a drug-like response if certain aspects of the environment are emphasized and a drug-opposite response if other aspects are emphasized (Eikelboom and Stewart, 1981; Staiger and White, 1988). And as noted above, in certain instances drug-like reactions may be replaced by drug-opposite ones if those aspects of the environment associated with the drug effects are presented repeatedly.

Nevertheless, it is clear that experience with a drug may cause reactions in the absence of any drug effect. These reactions may be similar or opposite to the effects of the drug and are likely to be an important factor predisposing a person to further drug use. The reactions may also influence the effects of a drug taken, particularly through conditioned tolerance.

PERSONALITY AND DRUG USE

While most people in contemporary Western society use drugs, the amounts used and the kinds of drugs used vary enormously. To many, drug use is a relatively small and unimportant part of their lives. Most people spend little time and effort in obtaining drugs, and while they might use something like caffeine on a fairly regular basis, they would also be able to tolerate its absence without too much difficulty.

On the other hand, there are many individuals whose drug use is a major part of their lives. If the drug is a legal one and readily obtainable this may not cause any problem in the short-term. Cigarette smoking is an example of this pattern. The behavior has severe long-term consequences and people have extreme difficulty giving up smoking, but it does not cause great disruption to the individual's overall lifestyle.

Frequent use of heroin, amphetamine, and a number of other drugs can create severe problems for the user. The drugs are difficult to obtain, can be dangerous because of variations in purity and dose, and can cause problems if taken in large quantities (see Chapter Five). Clearly, there are strong grounds for not engaging in such drug use. Why then does it occur? The evidence described above shows that drugs are very powerful reinforcers which have strong subjective and behavioral effects that contribute to their use. In addition, once begun, drug use may be hard to terminate because of physical dependence and the development of conditioned reactions.

There are also influential factors over which we have no control. Both our genetic heritage and our past history predispose us to behave in certain ways. Such predispositions may, in turn, alter our response to drugs. For example, a combination of certain genetic factors and early experience may make it more likely that a person will experience pleasant subjective effects after taking a particular drug. In turn, this may make continued drug use more likely. Similarly, a person with a history of anxiety may be more prone to use a drug that has the effect of relieving such anxiety than another without such a history.

How do past experience and hereditary factors influence our response to drugs? Although it is only speculation at this stage, it is presumably through influence on brain function. The manner in which the brain works can be determined broadly by hereditary factors and then molded by experience. Everything we do has the potential to alter brain function in the future. These changes may be subtle alterations in levels of certain neurotransmitters or the activity of certain cells, for example. Since the effect of a drug is dependent on such factors, its influence will be governed in part by the past history of the individual.

When discussing individual behavior, the sum of hereditary influences and past experiences is sometimes termed one's personality. People with similar personalities are likely to behave in similar ways given the same set of circumstances. Knowledge of an individual's history by an analysis of their personality should help predict how they will act in any given situation. If our interest is in drug use, it may help to predict a person's reaction to various drugs and to understand his individual reasons for drug use.

Reasons for Personality Research

There are a number of important practical reasons for investigating the relationship between personality and drug use. One of the most frequently cited is the ability to identify those who are likely to experience difficulties in managing their drug use. By itself, drug use is not necessarily a bad thing, but, as described in Chapter One, problems arise when drug use disrupts people's lives. It may be advantageous to detect those who are likely to fall into such a pattern of drug abuse. If this were possible, such individuals could be given appropriate help before the abuse problem began.

The second reason for investigating personality factors is to be able to match therapy to the individual. It is clear that not all users of a particular drug have the same reason for taking it. For some the pleasant subjective effects may be most important, whereas for others it may be the relief from stress, and for others simply an escape from normal life. Questioning a person may reveal such information, but we are not always accurate observers of our own behavior, nor do our reasons always correspond to those found to be important ultimately. A better diagnosis may come through the use of personality tests. Information about the reasons for drug use can then allow a therapist to design programs most suitable for an individual.

A third, and related, reason is to try to identify those individuals most likely to relapse into drug use after a drug-free period. As will be discussed in Chapter Six, getting a person to stop taking a drug is not always the hardest part. Rather, it is in ensuring that their use remains at a sufficiently low or nonexistent level. One important factor in the relapse process has already been discussed: the role of environments previously associated with drug use and drug withdrawal. However, certain people may be more prone to relapse than others. A particular group at risk are those for whom the drug met some unfulfilled need. For example, an individual may have a certain psychiatric problem that has never been dealt with adequately. This problem may predispose her to use of a particular drug type and may have led to abuse of the drug initially. If such an individual were to undergo therapy for this drug abuse problem alone, her psychiatric problem would remain. As a result, she may be very likely to return to drug use in order to try and control it.

Personality Theories of Drug Use

Very early views of drug problems held personality to be the primary factor. Those with an "addictive personality" were likely to end up as alcoholics, opiate addicts, or with some other drug abuse problem. In that this view predated much of the behavioral work described earlier in this chapter, differences in individual experience with a drug were not held to be of particular importance. The "addictive personality" was something like the "criminal personality"—once one had it, one's life pattern was said to be established. This, rather than the inadequacy of therapy, their experience with the drug, or their social situation, explained people's failure to limit their drug use.

More recent theories have rejected this notion. People have been shown not to be compelled to drug use, but may be more likely to develop drug problems than others because of certain personality characteristics. There have been a number of theories concerning the personality characteristics of heavy drug users. From these, several main themes emerge. (Lettieri, Sayers, and Pearson, 1980, is a useful source, containing brief summaries of a number of such theories.)

One is that drug users are less able to delay gratification. Rather than striving for longer-term goals which may be advantageous, they seek more immediate gratification. Drugs provide a powerful source of reinforcement which can often be obtained with relatively little effort and little delay. Few such powerful reinforcers are so immediate. One would also presume that because their focus is on short-term rather than long-term consequences, such people would be more likely to disregard the deleterious effect of drugs.

The origins of such behavior patterns are not clear. One suggestion is that the person is simply immature. Need for immediate reinforcement is a characteristic of children. As we grow older, this pattern is replaced by a more adult one in most individuals. However, some people are slower to develop adult characteristics and may lapse into drug use in order to get the more immediate gratification they are unable to find in the adult world. Perhaps when they do develop more mature patterns their drug use may simply stop.

A second theme concerns the personality disturbances that arise when an individual cannot cope with the demands placed on him. It may be that they are unable to meet the expectations of others, such as their parents. He may not be able to cope with the normal conflicts that arise during childhood and later development. The results of such difficulties can vary. The individual is likely to feel powerless and have relatively low self-esteem. Depression may develop as a result. The person may also experience anxiety above normal levels. The function of the drug in such individuals is to give greater feelings of power and control. This would then increase self-esteem and alleviate any anxiety or depression. The drug of choice may depend on the symptom which is most severe for the individual. For example, cocaine and amphetamine are often said to give the user feelings of self-confidence. Alcohol, barbituates, or benzodiazepines may be more effective in alleviating anxiety.

A third theme to emerge from personality theories is that drug users are less socially conforming than normal. Use of illegal drugs is one way of expressing such nonconformity and demonstrating one's rejection of the traditional culture. People with this type of personality often come together in social groups. They may engage in a number of antisocial activities. One member of a group may begin drug use in the process of experimenting with alternative modes of behavior and it may then spread to the other members. Such rejection is likely to occur in adolescent years but may continue for some time after.

These different views are not mutually exclusive. They may all describe at least some individuals prone to excessive drug use. In addition, these personality characteristics may exist in a combination in certain people. A person may have low self-esteem and be socially nonconforming, for example. At this stage these ideas remain theories. What is necessary is some actual data on personalities of drug users to confirm or refute them.

Personalities of Drug Users: Problems with Research

Before beginning a discussion of the research on this topic it is worth mentioning some of the difficulties encountered in this area (see also Sutker and Allain, 1988). At first blush it might seem simple — a researcher only has to go around giving personality tests to samples of drug users and compare them with the population norms. However, this does not tell us whether any deviation from the norm was either caused by drug use or existed prior to drug use, and was itself a cause of drug use. Finding that alcoholics are depressed may not be all that surprising. Large quantities of alcohol have a number of adverse effects which could lead to depression. Simply being reliant on alcohol and having to orient one's whole life around use of the drug create a dependency that induces depression in many individuals. The drug may also cause specific brain damage (see Chapter Five) which results in disorders of personality. Ideally, research in this area should include data on people that precede their drug use, so that one could determine if the personality disorder was present before the drug-taking began.

A second problem arises in the attempt to measure personality for this purpose. There are so many factors that affect the results of personality tests that one is never sure whether the result is either real or spurious. Demographic variables such as age, sex, and socioeconomic status are all important. To be certain of any findings it is necessary to have a sample which is not going to be biased due to over- or under-representation of any one of these factors. If for example, one went to a drug clinic in a poor, inner-city suburb and tested subjects there, it could be argued that any significant deviation from the norm revealed information about the types of people who live in such areas rather than the types of people who have drug problems.

Because of this difficulty there is a high incidence of contradictory findings in different studies. Often, it is only possible to be sure of a finding once a number of similar studies have been completed. The results of any single study should be treated with caution.

A third problem is simply that most research has been concerned with alcoholism. While this enables us to be more confident about results from this type of drug user, it is often difficult to determine whether the results are common to all drug users or relatively specific to those with alcohol problems. Even with respect to the issues described above, there is often very little information about people who use drugs other than alcohol. This is an important problem as it is not known whether there are personality characteristics general to all types of drug users (as the theories above would suggest) or whether characteristics are specific to users of each drug type.

Personalities of Drug Users: Results

Perhaps the most consistent findings, obtained by a number of different types of personality measures, are that drug users tend to be less socially conforming, more independent, and more impulsive (Cox, 1985). Most results have been obtained from alcoholics. They show that these characteristics are present before alcohol use begins, continue through the period of alcohol use, and remain even if alcohol use ceases.

Other types of drug users show a similar pattern. Again these are enduring personality characteristics and not solely a result of drug use. There is some evidence that these personality characteristics are also more common in people who have nondrug "addictions:" excessive gamblers and people with eating disorders. Even smokers have been found on average to have slightly less impulse control than the norm.

To some extent these characteristics are what might be expected based on theoretical grounds. Certainly the impulsivity is consistent with the delay-of-gratification hypothesis. What is perhaps most interesting is the lack of social conformity amongst alcoholics. In the Western societies in which these results were obtained, use of alcohol is a normal social custom regularly practised by the majority of adults. With other, illegal drugs, one could simply say that social nonconformity indicates a predisposition to experiment with forbidden practices, as was suggested above. The fact that it is common to alcoholics suggests that nonconformity predisposes a person to excessive consumption.

Anxiety and depression are common amongst drug users of all types. Even heavy caffeine users are more anxious and depressed than normal. However, in many cases the anxiety and depression are temporary, remaining only for the period of drug use. If this ceases then the anxiety and depression seem to diminish gradually. The levels of these disorders have been found to be quite high amongst those treated for heroin problems and there is some evidence that these problems may be more enduring amongst this population. While anxiety and depression are not beyond normal levels in prealcoholics, they are in those who go on to use illegal drugs such as heroin and amphetamine.

Low self-esteem is another characteristic of many drug users. It seems to be especially common amongst alcoholics, particularly female alcoholics. This low self-esteem often improves with abstinence. Most evidence indicates that the low self-esteem is a consequence of the drug problem. However, there is some evidence that it may be a precursor to drug use in certain individuals. Again, it seems to be amongst users of "harder," illegal drugs that this is most common.

These results confirm a number of the theoretical predictions discussed above, but also suggest a much more complicated picture than do the theories. For one thing, there are differences amongst users of the different types of drugs not always exhibited in the direction expected on the basis of theoretical considerations. The lack of social conformity amongst alcoholics is one such example.

These results have some important practical implications. They suggest that we have gone at least part of the way to identifying those people most likely to have drug problems. More impulsive and less socially conforming individuals are the most obvious group. However, a problem noted by Nathan (1988) is that this factor has relatively little predictive value because antisocial personality is so widespread in the population. The number of people identified in this way would be very great, and would certainly outnumber those who are likely to develop dependence problems. The research also suggests that people with disorders such as anxiety and depression should be identified and treated, in that they seem to have a higher risk of developing certain types of drug abuse problems. If drug abuse has already begun, these other problems should be dealt with in addition to actual drug use. Without such treatment the chances of relapse are likely to be much higher.

A word of caution should be expressed about these results. The differences are normative only. They do not indicate that *every* drug user is impulsive or lacks social conformity or shows any of the other characteristic traits.

While there may be a higher proportion of drug users with such traits, there will also be drug users who do not show them and people who do not have drug abuse problems, but who exhibit these same characteristics to an extreme degree. There is a danger that some people may still look for and think they can identify those with an 'addictive personality,' but one disguised in psychologically more sophisticated language. People with drug abuse problems are not a uniform group who can be labelled in a manner suggestive of a common personality type.

CONCLUSION

Like biological aspects, the various psychological factors are influential at every stage of drug use. One thought to be very important is personality. It is likely that more independent, rebellious adolescents may be more willing to try illegal drugs and to try drugs such as alcohol at an age when it is forbidden to do so.

Once an individual samples a drug the various subjective and behavioral changes it produces become major determinants of future use. Subjective changes may include alterations to sensation and perception (most apparent in the case of hallucinogens), changes in mood and feelings, plus a general subjective change, sometimes referred to as a *change of state.*

Given a reasonable dose, almost every aspect of behavior will be affected by the drug. The type of change depends on a number of factors, including the type of consequence maintaining the behavior (its motivation), the rate at which the behavior normally occurs, whether it is under strong environmental control, or whether it is a newly learned or established behavior pattern. Both the previous history of the behavior and other behavior in the person's repertoire may also play a role in this. Expectancy concerning the drug effect has also been claimed to influence behavioral changes. Because of this multitude of factors it is very difficult to make general statements about the manner in which any behavior can be affected by a particular drug. Instead, there will clearly be considerable variation depending on the particular individual and her situation.

The exact nature of behavioral change may also influence the course of tolerance. There is evidence to suggest that if a drug-induced behavioral change is for the worse (for example, a loss of reinforcement) then tolerance to that particular behavioral disruption will occur much faster than if the drug induced a beneficial behavior change, or one with no net effect. Tolerance will also be influenced by the circumstances in which the drug is used. The magnitude of drug-induced change will be considerably less if it is a situation in which the person has used the drug on previous occasions.

Once drug use has begun, a range of direct influences will modify its frequency. Both the cost (in money, effort expended, etc.) and the dose obtained influence drug use. Frequency of intake tends to decline with increases in cost, but in lower dose ranges, will increase with the amount in each dose. At higher dose levels frequency of intake (but not total intake) declines as the unit dose increases. Other factors include the history of prior drug use (making future use more likely) and the current conditions experienced by the individual. Particular personality characteristics (for instance, high levels of anxiety) may also predispose the individual to high level drug use. In addition, drug use is likely to diminish if there are negative outcomes associated with it. At the stage where a drug is being used repeatedly a pattern of drug use may develop. An important determinant of this pattern is the actual drug itself. Cyclic patterns are more common with certain drugs (for instance, amphetamine) while patterns of continuous intake tend to be found with others (such as the benzodiazepines). The termination of a period of drug use may be associated with the build-up of adverse effects. Conditioned withdrawal may also become an important motivating factor at this stage. Withdrawal-like reactions may occur if the user does not take the drug in a situation in which he had previously done so. The situation may be a physical environment, specific social circumstance, or a subjective state. These reactions may continue to occur even when use has stopped for a considerable period of time.

REFERENCES

ASNIS, S.F. & SMITH, R.C. (1979). Amphetamine abuse and violence. In D.E. Smith et al. (Eds.), *Amphetamine use, misuse, and abuse* (pp. 205–217). Boston: G.K. Hall.

BARRETT, J.E. (1977). Behavioral history as a determinant of the effects of d-amphetamine on punished behavior. *Science, 198,* 67–69.

BARRETT, J.E. & KATZ, J.L. (1981). Drug effects on behaviors maintained by different events. In T. Thompson, P.B. Dews, & W.A. McKim (Eds.), *Advances in behavioral pharmacology.* (Vol. 3, pp. 119–168). New York: Academic Press, 1981.

BIGELOW, G., GRIFFITHS, R.R., & LIEBSON, I. (1976). Effects of response requirement upon human sedative self-administration and drug-seeking behavior. *Pharmacology, Biochemistry and Behavior, 5,* 681–685.

BIGELOW, G. & LIEBSON, I. (1972). Cost factors controlling alcoholic drinking. *Psychological Record, 22,* 305–314.

BIGNAMI, G. (1966). Pharmacological influences on mating behavior in the male rat. *Psychopharmacologia, 10,* 44–58.

BLUNDELL, J.E. (1987). Structure, process and mechanism: Case studies in the psychopharmacology of feeding. In I.H. Iversen, S.D. Iversen, & S.H. Snyder (Eds.), *Handbook of psychopharmacology* (Vol. 19, pp. 123–182). New York: Plenum Press.

CALDWELL, D., MYERS S.A., DOMINO, E.F., & MERRIAM, P.E. (1969). Auditory and visual thresholds of marijuana in man. *Perceptual and Motor Skills, 29,* 755–759.

CATANIA, A.C. (1976). Drug effects and concurrent performances. *Pharmacological Reviews, 27,* 385–394.

CHAIT, L.D., EVANS, S.M., GRANT, K.A., KAMIEN, J.B., JOHANSON, C.E., & SCHUSTER, C.R. (1988). Discriminative stimulus and subjective affects of smoked marijuana in humans. *Psychopharmacology, 94,* 206–212.

CHAIT, L.D., UHLENHUTH, E.H., & JOHANSON, C.E. (1987). Reinforcing effects of several anorectics in normal human volunteers. *Journal of Pharmacology and Experimental Therapeutics, 242,* 777–783.

CICERO, T.J., MYERS, R.D., & BLACK, W.C. (1968). Increase in volitional ethanol consumption following interference with a learned avoidance response. *Physiology and Behavior, 3,* 657–660.

CORFIELD-SUMNER, P.K. & STOLERMAN, I.P. (1978). Behavioral tolerance. In D.E. Blackman & D.J. Sanger (Eds.), *Contemporary research in behavioral pharmacology.* (pp. 391–448). New York: Plenum Press.

COX, W.M. (1985). Personality correlates of substance abuse. In M. Galizio & S.A. Maisto (Eds.), *Determinants of substance abuse.* (pp. 209–246). New York: Plenum Press.

DAVIS, J.D. & MILLER, N.E. (1961). Fear and pain: Their effect on self-injection of amobarbital sodium by rats. *Science, 141,* 1286–1287.

DEWS, P.B. (1955). Studies on behavior. I. Differential sensitivity to pentobarbital of pecking performance in pigeons depending on the schedule of reward. *Journal of Pharmacology and Experimental Therapeutics, 113,* 393–401.

DEWS, P.B. (1958). Studies of behavior. IV. Stimulant actions of methamphetamine. *Journal of Pharmacology and Experimental Therapeutics, 122,* 137–147.

DEWS, P.B. & WENGER, G.R. (1977). Rate dependency of the behavioral effects of amphetamine. In T. Thompson & P.B. Dews (Eds.), *Advances in behavioral pharmacology.* (Vol. 1, pp. 167–227). New York: Academic Press.

DIETRICH, R.A. & SPUHLER, K. (1984). Genetics of alcoholism and alcohol actions. In R.G. Smart, H.D. Cappell, F.B. Glaser, Y. Israel, H. Kalant, R.E. Popham, W. Schmidt, & E.M. Sellers (Eds.), *Research advances in alcohol and drug problems.* (Vol. 8, pp. 47–98). New York: Plenum Press.

EDDY, N.B. & MAY, E.L. (1973). The search for a better analgesic. *Science, 181,* 407–414.

EIKELBOOM, R. & STEWART, J. (1981). Temporal and environmental cues in conditioned hypothermia and hyperthermia associated with morphine. *Psychopharmacology, 72,* 147–153.

ERWIN, V.G. & McCLEARN, G.E. (1981). Genetic influences on alcohol consumption and actions of alcohol. In M. Galanter (Ed.), *Currents in Alcoholism.* (Vol. 8, pp. 405–420). New York: Grune and Stratton.

FERSTER, C.B. & CULBERTSON, S.A. (1982). *Behavior principles.* 3rd ed. Englewood Cliffs: Prentice Hall.

GESSA, G.L., PAGLIETTI, E., & PELLEGRINI-QUARANTOTTI, B. (1979). Induction of copulatory behavior in sexually-inactive rats by naloxone. *Science, 204,* 203–204.

GRIFFITHS, R.R., BIGELOW, G.E., & HENNINGFIELD, J.E. (1980). Similarities in animal and human drug-taking behavior. In N.K. Mello (Ed.), *Advances in substance abuse.* (Vol. 1, pp. 1–90). Greenwich: JAI Press.

GRIFFITHS, R.R., BIGELOW, G., & LIEBSON, I. (1979). Human sedative self-administration: Double blind comparison of pentobarbital, diazepam, chlorpromazine, and placebo. *Journal of Pharmacology and Experimental Therapeutics, 210,* 301–310.

GRIFFITHS, R.R. & WOODSON, P.P. (1988). Reinforcing effects of caffeine in humans. *Journal of Pharmacology and Experimental Therapeutics, 246,* 21–29.

GRIFFITHS, R.R., WURSTER, R.M., & BRADY, J.V. (1975). Discrete trial choice procedure: Effects of naloxone and methadone on choice between food and heroin. *Pharmacological Reviews, 27,* 357–365.

HAERTZEN, C.A. (1965). Subjective drug effects: A factorial representation of subjective drug effects on the Addiction Research Center Inventory. *Journal of Nervous and Mental Disease, 14,* 280–289.

HAERTZEN, C.A. (1966). Development of scales based on patterns of drug effects, using the Addiction Research Center Inventory (ARCI). *Psychological Reports, 18,* 163–194.

HAERTZEN, C.A., HILL, H.E., & BELLEVILLE, R.E. (1963). Development of the Addiction Research Center Inventory (ARCI): Selection of items that are sensitive to the effects of various drugs. *Psychopharmacologia, 4,* 155–166.

HAERTZEN, C.A. & HOOKS, N.T. (1969). Changes in personality and subjective experience associated with the chronic administration and withdrawal of opiates. *Journal of Nervous and Mental Disease, 148,* 606–614.

HELLEKANT, G. (1965). Electrophysiological investigation of the gustatory effect of ethyl alcohol. II. A single fibres analysis in the cat. *Acta Physiologica Scandinavica, 64,* 398–404.

HENNINGFIELD, J.E. & GRIFFITHS, R.R. (1980). Effects of ventilated cigarette holders on cigarette smoking by humans. *Psychopharmacology, 68,* 115–119.

HINDMARCH, I. (1980). Psychomotor function and psychoactive drugs. *British Journal of Clinical Pharmacology, 10,* 189–209.

HOEBEL, B.G. (1977). The psychopharmacology of feeding. In I.H. Iversen, S.D. Iversen, & S.H. Snyder (Eds.), *Handbook of psychopharmacology.* (Vol. 8, pp. 55–129). New York: Plenum Press.

HOLTZMAN, S.G., SHANNON, H.E., & SCHAEFER, G.J. (1977). Discriminative properties of narcotic antagonists. In H. Lal (Ed.), *Discriminative stimulus properties of drugs.* (pp. 47–72). New York: Plenum Press.

JOHANSON, C.E., BALSTER, R.L., & BONESE, K. (1976). Self-administration of psycho-motor stimulant drugs: the effects of unlimited access. *Pharmacology, Biochemistry, and Behavior, 4,* 45–51.

JOHANSON, C.E. & SCHUSTER, C.R. (1981). Animal models of drug self-administration. In N.K. Mello (Ed.), *Advances in substance abuse.* (Vol. 1, pp. 219–297). Greenwich: JAI Press.

JOHANSON, C.E. & UHLENHUTH, E.H. (1981). Drug preference and mood in humans: Repeated administration of k-amphetamine. *Pharmacology, Biochemistry and Behavior, 14,* 159–163.

JOHANSON, C.E. & UHLENHUTH, E.H. (1980a). Drug preference and mood in humans: Diazepam. *Psychopharmacology, 71,* 269–274.

JOHANSON, C.E. & UHLENHUTH, E.H. (1980b). Drug preference and mood in humans: d-amphetamine. *Psychopharmacology, 71,* 275–279.

JONES, B.E. & PRADA, J.A. (1975). Drug-seeking behavior during methadone maintenance. *Psychopharmacologia, 41,* 7–10.

KALIX, P. (1987). Khat: Scientific knowledge and public policy. *British Journal of Addiction, 82,* 47–53.

KELLEHER, R.T. & MORSE, W.H. (1968). Determinants of the specificity of the behavioral effects of drugs. *Ergebnisse der Physiologie, Biologischem Chemie und Experimentallen Pharmakologie, 60,* 1–56.

KRASNEGOR, N.A. (1978a). *Self-administration of abused substances: Methods for study.* Rockville, MD: National Institute on Drug Abuse.

KRASNEGOR, N.A. (1978b). *Behavioral tolerance: Research and treatment implications.* Rockville, MD: National Institute on Drug Abuse.

LATIES, V.G. (1975). The role of discriminative stimuli in modulating drug action. *Federation Proceedings, 34,* 1880–1888.

LETTIERI, P., SAYERS, M., & PEARSON, H.W. (1980). *Theories on drug abuse.* Rockville, MD: National Institute on Drug Abuse.

LEVINE, D.G. (1974). Needle-freaks: Compulsive self-injections by drug users. *American Journal of Psychiatry, 131,* 297–300.

McKEARNEY, J.W. & BARRETT, J.E. (1975). Punished behavior: Increases in responding after d-amphetamine. *Psychopharmacologia, 41,* 23–26.

McKEARNEY, J.W. & BARRETT, J.E. (1978). Schedule-controlled behavior and the effects of drugs. In D.E. Blackman & D.J. Sanger (Eds.), *Contemporary research in behavioral pharmacology.* (pp. 1–68). New York: Plenum Press.

McKIM, W.A. (1981). Rate dependency: A nonspecific behavioral effect of drugs. In T. Thompson, P.B. Dews, & W.A. McKim (Eds.), *Advances in behavioral pharmacology.* (Vol. 3, pp. 51–73). New York: Academic Press.

MELLO, N.K. & MENDELSON, J.H. (1972). Drinking patterns during work-contingent and noncontingent alcohol acquisition. *Psychosomatic Medicine, 34,* 139–164.

MICZEK, K.A. (1987). The psychopharmacology of aggression. In L.L. Iversen, S.D. Iversen, & S.H. Snyder (Eds.), *Handbook of psychopharmacology.* (Vol. 19, pp. 183–328). New York: Plenum Press.

MIKSIC, S., SMITH, N., NUMAN, R., & LAL, H. (1975). Acquisition and extinction of a conditioned hyperthermic response to a tone paired with morphine administration. *Neuro-psychobiology, 1,* 277–283.

O'BRIEN, C.P. (1975). Experimental analysis of conditioning factors in human narcotic addic-tion. *Pharmacological Reviews, 27,* 533–543.

O'BRIEN, C.P., EHRMAN, R.N., & TERNES, J.W. (1986).   Classical conditioning in human opioid dependence. In S.R. Goldberg & I.P. Stolerman (Eds.), *Behavioral analysis of drug dependence.* (pp. 329–356). Orlando: Academic Press.

O'BRIEN, C.P., NACE, E., MINTZ, J., MEYERS, A., & REAM, N. (1980).   Follow-up of Vietnam veterans. Part 1: Relapse to drug use after Vietnam service. *Drug and Alcohol Dependence, 5,* 333–340.

O'BRIEN, C.P., O'BRIEN, T.J., MINTZ, J., & BRADY, J.P. (1975).   Conditioning of narcotic abstinence symptoms in human subjects. *Drug and Alcohol Dependence, 1,* 115–123.

O'BRIEN, C.P., TESTA, T., O'BRIEN, T.J., BRADY, J.P., & WELLS, B. (1977).   Conditioned narcotic withdrawal in humans. *Science, 195,* 1000–1002.

OVERTON, D.A. (1982).   Memory retrieval failures produced by changes in drug state. In R.L. Isaacson & N.E. Spear (Eds.), *The expression of knowledge: Neurobehavioral transformations of information into action.* (pp. 116–134). New York: Plenum Press.

OVERTON, D.A. (1984).   State dependent learning and drug discrimination. In L.L. Iversen, S.D. Iversen, & S.H. Snyder (Eds.), *Handbook of Psychopharmacology.* (Vol. 18, pp. 59–128). New York: Plenum Press.

PERNANEN, K. (1976).   Alcohol and crimes of violence. In B. Kissin & H. Begleiter (Eds.), *Social aspects of alcoholism.* (pp. 351–444). New York: Plenum Press.

PICKENS, R. (1977).   Behavioral pharmacology: A brief history. In T. Thompson & P.B. Dews (Eds.), *Advances in behavioral pharmacology.* (Vol. 1, pp. 229–257). New York: Academic Press.

POHORECKY, L.A. & BRICK, J. (EDS.) (1983).   *Stress and alcohol use.* New York: Elsevier.

POLING, A. & APPEL, J.B. (1979).   Procedures for reducing drug intake: Nonhuman studies. In T. Thompson and P.B. Dews (Eds.), *Advances in behavioral pharmacology.* (Vol. 2, pp. 229–263). New York: Academic Press.

POSCHEL, B.P.H. (1963).   Effects of methamphetamine on hunger and thirst motivated variable-interval performance. *Journal of Comparative and Physiological Psychology, 56,* 968–973.

RICKLES, W.H., COHEN, M.J., WHITAKER, C.A., & McINTYRE, K.E. (1973).   Marijuana-induced state-dependent verbal learning. *Psychopharmacologia, 30,* 349–354.

ROBBINS, T.W. (1981).   Behavioral determinants of drug action: Rate-dependency revisited. In S.J. Cooper (Ed.), *Theory in psychopharmacology.* (Vol. 1, pp. 1–63). London: Academic Press.

ROBBINS, T.W. & SAHAKIAN, B.J. (1979).   'Paradoxical' effects of psychomotor stimulant drugs in hyperactive children from the standpoint of behavioral pharmacology. *Neuropharmacology, 18,* 931–950.

RUBIN, H.B. & HENSON, D.E. (1979).   Effects of drugs on male sexual function. In T. Thompson & P.B. Dews (Eds.), *Advances in behavioral pharmacology.* (Vol. 2, pp. 65–86). New York: Academic Press.

RUBIN, H.B. & HENSON, D.E. (1976).   Effects of alcohol on male sexual responding. *Psychopharmacology, 47,* 123–134.

RUMBOLD, G.R. & WHITE, J.M. (1987).   Effects of repeated alcohol administration on human operant behavior. *Psychopharmacology, 92,* 186–191.

SANDLER, M. & GESSA, G.L. (1975).   *Sexual behavior: Pharmacology and biochemistry.* New York: Raven Press.

SANGER, D.J. (1986).   Drug taking as adjunctive behaviour. In S.R. Goldberg & I.P. Stolerman (Eds.), *Behavioral analysis of drug dependence.* (pp. 123–160). Orlando, Florida: Academic Press.

SCHUSTER, C.R. (1970).   Psychological approaches to opiate dependence and self-administration by laboratory animals. *Federation Proceedings, 29,* 2–5.

SCHUSTER, C.R. (1978).   Theoretical basis of behavioral tolerance: Implications of the phenomenon for problems of drug abuse. In N.A. Krasnegor (Ed.), *Behavioral tolerance: Research and treatment implications.* (pp. 4–17). Rockville, MD: National Institute on Drug Abuse.

SCHUSTER, C.R. & JOHANSON, C.E. (1986).   Efficacy, dependence potential, and neurotoxicity of anorectic drugs. In L.S. Seiden & R.L. Balster (Eds.), *Behavioral pharmacology: The current status.* (pp. 263–280). New York: Alan R. Liss.

SEPPINWALL, J.A. & COOK, L. (1978).   Behavioral pharmacology of antianxiety drugs. In L.L. Iversen, S.D. Iversen, & S.H. Snyder (Eds.), *Handbook of psychopharmacology.* (Vol. 13, pp. 345–393). New York: Plenum Press.
SHANNON, H.E. & HOLTZMAN, S.G. (1976).   Evaluation of the discriminative effects of morphine in the rat. *Journal of Pharmacology and Experimental Therapeutics, 198,* 54–65.
SHANNON, H.E. & HOLTZMAN, S.G. (1977).   Further evaluation of the discriminative effects of morphine in the rat. *Journal of Pharmacology and Experimental Therapeutics, 15,* 529–536.
SIDEROFF, S. & JARVIK, M.E. (1980).   Conditioned responses to videotape showing heroin-related stimuli. *International Journal of the Addictions, 15,* 529–536.
SIEGEL, R. (1977).   Hallucinations. *Scientific American, 232,* 132–140.
SIEGEL, S. (1983).   Classical conditioning, drug tolerance, and drug dependence. In R.J. Smart, F.B. Glaser, Y. Israel, H. Kalant, R.E. Popham, & W. Schmidt (Eds.), *Research advances in alcohol and drug problems.* (Vol. 7, pp. 207–246). New York: Plenum Press.
SIEGEL, S., HINSON, R.E., KRANK, M.D., & McCULLY, J. (1982).   Heroin "overdose" death: Contribution of drug-associated environmental cues. *Science, 217,* 436–437.
SMITH, J. & MISIAK, H. (1976).   Critical flicker fusion (CFF) and psychotropic drugs in normal human subjects — a review. *Psychopharmacology, 47,* 175–182.
STAIGER, P.K. & WHITE, J.M. (1988).   Conditioned alcohol-like and alcohol-opposite responses in humans. *Psychopharmacology, 95,* 87–91.
STEWART, J. & EIKELBOOM, R. (1987).   Conditioned drug effects. In L.L. Iversen, S.D. Iversen, & S.H. Snyder, (Eds.), *Handbook of psychopharmacology.* (Vol. 19, pp. 1–57). New York: Plenum Press.
STITZER, M.L., McCAUL, M.E., BIGELOW, G.E., & LIEBSON, I.A. (1983).   Oral methadone self-administration: Effects of dose and alternative reinforcers. *Clinical Pharmacology and Therapeutics, 34,* 29–35.
SUTKER, P.B. & ALLAIN, A.N. (1988).   Issues in personality conceptualizations of addictive behaviors. *Journal of Consulting and Clinical Psychology, 56,* 172–182.
TAKAHASHI, R.N. & SINGER, G. (1979).   Self-administration of $\triangle^9$-tetrahydrocannabinol by rats. *Pharmacology, Biochemistry, and Behavior, 11,* 737–740.
THOMPSON, D.M. & MOERSCHBAECHER, J.M. (1979).   Drug effects on repeated acquisition. In T. Thompson & P.B. Dews (Eds.), *Advances in behavioral pharmacology.* (Vol. 2, pp. 229–259). New York: Academic Press.
THOMPSON, T. & OSTLUND, W. (1965).   Susceptibility to readdiction as a function of the addiction and withdrawal environments. *Journal of Comparative and Physiological Psychology, 60,* 388–392.
WEISSMAN, A. (1959).   Differential drug effect upon a three-ply multiple schedule of reinforcement. *Journal of the Experimental Analysis of Behavior, 2,* 271–287.
WHEATLEY, D. (1981).   *Pharmacology of sleep.* New York: Raven Press.
WIKLER, A. (1965).   Conditioning factors in opiate addiction and relapse. In D.I. Wilner & G.G. Kassebaum (Eds.), *Narcotics.* (pp. 85–100). New York: McGraw Hill.
WILLIAMS, R.L. & KARACEN, I. (1976).   *Pharmacology of sleep.* New York: Wiley.
WOODS, J.H. & SCHUSTER, C.R. (1971).   Opiates as reinforcing stimuli. In T. Thompson & R. Pickens (Eds.), *Stimulus properties of drugs.* (pp. 163–175). New York: Plenum Press.
YOUNG, A.M. & HERLING, S. (1986).   Drugs as reinforcers: Studies in laboratory animals. In S.R. Goldberg & I.P. Stolerman (Eds.), *Behavioral analysis of drug dependence.* (pp. 9–67). Orlando: Academic Press.

CHAPTER 4

Social Aspects

The two previous chapters were concerned with the many biological and psychological factors which determine both the magnitude and nature of drug effects and patterns of drug use. The third type of influence comes from the social context in which the drug is taken. The importance of such social influences can be seen from the variety of drug use patterns both between societies and between different groups within a society. In addition, the behavioral effects of drugs seem to vary across different societies in a manner which does not seem to be accountable solely in terms of the biological and psychological factors discussed earlier.

These general differences in drug use and drug effects will be considered in the first section. Variation between societies, over time in different societies, and within a society will all be considered. Some of the factors that might account for this variation will be considered in the following two sections. The first of these will examine two important social factors: beliefs about drugs and the type of environment in which a drug is used. The second will examine how societies have attempted to control and regulate drug use. In particular, the controls adopted by Western societies in this century will be considered in some detail. The final section will examine the interaction of the drug user with society over the course of his or her drug-using career. Emphasis will be on those whose drug use causes major problems, rather than on the occasional or moderate user.

SOCIOCULTURAL INFLUENCES ON DRUG USE

Differences in Drug Use Between Societies

That there is and has been considerable variation in the use of drugs in different societies is evident from the discussions of various drugs in Chapter One. What is considered the norm in one country may be totally forbidden with heavy penalties in another. Variation between cultures is partly due to historical accident. It depended on the plants with psychoactive components which grew in the different regions and that were discovered to have effects. For example, naturally occurring hallucinogens such as muscimol are widely used among the Indians of Central America (where the plants grow), but are forbidden in Western societies. The same drug may also be used in quite different ways in different societies. When tobacco was first introduced to Europe it was used predominantly as a medicine in certain countries, but as a mild stimulant in others. In some, such as Russia, it was used as an intoxicant by means of deep and rapid inhalation.

Because alcohol consumption is such a widespread and common practise, it has been possible to study variations in the manner and context of its use among tribal societies (Bacon, 1976). These are societies whose drinking practises have been influenced to a minimal degree by contemporary societies, particularly from the West. Accordingly, they may reveal the "natural" variation in the way alcohol is used. The investigations suggest that aspects of alcohol use differ markedly across societies. What is common in modern Western societies cannot by any means be considered a norm.

One obvious difference in societies is the type of beverage used. In tribal societies this consists of some form of fruit wine or beer. The most important factor which determines the beverage used is simply the knowledge of which raw materials are available. Any one area may have an abundance of fruit or grains, but not always both.

The frequency of drinking varies from once a year, on a ceremonial basis, to regular, daily drinking in some tribes. Where drinking is only occasional, a relatively large amount is consumed each time, with the participants often ending up very drunk. Where drinking tends to be more frequent, it is also likely to be more moderate, though this is only a generalization.

Drinking occurs in many varied contexts. Ceremonies and rituals are common occasions for drinking amongst many people. As well as in tribal societies, this is the traditional pattern in India where regular use outside of such contexts has been relatively uncommon until very recently. The ceremonies may be religious or simply social occasions such as a marriage or birth. In some societies drinking traditionally accompanies food, in others it is done separately.

Approval of drunkenness varies considerably across different cultures. In some, drunkenness is approved, even encouraged. This is particularly the case where drinking has a ceremonial function. In others, drunkenness is much frowned upon.

The people who drink also vary. At one extreme are the cultures in which only adult males participate. They are almost always societies that have used alcohol from very early times. The other extreme consists of societies where drinking is virtually universal — where there are no strictures against women drinking and few against children. Most societies fall somewhere between these, with consumption occurring across the adult population, but to a greater degree amongst the men than the women.

While alcohol is an excellent example because of its widespread use, the same types of variation can be seen with other drugs. For example, use of marijuana also varies considerably, with ceremonial and religious use in some areas (for example, India), but not in others (Southeast Asia) (Rubin, 1975). Similarly, where use of a drug is a very old, traditional practice it is almost solely confined to the adult male population. This has been the case with opium use in many Arab countries.

The findings which have been obtained from the study of alcohol, many of which may be general to a range of drugs, suggest considerable cultural variation in drug use. It seems that there is no one characteristic way in which a particular drug is used. Rather, the manner and context adopted depend on both the drug and the nature of the society.

Changes in Drug Use Over Time

When a society is viewed in a historical context it can be seen that both the types of drugs used and the manner of their use have altered considerably (see, for example, Morgan, 1981). Indeed, the rate of such changes seems to be increasing all the time. Perhaps this is only to be expected. Increases in world trade have altered the pattern of use of a variety of commodities. Just as we now grow and eat various foodstuffs which originated from very distant places, we also consume drugs which were once localized to a small area of the world.

Changes in types of drugs used   The spread of drugs through legal and illegal trade has resulted in several important changes. One is that all people now have a much wider variety of drugs available to them than they had previously. As mentioned earlier, traditional societies tended to use only a very narrow range of drugs. In one form or another they are now offered a much wider range. Compare Western Europe of today with the same region several thousand years ago. The most common drug then would have been alcohol, with some use of plants producing hallucinogenic effects. While the Indians of South America used quite a variety of drugs, each tribal group employed only a limited number. Such barriers are now disappearing and people have access to a whole range of drugs which come from their region and from outside.

These changes have brought a degree of homogenization, and cultural differences in drug use are diminishing. Although this process has been occurring for some time, there is a tendency for new drugs or methods of using drugs to spread more rapidly now. Consider heroin. In a relatively short time (from the end of last century) it has been introduced to areas where opiates have not been used and has replaced opium in areas where that use is traditional. Modern pharmaceuticals have spread even more rapidly.

The final point of such change would seem to be a very large variety of drugs available all over the world. However, there are very strong barriers to such complete uniformity. For example, the ban on alcohol use by Muslims is unlikely to disappear. While weakening in some areas (for example, parts of North Africa), it is strengthening in others (in Iran or Malaysia, for instance).

Changes in manner of use   In addition to the actual drugs used, the manner in which they are used is also being altered in many societies. The clearest historical trend has been away from the oral route of administration toward routes that allow for a more rapid onset of the drug's effects. The first major change occurred with the spread of smoking from the American continent. Smoking was initially associated with the use of tobacco, but it was not long before the technique was adopted for use with other drugs. Opium and marijuana are the most outstanding examples.

The second major change occurred in the last century with the development of the hypodermic needle. Of all routes of administration, intravenous is the most efficient. Although smoking is about as fast, it is relatively wasteful of the drug because of heat destruction and loss to the atmosphere. With the intravenous route the loss is negligible and the effect is almost instantaneous. This method has become common for the use of opiates, stimulants, and barbiturates. However, it has not entirely replaced other routes of administration. For example, in Hong Kong smoking of heroin is more common than intravenous injection (Spencer and Navaratnam, 1981); the same is true in India (Adityanjee, Mohan, and Saxena, 1984).

The use of this route has also necessitated the supply of drugs in soluble powder form. Drugs previously used in their raw state now have to be processed in order for them to be injectable. One result of the popularity of intravenous administration has been the decreased demand for raw opium. It has been replaced in large part by the pure drugs morphine and heroin. From the suppliers' point of view, these also have the advantage of being less bulky and therefore easier to handle.

Despite this trend, the oral route is still the favored one for many drugs. Caffeine, for example, is taken in food or beverages, and also as an over-the-counter medicine. For many drugs, injection presents certain problems. The active ingredient in marijuana is an insoluble resin-like substance which is very difficult to administer by means other than smoking or ingestion. Thus, the change toward routes of administration allowing a rapid onset is not inexorable: For some drugs there is a limit on what methods can be used, while for others there does not seem to be any tendency to move away from the slower routes.

Other changes   Another change has been a lessening of association between drug use and cultural practices. In many societies the traditional use of drugs in religious ceremonies is becoming less frequent. In other cases, such use continues, but nonreligious use is increasing in the same culture. In addition, young members of many societies are not following the traditional drug use patterns of their parents. For example, in Western society marijuana has become a very common drug. Although hardly known a generation ago, it is now the most frequently used illegal drug in Europe, North America, Australia, and elsewhere. Contrast this change with that occurring in certain areas of Morocco where marijuana use is traditional. There, the more avant-garde youth have forsaken marijuana for alcohol, a drug not approved by their parents.

The breakdown of traditional patterns of use has important consequences. Many cultures have evolved means of handling and controlling drug use. This includes various social rules concerning the amount of drug which can be used, who can use it, the occasions on which it can be used, and acceptable behavior expected under the influence of the drug. In the normal course of events these (mostly unstated) rules would be learned during childhood and adolescence. When a change such as the introduction of a new drug occurs rapidly, then the culture does not have time to adapt: There is little time to develop social rules appropriate to the culture and hardly any opportunity for learning to occur. The result may be the creation of more widespread drug problems than were ever associated with traditional patterns of use.

Another notable historic trend seems to have been an increase in problems of drug abuse. Throughout history, alcohol has been the drug most commonly associated with such problems. Recognition of them and attempts to regulate alcohol sale and consumption date from ancient times. Nevertheless, even alcohol problems may have worsened. Examination of a range of societies suggests that patterns of excessive alcohol use are most prominent in urban, industrialized societies. In contrast to alcohol, other drug problems seem to have been rare in older societies. In some cases there were strictures on the use of opium, but these were concerned more with the prevention of overdose. Where coca leaves were chewed there is little evidence for overindulgence on the scale now observed with cocaine.

Future changes Having viewed historical changes, is it possible to predict what is likely to happen in the future? One clear trend that has been mentioned already and is likely to continue, is that routes of administration which allow faster onset of action will be used in preference to slower routes. In the last few years, one manifestation of this trend has been a move away from intranasal administration (snorting) of cocaine to smoking it (at least amongst those who prefer not to use needles). To do this, the cocaine is converted to free-base or 'crack' form. The change has occurred mainly in the United States, but is likely to occur in other parts of the world as well.

A second trend, described above, has been an increase in the rate at which drug use patterns spread across countries. Whether it is a new drug, a new method of preparation, or a new route of administration, if it gains a reasonable level of popularity in one country it is likely to spread rapidly to others. Compare the spread of such changes now with the rate several hundred years ago. This trend will undoubtedly continue, making it harder for any culture to adapt to new patterns of drug use.

A third pattern of change is one over which we have some control. It is clear from a historical analysis that drugs cannot be kept solely for medical use. The most common way for a new drug to be introduced has been as a medicine. Yet there is no drug which has any liability for abuse which has remained solely for medical use (except where there are already illicit drugs that have virtually identical actions, as in the case of certain opiates). The drugs that arouse most concern in contemporary Western society, heroin and cocaine, were both hailed as wonders of modern medicine late last century. Many years before them spirits were prescribed by doctors and used solely for medical reasons. In this century, both amphetamines and barbiturates have changed from medicinal to recreational drugs.

The message is particularly important in this era. The rate of introduction of new psychoactive pharmaceutical products has been very rapid in the last thirty years. The danger is clearly that we will continue to add more and more drugs which will eventually be found in the illicit drug trade. One hopeful sign is that new drugs are now tested for abuse liability (using methods such as self-administration and drug discrimination, described in the previous chapter), thus reducing the chances of introducing a new amphetamine or heroin.

The final trend is an increasing pattern of multiple drug use. Whereas most traditional patterns involve use of one or a very few drugs, use of a much larger number is now common. Caffeine use is virtually universal in Western society, while both alcohol and nicotine are very common. Users of illicit drugs tend to indulge in a number of legal and illegal drugs. Thus, it is very common for heroin users to take drugs such as benzodiazepines, barbiturates, cocaine, and alcohol. Sometimes these are combined specifically (for example, the "speedball"—a mixture of heroin and cocaine, and antihistamine-opiate combinations), but, more commonly, an individual simply uses a wide range of drugs. Evidence from treatment centers suggests that this *polydrug abuse* is increasing.

Differences in Drug Use Within Societies

It was mentioned briefly that patterns of use vary within traditional societies. Not all members engage in drug use to the same extent. For example, adult males may be the main users of drugs, rather than females or younger members of the society. An extreme case sometimes occurs with hallucinogens where the priest or shaman is the only one to use the drug. Other members of the group simply receive an interpretation of his experience.

In tribal societies the rules determining who does and who does not use a particular drug are clearly defined. Factors such as age, sex, and social position are all important. However, in modern societies the rules may neither be so clear nor so simple. In part this occurs because modern societies are frequently more diverse. Within the society there are groups varying in ethnicity and socioeconomic status as well as age, sex, and so on. Because of this greater variability it is often more difficult to specify the patterns of use.

Sex differences   Differences in drug use according to sex are common in tribal and modern societies. However, in most cases the differences are matters of degree rather than absolutes. For example, in modern Western societies one finds greater alcohol use among men than women, although this difference is diminishing. In contrast, barbiturate and benzodiazepine use is much higher amongst women than men. As these prescription drugs have many properties in common with alcohol it is interesting to speculate whether alcohol serves the same function for men as it does for women.

Alcohol has been a predominantly male drug in Western society for some considerable period of time. In earlier days the difference in patterns of consumption was somewhat more exaggerated. Drinking was socially proscribed for women in many countries. Often, there were no real alternative drugs with similar pharmacologic activity. However, drugs with different pharmacology were sometimes used. For example, in the latter part of the last century and early in this century, legal opiates were particularly popular amongst women from a wide range of backgrounds. Just as a benzodiazepine is now the common remedy for anxiety or insomnia, laudanum or some other opiate preparation served the same function at that time.

The frequency of consumption of illegal drugs also varies according to sex. Use of heroin, amphetamines, marijuana, and so forth has been shown to be predominantly male behavior patterns. The difference appears to begin in youth and then continues into later years, these 'deviant' activities being generally most frequent amongst young men.

Ethnicity Ethnic differences in drug usage may occur within a single country due to immigration patterns, which create ethnic diversity rather than homogeneity. Each group may have brought to any one country patterns of drug use in addition to other cultural practices. These may have then remained within that ethnic group, spread to the greater population, or been eliminated through prohibition or other means.

There are many examples of ethnic groups introducing drugs into a country where they had not been traditionally used. This is occurring presently in England, where certain groups have been importing khat leaves (Kalix, 1987). While not very common at this stage, use of khat may become more frequent amongst certain ethnic groups, spread to the wider population, or may be suppressed through law enforcement.

Some of the clearest examples of successful introduction of new drugs by ethnic minorities involve the spread of alcohol and tobacco by Western nations. The English, French, and other groups with empires over the world have introduced certain drug use practises that have had devastating effects on certain peoples. Alcohol use has caused major problems in parts of North America and the South Pacific for instance, where it was previously unknown.

The Chinese introduced the recreational use of opium to many parts of the world. Spread occurred within the Chinese empire, but also as a result of Chinese immigration. Large ethnic Chinese groups can be found throughout Southeast Asia and smaller groups in countries such as Australia, England, and the United States. For many immigrants, opium had been an unaffordable luxury in China. Greater prosperity in their adopted country allowed them to indulge. In some countries, there was a strong reaction to this strange drug habit and laws against opium use were introduced partly as a result of discrimination against, and fear of, these Chinese immigrants.

Ethnic groups may also differ in their drug consumption pattern. The United States is one country that has received immigrants from many parts of the world. Of these, the drinking habits of three prominent migrant groups, the Italians, the Jews, and the Irish, have been examined in some detail (see, for example, Knupfer and Room, 1967). In their home countries, all three consumed reasonable amounts of alcohol and the people who migrated continued to do so in their adopted country. However, the normal drinking patterns among the groups differ. While a high proportion of Italians are drinkers and their average consumption is high, there are few problems of abuse. The Jews tend to drink less and drinking is strongly associated with ceremonial occasions. They too have few drinking problems, even fewer than the Italians. However, amongst the Irish a smaller proportion of the migrants were drinkers, but they had a much higher proportion of problem drinking. The Irish drinking pattern tends to be one of occasional inebriation rather than drinking smaller amounts more regularly.

Amongst the first generation born in the United States the patterns began to break down. Perhaps the most significant change occurred amongst the offspring of Irish immigrants. In contrast to their parents, a very high proportion of them were drinkers. In addition, of the three offspring groups, this group manifested the highest frequency of drinking problems.

Socioeconomic status   In many places, ethnic differences are also associated with socioeconomic differences and it is not clear which is the more important factor. There are certain instances where both appear to be critical. For example, in the 1950s and 1960s there was widespread heroin use in the black ghettos of the United States (Chambers, 1974). The drug use patterns of other black groups did not change so dramatically, nor did those of poor white people. The factors which led to heroin use seemed to occur only in those of a certain socioeconomic and ethnic status.

Similarly, the use of marijuana in Jamaica is most common amongst the poor, black laborers. In this group approximately seventy percent of the people use the drug (Comitas, 1975). Use of marijuana in Jamaica is actually a sign of being lower class. Those who wish to be upwardly mobile stop using the drug so that they will not be identified with their poor rural relations. Interestingly, the blacks did not introduce marijuana, but adopted it from the laborers who came from India.

One other reason for this socioeconomic difference in marijuana use may be its association with physical labor. Poor laborers often indicate that marijuana helps them work in difficult circumstances (Comitas, 1975). For example, prior to ploughing a field they may smoke a little marijuana. In this sense it seems to function much as a tea or coffee break does in many societies.

One pattern which can be seen repeatedly across many countries and throughout history is the adoption of a new drug first by those of high socioeconomic status and only later by the lower socioeconomic groups. When spirits were first introduced to England it was only the upper class who could afford them. Use gradually spread, and it was eventually amongst the poor that the gin epidemic occurred. Europeans of high socioeconomic status served as the conduit for the introduction of marijuana and cocaine to that continent. In England, opium use was common amongst the wealthy before it became popular with the poorer people of certain areas. Other examples include the introduction of tobacco to England, Italy, and Russia, and ether to England as well.

The first people to use such drugs were not only of high socioeconomic status, they were frequently the more avant-garde, artistic members of society. Literary figures have been quite prominent proponents of drug experimentation, particularly in Europe. Many such people were also in the forefront of the increase in drug use among Western youth in the 1960s.

The same type of pattern can now be seen in many third world countries. The drugs of the West, like other aspects of that culture, are adopted by those who are of high socioeconomic status and are less tied to the traditional ways of their society. This is the case in several North African countries (for example Egypt, Morocco) where marijuana use is traditional. The wealthier groups are rapidly adopting alcohol use from the West, while many poor people continue to use marijuana to the exclusion of alcohol.

The changes in drug use that occur within a culture are not simply from high to low socioeconomic status. Many changes are of a quite different nature. One that has already been mentioned is the change in use of opiates in the United States. At the turn of the century, most users were white middle class females who employed them therapeutically. After a period in which the popularity of opiates diminished, the most frequent users are now residents of black ghetto communities. In contrast, the modern pattern of heroin use in Britain and Australia does not show such strong socioeconomic or ethnic trends.

What is clear is that a drug is not inevitably used by a certain group within society. We cannot say that a drug is definitely a poor man's or rich man's drug. Such patterns inevitably change over time and any explanation of the different patterns of drug use in society must take into account the changing nature of these patterns.

Age One strong association which does emerge is that between illicit drug use and youth. Where a drug is prohibited by law, and that law is properly enforced, use will occur predominantly amongst the younger members of the population, particularly those in the late teenage years. It seems that this is an age of general experimentation and drugs are simply one thing that is tried and tested.

Adolescent and young adult drug use received considerable attention in the West in the 1960s and early 1970s. At that time a number of new drugs were introduced to Western countries. Others changed from the preserve of small minority groups to be used by wide sections of society. The people who brought about these changes were indeed mostly in their late teens or early twenties. While the pattern was established in the United States, it was followed in some form in Europe, Australia, and elsewhere. Perhaps the most significant of all the changes was the increase in use of marijuana. From a drug used by very few in the West it changed to the most widely used illegal drug in a relatively short period of time (Josephson, 1974). It is now the case that a significant minority of young people in Western countries experiment with the drug at some stage. In contrast, older people in those countries have virtually no experience with it.

The evidence for youthful experimentation extends across time and cultures. As mentioned above, there is an increasing pattern of alcohol use in certain countries that have a predominately Muslim culture. Many who experiment with alcohol are younger people who defy the strictures of their parents in the same way as the marijuana smokers of the West. Earlier in this century, the outbreaks of amphetamine use in Japan and Scandinavia described in Chapter One occurred mainly amongst the young people of the countries involved.

Subcultures   The notion that drug use varies considerably within a culture and that it is concentrated amongst certain groups has led to the notion of drug subcultures (Johnson, 1973). Subcultures exist mainly where the drug used is illegal (for example, the subculture associated with illegal heroin use) but also where a legal drug is used in a socially unacceptable way (for example, abuse of alcohol).

Subcultures arise because of the punitive, sometimes prohibitionist reaction of the general society. This reaction is usually strongest where the groups within the society who use the drug have relatively little power (for instance, the poor). The users of cannabis in Jamaica are an excellent example. Long persecuted for their use of the drug, they regard the laws as discriminatory on the basis of both race and socioeconomic status. While use of the drug is widespread amongst this group, they grow and use it surreptitiously.

Membership of a subculture brings with it certain codes or norms of behavior to which the participant is expected to conform. Most obviously, participants are expected to use the drug on a regular basis and derive the same advantages from such use as the other members. For example, in the 1960s many young Western users of marijuana and hallucinogens regarded themselves as becoming more spiritually aware through their drug use. Members of this particular subculture had to report such personal changes in order to conform to the group norms.

Other norms are associated with particular subcultures. For example, members may be expected to actually grow or produce the drug or to distribute it. They may have to be willing to provide the drug to other members either free or with relatively little cost. Norms may also specify use of the drug in a particular ritualistic manner. For example, marijuana users may all sit in a circle around a water pipe, each inhaling once before passing the mouthpiece on. Heroin users have "cooking up" and sharing rituals.

Drug subcultures are similar to other subcultures within our society. They are groups of people with values different in some respects from the mainstream values of their society. In the case of most drug subcultures values diverge on the question of legitimate use of banned substances. Oppressive action forces these people even further away from the mainstream of society, but is the most common reaction. Subcultures, however, have little power to oppose these forces.

However, when a subculture spreads over a wide proportion of the population the punitive measures are frequently relaxed. For example, in some Western countries marijuana use has moved from a small minority activity (often of poor, ethnic groups) to one engaged in by a wide cross-section of youth. While it was easy to severely punish members of the small marijuana subcultures of twenty-five years ago, it is much more problematic to do the same to a significant minority of youth from all socioeconomic groups. The result, in many countries, has been a relaxation of the laws associated with marijuana use.

SOCIAL DETERMINANTS OF DRUG EFFECTS
AND DRUG USE

In the previous section the focus was on the broader, sociocultural influences on drug-taking. Here it is narrowed somewhat to two types of factors which may influence not only the use of a drug, but the effects it produces. One is the set of attitudes about the effects of the drug which are prevalent in the culture or subculture. Such beliefs may determine both how a person reacts to a drug and the likelihood of her using that drug. The second concerns the more immediate social environment. It has long been recognized that the situation in which a drug is used has a profound effect on the changes which it produces. This section will examine each of these influences in turn.

Cultural Attitudes

A number of factors which may contribute to individual variability in the effects of drugs have been described in Chapters Two and Three. In addition, there are broader social influences on the way people's behavior changes after drug use. For example, one may find the same drug producing quite different effects in one society or subgroup when compared to its effects in another. If a sample of people from each was asked to describe the effects of the drug they might seem to be discussing two different, although perhaps related, compounds. The same variability may be observed in a single culture over a long time-span.

This variability is most apparent, and has been best documented, in the case of alcohol. The effects of alcohol vary from general relaxation and agreeable lessening of social rules to the extreme breaking of virtually all social rules or aggressive outbursts. In different societies one or another may be the norm. There will, of course, also be variability between individuals within a society. One account of the basis for this variability suggests that beliefs about alcohol are a major contributing factor.

Beliefs about alcohol   People's views concerning the effects of alcohol include both positive and negative aspects. The positive aspects include relaxation, decreased tension and anxiety, and greater sociability. The negative ones include physical and behavioral impairment, transgression of social rules, and increased aggression and criminality. Since the time of the ancient Greeks and Romans many of these effects have been characterized in terms of alcohol-induced disinhibition.

Recently, it has been argued by an increasing number of people (for example, Marshall, 1979; Critchlow, 1986) that the effects produced by alcohol are determined to a large degree by people's beliefs about the nature of those effects. It is suggested that the direct effects of alcohol on behavior are only weak. Much more important is that people will act out the changes they believe to occur following alcohol ingestion.

This then is the explanation for differences in alcohol effects between societies and in the same society over time. Alcohol itself is not different, nor is the body tissue on which it acts (except perhaps to some small degree). What does vary between cultures and over time is people's beliefs about the effects of alcohol. To the extent that they determine the effects of alcohol actually manifested, the behavioral variation will be of a similar kind.

One of the major beliefs about alcohol is that it acts as a disinhibitor. That is, people do things under the influence of alcohol which they would not otherwise do. For example, they may be more aggressive than normal or engage in sexual activities perhaps considered "forbidden." The exact form this disinhibition takes will depend largely on the values of the society. What is allowable and what is suppressed will vary across cultures.

It has been argued by MacAndrew and Edgerton (1969), and others since them, that disinhibition does not result directly from alcohol ingestion. Alcohol is not a solvent for our moral standards. Instead, the drug provides an opportunity for people to engage in behavior which might otherwise be prohibited. This type of phenomenon can often be observed: A drunken person behaves in an objectionable way, but the episode may be laughed off simply because the person is inebriated.

Several arguments have been put forward in support of the theories that alcohol-induced disinhibition is principally a social rather than a pharmacological phenomenon. One is that there are always limits to the disinhibition. Drunken people don't usually behave with complete abandon. Rather, the social rules are simply stretched a little further. The exact limit depends on what the people in question believe the effects of alcohol to be. A second argument is that it is quite common for societies to provide a means whereby people can engage in normally proscribed activities. Ceremonial occasions sometimes serve this function. Thus, having periods in which social rules are stretched is a common phenomenon and use of alcohol is simply one means of arranging such periods. Indeed, the need for such periods may well motivate alcohol use in some instances.

More recently, evidence from studies of alcohol-induced behavioral changes and placebo effects using the balanced-placebo design (discussed in Chapter Three) have been suggested as supportive evidence for this argument. A number of these studies have purported to show that changes in behavior occur when people believe that they have received alcohol and not if they don't. Whether they actually receive the drug or not makes little difference. For example, people might be observed to become more aggressive if they are told that they have received alcohol, but the alcohol itself may have little effect on the level of aggression. Such results would support the argument that the pharmacological effect of alcohol is relatively weak compared to the effect of people's beliefs or expectancies about alcohol.

Some researchers have attempted to go further and influence people's beliefs about what alcohol is going to do to them (Wilson and Lawson, 1976; Keane and Lisman, 1980). For example, people may be told that alcohol is going to either increase or decrease their sexual arousal. Half the subjects in a given group are then given alcohol, and half are not. The aim is to determine whether subjects' expectancies and beliefs about alcohol, as influenced by the experimenter, determine the nature of the effect observed.

In general, results from both types of studies are not entirely supportive. As mentioned in the previous chapter, methodological difficulties with many studies employing the balanced placebo design have been noted by researchers. In those studies where the most stringent procedures have been adopted, some placebo effects have been noted, but these are usually in addition to the effects of alcohol itself. Where attempts have been made to influence people's beliefs directly, there is little evidence of the effect of alcohol being altered.

In summary, the problem is to explain the considerable variability in the effects of a drug such as alcohol. Reactions may range from quiet amusement to explosive violence and destruction. One view, described here, is that this variability stems from differences in people's beliefs about alcohol. To the extent that beliefs influence our behavior, the reactions to the drug will correspond to those beliefs.

Problems with beliefs   Several arguments can be weighed against this approach. One is that there is already extensive evidence on causes of variability in the behavioral effects of drugs. In the previous chapter it was noted that a number of factors determined the way in which a behavior is influenced by a drug. These include the rate at which the behavior occurs, what the consequences of that behavior are and have been, and whether the behavior is new or is already well learned, etc.

In the case of disinhibited behavior there are several determining factors. One is the degree of inhibition. If behavior is completely suppressed (in other words, punishment has been totally effective) then a drug is unlikely to increase the probability of that behavior occurring. Disinhibition appears to occur only if there is some likelihood of the behavior occurring anyway. Thus, in societies where aggression simply never appears we would not expect alcohol to turn people into violent criminals. However, in those societies where there is a high degree of suppressed aggression, then alcohol (or some similar drug) may produce dramatic increases in this behavior. Accordingly, we do not have to resort to theories about beliefs to explain variability in the effects of alcohol—there are many other factors to consider first.

A second argument is that beliefs themselves are somewhat troublesome if it is not also acknowledged that alcohol has powerful behavioral effects. Otherwise, where do the beliefs originate? The evidence that alcohol does increase suppressed behavior (see Chapter Three) suggests that beliefs about alcohol-induced disinhibition may match reality. If these direct behavioral effects are not acknowledged then it is necessary to explain how these beliefs arose in the first place.

As a result of these problems the role of beliefs remains a little unclear. However, research in this area has shown that different societies tolerate different behavioral excesses from intoxicated persons. Such excesses may even be encouraged. For example, in some societies where social interaction is very restrained (at least by our standards), much freer interaction may be allowed and even encouraged when members are under the influence of alcohol. Clearly then, while alcohol has a direct effect, this may be moderated or enhanced by the actions of others in the society. It is interesting to note the similarity between this view and the notions of behavioral tolerance and sensitization discussed in Chapter Three. A drug can have a direct effect on behavior, but the magnitude of that effect depends on the consequences of the behavior change for the individual. A behavior change that meets with approval may be amplified, while one that meets with disapproval is likely to diminish following such consequences.

Implications   Acceptance of drug-induced behavior change has important implications for understanding drug use. If a person is allowed to do things under the influence of a drug that would otherwise be prohibited, and if some of those actions are attractive to the individual, then they may well use the drug at least partly to engage in these actions. The drug is essentially functioning as a license to engage in prohibited behavior, then. The more acceptance there is of such deviation in a society, the more likely it is that people will take drugs for exactly that reason.

One form this deviant behavior takes is to abandon all normal responsibilities. People may use a drug habitually and be labelled a "junkie" or "alcoholic." This is virtually a license to "drop out" of normal life and be excused of all sorts of otherwise unacceptable behavior. Because people are allowed this escape they may actually continue to take the drug simply to avoid dealing with their responsibilities. This phenomenon has been noted both by drug users and by those around them. As long as society treats drug users differently and tolerates behavior that would otherwise be unacceptable, some people will be motivated to continue drug use for this reason.

The difficulty for both society in general and those most closely associated with drug users is to draw a reasonable boundary between what is and what is not acceptable. On the one hand it is necessary to acknowledge that drugs do affect behavior and we cannot expect a person to act in exactly the same manner when intoxicated. On the other hand, the more allowance that is made for intoxicated persons the more such intoxication is encouraged.

The Immediate Environment

It has long been recognized that physical and social aspects of the environment at the time of drug use alter both the effect of the drug and the amount of drug used. Unfortunately, much of the data are at the experiential level—there is little empirical evidence. The effects of the setting in which the drug is taken have been reported to be particularly strong in the case of marijuana (Goode, 1973). Users indicate that a setting incorporating shared use and sensory stimulation (particularly music) is most conducive to enjoying the effects of the drug. In other situations the effect of the same dose may be small and even barely noticeable. This has caused some problems for researchers wanting to investigate the effects of marijuana in a laboratory setting.

It also seems that certain effects of a drug may be more apparent in one type of situation than another. For example, people report more physiological symptoms of alcohol when drinking alone, but more subjective changes (for example, emotional reactions) when in a group setting (Pliner and Cappell, 1974).

Many drugs induce some distress in the inexperienced user. For example, the first time user of marijuana or opiates who takes a relatively large dose may feel as though he or she has lost control and the drug has taken over. Such reactions reach an extreme in the case of hallucinogens, where they may even occur among experienced users. Anecdotal reports suggest that such reactions are more likely in unsupportive or frankly hostile environments. If the setting for drug use includes friends, is familiar, and involves shared use, this type of experience is much less likely to occur. Such an environment may also reverse a "bad trip" which has already begun.

While there has been relatively little study of the influence of the immediate environment on actual drug effects, there has been some examination of its role in modulating the amount of drug used. With many drugs (heroin, for example) only a single dose is taken at a time and there is unlikely to be much effect of the immediate environment on this dose. However, other drugs are taken in a more continuous manner and the rate of use and amount used may alter according to the setting. This is most obviously the case with alcohol and it is this drug that has received the most attention (see McCarty, 1985, for a review). Alcohol is also an interesting drug for study because it is used in a very wide range of circumstances.

Determinants of alcohol use   Alcohol use occurs predominantly in group situations. For most people solitary use is infrequent. The groups most likely to share drinking are close friends and family, and the home is the most common location. In this sense it is more often a private rather than public behavior. Drinking is also more common on weekends than weekdays.

Virtually all drinkers use the drug outside of these high frequency situations on some occasions. However, exceptions are most often found in the case of heavy rather than light or moderate drinkers. These people drink more often when alone and when in public places (especially bars). This drinking frequently occurs on top of the more common patterns of drinking at home and with friends or family. With heavier drinkers then, drinking seems to range across a wider variety of circumstances.

One way in which the immediate environment has been studied is by observation of drinking in bars. Such observation has highlighted strong social influences on drinking. For example, people drinking in a bar in groups tend to drink more than those who drink alone. This appears to be due mainly to a longer time spent drinking, although drinking rate may also be affected. Several factors may contribute to this difference. One is the norms associated with drinking groups, and a second is the simple *modeling* or *imitation effect.*

Drinking norms vary considerably from culture to culture, but in many Western countries high status among masculine drinking groups is associated with heavy drinking, accompanied by little behavioral change. The individual who drinks less than the average is looked down upon, as is the person unable to "hold" his alcohol. The actual norm in a group varies with factors such as the age and socioeconomic status of the members.

While people respond to social norms, there is a more direct effect due to modeling. A drinker will increase his or her rate in the presence of someone who is consuming alcohol more rapidly. Experiments have been conducted in bars where a confederate of the researcher sits close to a solitary drinker (see for example, Reid, 1978). Any change in drinking rate as a result of the presence of the confederate is recorded.

One important factor moderating the degree to which people are influenced by the drinking of those around them is the behavior of the other individual. If a confederate is open and friendly, then a drinker is more likely to increase his drinking to the level of the confederate; if unfriendly or neutral there is less likely to be an effect. This conforms with other research in modeling which shows that it is much more likely that a person will be imitated if he is liked than if he is disliked.

While the discussion here has concentrated on alcohol consumption, the same principles are likely to be relevant to understanding use of other drugs. There is some research to suggest that it is the case. For example, the modeling effect occurs with cigarette smokers in a similar manner to drinkers (Glad and Adesso, 1976).

CONTROL OF DRUGS

One factor which may account for some of the differences in drug use between societies and over time concerns controls over drug use. The discussion here will be concerned mainly with formal controls—that is, the laws relating to drug production, sale, and consumption. Other, less formal controls exist and will be considered briefly.

The control of drugs by rulers and governments is not a modern phenomenon. The code of Hammurabi, the oldest known set of laws, includes some which regulate the sale and consumption of alcohol. Many of the problems faced by the Babylonians in framing such laws would be similar to those we still face today. No perfect means has been discovered for regulating drug use. Indeed, in contemporary societies the problem has worsened through the introduction of a much wider range of drugs.

The Nature of Drug Control

Legislation on drug use has a variety of functions. The most obvious function, and the one most frequently given by legislators, is simply to decrease the amount of drug used. It may be the intention to reduce this as close as possible to zero or to simply maintain an acceptable rather than excessive level of consumption.

A second function is to raise revenue. Drugs are important commodities in any economy and, with the exception of those used in a medical context, most legal drugs are taxed. If revenue raising is the sole purpose, careful legislation may enable a government to increase its income without disrupting the consumption patterns to an excessive degree. However, since drug consumption may decrease with increases in price (see below), taxes can be said to have a dual purpose of both raising revenue and decreasing consumption of harmful products.

Measures taken to limit drug use may also serve other economic functions. For example, a drug which has to be imported may be a drain on the country's economy compared to another form of the drug or another drug which is home grown. The response may be to limit use of the imported drug. Such responses occurred when coffee was first introduced to Europe. As it could not be grown in the European climate it was necessary to import it. The Germans saw it as a threat to their beer industry, and its importation as a drain on funds. Various measures, including taxation, were taken to reduce coffee consumption. In Britain, heavy taxes were imposed on coffee, but not on tea because the latter was produced in British colonies. The result was a shift to tea-drinking en masse.

Depending on the purpose, drug control may range from complete prohibition at one extreme (as is the case with heroin, for example), to complete freedom (tea and coffee in countries where it is untaxed). Prohibition has degrees of severity. In many countries penalties for use vary according to the type of drug. For example, marijuana use is generally treated with greater leniency than use of opiates, stimulants, etc.

A drug generally prohibited for use may be allowable if used medically. For example, opiates and barbiturates can be taken providing they are obtained through a doctor's prescription. Indeed, only a few prohibited drugs cannot be prescribed medically. Depending on the country, this group is likely to include heroin and cocaine.

Other drugs are subject to partial controls. Some are drugs used for medical purposes but sold over-the-counter by pharmacists. Examples include antihistamines and mild stimulants (caffeine in tablet form, ephedrine). The main drug which is not used for medical purposes but is subject to partial control is alcohol. Perhaps the most regulated drug in history, its popularity has prevented prohibition in all but a few countries, and then often only temporarily. However, to control its use a very wide range of regulations have been introduced. These will be discussed in some detail below.

Nicotine in tobacco products is subject to partial regulation in some countries. Taxes and import duties are often very heavy on such products. Sale may be limited to adults, although such laws are not always strictly enforced. Increasingly, the practice of smoking is being limited to certain areas. For example, smoking may be forbidden in certain public places such as restaurants, and also in places of work. Indeed, in some Western countries controls over smoking are becoming as complex as those for alcohol.

The various legal industries associated with the production and distribution of drugs are among the most highly regulated. Companies are specially licensed and the degree of control by government is greater with this, than with many other industries. Penalties may thus accrue to manufacturers and distributors as well as users.

Assumptions Underlying Drug Control

Legislative control of drug use is based on certain key assumptions. One concerns the balance between individual rights and the broader interests of society. Critics of current government policies argue that simple use of a drug is a victimless crime which has no major adverse consequences for the rest of society. According to this view, drugs should be available to those who wish to use them, and it is not the business of government to interfere in this aspect of people's lives (see for example, Richards, 1982).

Against this, and in favor of controls, two arguments are raised. One is that there are some victims of drug use. Those that die or are injured in car accidents caused at least partially by the influence of drugs on the driver are examples. Already, an excessive level of alcohol in a driver attracts a penalty in many countries. There are also other victims, for example, those who suffer violence at the hands of someone under the influence of alcohol. Evidence now suggests that nonsmokers suffer health problems by being in the vicinity of those who smoke. In a wider sense, all such drugs can produce adverse effects on the user, which may in turn have consequences for the rest of society. This may be in the provision of health services, and in police and general welfare services. All have to be paid for by the general population, but may be used by drug users to a much greater degree.

A second argument in favor of regulation of drug use is that governments are charged with enhancing the general welfare. Having within a population a large proportion of drug users may not be advantageous for the society as a whole. It may be less able to compete economically, for example, because of reduced work output by drug users and the need to divert resources to health, welfare, etc. Therefore, the interests of a few have to be sacrificed in order to benefit the majority. The problem, of course, is that the balance between individual freedom and general welfare is not easy to strike. While most people would support the argument above in some form, there would be considerable disagreement about the exact nature of regulation.

The position taken by most governments has been to try to differentiate problem from nonproblem drug use. No government has a consistent policy which either allows or prohibits all drug use. The general approach has been to allow those drugs which are perceived not to cause problems (caffeine, for example) and those which are impossible to prohibit (alcohol, for example) and to ban others which are perceived to cause problems (opiates, marijuana, etc.). Furthermore, those that are allowed but which may cause problems are regulated in such a way as to try to minimize those problems.

One implication of this approach is that there is a clear division in society. On the one hand are those who use illegal drugs or who use the legal ones in a socially prohibited manner (in the case of excessive alcohol use, for example). On the other are those who confine their drug use to socially acceptable practices. The division is, of course, very artificial. The various reasons for regarding a drug as acceptable or not acceptable are mainly historical rather than pharmacological in nature. In the case of certain drugs, it can be argued that users are persecuted not because their drug is any more harmful, but simply that this drug has been introduced to the society more recently.

In the case of legal drugs it is assumed that problem drug use can be clearly differentiated from nonproblem drug use. This assumption is most important when considering regulation of alcohol use. Alcohol is probably the most dangerous of the drugs legally available in a wide range of societies. It causes problems which are quite obvious, but has not been prohibited due to its popularity. The rationalization for partial control is to try to minimize problem drinking while allowing people to engage in nonproblem drinking.

This assumption is often associated with the disease model of alcohol use, which itself has been strongly criticized for a number of reasons (Alexander, 1987). However, the point most relevant here is that a survey of alcohol use among the general population will not show one large nonproblem drinking group and a second, much smaller problem drinking group. Instead, there is a continuum from no drinking to severe problem drinking (alcoholism) with people ranging at all stages in between. This continuity has been observed in a number of countries, with varying average consumption levels (Epstein, 1979).

A second perspective has been to see problem drug use as deviance (Cahalan and Cisin, 1976). It is argued that problem drug users could change their ways if they really wanted to. They do not have to continue to behave in that way and with a little extra will-power and moral conviction their problems could be solved. If we do not single out these people they will have no reason to change their ways. Accordingly, the law functions as a moral stiffener. A variant on this theme sees the problem drug user as one who suffers as a result of social problems within our society. Alienation, or sense of lack of power over their lives, and the stresses of modern industrial society affect some individuals more than others. Those who cannot cope resort to drug use to ease their problems. Whether the fault lies within society or within the individual, in the end these drug users have marked themselves as different from the rest of us through their pattern of drug use.

These are the underpinnings of modern drug legislation. They can be criticized on a number of grounds, but it is perhaps more instructive to see how they came about. To understand this better it is necessary to look at changes in the international scene, particularly of this century.

International Controls on Drug Use

Up until the early part of this century use of many drugs was not strictly regulated. There were some controls, but they varied considerably from country to country and many of the drugs banned today were allowed freely then. Examples included marijuana, cocaine, and opiates. By contrast, strict anti-drug legislation is now worldwide. Penalties for use and trade in drugs are often very harsh—even the death sentence is enforced in some places. What has occurred to bring about this dramatic change?

The story is one of international "cooperation," cooperation in controlling the drug trade that is described in detail by Bean (1974). It began in 1909 with a meeting of representatives from thirteen countries in Shanghai. Little came directly from this, but the stage was set for the First International Opium Convention held at The Hague in 1912. The result was a treaty in which the signatories agreed to control the production and distribution of opium. Some countries simply banned opiates completely, while others allowed some trade under very tight controls. The group was unable to come to any agreement on cannabis.

This led to two landmark pieces of legislation. One was the *Harrison Act* in the United States and the other the *Dangerous Drugs Act* in Britain. The effect of the former was complete prohibition of opiates and cocaine. It is not clear that this was the intention of the legislators who passed the bill, but the interpretation made by the courts produced such a result. Much drug use was driven underground by the Harrison Act. In contrast, the British legislation allowed medical supply of drugs to addicts, who were to be registered. The difference then, was that the British system treated drug dependence as a medical problem whereas the American system treated it as a criminal one.

Many reasons have been given for the decision to select certain drugs for prohibition. Some suggest that opium came to be regarded as a pernicious influence because of prevalent antiChinese attitudes. It has also been argued that production and supply of the entrenched drugs (alcohol, nicotine, caffeine, etc.) were controlled by the wealthy and powerful in society. Other drugs were, if anything, a threat to businesses. Another view is simply that it was old, well-established drugs versus new ones. Given that there was some concern about the widespread use of drugs in society and the increasing number available, it was the latter group that had to go.

Whatever the reason or reasons, the process continued unabated. International control has developed under the aegis of first the League of Nations and later the United Nations. The number of drugs controlled through international treaties has escalated tremendously — from a handful in 1920 to twenty-one in 1945 and over one hundred by 1970. Restrictions have also been tightened considerably. Early treaties specified restrictions on trade only. It was left up to member countries to make their own decisions regarding controls on internal consumption. More recently, agreements have been made which encourage a common approach to domestic drug use.

The main aim of the international controls, elimination of the illegal traffic in drugs, has not been achieved. The degree of success is hard to measure, in that one does not know what the level of trade would be without restrictions, or even what exactly it is now. However, it is clear that there is still a multibillion dollar international trade in heroin and cocaine alone. The heroin, mainly from Southeast Asia, and the cocaine from Central and South America are sent all over the world. The biggest market for both drugs is the United States.

The restrictions on drug use do have some cost, particularly a loss of individual freedom. The operations of police and customs agents are objectionable to many people who feel that their right to privacy is being violated. In many countries regulating authorities who are, under most circumstances, tightly controlled, are given a virtual carte blanche in drug investigations. Of course, those whose freedom has been affected most directly are the drug users themselves, who have become criminals.

A second negative effect of controls is that they foster an increase in the price of drugs to extreme levels. The street price of drugs is almost totally unrelated to their costs of production. One result is that drug use is often difficult to maintain on a normal income. People may have to resort to criminal activities to finance their drug use. This occurs most commonly in individuals physically dependent on the drug.

A third negative effect is the absence of control over the quality of street drugs and the conditions of drug administration. Street drugs are inevitably adulterated with other substances, some of which are quite toxic and may cause serious health problems in the user (see Chapter Five). Drug administration is also a problem, particularly the reuse of needles and syringes. Dirty needles have long been known as a medium for the spread of hepatitis and, more recently, they have been shown to play a role in the spread of AIDS.

Regulation of Alcohol Use

Except for a few countries, one drug which has not been banned is alcohol. Despite the adverse effects of this drug and the dependence problems inevitably associated with its use, it remains extremely popular. However, as mentioned, alcohol is usually tightly regulated. There are a number of ways in which this is done and these will be discussed in the following paragraphs. More detailed reviews can be found in Popham, Schmidt, and de Lint (1976), Moore and Gerstein (1981), and Holder (1987).

Monopoly vs. competition   It has been argued that the competitive nature of the alcohol business in many countries serves only to stimulate consumption. The different alcohol producers use advertising and marketing techniques in order to promote consumption of their own brand. If this competitive element was removed then overall consumption could decline.

The best known experiments with a monopoly system have been in Sweden (see Chapter One). The Gothenberg and later the Bratt system involved both monopolies and individual rationing. There is good evidence that the approach was effective. However, individual rationing rather than a monopoly may have been the key element in the system.

It is interesting to note that alcohol consumption does not appear to be any lower in countries that do not have a capitalist economic system. In the U.S.S.R., for example, consumption is high and alcoholism is a major social problem. However, one does not know what the situation would be if more competition were allowed amongst the alcohol businesses of that country.

The only other evidence comes from a comparison of states in the United States which have a monopoly distribution system, with those that have a competitive system. Comparisons between the two groups shows no difference in levels of consumption or indicators of alcohol damage such as mortality from cirrhosis of the liver (Popham, Schmidt, and de Lint, 1976). However, it should be noted that this comparison has limited utility in that many aspects of the alcohol business remain competitive in the monopoly states. In particular, advertising is the same in the two sets and there is approximately the same choice of products. Controls are often exercised over spirit distribution only, and not on distribution of wine and beer.

Outlets Governments have sought to control drinking by limiting the number of outlets for alcoholic beverages. Special licenses are usually required to do this and they are usually difficult to obtain. In fact, the evidence suggests that with one exception, there is no relation between level of consumption and outlet density (Popham, Schmidt, and de Lint, 1978). People do not drink more if alcohol is available from a greater range of locations.

The exception arises when outlet density is very low. That is, it is not merely inconvenient to get to one, but nearly impossible. In such cases, as with total prohibition, consumption seems to drop, but there is also an increase in illegally produced alcohol. Including this source, the total amount consumed is usually less than would be the case if alcohol was more widely available.

Above these minimal densities there seems to be little relation. Some studies have found a slight increase in consumption with increased outlet density, while others have detected a slight decrease. These findings have encouraged liberalization in many parts of the world, with alcohol sold in a wide variety of establishments.

Another recent trend of this kind has been to increase the number of hours and days during which alcohol is available for sale. Rather than the enforcement of strict regulations, a more permissive view is taken. Unfortunately, there is little evidence on the effects of such changes. That which exists suggests that certain types of changes (for example, allowing Sunday trading) may lead to an increase in consumption and associated problems, while others (extending daily hours) may alter drinking patterns while having little effect on overall levels of consumption. Outlets have also been regulated in other ways. For example, in many places they are not to be located near schools, churches, etc. Whether this influences consumption either in the short- or long-term is not known.

Drinking age One of the main controls over availability concerns the customers rather than the drinking establishments. Laws regarding the minimum age at which alcohol can be bought and consumed in public exist almost everywhere. The usual age is in the eighteen to twenty-one year range. The situation is slightly more complex in some places (for example certain states of the United States) which differentiate between beer and wine (which may be sold to anyone over eighteen) and spirits (which may be sold only to those twenty-one and over).

Those in favor of a higher drinking age argue that it protects the young at a time when they may be vulnerable to external influences. In addition, they suggest that lowering the drinking age to eighteen really means allowing sixteen and seventeen year olds to drink, as laws are often very difficult to enforce. The opposing view is that the young drink anyway, so why shouldn't this be brought out into the open. Controls, they believe, may only encourage young people to drink in a secretive manner, rather than an open, more natural way.

In recent years the latter view has been most influential and the legal drinking age has been reduced in many places. This has provided scientists the opportunity to collect data concerning the effects of such changes. One of the main measures has been the frequency of alcohol-associated road accidents involving eighteen to twenty year old drivers. Data collected in Australia, Canada, and the United States show an increase in such accidents when the drinking age is reduced from twenty-one to eighteen (Douglass, 1980). Furthermore, where this change has been reversed (for example in the state of Michigan) such accidents have decreased (Wagenaar, 1982).

Although seemingly conclusive, some caution should be expressed concerning these results. One confounding factor is that other liberalizations are often associated with lowering the drinking age. For example, the same piece of legislation may change the age from twenty-one to eighteen and extend the hours in which alcohol may be sold. It would be presumed that the former would be responsible for changes in the accident rate of eighteen to twenty year-old drivers, but this cannot be proven. It is also important to note that increases in accidents may only be temporary. Some people have argued that longer-term changes are not nearly so significant (Miller, Nirenberg, and McClure, 1983).

This latter conclusion may well be expected on the basis of psychological research reported in the last chapter. Drivers inexperienced in the use of alcohol will be those most disrupted by the drug. With increasing experience of driving while intoxicated, behavioral tolerance should develop and the impairment due to alcohol diminish. A dramatic jump in accident rate should be expected when the whole group of eighteen to twenty year olds suddenly begins driving under the influence of alcohol for the first time. After a while it should only be the eighteen year olds who are affected in this way—by the time they get to nineteen some behavioral tolerance should have developed.

Other evidence has shown increases in juvenile crime rates and general levels of consumption at a lower drinking age. Although there are problems with interpreting all these data, the evidence certainly suggests increased problems stemming from lower drinking age. Perhaps the most important question, and one that remains to be answered, is whether the changes will persist, or are only temporary.

Taxes and price control   One of the oldest types of controls on drug use has been the imposition of taxes by government. Taxes have the additional benefit of increasing government revenue and discouraging overpricing. They have been implicated in the reduction of excessive drinking dating back to the London gin epidemic of around 1720–1750.

The effectiveness of taxes in curbing consumption relates to an issue raised in Chapter Three: *price elasticity,* that is, whether consumption changes markedly with price (the item is termed price elastic) or whether price has little effect on demand and consumption (the item is then price inelastic). Many would argue that drug use in general is price inelastic, particularly among heavy users. At least with alcohol this may not be the case, however.

Evidence from a number of countries at various times shows that alcohol consumption changes with price (Popham, Schmidt, and de Lint, 1978; Moore and Gerstein, 1980). The most common change, an increase in price, results in a decrease in consumption. What is of particular interest is that heavy drinking rates decrease. It is not just a matter of light and moderate drinkers changing their behavior, the heavy drinkers do so as well. In addition, the deleterious effects of drinking seem to diminish when prices are increased through taxation. These include deaths from cirrhosis of the liver and car accidents involving intoxicated drivers.

These findings certainly suggest that taxation on alcoholic beverages can be an effective instrument of public policy. Higher prices diminish drinking and its adverse effects. Some have suggested that governments ought to adopt a rational pricing policy with respect to alcohol. Such a policy may involve adjustments to prices in response to changes in income, and also equating the costs of different drink types (beer, wine, and spirits) in terms of alcohol content. However, there is a problem with price controls — the poor are generally affected more than the wealthy (though see Ashton, Casswell, and Gilmore, 1989, for a contrasting example).

One view is that a policy encouraging beer drinking could be beneficial. Such a policy could lessen the differential effect on the poor. However, there are difficulties with this. In particular, its proponents assume that beer is not used for heavy intoxication and is not used by alcoholics. While this may be true in some countries, it is certainly not true in others, such as Australia.

In considering differential pricing for the various types of beverages, another confounding factor is that price elasticity may vary according to the particular beverage. There is evidence for example, that beer is more price inelastic, and spirits the most price elastic (Ornstein, 1980). The generality of these findings needs to be confirmed.

Drinking consequences   Some laws are not concerned with the regulation of drinking itself, but with certain consequences of drinking. Two such laws refer to public drunkenness and driving while intoxicated. A third relates to the responsibility of the premises on which the alcohol was consumed.

Public drunkenness is a very old offense. However, it has become less common recently with many governments removing it from their statutes.

Several reasons have been given for this change. One is simply that the law is ineffective. For the most part it is a small group of repeat offenders who make up the majority of cases. Despite continued convictions they do not seem to change their drinking practises. Secondly, it is said that an "enlightened" view does not perceive such people as criminals, but rather as individuals who have a specific illness.

The effects of such legal changes are largely unknown. There seems to have been little attempt to systematically study them. The issue is also complicated by the fact that in many places public drunks are taken into protective custody until they sober up—usually this lasts until the following morning. The treatment is similar, but the difference is simply that the person is no longer charged with an offense.

One of the major adverse consequences of alcohol use is the increase in frequency of motor vehicle accidents, with its associated deaths and injuries. In many places attempts have been made to reduce this toll by heavy penalties (fines, suspension of license, jail) for driving while intoxicated (see Ross, 1984, and Homel, 1988, for reviews). While some laws governing this behavior have been around for a long time, they were supported by the police judgment of intoxication. The invention of the breathalyzer, a device for measuring blood alcohol level through breath samples, made drunk-driving laws much easier to enforce.

A number of studies have been carried out to determine the effect of introducing drunk-driving laws based on use of the breathalyzer. Particular interest has focused on random breath-testing—allowing the police to pick drivers at random to determine their blood alcohol level. Frequently, the results have been disappointing. They show a large decrease in the frequency of intoxicated drivers for a few months following introduction of the law. However, after a period of time the frequency gradually returns to its old level. The only exceptions seem to occur where the rate of testing is very high, so that virtually all drivers have been tested at least once. It appears that people respond to initial warnings at the time of introduction, but if they have no personal experience being tested, eventually return to their normal practices.

The final type of regulation involves the source of the drinks rather than the drinker. It is increasingly argued that places that sell alcohol have a responsibility not to serve an intoxicated customer. And it goes without saying that customers should not be allowed to drink to an intoxicated state while in an establishment.

Government efforts have been directed mostly toward training staff employed on licensed premises. The staff are instructed to differentiate levels of intoxication and to handle customers who become difficult when refused a drink. While there are a few regulations concerning such practices, action in the courts may come mainly through civil cases. A person suffering injuries from an accident with a car controlled by an intoxicated driver may sue the licensed premises that allowed the person to become so intoxicated. Such attempts at civil action have only just begun appearing, but have the potential to markedly change the practises of bars, restaurants, and the like.

Perspectives on alcohol controls   This brief review has indicated the very broad nature of attempts to control alcohol use. Some have met with little success, while others have had a demonstrable effect. Even these could be improved so as to make them more effective and such changes are likely to occur gradually. However, any discussion should be kept in perspective: Alcohol problems are still very common in many societies and adverse consequences of drinking cause major personal, social, and economic difficulties. It is unlikely that this can be changed to any major extent in the near future.

A second issue concerns other drugs. Many agree that prohibition is not working with marijuana and other drugs, and we need to look at alternatives. One is to legalize the drugs, but with strict controls. Can anything be learned about the possibilities for control from our experience with alcohol? The answer depends to a great extent on the drug under consideration. Alcohol is a potent drug that produces marked changes in behavior (many of them adverse), has dangerous physical effects, and can induce strong physical dependence. It is unlikely that we would ever completely legalize any other drug that fits that description. Opiates may be made available from highly controlled medical sources, but controls are unlikely to be lessened to any greater extent. Similarly, the problems associated with amphetamine and cocaine use are of sufficiently greater magnitude to warrant a degree of caution.

More realistically, the drug most likely to be legalized in Western societies is marijuana. It does not have the range of adverse effects produced by alcohol, does not result in the same marked behavioral changes (at the doses usually taken), and does not induce strong physical dependence. Nevertheless, if it were to be legalized controls would need to be exercised. Indeed, one course would be to legalize with a maximum degree of control and, gradually, as the drug became more accepted into the culture and assuming no major problems ensued, to lessen the controls.

A successful control system might incorporate a monopoly rather than competition in the distribution and sale of the drug. If possible, a system of individual records of purchase would be kept. Availability may be limited to certain outlets and the drug only sold to those of a certain age. Taxation would be used to ensure a relatively high price. The basis of comparison may have to be the cost of alcohol, at least in the first instance. Penalties may be invoked for driving or operating other machinery under the influence of the drug.

The difficulties associated with both prohibition and complete freedom of drug use suggest that legislation designed to allow drug use, but to limit it as far as possible, may be the best solution. The basis of any such plan must be the information we have obtained from years of experience in dealing with alcohol—a drug which, if it had been invented only yesterday, would certainly have been outlawed.

The Role of Medicine

Throughout history medicine has been intimately involved in both the spread and control of drugs. It was noted in Chapter One that perhaps the only thing shared by the majority of drugs described there was that they had at one time been used for medicinal purposes. Many still are, while others are no longer used, either because they have been found to be ineffective (for example, tobacco) or have been replaced by other drugs (for example, heroin).

Nonmedical use has both preceded and followed medical use. In some cases a drug introduced for recreational, religious, or other reasons may later be reckoned to have medicinal properties. This is relatively uncommon, but probably occurred in some countries with the use of tobacco. Alternatively, a drug may be used at first for medicinal purposes and then only later be diverted for recreational pursuits. In some countries this seems to have been the case with opiates; it is certainly the case with a number of modern pharmaceuticals including amphetamine.

Medicine has long held a position of power over the distribution of drugs. While this has been most obvious in recent times with the delineation of precise legal roles for medical practitioners, it is not an altogether new phenomenon. Doctors have jealously guarded their privileges over the centuries. For example, the general use of opium in Western countries in the last century and early in this century was opposed by doctors who saw self-medication as a threat to their profession (Parssinen, 1983). Such attempts at control can be traced back even further to the shamans. Half doctors, half priests, in various societies they have regulated and controlled drug use. In some South American societies such control was extreme — to the point where they were the only ones who used certain hallucinogenic drugs. The justification for their usage was attributed to their ability to communicate with the gods while in a drug-intoxicated state.

The medical profession has always guarded its power very carefully. As long as people are unable to obtain certain drugs without a doctor as an intermediary, medicine reaps an enormous economic reward. Accordingly, they have a strong vested interest in tight control over the availability of drugs. This has been demonstrated repeatedly in the lobbying for new drug restrictions. While the medical profession provides a body of expert opinion on drugs, it should also be acknowledged that they have their own interests to protect.

In modern times the control of medicinal drugs has largely been effective. There are certain recognized problems, such as the overprescribing of antianxiety drugs. And new drugs seem to bring new problems, although these are not always recognized immediately. However, the pharmaceutical industry, the medical profession, and the research community have combined to introduce drugs superior to those of earlier generations. These include safer drugs (for example, the benzodiazepines) and drugs that have lower abuse potential (newer opiates). This process is likely to continue.

Other Controls

Most of the controls considered up to this point are legal controls. They are determined by governments and enforced by the police and other apparatuses of the state. However, many more informal mechanisms of control exist in addition to these formal, legal ones. One source of such control is religion.

Perhaps the best known and most effective religious ban on drug use is the Muslim injunction against alcohol. This began with Mohammed (A.D. 570–632), reputedly because of extensive alcohol abuse at the time, and continues to the present day. While it carries the force of law in some countries (Saudi Arabia, for instance), in many others the ban is maintained solely by the force of religion.

Religion may also help moderate drug use. Earlier it was mentioned that drinking problems tended to be infrequent in societies where alcohol was strongly associated with ceremonial (often religious) occasions. The religions of Central and South America also played an important role in regulating the use of hallucinogens, and perhaps in the regulating of coca as well.

Other sources of control are discussed elsewhere in this chapter. They include sociocultural controls, which are often associated with religious controls, and parental control over drug use in the young. Such controls are not always uniform throughout a society (as laws are), particularly in modern societies. Nevertheless, they can be as real and as strong as the more formal regulations.

THE NATURAL HISTORY OF DRUG USE

A number of different types of social influences governing the use of drugs have been described above.

This section will examine how social and other factors come together to influence the behavior of the individual with a drug problem. In particular, what is the background of people who develop drug problems? What happens during the period of the drug problem, and how do they give it up, if at all? Some related material has already been covered — in the previous chapter personality factors associated with drug use were discussed. While these will not be considered in detail again, various factors which predispose an individual to drug use will be considered.

Predisposing Factors

One factor over which an individual has no control is genetic heritage. A difficulty in studying the role of inherited factors has been the problem of the relatively low incidence of many types of drug problems, such as heroin or amphetamine abuse. Much greater frequencies are needed for any sort of genetic analysis. For this reason alcohol problems are the only ones that have been subject to detailed genetic analysis (see Crabb, McSwigan, and Belknap,

1985, and Schuckit, 1987, for reviews; Peele, 1986, presents a somewhat critical perspective).

Some of the most convincing evidence comes from studies of adopted children. The results show that a child's chances of eventually developing alcoholism are considerably enhanced if they have an alcoholic biological parent, but not if they have an alcoholic adopted parent. Estimates vary, but for males there may be four times the risk of developing alcoholism as a consequence of having alcoholic biologic parents.

Other studies have used different methods — comparing monozygotic with dizygotic twins, for example. There is also support from animal studies showing that rat strains differ in their preference for alcohol and this characteristic can be selected by appropriate breeding. However, it is also clear that inheritance is likely to be complex. For example, there may be a different mode of inheritance for men and women. It has also been suggested that genetic factors only play a role in a certain subset of alcoholism cases. Exactly what is inherited (a different way of metabolizing alcohol, greater inherited tolerance, etc.) is also a matter for investigation. Thus, while it is clear that genetic predispositions are important, their exact nature and role have yet to be determined.

A number of sociodemographic factors have been shown to have some relation to later drug use. For example, several studies have noted a much higher incidence of illegal drug use amongst people raised in urban rather than rural environments (Vaillant, 1966; Nyberg, 1979). Drug use is often identified with particular social classes, and religious and ethnic groups. However, it is not possible to give clear statements about the role of such factors. The nature of the association between use of a particular drug and various socio-demographic factors depends on the particular country and the particular historical time. For example, in the United States heroin is used in large part by black and Hispanic people who live in poor urban environments. In contrast, heroin use in Australia spreads across the socioeconomic range and is not found to any great extent in any one particular group. Nevertheless, certain environments may provide both access to the greater availability of drugs and pressure to use them.

A more immediate influence is the drug use of an individual's parents. Some have suggested that children's modeling of their parents is very general, and what they learn primarily is to rely on drugs in much the same way (Smart and Fejer, 1972). Rather than solving problems by other means, drugs are instead used to provide immediate relief. According to this view, children may use different drugs than their parents, but they use them in a similar manner.

There is some evidence to suggest that this is the case. A direct modeling effect occurs whereby children are likely to use the drugs used by their parents, whether they are legal or not. There are also cross-drug effects; parents' high-level use of alcohol for instance, predisposes their children to use of illegal drugs (Kandel, 1974).

Other aspects of parental behavior can play an important predisposing role. For example, a number of prospective studies examining the development of alcohol problems have shown that the presence of marital conflict, a lack of contact between child and parents, and poor parental style (for example a lack of affection or interest) are all significant predisposing factors (Zucker and Gomber, 1986). It has been suggested that the best protection against drug problems is a cohesive family structure with a proscriptive parental style (Blum and Associates, 1972). In such environments, development of self-control is encouraged and there is respect for such traditional institutions as the law. It may be that children raised in such environments are likely to be less independent and rebellious, and consequently less likely to experiment with drugs (see Chapter Three discussion on personality). To date this can only be regarded as an hypothesis. Nevertheless, there is clear evidence that certain elements in the family environment contribute to drug use.

The Development of Drug Abuse

As mentioned above, one characteristic of problem drug use that is reasonably predictable is the age at which it begins. It appears that the period from adolescence to the early twenties is the main time in which drug problems develop, with the late teens being the greatest period of risk. A person without any drug problems by the midtwenties is very unlikely to develop them. One exception may occur with alcohol. Heavy drinking patterns usually develop in this late teens through early twenties period, but escalation to alcoholism often occurs later in life (Vaillant, 1983).

As described in this and in the previous chapter, many people who develop drug problems have certain backgrounds and personality characteristics. One question is whether these differences also lead to other kinds of deviant behavior in childhood and adolescence. If there is continuity, then those who are going to become drug abusers should manifest certain behavioral characteristics prior to commencement of their drug careers.

There is some evidence that this is the case. The rebelliousness characteristic of many drug abusers is often apparent at the childhood and adolescent stage. It may be manifested in a number of ways, such as in their having problems with authority while at school, poor academic performance, more frequent absences from school, greater involvement in petty crime, and a high frequency of aggressive acts (Kandel, 1978; Zucker and Gomberg, 1986).

Such behavior patterns may begin at a very early age and continue through the teenage years. Research is continuing on this issue, but some investigators have suggested that we may eventually be able to detect children with a higher than normal probability of developing drug problems as early as kindergarten years (Kellam, Simon, and Ensminger, 1983). However, not everyone who has drug problems will have had a rebellious childhood or youth — such behavior cannot be regarded as a perfect predictor of later drug use.

One factor that will determine whether a teenager begins use of a drug and then develops a pattern of drug abuse will be whether or not she has been exposed to drugs. This can occur via family or friends. As mentioned above, the influence of family is most direct in the case of drugs actually used by the parents. Whether it is a marijuana infusion given to children in Jamaica, tea given to Western children, or wine given to children in countries such as France and Italy, early exposure is likely to predispose a person to later use.

The other influence on initiation and patterns of drug-taking is peer interaction. This process has been most closely studied in the case of marijuana (Kandel, 1974). Research has shown that marijuana use by close friends is the strongest determiner of use. Marijuana users have many more friends who use the drug than do nonusers, and the likelihood of marijuana use increases with the number of drug-using friends. This does not imply that there is an automatic effect however; there are many nonusers who have a number of marijuana-using friends.

Although there is considerably less evidence for other drugs, the situation is almost certainly the same. Introduction to illicit drug use occurs mainly via friends and the likelihood of such use is dependent on the number of drug-using friends in the person's environment. Continued use relies on the maintenance of a group of drug-using friends. The association of drug use with certain identifiable groups in society (for instance certain socioeconomic classes, geographical groups, ethnic groups) may be explained partly by such patterns of influence. Once drug use begins within a group, then an increasing number of individuals in the group are likely to be initiated into drug use around the time they reach adolescence. Where the spread of use is especially rapid people have employed the term 'epidemic' because of similarity to the spread of a contagious disease.

The progression from initiation to drug abuse is a relatively long one in most cases. Popular accounts often suggest that users are 'hooked' from their first use of heroin and alcoholics doomed from their first drink. However, estimates from the actual experience of addicts suggest a much longer period. In the case of heroin, reports vary, with averages centering around a year. However, the variability is considerable: Some people progress to physical dependence in a few weeks while others may be occasional users for many years before escalating their use (Winick, 1974; Robins, 1979). An unknown but significant number never progress to heroin dependence, but maintain a pattern of occasional use. A description of this rarely studied group is given in Zinberg (1979). In countries such as Australia the majority of heroin users fall into this category.

The same pattern is seen with alcohol. The progression from a moderate to a heavy drinker may take many years, but the variability is considerable (Polich, Armor, and Braiker, 1981; Vaillant, 1983). Unfortunately, we lack detailed knowledge of this progression for any drug. The factors that determine whether this progression occurs at all and the rate at which it occurs are poorly understood.

Patterns of Abuse

The actual pattern of use varies considerably according to the drug taken (see Chapter One). For example, amphetamine abuse is often characterized by repeated binges of several days' duration interspersed with periods of abstinence lasting days or weeks. Chronic amphetamine users who regulate intake so as to maintain relatively constant blood levels are rare. On the other hand, opiate users are usually characterized in this way and many heavy barbiturate users probably can be seen to show the same pattern.

Changing patterns of use　While there may be a general pattern of use associated with each particular drug, not everyone conforms to this pattern exactly. There is considerable variability both between individuals and in many individuals over a long time span. Both types of variation can be illustrated using data on alcoholism. First however, certain limitations of the data should be noted. The type of individual history obtained in a study is influenced strongly by the nature of the initial sample. Ideally, one should obtain a representative sample of prealcoholic days. This is not always possible, and certain biases have been introduced in studies where the sample is a group detected at treatment stage, for example. Demographic characteristics of the sample, such as age and socioeconomic status, may also have some bearing on the results. The biases of the researchers are also worth considering—debates on the nature of alcoholism arouse intense passions on both sides.

Two main views have emerged concerning the development of alcoholism. A traditional view holds that it is progressive and ends only in death. A typical scenario would involve introduction to regular alcohol use in the early teens, problem drinking with frequent heavy bouts in the late teens, and a gradual worsening as the person becomes less able to control his drinking. Unless he breaks the pattern by giving up altogether then he is doomed to continue in this manner. An alternative view is that there is no clear progression to the state of alcoholism. It is argued that the stages that some have suggested have not been borne out by close examination of the actual lives of alcohol abusers. The many who give up drinking entirely and those who return to a more normal drinking pattern after many years are also cited in evidence.

In truth, both views could be supported if one selects the appropriate group of alcohol abusers (Vaillant, 1983). There are those who seem to go on getting worse and for whom there seems little hope. There are also those who show little 'progression' and are eventually able to alter this behavior in favor of abstinence or more normal drinking patterns.

One argument against the progression notion concerns the variability in amount used by an individual over time. It is often thought that the pattern of intake of an alcohol abuser is relatively stable from day-to-day. Some tend to drink constantly through the day while others drink at a high rate for short periods (for example, first thing in the morning or in the evening after work). However, it appears that these patterns are not constant. Instead, most spend a considerable part of every year abstinent. Drinking in another portion of each year would more closely resemble the pattern of a moderate drinker rather than an abuser. Thus, perhaps only a part, or a little over half of each year of heavy drinking could be termed an alcoholic pattern.

Those arguing against the progressive nature of alcohol abuse cite these findings as evidence in their favor. They suggest that drinking is periodic rather than progressive. In many cases the periods of abstinence or normal drinking become longer until, finally, the individual does not return to problem drinking again.

There is also evidence that a similar, changing pattern of use occurs with other drugs. Initial opiate use generally remains occasional for some time. While many cease using the drug at this point or continue to use at this frequency, in some there is escalation to more regular use and, eventually, physical dependence. Even at this stage there are periods of abstinence and even regression to occasional use, as is the case with alcohol. The abstinence periods sometimes last as long as several months (Winick, 1974; Robins, 1979).

There are a number of reasons why a person physically dependent on a drug such as heroin or alcohol may cease using it for a period of time. Cost of the drug is one factor, particularly where the substance is an illegal one. Being able to supply the money necessary to maintain a heroin habit can eventually become too difficult. Alcohol is less of a problem, but money considerations may nevertheless be important. Social pressure from family, employer, or friends may be a major contributor. Health problems resulting from drug use may also be influential. The drug abuser has an impact on society during the period of his or her use. This influence is felt most by those directly involved with the individual—his or her family and friends—but also by the wider society through increased crime and greater health problems, etc. The interaction goes, of course, both ways. Those affected by drug abuse endeavor to influence the drug abusers (for instance attempt to persuade an individual to stop, fund treatment centers, provide pressure to increase penalties for use) and this in turn, alters what the drug abuser does. The effects on families and one major impact on general society—the crime committed by drug abusers— will be discussed in the following paragraphs.

Drug abuse and families   The families of drug abusers suffer considerably. Both divorce rate and general marital instability are higher among alcoholics and heroin addicts than in the general population, and the same is likely to be true for other drug abusers (Robins, 1979; Vaillant, 1983). A number of reasons could be given for this. One is that frequent use of either drug may result in considerably impaired sexual functioning in males. Another result of frequent drug use may be financial problems. These may be due simply to the cost of the drug, or the inability of the heavy user to maintain stable employment.

An alternative view is that marital difficulties are inevitable due to the predisposition of people who become dependent on a drug. Those who would argue for personality 'defects' amongst heavy drug users may also suggest that marital difficulties are more likely because of those personality problems, even apart from the effects of prolonged, heavy drug use (see Paolino and Mc-Crady, 1977). Unfortunately, there is little evidence that can be used to judge this view. An older variant of the idea that the marital difficulties are predetermined held that it was the wives of alcoholics who had psychological problems. It was argued that no one should opt to marry an alcoholic—therefore, anyone who did must be disturbed in some way. This view has not been backed up by any clear, substantive evidence.

Children of drug abusers suffer as a result of the practices of their parent or parents. As was noted earlier, people who lead an abnormal lifestyle tend to influence their children in that direction. In addition, the children are brought up in an environment which frequently involves marital instability, financial difficulties, violence (in the case of alcohol), crime (particular if the drug is an illegal one), and various health and psychiatric problems which the user may suffer. Many of these children grow up to be content, well-adjusted adults, but the frequency of social and psychological problems is higher than average amongst this group (see for example, Schaeffer, Parsons, and Yohman, 1984).

While the fact that a person is using drugs excessively may have a considerable influence on those in his or her immediate family, the influence may also work in the opposite direction. Spouses and children may alter the course of a drug abuser's career, primarily for the better. There are many instances of addicts giving up following or prior to marriage, or under strong pressure from a spouse. Thus, the duration of heavy drug use may be influenced strongly by the reaction of the immediate family.

Drug abuse and crime   A common view sees the drug user as a criminal who creates havoc in our otherwise orderly society. Drug use is seen as being confined to those who use illegal drugs, although alcohol abusers may also be included. While there is an association between crime and drug use (apart from the obvious criminal act of using illegal drugs), the situation is somewhat more complex than such views might suggest. There is considerable variation in the type of crime a drug abuser is likely to commit. There is also the question of etiology: Perhaps the criminal behavior actually precedes the drug abuse and the latter is simply a manifestation of the former. These issues have been discussed in detail by McGlothlin (1978).

The relationship between crime rates and use of certain drugs is well established. For example, crime rates appear to be several times higher in marijuana users as compared to nonusers. The same type of relationship exists for alcohol users as compared to nonusers. However, the type of crime differs somewhat. There is a clear association between alcohol and violent crime (at least in those Western countries where surveys have been done). Only the barbiturates—which share a number of properties with alcohol—seem to influence violence in the same way. No such relationship exists for marijuana users.

There is evidence that use of illegal drugs is simply one aspect of a general pattern of delinquent behavior. Teenagers who begin illegal drug use are also likely to have committed other criminal acts beforehand, whether or not they have been caught. It is likely that this relationship may be sufficient to explain the higher crime rates of marijuana users. It is not so much that marijuana use causes crime (except, of course, the crime of using the drug), but that those who use marijuana are also the type of people more likely to commit criminal acts. Thus, the drug itself is benign and cannot be associated directly with heightened criminal behavior.

The same relationship exists in the case of other illegal drugs. Those likely to break the law in taking the drug are also likely to have a preexisting pattern of delinquency which is the antecedent of both drug use and criminal behavior. In beginning drug use the pattern of criminal and delinquent behavior does not change greatly.

Some drug users may have little preexisting criminal tendency but resort to crime when the cost of the drug forces them to do so. Many heroin users may fall into this category. It is known that the crime rate of users increases with the beginning of their drug careers and declines when they cease taking the drug. Furthermore, even during their drug-using careers crime rates drop off during periods of low or no drug use. The nature of the crime also suggests that it functions mainly to generate income. In the case of a drug like heroin, both preexisting criminal tendencies and the need to finance an expensive habit seem to account for the criminal behavior which is associated with use of the drug.

Only in the case of alcohol and barbiturates is there any evidence of a direct causal link between drug use and criminal behavior. The evidence that aggressive behavior is heightened under the influence of these drugs is consistent with the results of experimental work with animals, indicating that alcohol enhances aggression (Berry and Smoothy, 1986). It is also consistent with a general disinhibiting effect whereby suppressed behavior becomes more probable (see Chapter Three). Rates of criminal behavior probably underestimate the level of violence associated with alcohol use in that much of it appears to occur in private. It is also worth noting that high levels of alcohol intoxication may also predispose a person to be a victim of violent crime (Welte and Abel, 1989). Those most closely connected with problem drinkers often suffer considerably in this respect.

Terminating Drug Use

Earlier, it was suggested that the onset of problem drug use usually occurs in the late teens or perhaps early twenties. Exceptions may occur, but this seems to be the most common time, particularly in the case of illegal drugs. Evidence has been presented showing that the career of a drug abuser is not a continuous progression but a series of stops and starts. Is this pattern never-ending, or do people eventually cease their drug use?

In the case of heroin users, it seems that there is a limit for most people (Robins, 1979). The average period of use is around ten years or less. The variation is considerable: Some people are dependent for only a few years while others may continue high rate usage for twenty years. The typical, average pattern involves onset around age twenty and termination around age thirty. Older addicts have either started later or are those with a longer career than the mean.

On average the careers of alcohol abusers seem to be longer (Vaillant, 1983). Rather than giving up in their late twenties or thirties, they seem to continue on into their forties. Some data indicate that a considerable number of alcohol abusers cease or moderate their drinking by about age fifty, but there is some disagreement on this point. While it appears that many do, there are also a number who continue drinking until they die at a relatively young age, often in their fifties.

There is relatively little information about the careers of other types of drug users. One problem is that many drugs have not been widely available for a long period of time. As a result, it has not been possible to trace the full careers of a significant number of individuals. For example, cocaine has become fashionable again in the West only in recent years. In the areas from which it originates moderate use throughout an individual's lifetime is the norm. The patterns of abuse sometimes seen in other countries do not seem to have a parallel among traditional users.

If it is true that many drug abusers eventually stop, how do they do so? One suggestion is that the natural breaks in their drug-taking simply become longer. Eventually, a break occurs that is not terminated by resumption. Some of these breaks may be serious attempts at giving up. Repeated attempts are also the norm even where there are few or no natural breaks. For example, smokers tend to have had several serious, but unsuccessful attempts at stopping prior to a successful one (Schachter, 1982).

It appears from these observations that a person does not simply cease taking a drug in a sudden manner. The repeated attempts may occur over many years, each associated with a strong level of commitment and effort.

Some of these are accompanied by therapy provided by a clinic, counseling service, doctor, or other agency. Such repeated attempts refute the notion that "willpower" is all that is needed. It would appear that if that were the case then most addict careers would be considerably shorter.

One question is whether people are actually helped by treatment or not. While it will be considered in more detail in Chapter Six, the question is of some relevance here. Assessment of the effectiveness of treatment is very difficult to gauge, in that those who present for therapy are often those with the worst problems. Nevertheless, there is evidence that therapy is of some use in helping people moderate or completely eliminate their drug use. Undergoing therapy is only one factor, however, and there are many others which may also enhance the chances of success. For example, changed family or employment circumstances may provide the incentive for an individual to stop drug-taking.

Two possible outcomes often result from ending a pattern of drug abuse. One is to adopt a pattern of moderate or low rate use and the other is to remain completely abstinent. While many people adopt the latter course, the former is also quite common. Heroin users may cease their pattern of multiple daily use, but continue to use the drug on occasions—perhaps once a week. Former alcoholics are sometimes able to develop a pattern of moderate drinking in which they can conform to the norms of society. The relative merits of abstinence and controlled drug use will be considered again in Chapter Six.

CONCLUSIONS

Material presented in this chapter has shown that social factors have a profound influence on patterns of drug use. Clearly, both the availability and acceptability of drugs are determined largely by sociocultural factors. What is readily available and widely used and accepted in one society may not be in others. Similarly, an accepted form of drug use at one time may be prohibited by law at a later time, or vice versa. For any one drug, the exact way in which it is used varies across time and cultures. There are different routes of adminis-tration (with a trend towards those that produce a faster onset of action) and different patterns of use (varying from occasional, ceremonial, to regular, or frequent use). Who is permitted to use the drug may also be precisely defined.

All individuals then, are raised in a social context with its implications for both availability and the socially accepted patterns of use. In addition, certain aspects of the particular family environments may be important influ-ences. These include the individual's genetic heritage, the drug use of the parents, and the nature of the family environment. At a later stage the influence of peers becomes more important and this provides an immediate influence on drug use, possibly leading to an adoption of the peers' drug use patterns.

Once drug use has begun, the reaction of those in the individual's environment becomes influential. In particular, it has been noted that the behavior change resulting from drug use may be determined partly by what is and what is not acceptable in a society. The behavior of someone intoxicated with alcohol can take a number of different forms; the exact form is influenced strongly by the reaction of those in the social environment.

Controls on drug use may modify the practices of the individual user. Strict laws may make obtaining the drug too costly: It may be expensive, difficult, or even dangerous to obtain. In such cases controls are likely to act as a suppressant. However, controls may have the opposite effect if a drug is regarded as 'forbidden fruit:' a prize that is to be obtained if one is prepared for the risk. Very strict controls make drug users criminals, and may force them into a certain lifestyle often associated with further illegal activities. Whether or not this cost is balanced by apparent suppression of drug use should be a matter for continued debate.

For those developing dependence on a drug, their pattern of use is very often a fluctuating one which includes periods of abstinence. Permanent return to abstinence or moderate use may be helped by a variety of factors, including experience of adverse effects, difficulty in maintaining supply, and the influence of significant others (family, friends) and professionals.

REFERENCES

ADITYANJEE, MOHAN, D. & SOXENA, S. (1984). Heroin dependence: The New Delhi experience. *Indian Journal of Psychiatry, 26,* 213-316.

ALEXANDER, B.K. (1987). The disease and adaptive models of addiction: A framework evaluation. *Journal of Drug Issues, 17,* 47-66.

ASHTON, T., CASSWELL, S., & GILMORE, L. (1989). Alcohol taxes: Do the poor pay more than the rich? *British Journal of Addiction, 84,* 759-766.

BACON, M.K. (1976). Alcohol use in tribal societies. In B. Kissin & H. Begleiter (Eds.), *Social aspects of alcoholism.* (pp. 1-36). New York: Plenum Press.

BEAN, P. (1974). *The social control of drugs.* London: Martin Robertson.

BERRY, M.S. & SMOOTHY, R. (1986). A critical evaluation of the claimed relationships between alcohol intake and aggression in infrahuman animals. In P.F. Brain (Ed.), *Alcohol and aggression.* (pp. 84-137). London: Croom Helm.

BLUM, R.H. & ASSOCIATES (1972). *Horatio Alger's children.* London: Jossey-Bass.

BRAUCHT, G.N., BRAKARSH, D., FOLLINGSTAD, D., & BERRY, K.L. (1973). Deviant drug use in adolescence: A review of psychosocial correlates. *Psychological Bulletin, 79,* 92-106.

CAHALAN, D. & CISIN, I.H. (1976). Drinking behavior and drinking problems in the United States. In B. Kissin & H. Begleiter (Eds.), *Social aspects of alcoholism.* (pp. 77-115). New York: Plenum Press.

CHAMBERS, C.D. (1974). Some epidemiological considerations of the onset of opiate use in the United States. In E. Josephson & E.E. Carroll (Eds.), *Drug use: Epidemiological and sociological approaches.* (pp. 65-82). Washington: Hemisphere.

COMITAS, L. (1975). The social nexus of ganja in Jamaica. In V. Rubin (Ed.), *Cannabis and culture.* (pp. 119-132). The Hague: Mouton Publishers.

CRABBE, J.C., McSWIGAN, J.D., & BELKNAP, J.K. (1985). The role of genetics in substance abuse. In M. Galizio & S.A. Maisto (Eds.), *Determinants of substance abuse.* (pp. 65-99). New York: Plenum Press.

CRITCHLOW, B. (1986).   The powers of John Barleycorn: Beliefs about the effects of alcohol on social behavior. *American Psychologist, 41,* 751-764.

DOUGLASS, R.L. (1980).   Legal drinking age and traffic casualties: A special case of changing alcohol availability in public health context. *Alcohol and Health Research World, 4,* 18-25.

EPSTEIN, F.H. (1979).   Alcohol and alcoholism: Epidemiological and preventive approaches. In P. Avogaro, C.R. Sirtori, & E. Tremuli (Eds.), *Metabolic effects of alcohol.* (pp. 13-25). Amsterdam: Elsevier/North Holland.

GLAD, W. & ADESSO, V.J. (1976).   The relative importance of socially induced tension and behavioral contagion for smoking behavior. *Journal of Abnormal Behavior, 85,* 119-121.

GOODE, E. (1973).   *The drug phenomenon: Social aspects of drug taking.* Indianapolis: Bobbs-Merrill.

HOLDER, H.D. (Ed.) (1987).   *Control issues in alcohol abuse prevention: Strategies for states and communities* (Advances in substance abuse: Behavioral and biological research. Suppl. 1), Greenwich, Conn.: JAI Press.

HOMEL, R. (1988).   Policing and punishing the drinking driver: *A study of general and specific deterrence.* New York: Springer-Verlag.

JESSOR, R. & JESSOR, S. (1978).   Theory testing in longitudinal research on marijuana use. In D. Kandel (Ed.), *Longitudinal research on drug use.* (pp. 135-172). Washington, DC: Hemisphere.

JOHNSON, B.D. (1973).   *Marijuana users and drug subcultures.* New York: Wiley.

JOSEPHSON, E. (1974).   Trends in adolescent marijuana use. In E. Josephson & E.E. Carroll (Eds.), *Drug use: Epidemiological and sociological approaches.* (pp. 177-206). Washington: Hemisphere.

KALIX, P. (1987).   Khat: Scientific knowledge and public policy. *British Journal of Addiction, 82,* 47-53.

KANDEL, D. (1974).   Interpersonal influences on adolescent illegal drug use. In E. Josephson & E.E. Carroll (Eds.), *Drug use: Epidemiological and sociological approaches.* (pp. 207-240). Washington: Hemisphere.

MARSHALL, M. (Ed.) (1979).   *Beliefs, behaviors and alcoholic beverages: A cross-cultural survey.* Ann Arbor: University of Michigan Press.

McGLOTHLIN, W.H. (1978).   The etiological relationship between drug use and criminality. In Y. Israel, F.B. Glaser, H. Kalant, R.E. Popham, W. Schmidt, & R.G. Smart (Eds.), *Research advances in alcohol and drug problems.* (Vol. 4, pp. 376-388). New York: Plenum Press.

MILLER, P.M., NIRENBERG, T.D. & McCLURE, G. (1983).   Prevention of alcohol abuse. In B. Tabakoff, P.B. Sutker & C.L. Randall (Eds.), *Medical and social aspects of alcohol abuse.* (pp. 375-397). New York: Plenum Press.

MOORE, M. H. & GERSTEIN, D.R. (Eds.) (1981).   *Alcohol and public policy: Beyond the shadow of prohibition.* New York: National Academy Press.

MORGAN, H.W. (1981).   *Drugs in America: A social history 1800-1980.* Syracuse, New York: Syracuse University Press.

NYBERG, K.L. (1979).   Drug abuse and drug problems in rural America. In R.I. Dupont, A. Goldstein, & J. O'Donnell (Eds.), *Handbook on drug abuse.* (pp. 287-292). Bethesda, MD: National Institute on Drug Abuse.

ORNSTEIN, S.I. (1980).   The control of alcohol consumption through price increases. *Journal of Studies on Alcohol, 41,* 807-818.

PARSSINEN, T.M. (1983).   *Secret passions, secret remedies: Narcotic drugs in British society 1820-1930.* Philadelphia: Institute for the Study of Human Issues.

PEALE, S. (1986).   The implications and limitations of genetic models of alcoholism and other addictions. *Journal of Studies on Alcohol, 47,* 63-73.

PLINER, P. & CAPPELL, H. (1974).   Modifications of affective consequences of alcohol: A comparison of social and solitary drinking. *Journal of Abnormal Psychology, 83,* 1, 418-425.

POLICH, J.M., ARMOR, D.J., & BRAIKER, H.B. (1981).   *The course of alcoholism.* New York: Wiley.

POPHAM, R.E., SCHMIDT, W., & DE LINT, J. (1978).   Government control measures to prevent hazardous drinking. In J.A. Ewing and B.A. Rouse (Eds.), *Drinking.* Chicago: Nelson-Hall.

POPHAM, R.E., SCHMIDT, W., & DE LINT, J. (1976). The effects of legal restraint on drinking. In B. Kissin & H. Begleiter (Eds.), *Social aspects of alcoholism.* (pp. 579-625). New York: Plenum Press.

REID, J.B. (1978). Study of drinking in natural settings. In G.A. Marlatt & P.E. Nathan (Eds.), *Behavioral approaches to alcoholism.* New Brunswick, N.J.: Rutgers Center of Alcohol Studies.

RICHARDS, D.A. (1982). *Sex, drugs, death and the law.* Totowa, New Jersey: Rowman and Littlefield.

ROBINS, L.N. (1979). Addict careers. In R.I. Dupont, A. Goldstein, & J. O'Donnell (Eds.), *Handbook on drug abuse.* (pp. 325-336). Rockville: MD: National Institute on Drug Abuse.

ROSS, H.L. (1984). *Deterring the drinking driver: Legal policy and social control* (rev. ed.), Lexington: Lexington Books.

RUBIN, V. (1975). *Cannabis and culture.* The Hague: Moulton Publishers.

SCHACHTER, S. (1982). Recidivism and self-cure of smoking and obesity. *American Psychologist, 37,* 436-444.

SCHAEFFER, K.W., PARSONS, O.Q., & YOHMAN, J.R. (1984). Neuropsychological differences between male familial and nonfamilial alcoholics and nonalcoholics. *Alcoholism: Clinical and Experimental Research, 8,* 347-358.

SCHUCKIT, M.A. (1987). Biological vulnerability to alcoholism. *Journal of Consulting and Clinical Psychology, 55,* 301-309.

SMART, R. & FEJER, D. (1972). Drug use among adolescents and their parents: Closing the generation gap in mood modification. *Journal of Abnormal Psychology, 79,* 153-160.

SPENCER, C.P. & NAVARATNAM, V. (1981). *Drug abuse in East Asia.* Kuala Lumpur: Oxford University Press.

VAILLANT, G.E. (1983). *The natural history of alcoholism.* Cambridge, Mass.: Harvard University Press.

VAILLANT, G.E. (1966). A twelve year follow-up of New York narcotic addicts: Some social and psychiatric characteristics. *Archives of General Psychiatry, 15,* 599-609.

WAGENAAR, A.C. (1982) Aggregate beer and wine consumption: Effects of changes in the minimum legal drinking age and a mandatory container deposit law in Michigan. *Journal of Studies on Alcohol, 43,* 469-487.

WELTE, J.W. & ABEL, E.L. (1989). Homicide: Drinking by the victim. *Journal of Studies on Alcohol, 50,* 197-201.

WILSON, G.T. & LAWSON, D.M. (1976). Effects of alcohol on sexual arousal in women. *Journal of Abnormal Psychology, 85,* 1, 489-497.

WINICK, C. (1974). Some aspects of careers of chronic heroin users. In E. Josephson & E.E. Carroll (Eds.), *Drug use: Epidemiological and sociological approaches.* (pp. 105-128). Washington, DC: Hemisphere.

ZINBERG, N.E. (1979). Nonaddictive opiate use. In R.I. Dupont, A. Goldstein, & J. O'Donnell, (Eds.), *Handbook on drug abuse.* (pp. 303-313). Bethesda, MD: National Institute on Drug Abuse.

ZUCKER, R.A. & GOMBERG, E.S.L. (1986). Etiology of alcoholism reconsidered: The case for a biopsychosocial process, *American Psychologist, 41,* 783-793.

CHAPTER 5

Medical Consequences of Drug Use

Drug use brings with it certain risks. The user is introducing a chemical into his or her body which may have harmful effects on the body tissue or may cause harm through its central nervous system effects. The latter may be direct — through the induction of psychosis, for example — or indirect, as in the case of an intoxicated driver injured due to an accident.

Certain adverse effects may occur on any occasion in which the drug is taken. These are the acute toxic effects of the drug. Even the first-time user risks such effects. For example, an opiate overdose will result in a depression of respiration which can be fatal if the dose is large enough.

Other adverse effects arise only with chronic drug use. In most cases these have a gradual onset. Each time the drug is taken it worsens the situation a little. One such example is liver cirrhosis induced by heavy alcohol consumption. Some chronic effects are reversible while others remain even when drug use ceases.

An understanding of the adverse effects of drugs is of interest for several reasons. First, people frequently change their drug-taking practices as a result of adverse effects. These may be mainly medical (as described in this chapter), social or behavioral (described here and earlier), or a combination of these. Secondly, treatment of adverse drug effects is one of the two aspects of general therapy for problem drug use; the second is aimed at reducing or eliminating that use. Finally, consideration of the adverse effects of drugs is essential if society is to make rational decisions about the control of drug use. Clearly, if a drug were to be virtually free of adverse effects then it should be looked on more favorably than one likely to cause widespread medical problems.

The chapter is divided into two sections. The first is concerned with acute effects and the second with effects which arise with chronic administration. Although some mention is made of treatment in certain areas, discussion will be confined mainly to the actual effects themselves. Where it is possible, treatment for most of the problems described here should be carried out by appropriate medical staff.

ACUTE ADVERSE EFFECTS

There are three main types of adverse drug effects following acute administration. Two of these — idiosyncratic reactions and allergic reactions — are relatively rare and occur only in certain individuals. Such reactions can occur as a result of taking virtually any chemical introduced to the body, whether it be a drug (therapeutic or otherwise), a component of food, or some other compound. One of the best known and perhaps most common is the reaction to penicillin exhibited by certain individuals. Idiosyncratic and allergic reactions will not be considered here in any detail, although it should be noted that the risk of them occurring is always present.

Much more common are adverse effects which are simply an extension of the usual effects of the drug. For example, moderate doses of barbiturates often produce mild sedation and larger doses a more profound sedation, but very large doses can result in coma. Moderate doses of opiates will depress respiration, but an overdose can cause death due to the fact that the person stops breathing entirely. Of course, not all effects are seen at all doses. Amphetamine can induce a psychotic-like state, but there is no 'minipsychosis' at smaller doses. Rather, with adverse effects such as these, there is a threshold dose below which the effect cannot be seen.

Just as the usual effects of each drug are quite diverse (see Chapter One), the toxic or adverse effects can be quite varied. Each drug will have many adverse effects, not all of which will appear on any one occasion. A broad range of factors influence this, including the route of administration (some effects may only appear with rapid onset of action, for example), the dose taken, and the predisposition of the individual who self-administers it.

The degree of unpredictability is increased dramatically when drugs are taken in combination. The subject of drug interaction will not be covered here as it is a very extensive topic and requires more detailed analysis of the biological effects of drugs (see, for example, Griffin and D'Arcy, 1984). It is sufficient to note that even now we have little understanding of the many types of drug interactions. When a person uses several drugs simultaneously it is very difficult to analyze the cause of any toxic effects and to also treat them.

A related issue is the *adulterants* which often accompany drugs. These may be innocuous (as is the case with pharmaceuticals in tablet form), but can also be highly toxic. This is an important problem with illegal drug use. Various adulterants are added, usually to dilute the drug, but sometimes to try and magnify the effects of the drug (for example, PCP added to marijuana). A person suffering adverse effects of drug use may actually be suffering from the effects of these adulterants. Unfortunately, the adulterants are often unknown, again making treatment difficult. In other cases the adulterants are known and their effects have been analyzed. For example, while the toxic effects of nicotine itself are well understood, studies have also analyzed tobacco smoke and its various constituents. Tobacco is virtually the only means by which nicotine is used, so that the toxicity of tobacco is more important than the toxicity of nicotine alone.

Acute toxic effects of drugs will be considered under three broad headings here. The first concerns the direct biological effects and their treatment. Some of the major toxic effects of the various drug types will be described (many have already been mentioned in Chapter One) together with general approaches to treatment of drug toxicity. The second deals with impairment of psychomotor function by drugs. The third concerns one of the major types of indirect adverse effects of drugs: injuries resulting from drug use. These may be deliberate (for example, suicide) or may be a consequence of the psychomotor impairment.

Treatment of Acute Toxicity

If a sufficiently large dose of a drug is taken the adverse effects may be very severe, even life-threatening. In such cases the person may seek medical treatment, or someone may take him or her to such treatment. An overdose may be accidental, an attempt at suicide, or someone else's attempted homicide.

The first step in treatment involves identification of the drug. This may be possible if the person is conscious, or if they are accompanied by someone who knows what happened. Drug samples may be occasionally left about the person (for instance, cocaine around the nose after intranasal administration) or it may be possible to do a blood test. Treatment is much simpler if there is a single drug involved and if this is known from the start.

In the case of many drugs the principal and most effective treatment is the administration of an antagonist. Compounds that are highly specific, pure antagonists block the drug at the site of action. This immediately reverses the effects of the drug and prevents further adverse effects for as long as the antagonist remains in the body. Perhaps the best example is the opiate antagonist naloxone. This can immediately reverse the effects of an opiate overdose. However, some caution has to be exercised if the person is physically dependent in that a sufficiently large does of the antagonist will precipitate withdrawal.

Unfortunately, there are many drugs for which antagonists are not available, or if they are, they do not block all effects of the drug. In such cases one approach is to try and minimize the amount of drug in the body; this means decreasing absorption or increasing the rate of drug elimination from the body.

Decreasing absorption is usually possible only if the oral route of administration has been used. With intravenous administration, inhalation, etc., absorption is too rapid and it is virtually impossible to remove the drug in these cases. One method is to remove the drug from the stomach by gastric lavage or the induction of vomiting. Activated charcoal may also be put in the stomach to try to adsorb as much of the drug as possible.

There are a number of ways of increasing elimination rates. One is to use dialysis to filter the drug from the body. Whether this is possible depends on the particular drug. A second is to force an increased rate of urine production by intravenous administration of fluid and diuretic drug. A third is to change the acid/alkaline level of the urine by administration of a suitable substance. Depending on the chemical characteristics of the particular drug this may alter the rate of elimination (see Chapter Two).

Finally, treatment may be concerned with the specific symptoms the individual exhibits. This is sometimes the only form of treatment if the drug is not known. Examples include administration of a benzodiazepine to stop convulsions, artificial ventilation and administration of oxygen in the case of respiratory depression, and fluid administration for hypertension. Such treatment may continue for a considerable time after the patient is admitted. While treatment may focus on the most important or life-threatening dysfunction, a number of symptoms may have to be treated simultaneously.

Specific Drugs

Outlined below are the characteristic toxic symptoms and associated methods for treatment for each of the major drug classes. Note that only a general approach is described. In many cases this has to be modified according to the specific drug. For example, the acid or alkaline character is dependent on the drug in question and is not general to each drug class. Thus, any treatment aiming to increase elimination by altering urine acidity must be based on knowledge of the specific chemical properties of the drug in question. More detailed descriptions of symptoms and treatment can be found in a number of sources, including Hanenson (1980) and Gossel and Bricker (1984).

Barbiturates   At one time barbiturates were the main drug group prescribed for treatment of anxiety and insomnia. Accidental and intentional overdose was then very common. As their use has declined, so has the frequency of barbiturate poisoning. Nevertheless, they are still widely used both legally and illegally. Most legal administration is oral, whereas certain illicit users administer the drug intravenously. Their highly toxic effects when administered in overdose ensure that they remain one of the major causes of drug poisoning.

While mild barbiturate intoxication is similar to drunkenness, respiration is depressed and the person may lapse into a coma at higher doses. Very high doses can induce a wide range of untoward symptoms including low blood pressure and loss of reflexes. Death is usually due to respiratory depression.

Unfortunately, there is no specific antagonist for barbiturates. Treatment usually consists of prevention of absorption (for example, by gastric lavage), increasing the rate of drug elimination (the method depending on the particular barbiturate in question) and supportive treatment for symptoms such as respiratory depression.

The duration of barbiturate toxic effects varies enormously. In the case of the short-acting drugs it may be only a few hours, while the long-lasting ones may continue to produce toxic symptoms for many hours or days. However in either case, recovery is likely to take a number of days, particularly if a deep stage of coma has been reached.

Benzodiazepines   One of the major advantages of benzodiazepines over barbiturates is their lower toxicity. With rare exceptions, overdose of an orally administered benzodiazepine is not fatal. However, intravenous administration is considerably more dangerous and death can result. Danger may also be heightened and recovery made more difficult if they are combined with other drugs. Administration of alcohol together with a benzodiazepine is common and is considerably more dangerous than taking a benzodiazepine alone.

Many of the symptoms of benzodiazepine overdose are similar to the effects of mild barbiturate poisoning. They include drowsiness and lack of response to external stimuli. The person may reach a comatose state where even painful stimuli do not arouse them. However, there is usually no respiratory depression or impairment of cardiovascular function. Therapy is usually of a supportive nature, dealing only with specific symptoms.

Opiates An overdose of an opiate drug produces a wide range of symptoms, including sedation, respiratory depression, lowered heart rate, nausea, and vomiting. Death usually results from respiratory depression. This can occur in a seemingly conscious patient and without any indications of struggle or difficulty — breathing simply becomes less frequent, and finally stops.

The most important aspect of treatment is administration of an antagonist, usually naloxone. This is generally given intravenously, to hasten the process, and gradually, so as not to precipitate a severe withdrawal syndrome if the person is physically dependent. Naloxone reverses virtually all major effects of opiates. Due to its relatively short duration of action compared to many opiates (for example, methadone) it may need to be given several times to ensure that overdose symptoms do not return. Other therapy is supportive. Frequently, respiratory support has to be given immediately and until the naloxone takes effect.

In practice, a person brought to a hospital for treatment of an opiate overdose is likely to remain under care for some further time to check for any complications of their opiate use or of the overdose. These may include renal disorders, hepatitis, pneumonia, cardiac disorders, and more recently, acquired immune deficiency syndrome (AIDS).

Amphetamine Overdose of amphetamines or amphetamine-like compounds can cause severe symptoms and even death. When used in a medical context there seem to be very few problems with these drugs. However, illicit use, particularly intravenous use, appears to be much more dangerous.

The most problematic symptoms are those associated with the cardiovascular system. They include increased heart rate, blood pressure, and cardiac arrhythmias. The person may also complain of chest pain similar to angina. Lethality usually results from cerebro-vascular hemorrhage or a general collapse of the cardiovascular system.

Very obvious changes are associated with the central nervous system effects of the drug. Symptoms of a mild overdose include restlessness, tremor, insomnia, and euphoria. Higher doses are likely to result in confusion, hyperactivity, paranoia, and purposeless, repetitive movements. At this stage the individual may appear to be in a psychotic state, and has varied symptoms ranging from self-injury and aggressive behavior to paranoid behavior.

A number of other bodily symptoms are exhibited, including elevated temperature and rapid breathing. The person may experience nausea and vomiting.

The most important aspect of treatment is the administration of an antipsychotic drug. These drugs reverse virtually all effects of the amphetamine group, particularly those that are life-threatening. Diazepam is sometimes used in the case of low level amphetamine poisoning.

Other therapeutic measures are concerned with specific symptoms. For example, placement of a patient in a cold room and the minimizing of physical activity may be necessary to reduce body temperature. Some effort may also be directed towards preventing further absorption and increasing the rate of elimination of the drug. The latter is usually achieved by acidification and forced diuresis.

Cocaine.   The toxic effects seen after cocaine overdose are very similar to those characteristic of amphetamine. Symptoms such as increased heart rate and blood pressure, rapid breathing, cardiac stimulation and excited, agitated behavior are common to both. However, cocaine usually has a shorter onset and a much briefer duration of action. Therapy is supportive and concerned with the more dangerous effects, particularly convulsions, cardiovascular effects, and the elevated temperature. Various drugs may be given to control particular symptoms.

Nicotine.   Severe poisoning does not commonly occur following use of tobacco products. It sometimes results from ingestion of tobacco by children or the use of nicotine as a pesticide.

Caffeine.   Acute caffeine overdose is also not a major problem. However, ingestion of large amounts can result in headache, dizziness, tremor, insomnia, anxiety, and irritability. Heart rate may be elevated; cardiac arrhythmias may be experienced at very high doses. Nausea, vomiting, and diarrhea may also occur. Treatment is supportive, and diazepam is generally given if convulsions occur.

Hallucinogens.   Although death can result from the direct effects of an overdose of an hallucinogen (one of the LSD group or PCP), it is relatively rare. Symptoms of LSD poisoning include a psychotic-like state characterized by anxiety and fear, elevated heart rate and blood pressure, and tremor. PCP can also induce a psychotic-like state, but one much closer to acute schizophrenia. Other PCP symptoms are elevated blood pressure, aberrations of movement (muscular rigidity, repetitive movements, etc.) and nystagmus (involuntary eyeball movement). Treatment is mainly supportive, but may also include attempts to decrease absorption and increase elimination, particularly in the case of PCP.

Marijuana.   The acute toxic effects of marijuana include anxiety, disorientation, and occasionally a more severe paranoid reaction. Heart rate is usually elevated and respiration depressed. The individual may experience nausea. These effects rarely pose a major overdose problem and can be treated symptomatically.

Anticholinergics.   A variety of symptoms follow anticholinergic overdose. These include anxiety and delirium, often associated with hallucinations, poor muscular coordination, and incoherent speech. Heart rate and blood pressure are elevated, vision is blurred, respiration depressed, the mouth is very dry, and the person complains of thirst. Although the fatal dose is relatively high, death may occur after the person lapses into a coma.

The symptoms of anticholinerginic poisoning can be reversed by administration of *physostigmine.* However, it needs to be used very carefully in order not to produce adverse effects of the opposite kind (for instance, CNS depression and reduced heart rate). Unlike antidotes such as naloxone, physostigmine itself has strong toxic effects. Other treatment includes supportive measures for specific symptoms, and forced diuresis to increase excretion rate.

Inhalants.   The various solvents and aerosols which comprise this group are a diverse range of substances which have a wide variety of effects. Accordingly, it is not always possible to predict the exact toxic effects unless the actual substance used is known. Nevertheless, there are some general symptoms common to overdose with a number of inhalants. These include depression (which usually follows the initial excitement and euphoria), hallucinations, confusion, blurred vision, and slurred speech. Respiratory depression, nausea, vomiting, diarrhea, and pain may also occur. One potentially fatal complication is choking following vomiting. It is due in part to relaxation of the throat and tongue muscles, and weak breathing. However, the most serious symptom is the presence of arrhythmias which may lead to cardiac arrest and death. Treatment is of a supportive nature and, at least initially, is concerned mainly with the cardiac arrhythmias.

Impairment of Psychomotor Function

Casual observation of people who have used drugs suggests that their ability to react to the outside world is impaired. They do not respond normally, are very slow or make a lot of mistakes. The drunk who fails to notice oncoming traffic, is slow to react when it is right upon him and even goes the wrong way once he does react provides an obvious example. These observations are confirmed by studies of psychomotor function.

Studies of drug effects on psychomotor performance are of interest in themselves in that they indicate one type of change in behavior which occurs following drug administration. However, they have enormous practical importance due to their relevance to the execution of skilled behavior in the natural environment. One of the most important adverse effects of drugs is the increased accident rate amongst users. The most publicized example concerns motor vehicle driving while under the influence of alcohol. But people use a variety of other drugs and engage in a wide range of skilled behavior which may be impaired by drug use. In some cases there may be considerable physical danger involved (for example, in operating machinery), while in others it may simply be that performance is impaired (an office worker). In both cases the drug alters performance in a manner which may have direct adverse consequences (for instance injury) or indirect ones (loss of job through poor performance).

Psychomotor performance.   Some effort has been devoted to breaking down psychomotor function into a number of different components or aspects (see, for example, Welford, 1968; Lindsay and Norman, 1977). One such aspect can be seen as the ability to use information provided by the environment, or *sensory processing ability*. If an individual cannot detect what is going on in his or her environment with a fair degree of accuracy, then their response to it will often be inappropriate.

At the opposite end is the ability to actually control the musculature in order to execute appropriate behavior. A person may be limited in their ability to respond to the environment simply because their motor control is poor. This can be assessed using tests of motor performance or motor control. These are usually designed specifically to test fine motor control (for example, small finger movements) or gross motor control (being able to stand steady, for instance).

An important aspect of the response is the speed at which it is done. In many situations speed is absolutely essential and any kind of drug or other influence which decreases speed will impair the person's interaction with their environment. Speed can be measured in reaction time tasks where a person is asked to respond as rapidly as possible to a particular stimulus event (for example, onset of a light). In some cases there are a number of possible responses, each appropriate for a different stimulus event. This is known as choice reaction time.

Various tasks are also said to incorporate a number of aspects of psychomotor function. In particular, impairment of any one aspect of psychomotor function will diminish performance on other naturalistic tasks such as driving a car. Detection of information in the environment (signs, cars, etc.), executing appropriate and accurate responses (steering, braking, etc.) and doing so at an appropriate speed are all important. Deficiencies in any one will obviously impair overall performance.

Drug effects. An important determinant of the severity of drug effects is the dose administered. The description of the drunk given earlier indicates one extreme — a dose so high that all aspects of psychomotor function will be impaired. Anyone who is seeking the sort of treatment for acute toxicity described in the previous section would certainly fall into this category. At the other end is the person who has taken a normal dose of what appears to be an innocuous drug, such as a benzodiazepine. It is important to determine whether their psychomotor performance is impaired as a result of such drug administration.

Research in this area has been concerned mainly with the latter case (see Hindmarch, 1980, and Nicholson and Ward, 1984, for detailed summaries). People who exhibit the obvious behavioral effects of a drug can be readily shown to have impaired psychomotor abilities. They run the risk of major adverse consequences if they attempt to engage in any behavior which requires some degree of skill. On the other hand, those less clearly intoxicated may be in some danger as they may be unaware of any possible impairment. If they continue on as normal, and engage in activities such as driving a car, then they may suffer adverse consequences.

Impairment of sensory ability will not be discussed in detail here, in that it has already been considered in Chapter Three. There it was suggested that a number of drugs could alter sensory functioning. While in certain cases improvement is noted (for example, where stimulants are used prior to doing a task which requires continued attention over long periods of time), most drugs impair sensory functioning. While the doses which produce obvious sensory impairment are relatively high, performance on more complex tasks involving attention to two or more stimuli is affected at much lower doses. Drugs such as alcohol, benzodiazepines, and marijuana all impair performance on these divided attention tasks. Similarly, performance on a driving simulation is impaired by drugs at lower doses if the individual is required to simultaneously attend to a second task at the same time. These results indicate that drugs may play a role in accidents partly because they increase the incidence of attention failure — a major cause of road accidents (Johnston, 1982).

Studies of motor function frequently show negative results. That is, moderate doses of many drugs do not significantly impair a person's ability to actually execute a response. However, some effects have been noted. For example, stimulants may worsen performance on tasks requiring fine motor control (for example, accurate firing of a pistol, handwriting) and in general they seem to reduce hand steadiness. In contrast, benzodiazepines may improve hand steadiness, at least in people who are already anxious.

Another motor function that has been shown to be impaired by drugs is *saccadic eye movements.* These are eye movements which involve jumps from one point to another rather than smooth graduated movements. (Although it should be noted that we are not usually aware of the jumps). A wide variety of drugs have been shown to alter various characteristics of the saccades. These include alcohol, barbiturates, benzodiazepines, opiates, and amphetamine. The most robust effect appears to be a decrease in saccade velocity associated with the administration of barbiturates. In some studies opiates have been shown to produce a similar effect. Amphetamine had no effect on speed by itself, but reduced the effects of fatigue. (Griffiths, Marshall, and Richens, 1984). The reductions in velocity would presumably indicate difficulty in maintaining visual activity at the normal rate. This may be reflected in reduced speed of reading, for example.

More complex tasks such as those requiring arithmetic computation and various other aspects of intellectual functioning reveal varying degrees of impairment due to the effects of drugs. The precise effects are highly dependent on dose. For example, low doses of benzodiazepines usually produce little effect and sometimes even an improvement in performance, whereas higher doses usually reduce performance level. In addition tolerance develops quite rapidly to any worsening. One factor which increases drug effects has already been mentioned—simultaneous involvement in two or more tasks. Another is the concurrent use of several drugs. For example, doses of alcohol and a benzodiazepine which by themselves have little effect may produce a significant impairment when coadministered. However, this seems to be highly dependent on the actual benzodiazepine, with some (for example loprazolam) even appearing to counteract the effects of alcohol (Mattila, 1984). Alcohol and marijuana have also been shown to have additive effects.

Stimulants have been noted to improve performance in a number of tests of intellectual functioning. Amphetamine and amphetamine-related compounds, caffeine, and nicotine have all been observed to have such effects. The opposite effects have been observed with sedative-hypnotics such as the benzodiazepines and alcohol.

Examination of performance in more naturalistic situations (for example, studies of driving behavior) has also shown that factors such as the dose, various characteristics of the person, and the presence of other drugs all play a role (Ferrera, 1987). Thus, it is not possible to say that a certain type of drug, even a certain dose, will always impair performance unless the dose is one high enough to produce clear intoxication. Unfortunately, we are a long way from being able to predict what type of impairment in psychomotor performance is produced by the various drug types and under what conditions the impairment occurs.

Injury and Death

Some of the adverse effects which follow acute intoxication are not direct effects of the drug, but are a result of the behavioral changes the drug induces. One type is accidental injury, which occurs when driving cars, operating machinery, or simply carrying out normal activities. People intoxicated with a drug may experience a higher rate of such injury, at least partly because of the impairment of psychomotor functioning described above. The second type is intentional injury, the most severe being suicide and homicide. There seems to be a strong involvement of at least some drugs in deaths of this nature.

Unfortunately, there is not a great deal of information on the involvement of drugs in both accidents and violence. Most information available concerns alcohol, with very little on other drugs. In part, this is due to the fact that use of a number of other drugs is a relatively infrequent phenomenon. In most Western societies the proportion of people who regularly use opiates, for example, is actually very small. This makes the detection of injuries and death attributable to the drugs extremely difficult. Accordingly, most of the discussion here will be concerned with alcohol.

One major group of injuries are those arising from motor vehicle accidents. They are a major cause of death and injury in many societies throughout the world and there is unequivocal evidence that alcohol contributes to these accidents. Surveys in various countries over the last few years have indicated that alcohol is involved in at least half of all road accident deaths. Data from the United States indicate that whereas around four percent of drivers randomly sampled have blood alcohol levels over one-tenth percent, about forty percent of the drivers in two vehicle accidents deemed responsible for the accident, and fifty-five percent of drivers in single vehicle accidents have levels this high (Waller, 1976).

There seems to be a threshold point around the five-hundredths percent blood alcohol level (Howat and Landauer, 1983). Below that, there is relatively little increased risk of accident. Above that level the risk rises exponentially. This accords with laboratory studies showing little impairment of psychomotor function at low blood alcohol levels.

Interestingly, a large number of pedestrians killed on the roads also have high blood alcohol levels. Some surveys show that one quarter to one half of all such pedestrians have blood alcohol levels over one-tenth percent (Waller, 1976; Denney, 1979). Again, this would seem to follow naturally from the impaired psychomotor functioning produced by alcohol. Crossing a road is a complex task — it requires divided attention, judgment of speeds and distances and so forth.

Some data are now emerging to suggest the involvement of other drugs in road accidents. One group that has been implicated comprises sedatives prescribed for medical purposes. Benzodiazepines are known to impair psychomotor skills related to driving and are likely to play a causal role in some accidents. Concurrent use of alcohol will almost certainly exacerbate these effects. Other drugs which have an adverse influence on driving include marijuana and antidepressants (Ferrara, 1987).

In other types of injuries (for example, accidental falls) alcohol seems to be a factor. A higher proportion of people who suffer such injuries are intoxicated than might normally be expected. The more serious the accident, the more possible it is that alcohol has been used by the person (or persons) involved. Where an individual is at least partly responsible for their injury it is also highly probable that they have been using alcohol (Waller, 1976).

Death through accident is much higher in alcoholics than in non-alcoholics. The type of accident is varied and includes falls, fire, and poisonings in addition to motor vehicle accidents. While a number of explanations could be given for this elevated frequency, including various deficits caused by chronic alcoholism (discussed below), at least some of the accidents are likely to be due to alcohol intoxication.

Alcohol has also been implicated in a large proportion of homicides. Becoming intoxicated appears to increase the risk of dying by someone else's hand. Approximately half of all homicide victims have positive blood alcohol levels (Pernanen, 1976). In addition, there is evidence that the victim's intoxication contributes directly to his or her death. In one study (Wolfgang, 1967) it was shown that where the victim was a direct precipitator of the murder, seventy-four percent of the victims had detectable blood alcohol levels. Where the crime was not clearly victim-precipitated, alcohol was involved in sixty percent. Drinking immediately prior to the murder also increased the likelihood of the victim precipitating his or her death. It is also interesting to note that studies of animal social behavior show that an individual intoxicated with alcohol has an increased likelihood of attacking and of being attacked (Miczek, 1987).

Data on other drugs are relatively scarce. There is no clear evidence for increased death through homicide amongst people who have detectable blood levels of other drugs. In surveys of homicide victims no particular drug seems "overrepresented." This may be expected on the basis of findings presented in Chapter Three. While alcohol appears to increase aggressive behavior, most other drugs do not have this effect.

Drugs are frequently found in blood samples taken from suicide victims. However, it is often difficult to determine the relationship between drug use and suicide. A drug may be used to effect a suicide, or to make the act easier; suicide may also have occurred spontaneously under the influence of the drug or the presence of the drug may be incidental. Survey data show that alcoholics have a higher rate of suicide than the normal population. However, this could be due to a number of factors, including social isolation through loss of family, employment, etc., and also the high frequency of severe depression among alcoholics (see Chapter Three). Acute alcohol intoxication may play a role, in that it is known that drinking actually tends to increase anxiety and depression in alcoholics (Adesso, 1980). Similarly, chronic intravenous amphetamine users frequently die as a result of homicide or suicide. The extent to which this is due to actual amphetamine intoxication is not clear.

ADVERSE EFFECTS FOLLOWING CHRONIC ADMINISTRATION

Many adverse effects of drugs do not occur, or at least are not revealed, after a single administration. Rather, they can only be found when the drug is used repeatedly. Some symptoms may occur following occasional use for some period of time, while others require excessive use for many years. In any case, there is considerable variability from individual to individual. It is simply not possible to say that a certain amount of drug will inevitably produce a certain pathological state.

The effects may be similar superficially to those which follow a single large dose (for example, impaired psychomotor function), but may also be quite different (cancer, for example). For this reason separation of acute from chronic effects requires that the person be tested or examined when not under the influence of the drug.

Some adverse effects are permanent. That is, even if the person were to stop using the drug the problem would remain. With others, the problem gradually disappears if use stops. Many are in between—the symptoms improve if drug use ceases, but never completely revert to the predrug state.

Types of Adverse Effects

The drugs considered here have their main site of action in the brain. It seems logical, then, to examine whether they adversely affect that organ in any way. While an ideal situation would be to examine the brain directly for evidence of such pathology, this can only be done to a very limited extent, particularly when looking for effects in humans. Instead, most evidence of nervous system dysfunction comes from alterations to behavior.

Aspects of behavior found to be impaired as a result of chronic drug use include learning ability, memory function, and psychomotor performance. It is often difficult to detect whether such impairment has occurred in a particular individual because the individual's ability level before drug use is generally not known. The natural variability in the population means that there has to be a high level of dysfunction in order to provide convincing evidence of drug-induced impairment.

Other evidence may come from psychiatric examination and personality testing. This type of evidence has been discussed in Chapter Three. It was noted that there are many difficulties in deciding the origin of any personality or psychiatric problem. When trying to determine the effects of chronic administration, the issue to be focused on is whether or not any problems present existed prior to drug use, or developed with usage instead. The research discussed in that chapter suggested that certain changes in personality developed with a pattern of chronic high level drug use, but most of these disappeared when drug use stopped. Nevertheless, certain types of problems may remain, indicating a permanent effect of drug use.

A second type of problem which may or may not be related to brain dysfunction is impaired sexual and reproductive functioning. This has also been discussed to some extent in Chapter Three. Such impairment can arise through many means and can take a number of different forms. It may be that hormonal levels are altered or sensitivity of certain bodily tissues to hormones has changed. This may lead to a loss of libido, impaired sexual performance, or the impaired ability to reproduce.

Many drugs alter cardiovascular functioning following acute administration. Some also have the potential for chronic impairment of cardiovascular functioning. Heart disease has received considerable attention in recent years and much discussion has been devoted to the various risk factors associated with it. Use of drugs, particularly alcohol and tobacco, has been highlighted as a risk factor which is in each person's own control. In some cases of drug-induced cardiovascular impairment it seems that adverse effects are permanent. While stopping drug use reduces the risk, it does not eliminate the effects of previous use.

A second type of disease which is of considerable public concern is cancer. Again, much time and effort has been devoted to isolating the risk factors associated with cancer development. Two of the most commonly used drug products, alcohol and tobacco, have again been implicated. Certainly, there is a long history of research on the relationship between cigarette smoking and lung cancer which has been very influential in altering smoking habits in recent years.

Other types of disease or damage to organs may also occur because of drug use. A drug may have a direct toxic effect on a particular organ or part of the body. Repeated use of the drug may result in altered structure and/or function of the organ and consequent health problems. Alternatively, the effect of the drug may be to enhance or increase the likelihood of a disease process which can occur in the absence of drug use. Liver cirrhosis induced by excessive alcohol consumption would be an example of this.

One area of recent concern has been genetic damage due to drugs. Unfortunately, such damage is very difficult to assess. Many things in our environment have the potential to induce chromosomal damage — drugs are only one such factor. Even when it is possible to isolate drug-induced genetic change, the implications of such damage are not always clear.

Finally, drugs do not have adverse effects solely on the person him- or herself, but may also affect their offspring. This is particularly the case when a pregnant woman uses drugs which can affect the development of the fetus. These effects will be discussed in detail in a separate section.

Research Problems

Determining whether or not repeated drug use causes specific adverse effects is difficult to prove. A number of problems and issues must be resolved before a statement of this nature can be made conclusively. Simply finding that people who use a certain drug also tend to have a certain type of problem is not sufficient. There are many correlational findings of this kind, but they are really only a first step. Determining the actual cause of the problem, whether it be a drug or something else, takes considerably more time.

One of the major difficulties is that users of a particular drug are not a random sample within the population. When they begin drug use they already have certain genetic backgrounds, personal histories, and current circumstances. These factors may be more influential in the development of particular adverse effects than use of the actual drug itself. This issue has already been discussed in Chapter Three, with reference to personalities of drug abusers, but it also arises when considering other types of adverse effects. For example, people who use alcohol excessively often report that they do so to relieve anxiety. If this anxiety is the result of a stressful lifestyle then these people may also be expected to have a high rate of heart disease (Glass, 1977). A simple correlation may show increased heart disease amongst heavy alcohol users, but these people may have been more likely to have such an elevated rate independent of any alcohol use.

It was noted in the previous chapter that drug use is often distributed unevenly across various sociocultural groups in various societies. Studies of adverse effects have to take account of these differences. For example, a particular drug may be used mostly by one ethnic group. That group may be comprised mainly of lower income people who have relatively poor nutrition. The poor nutrition may, in turn, increase the likelihood of a number of diseases. A correlational study which looked only at drug use and disease state, without considering sociocultural factors, may falsely conclude that drug use increased the rates of certain diseases.

Drug use may impose a certain lifestyle which has unhealthy consequences. This is the case particularly with users of illegal drugs. The need to spend large sums of money on drugs (rather than on food, clothing, shelter, etc.) may have its own adverse consequences. In addition, the actual obtaining of the money may cause problems — prostitution is an obvious example of an occupation which has great health risks.

One very important correlated factor is other drug use. Most drug users do not confine themselves to one particular drug. Instead, they sample from a range of drugs, any or all of which may have adverse effects. This issue has arisen when researchers have tried to determine whether alcohol has a role in the causation of certain cancers. Almost all heavy drinkers are cigarette smokers as well. Accordingly, it is difficult to determine whether the cancer is due to the cigarettes alone (which have known carcinogenic potential) or whether alcohol has a contributory effect. A related problem is that there may be impurities or adulterants that cause adverse effects rather than the drug itself.

Finally, any adverse effects may be an indirect rather than direct consequence of drug use. For example, alcohol impairs the absorption of food.

This, together with the bad dietary habits of most alcoholics, may cause nutritional problems. In addition, excessive alcohol use causes *apnea,* or long periods without breathing, during sleep. How is it possible to separate the nutritional difficulties, oxygen deprivation, and direct toxic effects of alcohol? This may not make any difference if one is simply considering the adverse effects of particular drug habits, but it is of critical importance if someone is trying to reverse or prevent those effects. Furthermore, people physically dependent on a drug may frequently suffer withdrawal. It was noted in Chapter Two that withdrawal may itself be dangerous. If a person goes through repeated withdrawal during a history of drug use this may have major long-term adverse effects in itself. Unfortunately, this question has received relatively little attention to date.

Adverse Effects of Specific Drugs

It is clear from the problems described above that convincing evidence of an adverse effect caused by a drug is difficult to obtain. Accordingly, it is only worth pursuing such investigations if the effect is an important one, is found in a significant percentage of users, and if there is reason to believe that it is not caused by any other factors. For many of the drugs discussed, there are no effects to satisfy these criteria. This should not be taken to mean that they do not have any adverse effects.

The discussion below will be concerned principally with major adverse effects for which there is convincing evidence of the drug having a causative role. Some adverse effects of chronic administration which have already been discussed, particularly physical dependence, will not be considered here.

Opiates.   Chronic use does not seem to lead to major adverse effects. Most heroin addicts seem to recover normal health once they cease using the drug (Robins, 1979). A number of chronic effects are simply an extension of the acute effects of the drug and disappear once use ceases. These include sexual impairment, constipation, and pinpoint pupils. Users of illicit opiates have a range of health problems associated with contaminants, needle sharing, etc.

Benzodiazepines and barbiturates.   These drugs are mostly used on a chronic basis and the incidence of dangerous adverse effects is very low. Some are extensions of the acute effects (for example, tiredness), but there are also a variety of reactions with very low incidence which could probably be best described as allergic or idiosyncratic. These include blood and liver disorders.

Alcohol.   Considerable attention has been paid to the deleterious effects of chronic alcohol use (see Popham, Schmidt, and Israelstam, 1984, for a review). The most obvious evidence indicating the severity of such effects is the high mortality rates of heavy drinkers. It is also important to note that health does not necessarily return to normal when a person ceases heavy drinking. Depending on the period of use and the age of giving up, even an ex-alcohol abuser may have impaired health and reduced life-span. The hazardous effects seem to be confined to heavy drinkers: there is no convincing evidence of danger to moderate drinkers, or that abstinent persons fare better.

Cirrhosis of the liver is a potentially fatal disorder which occurs with much greater frequency among alcoholics. This increased susceptibility is due to the direct toxic effect of alcohol on the liver, although the poor nutrition of many alcoholics may also exacerbate the problem. Other liver disorders with elevated rates in heavy drinkers include hepatitis and fatty liver.

Cardiovascular disease is also increased among heavy drinkers. While several mechanisms involving the various toxic effects of alcohol have been proposed, it is still not clear whether other, correlated factors contribute in some way (Ashley, 1984). These may include personality factors, as mentioned above.

A number of different cancers appear with greater frequency amongst alcoholics. These include cancers of the liver, lung, and upper digestive and respiratory tracts. Unfortunately, it has been difficult to separate the effects of alcohol and smoking, mostly for the reason that almost all heavy drinkers also smoke. However, while there is some doubt as to whether alcohol, by itself, directly causes cancer, it appears to act synergistically with tobacco. Thus, drinking will significantly increase the risk of cancer associated with cigarette smoking. For some cancers it may also have an independent action.

A variety of gastric disorders have been associated with chronic alcohol use. These include gastritis, peptic ulcer, and pancreatitis. The latter two are potentially fatal, but mortality is relatively low. As yet there is no clear evidence for an underlying mechanism which directly involves alcohol.

A number of endocrine changes may be produced by alcohol. These are revealed in male heavy drinkers by two distinct syndromes: *hypogonadism* and *feminization*. Symptoms of the former include reduced testicular size and diminished fertility, and in some cases, reduced libido and loss of secondary sexual characteristics. These changes appear to result from a direct toxic effect on the testes and possibly an impairment of pituitary function. Feminization involves the assumption of various female secondary sexual characteristics, including breast enlargement and pelvic fat deposits. The reasons for this are unclear (Morris, 1984).

Some of the major adverse effects resulting from chronic alcohol use involve brain dysfunction. Perhaps the worst, and most clearly defined, is *Wernicke-Korsakoff syndrome*. People with this disorder have distinct brain lesions associated with memory impairment, ataxia, ocular problems, and general confusion. The disorder may be so severe that the people involved are unable to live without care. The changes are usually permanent, but there is an acute form. The main cause is thiamine deficiency although direct toxic effects of alcohol on the nervous system may also contribute.

Less severe deficits may be more common. A large number of alcohol abusers have impaired intellectual ability and/or psychomotor function. While some of these disappear when alcohol use ceases, symptoms often remain. These changes also occur in conjunction with brain pathology, particularly lesions and atrophy in the cortex. Impairment is often associated specifically with sensory and/or motor nerves. This may result in impaired motor function, pain, and other problems.

It is likely that there is actually a continuum of deficits, from mild and reversible to the severe, irreversible Wernicke-Korsakoff syndrome (Ron, 1984). While many alcoholics may have subtle deficits, very few develop the full Wernicke-Korsakoff syndrome. In addition, severity is not always related to an amount ingested. Many people with long histories of very heavy drinking seem to escape this type of impairment.

For all these neurological disorders questions remain about the precise etiology. While it seems likely that a direct effect of alcohol (or its metabolites) and dietary deficiency (particularly thiamine deficiency) are involved, increased incidence of head injury and other possible causes may also play a role. Even when experimental studies have been done with animals these factors were shown to be difficult to control.

Amphetamine and cocaine.   During the many years it was available through prescription, amphetamine was regarded as relatively benign. Similarly, methylphenidate and other amphetamine-related compounds are given to children for the control of hyperactivity. Despite daily use, no major chronic health effects have been noted. The coca chewers of South America do not manifest any major effects from that drug, either.

However, chronic use of high doses of amphetamine and cocaine can induce brain abnormalities, including long-lasting depletion of the neurotransmitter dopamine. Disorders of posture and movement, depression, and an amotivated state may be associated with such changes. Other effects are simply extensions of the acute effects of these drugs. They include disturbances to eating and sleep. Intranasal administration of cocaine may result in problems with the nose, varying from excessive mucus secretion to ulceration of the tissue.

Nicotine.   The health effects of chronic tobacco usage have received extensive coverage in the popular media. Public health authorities have attempted to publicize these effects in order to reduce tobacco usage. Considerable research effort has been devoted to this problem, much of it documented in the United States Surgeon-General's report (United States Department of Health, Education and Welfare, 1979). There are a number of diseases which become more likely with chronic use of tobacco, and the risk is related to the amount of tobacco consumed and the manner of use. Cigarette smoking seems to be the most dangerous form, with cigar and pipe smoking and other forms of tobacco usage somewhat less so. The probability of developing most of the diseases declines once tobacco usage stops.

Cardiovascular disease is a major cause of death. It can take a variety of forms, including coronary artery disease and cerebrovascular disease. Carbon monoxide and possibly nicotine as well, seem to be the constituents of tobacco smoke most responsible for these disorders. Cancer is the second major disease problem. Lung cancer has received the most attention, but cancers of the mouth, throat, larynx, esophagus, and bladder all occur with greater frequency in smokers. These are assumed to be due to one or more of the various carcinogens present in tobacco and tobacco smoke. Interestingly, tobacco chewers have a high incidence of lip and mouth cancer, indicating problems with unburnt tobacco. The final major cause of increased mortality is chronic lung disease. Again, this occurs much more frequently amongst smokers, particularly cigarette smokers, and is presumed to be due to the build up of tar from the smoke.

While these effects are all potentially fatal, smokers may also notice less severe effects. These include shortness of breath and excessive coughing. Most heavy smokers have difficulty exercising because of impairment to breathing. Gastric disorders may also be worsened due to enhanced acid secretion.

Caffeine. Consumption of caffeine, mainly through tea and coffee, is extremely widespread. In general, these drinks have been regarded as relatively benign and not a major cause of health problems. However, in recent years some findings have emerged which suggest that they do have important health consequences (James and Stirling, 1983; Abbott, 1986). Unfortunately these findings have been difficult to assess for associated drug use (particularly smoking), and also difficult in determining the doses required to produce the various degrees of effect.

Chronic caffeine use is associated more closely with a number of less severe symptoms, many of which seem to be extensions of its acute effects. These include anxiety, insomnia, headache, tremulousness, and loss of appetite. Caffeine enhances gastric secretions and this can induce nausea and may increase the probability of peptic ulcer.

Hallucinogens. While there has been some concern over the effects of chronic hallucinogen use, it should be noted that the most common pattern is one of occasional use only. These drugs are rarely, if ever, taken on a regular basis in the same way as alcohol or caffeine, for example. While the possibility of LSD-induced chromosomal damage has aroused some interest, there is no convincing evidence of major effects from repeated hallucinogen use. Naturally, repeated use may exacerbate certain symptoms of acute administration and increase the possibility of a "bad trip."

Marijuana. Although the effects of chronic marijuana use have been studied extensively in both humans and animals (Jones, 1978; Maykut, 1984), a number of questions remain unanswered. The issue is also complicated by the fact that marijuana is both smoked and ingested (drunk as an infusion or eaten). As will be noted below, the health consequences may be quite different for the two routes of administration.

Marijuana appears to have no major long-term effects on the cardio-vascular system. However, there is an increased risk of a number of pulmonary disorders, including bronchitis and emphysema. Lung cancer is also more common. These changes appear to be associated with marijuana smoke and should not be expected if ingested. They are similar to the adverse effects of tobacco smoke on the pulmonary system.

It has been argued that chronic marijuana use depresses the immune system. However, the results are far from clear. For one thing, it is difficult to control for other differences between users and nonusers which may account for the finding. Confounding factors such as nutritional status, general living conditions, and other drug use may all play a role.

Some endocrine changes occur following chronic marijuana use. In males, levels of luteinizing hormone and testosterone are depressed slightly, but they are still within the normal range and return to previous levels once smoking stops. There is some evidence suggesting that very high rate use may impair sexual functioning. In females, levels of a number of hormones are changed slightly by chronic marijuana use. The significance of such changes is not clear, although there may be some alteration to the menstrual cycle.

Arguments against marijuana use are sometimes based on various types of brain damage, psychosis, and an "amotivational" syndrome induced by chronic marijuana use. While some evidence is given for the existence of these disorders, it is often flawed by failure to control for differences between users and nonusers which do not result from taking the drug. In general, there is no convincing evidence that such disorders are caused by chronic marijuana use.

Inhalants.   Patterns of inhalant use vary considerably. Although most use is occasional, there are instances of chronic high rate use. This is of particular concern in that many inhalants are very toxic. Unfortunately, it is difficult to describe the adverse effects exactly; they vary considerably from substance to substance. Many adverse effects result not so much from the inhalant itself as the presence of metals (for example lead) and chemicals (such as vinyl chloride) which are themselves highly toxic.

Some inhalants (particularly solvents) are suspected of having detrimental effects on the nervous system. Changes in both the peripheral and central nervous system have been detected. In most cases the changes are reversible, but there is some suggestion of irreversible damage due to the presence of lead or because of high-rate use over a long term. Psychological testing also shows deficits amongst populations of inhalant users, but the question as to whether these differences are due to the actual inhalant or not has not been fully answered. Perhaps the most serious effects are seen with chronic gasoline sniffers. Their symptoms include confusion, slurred speech, movement disorders, and intellectual impairment. Many of these are permanent and most are thought to be due to lead in the gasoline.

Damage may also occur to various internal organs, particularly the liver and kidney. This is generally reversible, but some inhalants (such as cleaning fluid, fluorocarbons) may induce permanent changes. Other toxic effects are specific to one or a small group of inhalants. For example, benzene is associated with elevated rates of leukemia and with damage to bone marrow.

EFFECTS ON OFFSPRING

Some adverse effects of drug administration are produced in the offspring of an individual. The most common way for this to happen is for a drug taken by a pregnant woman to alter the development of her fetus in such a way that it manifests some morphological, biochemical, or behavioral abnormality at or sometime after birth. In most cases such effects only arise as a result of repeated administration. A single dose is unlikely to produce clear effects unless it is very high.

There are a number of types of defects which can be produced by drugs. The most severe is *prenatal* or *perinatal death*. This probably occurs relatively often, but may not be noticed if it happens early in pregnancy. The causes of prenatal death are not well understood. Growth retardation may also result from drug use. The baby may be born light and may continue to have impaired development for some time. The defect may be a specific malformation present at birth, and examples include absent or deformed body parts. Functional malformations are less obvious, but may be just as damaging. These may take the form of biochemical aberration (which may affect nutritional status, for example) or the behavior of the child may differ from normal in some respect.

The effect of a drug will usually be some combination of these various types. For most drugs we have only some idea of exactly what effects are produced. However, in a few cases (alcohol being a notable example) there is a distinct syndrome with a well-defined set of symptoms.

Mechanisms

There are a number of ways in which offspring can be damaged by drug intake. Although we normally think of maternal drug intake as being important (and the vast majority of research has been in this area), paternal intake prior to conception should also be considered. For example, both paternal alcohol consumption and smoking have been shown to have an adverse effect on the developing fetus (Joffe, 1979). In animal studies the proven teratogen thalidomide adversely affects offspring when given to males prior to mating and conception (Lutwak-Mann, 1964). At present, we have little idea as to how such changes can occur. Possible mechanisms include transmission of the drug in seminal fluid and damage to sperm.

Female drug intake may affect offspring when it occurs prior to conception, during gestation, and if the baby is breast fed, following birth. Most research has been concerned with the effects during gestation. This arises when a drug taken by the mother crosses the placental barrier and reaches the fetus. Virtually all the drugs being considered here pass through the placenta in this way. The drug effects may be magnified in the fetus because of poorly developed enzyme systems. The resultant lower rates of metabolism may mean that the drug remains in fetal circulation for longer than it does in maternal circulation. This is believed to be the case with diazepam (Mandelli et al., 1975).

Fetal damage may also occur if a drug affects placental function. Some drugs may not be directly toxic to the fetus, and may not even enter fetal circulation, but may alter normal development. If, for example, blood flow across the placenta is impaired in any way then the fetus will be deprived of oxygen and nutrients.

Drugs may directly influence the health status of the mother and then indirectly impair fetal health. These changes may be brought about through altered hormone levels, changed nutritional status (if the drug reduces food intake), alteration to the immune system, impaired cardiovascular functioning, etc. Any of the chronic effects of drugs may rebound on the developing fetus.

Finally, maternal drug use during pregnancy may alter development after birth if the drug induces physical dependence. The baby will be born physically dependent if the mother has been using the drug sufficiently often, and will then undergo withdrawal unless treated appropriately. Withdrawal can be particularly damaging in the newborn if it is sudden, and medical care is necessary to avoid death or damage to the infant. This may involve administration of gradually reducing amounts of drug to the infant as well as supportive care.

Considerably less attention has been paid to the effects of maternal drug intake prior to conception and during breast feeding. The effects prior to conception may parallel the effects of paternal drug use, although the mechanisms may be somewhat different. While it is known that drugs are secreted in varying quantities through mother's milk, the effects are largely unknown. In practice, drug use often occurs prior to, during, and after pregnancy. As a result, it is difficult to isolate any one time period.

Research Problems

As in so many areas of drug research there are important methodological problems which make conclusions about whether or not a drug has teratological effects very difficult. This makes discussions regarding the nature of these effects that much more difficult. While some types of research can be done using data from humans, many types of studies are done instead, on animals. This brings its own problems, including the considerable variation in teratogenic potential between species. The best known example is *thalidomide,* a drug given to pregnant women before it was found to cause major morphological malformation in the offspring. While highly teratogenic in some species, it has little or no effect in others (Fabro, 1981). Unfortunately, prior to release it had not been tested for teratogenicity in sensitive species.

One complication in assessing the teratogenic potential of a therapeutic drug is separating the effects of the drug from the effects of the medical disorder for which it was prescribed. For example, a drug given for treatment of anxiety may be suspected of being teratogenic. How is it possible to separate the effects of this drug from the effects of anxiety per se? Anxiety may be important because anxious people often have lower food intake and altered hormonal levels. Either of these could modify fetal development independently of the drug. While it is possible to separate such factors (and animal research may be particularly useful here), it is not always easy.

Another problem is that teratogenic potential depends critically on both the amount of drug administered and the stage of fetal development at which it is given. Accordingly, one might conclude that a drug has teratogenic potential only if the offspring of women who took a certain minimum amount at a certain stage of pregnancy were examined. If all women who used the drug were considered, the offspring may not appear to be much different from normal.

Fetal abnormalities may be difficult to detect. One example of this is spontaneous abortion very early in pregnancy. Any drug which produces such an effect may not be recognized. Also difficult to recognize are drugs that produce abnormalities at a very low rate of occurrence. The high frequency teratogenic effects have been hard enough to identify. If a drug produces effects in offspring that are severe, but occur very infrequently, then the chances of recognition are small.

Specific Drugs

Information concerning specific drug effects on offspring varies considerably. In some cases we have a reasonable idea of the effects produced, while in others there is relatively little information. As with chronic effects, it should not be assumed that those about which we know little have negligible effects. More detailed information can be found in the volumes by Briggs et al. (1983), Chiang (1985), and Pinkert (1985), and the chapters by Finnegan and Fehr (1980) and Rossett (1980).

Opiates. It has been difficult to separate the effects of opiates from the general lifestyle and living conditions of most people dependent on them. They frequently have poorer nutritional status, more illnesses than average, and ingest a range of other drugs. Study of the offspring of heroin-dependent mothers has revealed problems of low birth weight, prematurity, perinatal complications, and a range of abnormalities. Their general development may be slower. However, as mentioned, there are many confounding factors which make evaluation of the effects of heroin itself very difficult. One approach has been to compare people using street opiates with those on methadone maintenance programs (see Chapter Six). The findings show that while there is a higher risk of these problems with street opiate users, the offspring of methadone users are very close to normal. These different outcomes may be partly due to heroin-methadone differences, but the poorer health and higher frequency of withdrawal experienced by heroin users may also be factors. Opiate withdrawal is important as it results in reduced oxygen supply to the fetus. In animal studies abnormalities can be produced by administration of very high doses, but doses equivalent to those taken by humans result only in decreased birthweight and increased perinatal mortality.

Barbiturates. There is some evidence of morphological and behavioral impairment as a result of maternal barbiturate administration. However, studies in humans should be treated tentatively, in that many barbiturate users self-administer other drugs. In addition, many use the drug to control epilepsy, and the occurrence of seizures may have a deleterious effect on the fetus. Some results suggest behavioral impairment in the form of delayed development of the sucking response.

Benzodiazepines. There are reports of a number of different kinds of birth defects in children born to benzodiazepine-using mothers. Animal studies also suggest the possibility of a wide range of effects. The strongest evidence is for a higher incidence of cleft palate. It is not clear whether this is common to all benzodiazepines or whether only some have this effect. The evidence is most convincing in the case of diazepam.

Alcohol. The most clearly defined set of effects produced by maternal drug intake is that associated with alcohol use. Fetal alcohol syndrome is characterized by abnormal facial appearance, growth retardation, cardiovascular defects, various other morphological defects, and damage to the central nervous system. It is one of the major causes of mental retardation. While the complete syndrome only occurs with heavy drinking women, it now seems that lower drinking levels may produce some effect. Damage to the central nervous system, manifested as behavioral abnormalities, may be the most common result. Advice to women intending to conceive suggests that they reduce their consumption to two drinks per day at most, but preferably less. In that most damage occurs in the first sixty to ninety days, waiting until pregnancy is suspected or confirmed may be ineffective.

Amphetamine and cocaine.   Animal studies have suggested that maternal amphetamine administration induces a wide range of abnormalities. Even at quite low doses there are behavioral differences in the offspring of mothers who have administered amphetamine. The most notable change is an increase in excitability. However, the results from studies of humans are less conclusive. It seems that there are effects, including cleft palate, but these occur with a relatively low frequency. Research is made more difficult by the fact that amphetamine and related stimulants are no longer widely prescribed for adult women. Research into the teratogenic effects of cocaine is in its early stages at present. To date, there are indications of a range of adverse effects including higher rates of spontaneous abortion and low birth weight. Behavioral problems in infancy may be caused by the CNS effects of cocaine *in utero*. Certain malformations may be more common. For example, both human and animal studies indicate that urogenital anomalies may be related to maternal cocaine use. However, it should be noted that much research is yet to be done. In many cases the appropriate controls are missing, and there are reports of no detectable problems in the offspring of cocaine-using mothers. Hopefully, these issues will be clarified over the next few years.

Tobacco.   The risk of spontaneous abortion is much higher in smokers than in nonsmokers. It seems that smoking can induce malformations which are sufficiently large so that death results at an early stage. If the fetus does survive then it will be (on average) ten to fifteen percent lighter than would be expected. This difference appears to continue at least for some years, but the death rate is no higher amongst these children than among the children of nonsmokers. This body weight difference has been confirmed in animals, and the magnitude has been shown to be related to the amount of maternal exposure to tobacco smoke. There is no convincing evidence of particular morphological or other abnormalities.

Caffeine.   The evidence on the effects of caffeine is somewhat contradictory. While many studies have shown no effect, there is evidence that high caffeine intake levels (approx. six hundred milligrams per day or more) may result in higher rates of spontaneous abortion and possibly certain congenital abnormalities. While the data from animal studies support such conclusions, it should be noted that other factors unrelated to caffeine intake have not been ruled out in the human studies.

Hallucinogens.   The effects of maternal hallucinogen use are not clear. While LSD is capable of inducing chromosomal damage, at normal human dosage levels this does not seem to occur. Some evidence has been obtained suggesting that structural abnormalities, particularly of the limbs, may be more frequent in offspring of LSD users. Again, however, the lack of control studies makes this suggestive only. LSD teratogenicity varies considerably from species to species. Little is known of the effects of other hallucinogens.

Marijuana.   Like LSD, marijuana has been observed to induce chromosomal damage at high doses, but it is not clear that it has such effects in humans taking normal doses. Little evidence exists concerning the effects of maternal marijuana use in humans. Animal studies have described increased perinatal mortality and reduced birthweight. Differences in behavior have been noted when comparing offspring of both marijuana-treated and control mothers. There is evidence that the behavioral effects may be due to the main active ingredient, $\triangle^9$-THC. It is suspected that other effects may be due to the various other constituents of marijuana smoke.

Inhalants.   There is little evidence concerning these compounds. Given their toxicity, effects on offspring are highly likely with these drugs, particularly where contaminants such as lead are involved. However, since inhalant use is mostly confined to younger teenagers, there may be relatively few affected children. Nevertheless, there are reports of profound effects on the offspring of teenage mothers who have been inhalant abusers (see Hunter, Thompson and Evans, 1979).

CONCLUSIONS

This brief survey has indicated the wide variety of adverse effects that drugs can produce. The types of effect depend on a range of factors including the type of drug, the amount taken, and the pattern of intake, and on the various characteristics of the individual using the drug. This multiple determination means that it is hard to predict the effects on any one individual (or that individual's offspring). Although acute effects are reasonably predictable, the difficulty becomes apparent when the effects of chronic administration are considered. We can only speculate as to why one heavy user suffers considerable damage while another seems to escape almost unscathed.

The adverse effects of drugs are an important consideration when decisions are made concerning drug availability, price, advertising, and related matters (see Chapter Four). While some may condemn drug use per se as morally or psychologically 'unhealthy,' most people would view the adverse effects of drugs as the main reason for regulating and controlling their use. What is apparent from the material here is that there is no rational basis for current regulations. As was suggested in Chapter Four, it is not the dangerous drugs that are prohibited, but those less firmly entrenched. Bans which meet considerable resistance are less likely to be enforced than those which meet resistance from a small, relatively powerless group in society.

One conclusion which could be supported from the information presented here is that all drugs should be banned. All produce adverse effects which are sufficiently severe to warrant such action. However, these results need to be put into some perspective. Just as the adverse effects of various drugs have been described, the same could have been done for vitamins, drugs regarded as virtually harmless and freely available (aspirin, for instance), and pollutants in our air, water, and food to which we are all exposed. Virtually any chemical introduced to our bodies is toxic if given in large enough quantities and for a long enough period of time. The issue is not so much whether there are any adverse effects but instead, at what amount do these substances become toxic? Drug use involves risks as do many other activities. What is important to society is determining both the level of risk, and the potential consequences.

The ability of medical and other services to deal with drug-induced problems varies considerably. While the chances of a drug overdose patient surviving are relatively good, and certainly better than they were, many effects of chronic drug use are more difficult to treat. Furthermore, a number of adverse effects are simply not reversible. For example, damage to brain tissue resulting from alcohol abuse cannot be reversed through medical treatment. A patient with severe Wernicke-Korsakoff syndrome for instance, simply has to be in care for the rest of his or her life. Certain effects on offspring too, may be extremely difficult to correct.

Clearly, the treatment of people whose drug use has been excessive (either on an acute or chronic basis) is only partially effective. Even with considerable advances in science and medicine this is likely to remain the case. Because of this, many have argued that it is better to concentrate on reducing drug abuse, both by preventative measures and by treatment aimed not so much at the adverse effects but at drug use itself. This is the subject of the following chapter.

REFERENCES

ABBOTT, P.J. (1986). Caffeine: A toxicological overview. *Medical Journal of Australia, 145,* 518–521.

ADESSO, V.J. (1980). Experimental studies of human drinking behavior. In H. Rigter & J.C. Crabbe (Eds.), *Alcohol tolerance and dependence.* (pp. 123–155). Amsterdam: Elsevier.

ASHLEY, M.J. (1984). Alcohol consumption and ischaemic heart disease: The epidemiological evidence. In R.G. Smart, H.D. Cappell, F.B. Glaser, Y. Israel, H. Kalant, R.E. Popham, W. Schmidt, & E.M. Sellers (Eds.), *Research advances in alcohol and drug problems.* (Vol. 8, pp. 99–147). New York: Plenum Press.

BRIGGS, G.G., BODENDORFER, T.W., FREEMAN, R.K., & YAFFE, S.J. (1983). *Drugs in pregnancy and lactation: A reference guide to fetal and neonatal risk.* Baltimore, MD: Williams and Wilkins.

CHIANG, N.C. (Ed.) (1985). *Prenatal drug exposure: Kinetics and dynamics.* Rockville, MD: National Institute on Drug Abuse.

DENNEY, R.C. (1979). *Drinking and driving.* London: Robert Hale.

FABRO, S. (1981). The biochemical basis of thalidomide teratogenicity. In M.R. Juchau (Ed.), *The biochemical basis of teratogens.* (pp. 159–178). New York: Elsevier North Holland.

FERRARA, S.D. (1987).   Alcohol, drugs and traffic safety. *British Journal of Addiction, 82,* 871–883.

FINNEGAN, L.P. & FEHR, K.O. (1980).   The effects of opiates, sedative hypnotics, amphetamines, cannabis and other psychoactive drugs on the fetus and newborn. In O.J. Kalant (Ed.), *Alcohol and drug problems in women.* Research advances in alcohol and drug problems. (Vol. 5, pp. 653–723). New York: Plenum Press.

GLASS, D.C. (1977).   *Behavior patterns, stress, and coronary disease.* Hillsdale, NJ: Lawrence Erlbaum.

GOSSEL, T.A. & BRICKER, J.D. (1984).   *Principles of clinical toxicology.* New York: Raven Press.

GRIFFIN, J.P. & D'ARCY, P.F. (1984).   *A manual of adverse drug interactions* (3rd ed.). Bristol: Wright.

GRIFFITHS, A.N., MARSHALL, R.W., & RICHENS, A. (1984)   Saccadic eye movement analysis as a measure of drug effects on human psychomotor performance. *British Journal of Clinical Pharmacology, 18,* 735–825.

HANENSON, I.B.   (Ed.) (1980).   *Quick reference to clinical toxicology.* Philadelphia: J.B. Lippincott Company.

HINDMARCH, I. (1980).   Psychomotor function and psychoactive drugs. *British Journal of Clinical Pharmacology, 10,* 189–209.

HOWAT, P.A. & LANDAUER, A.A. (1983).   *Blood alcohol concentrations and motor vehicle accidents: A review of the evidence.* Perth, Western Australia: Western Australia Institute of Technology.

HUNTER, A.G., THOMPSON, D., & EVANS, J.A. (1979).   Is there a fetal gasoline syndrome? *Teratology, 1,* 75–79.

JAMES, J.E. & STIRLING, K.P. (1983).   Caffeine: A survey of some of the known and suspected deleterious effects of habitual use. *British Journal of Addiction, 78,* 251–258.

JOFFE, J. (1979).   Influence of drug exposure of the father on perinatal outcome. *Clinics in Perinatology, 6,* 21–36.

JOHNSTON, I.R. (1982).   The role of alcohol in road accidents. *Ergonomics, 25,* 941–946.

JONES, R.T. (1978).   Marijuana: Human effects. In L.L. Iversen, S.D. Iversen, & S.H. Snyder (Eds.), *Handbook of Psychopharmacology.* (Vol. 12, pp. 373–412). New York: Plenum Press.

LINDSAY, P.H. & NORMAN, D.A. (1977).   *Human information processing* (2nd ed.). New York: Academic Press.

LUTWAK-MANN, C. (1964).   Observations of progeny of thalidomide treated male rabbits. *British Medical Journal, 1,* 1090–1091.

MANDELLI, M., MORSELLI, P.L., NORDIO, S., PARDI, G., PRINCIPI, N., SERENI, F., & TOGNONI, G. (1975).   Placental transfer of diazepam and its disposition in the newborn. *Clinical Pharmacology and Therapeutics, 17,* 564–572.

MATTILA, M.J. (1984).   Interactions of benzodiazepines on psychomotor skills. *British Journal of Clinical Pharmacology, 18,* 21S–26S.

MAYKUT, M.O. (1984).   *Health consequences of acute and chronic marijuana use.* Oxford: Pergamon Press.

MICZEK, K.A. (1987).   The psychopharmacology of aggression. In L.L. Iversen, S.D. Iversen, & S.H. Snyder (Eds.), *Handbook of Psychopharmacology.* (Vol. 19, pp. 183–328). New York: Plenum Press.

MORRIS, A.I. (1984).   Sexuality, alcohol, and liver disease. In N. Krasner, J.S. Madden, & R.J. Walker (Eds.), *Alcohol-related problems.* (pp. 251–258). Chichester: Wiley.

NICHOLSON, A. & WARD, J. (Eds.) (1984).   Psychotropic drugs and performance. *British Journal of Clinical Pharmacology, 18,* 1S–140S.

PERNANEN, K. (1976).   Alcohol and crimes of violence. In B. Kissin & H. Begleiter (Eds.), *Social aspects of alcoholism.* (pp. 351–444). New York: Plenum Press.

PINKERT, T.M.   (Ed.) (1985). *Current research on the consequences of maternal drug use.* Rockville, MD: National Institute on Drug Abuse.

POPHAM, R.E., SCHMIDT, W., & ISRAELSTAM, S. (1984).   Heavy alcohol consumption and physical health problems: A review of the epidemiologic evidence. In R.G. Smart, H.D. Cappell, F.B. Glaser, Y. Israel, H. Kalant, R.E. Popham, W. Schmidt, & E.M.

Sellers (Eds.), *Research advances in alcohol and drug problems.* (Vol. 8, pp. 149–182). New York: Plenum Press.

ROBINS, L.N. (1979). Addict careers. In R.I. DuPont, A. Goldstein, & J. O'Donnell (Eds.), *Handbook on drug abuse.* (pp. 325–336). Rockville, MD: National Institute on Drug Abuse.

RON, M.A. (1984). Brain damage in chronic alcoholism. In N. Krasner, J.S. Madden, & R.J. Walker (Eds.), *Alcohol-related problems.* (pp. 243–250). Chichester: Wiley.

ROSETT, H.L. (1980). The effects of alcohol on the fetus and offspring. In O.J. Kalant (Ed.), *Alcohol and drug problems in women.* Research Advances in Alcohol and Drug Problems. (Vol. 5, pp. 595–652). New York: Plenum Press.

U.S. DEPT. OF HEALTH, EDUCATION, AND WELFARE (1979). *Smoking and health: A report of the Surgeon General.* Washington, DC: U.S. Government Printing Office.

WALLER, J.A. (1976). Alcohol and unintentional injury. In B. Kissin & H. Begleiter (Eds.), *Social aspects of alcoholism.* (pp. 307–349). New York: Plenum Press.

WELFORD, A.T. (1968). *Fundamentals of skill.* London: Methuen.

WOLFGANG, M.E. (1967). Victim-precipitated criminal homicide. In M.E. Wolfgang (Ed.), *Studies in homicide.* (pp. 72–87). New York: Harper and Row.

CHAPTER 6

Therapy for Dependence Problems

In addition to management of drug-induced medical problems, treatment for drug dependence may also involve attempts to reduce drug intake itself. This may be necessary because the deleterious effects of the drug (medical, psychological, social) become sufficiently severe that the person seeks out such treatment. A second reason is that the drug used is an illegal one and potential or actual legal problems may provide a reason for cessation of use.

Such treatment has a considerable history. Many early "cures" involved substituting one drug for another. Last century Freud was experimenting with the use of cocaine as a substitute for opium in physically dependent individuals (Byck, 1974). Another example has been the use of opium or opiates for alcohol problems (Siegel, 1986).

Modern approaches are quite diverse. They have arisen from a range of theoretical perspectives and are used by people with very different training and backgrounds. While many therapists combine elements from the different approaches, others adopt only a single approach and use only a limited range of techniques. Accordingly, each of the major approaches (medical, psychotherapeutic, social, and behavioral) will be considered separately below. Before doing so, certain preliminary matters, covering general aspects of the treatment process, need to be examined. After discussion of each individual treatment type some consideration will be given to selection of an appropriate treatment, combining approaches, and dealing with the problem of relapse. Finally, prevention will be considered as a means for reducing problems of drug abuse before they reach the treatment stage.

PRELIMINARY CONSIDERATIONS

Types of Treatment Facilities

In modern societies a vast range of individuals and facilities offer treatment to drug users (see, for example, the discussion of alcohol treatment facilities by Pattison, 1979). One of the important ways in which they differ is by the type and training of staff. Medically trained staff are present in hospital settings and in private practice. The first point of contact for an individual may be through their normal doctor. He or she may offer some treatment, or may refer the person to a psychiatrist, hospital, or outpatient facility specializing in drug problems. Some general hospitals also have facilities for such treatment and are usually staffed with medical personnel. However, individuals who have a variety of backgrounds (social workers, psychologists, counsellors, etc.) often work together with medically trained staff in these settings.

Other facilities have little input from medical personnel. Therapeutic communities, halfway houses, and various community facilities tend to involve doctors only when clear medical problems are present. The majority of staff may be drug counsellors or have training in psychology. Many former drug users are employed as counsellors. These are people who had a drug abuse problem, resolved it, and now wish to help others who have such problems. The suggestion is that those who have themselves been through the experience can best understand what it is like and therefore relate to the drug user. A number of facilities have both ex-users and professional staff such as psychologists as counsellors.

As well as the type of people involved, facilities vary according to their source of funding. Many medical facilities rely on payment from the individual, although this depends on the nature of the health system in the particular country. Some may be reimbursed or paid for by government, and may allow free treatment to anyone who enters. Others, such as certain therapeutic communities, rely both on charity and payment from users.

A related issue concerns the financial organization of the facility. Some are profit-making, others are not. Private medical, psychiatric, and psychological consultations would have to be included under profit-making organizations. Generally, private hospitals are profit-making, whereas those funded by government agencies are not. Therapeutic communities vary considerably, with some clearly making profit and others acting more in the manner of self-help groups.

Some facilities treat only on an outpatient basis whereas others offer inpatient facilities. The latter are used mainly for detoxification and for treatment of the medical consequences of drug use. While inpatient treatment has been popular, particularly for the treatment of alcoholism, some doubt has been cast on its cost effectiveness (Miller and Hester, 1986). It is considerably more expensive than outpatient treatment, but a number of studies have shown no real benefit in terms of overall outcome. However, as will be discussed below, it may be best suited to certain individuals, particularly those with more severe problems.

Finally, facilities may be specialized for one type of drug problem or may treat a range of problems. For example, many private hospitals deal with alcohol problems only, while methadone clinics specialize in treatment of opiate dependence. Therapeutic communities are often specialized, as well. However, most private therapists deal with a range of drug problems.

Entry to Treatment

People arrive at drug treatment facilities in a number of different ways. In some cases it is a referral from a court system which results in clinic attendance. Compulsory treatment for drug problems is sometimes prescribed by courts as an alternative to a jail sentence or heavy fine. Such people may be reluctant patients. They do not necessarily have any wish to cease drug use and may resist attempts which try to get them to do so.

Other people may be referred by employers. Poor work performance over some time may have been attributed to drug use of some kind. The employer may suggest the person attend a drug treatment facility or the organization may be involved in an occupational assistance program which provides trained counsellors. Such programs are becoming more common in a number of countries. They provide a means by which drug problems can be dealt with before the person reaches the stage of losing his or her job. Details of the operations of such programs can be found in Shain and Groeneveld (1980) and Myers (1984).

Drug treatment may also be suggested by a doctor, social worker, or other professional with whom the person comes in contact. For example, in the course of medical examination and testing, a doctor may discover a liver disorder which he or she suspects has an alcoholic etiology. The doctor may decide to deal with the person's alcohol problem themselves or may refer them to some other facility for more specialized attention.

Finally, people may simply approach a treatment facility on a voluntary basis. Usually, the pressure to do so will have arisen because of adverse medical or social effects of drug use. However, in some cases antidrug advertising and information may prompt a person to seek help before such effects arise. For example, people may seek help in giving up smoking even though they have no symptoms of lung cancer, heart disease, or emphysema. The threat of these may be sufficient in some cases.

Diagnosis

Once a person reaches a treatment facility the first step is diagnosis or assessment. Although superficially simple (for example, the person may be classified as heroin dependent, or a binge drinker) adequate assessment is a complex task. Its importance is as a guide for the design of therapy. While in some situations people are given a 'standard package' of treatment, the ideal is individualized therapy based on assessment.

The most obvious part of assessment concerns the actual drug use. Questions should relate to current use (how much?, how often?, etc.) and history of use. Other drugs used should also be investigated, in that therapy may have to be concerned with them as well. Symptoms of withdrawal should be assessed, particularly where the syndrome can be physically dangerous (as with alcohol or barbiturate withdrawal). Other consequences that need to be assessed include any social problems or health problems which have resulted from drug use. These may include loss of employment, arrest, various medical problems, etc. Other aspects of assessment will depend on the particular therapeutic approach, and will be considered below.

The form assessment takes can vary considerably. The most basic involves obtaining information from the patient in a simple question-and-answer format. Various structured questionnaires may be used to provide more detailed and perhaps more accurate information in certain areas (see Sobell, Sobell and Nirenberg, 1988 for a review of these). For example, certain questionnaires attempt to more accurately characterize the various adverse consequences of excessive alcohol consumption an individual may have experienced. A clinician may also decide that additional information is needed. This could take the form of discussions with other people (for example, the client's spouse), medical tests (perhaps to assess liver function), or psychiatric examination.

One area where diagnosis has been controversial is differentiation of alcoholism from less severe problem drinking. Many attempts have been made at devising appropriate criteria, but none have proven to be valid and reliable or to have good predictive value (Mendelson and Mello, 1979).

The main criterion used has been the amount consumed. However, there are no clear divisions between alcoholics and nonalcoholics. Rather, there is a continuum of amount drunk, and any attempt to divide that continuum must be somewhat artificial. It should also be noted that on this basis many would argue that there should be no category of "alcoholic" (see Editorial and Commentaries, 1987). Furthermore, there are cultural differences in drinking norms, as was indicated in Chapter Four. What may be heavy drinking in one culture may only be regarded as moderate in another. In many modern societies composed of a number of different cultural groups this can be a considerable problem.

A second, related criterion is the presence of physical dependence. An alcoholic is sometimes defined as a person who is physically dependent on alcohol. One problem is in actually defining and assessing physical dependence. One can assess opiate dependence by administering an antagonist and observing any withdrawal signs. However, the only reliable way with alcohol is to prevent intake for a period of time — something which is often much harder than simple antagonist administration. A further difficulty is that physical dependence itself varies considerably in strength. Many people who have very serious drinking problems do not have strong physical dependence.

Another major diagnostic criterion is the degree of impairment to health and social functioning. One could simply argue that alcoholics are those people whose health and/or social functioning has been seriously impaired as a result of alcohol intake. A number of obvious difficulties arise in the use of such a criterion. For example, at the time of first consultation a person may have no serious health problems, but may develop fatal liver cirrhosis if allowed to keep drinking for another five years. While medical tests can sometimes help predict such changes, they are far from perfect.

Alcoholism is sometimes defined in terms of lack of self-control over drinking, but this is virtually impossible to use as a reliable diagnostic criterion. Clearly, there is no unambiguous means of differentiating alcoholics from nonalcoholics. In practice, the main diagnostic criteria used are consumption levels and adverse effects. Consumption data should include the pattern of drinking as well as overall intake. The entire range of adverse effects should be taken into account. By combining these it is possible to get some indication of the severity of the drinking problem.

Treatment Goals

There are two main types of goals to aim for in treatment. One is complete abstinence and the other is moderate, controlled use of the drug. There has been considerable controversy concerning the feasibility of controlled drug use, particularly as it applies to alcohol use (see Heather and Robertson, 1981). It has been argued that it is too risky for an alcoholic to attempt controlled drinking, and any true alcoholic will fail at such an attempt.

Those who favor controlled drinking as an alternative suggest that it is only appropriate for people without alcohol induced disease (including liver disease), for whom moderate drinking is not dangerous, and who feel capable of the self-control and decision-making required of a controlled drinker. A certain proportion of people find controlled drinking impossible; abstinence is the only alternative for them. In general, consumption levels are higher amongst this latter group and they are more likely to have a family history of alcoholism.

One major advantage of offering controlled drinking programs is that many more people with severe drinking problems are likely to seek help to reduce their consumption levels. There are a number of people who do not wish to be abstinent and for whom drinking is virtually essential. For example, male heavy drinkers in their late teens or early twenties are frequently involved in social groups that regard drinking as the norm. Any who stopped drinking would find it difficult to remain in the group. For such individuals a reduction of their intake may be possible, but abstinence would command too high a price.

Controlled drug use has been tried to a limited extent in other areas. Many smokers have found abstinence to be an impossible goal. They may have tried and failed a number of times, even with help. Such people are often successful at reducing their intake of nicotine and other tobacco products. They can learn to do this in several ways (Frederiksen, 1979). One is to reduce the number of cigarettes smoked each day. A second is to alter their pattern of intake so that inhalation is more shallow and lasts for a shorter period of time. While abstinence may be preferable in the case of cigarettes, safer use appears to be a viable alternative when all else fails. It may, of course, be a stepping stone to later abstinence.

MEDICAL APPROACHES

Many medically-trained personnel regard certain drug use patterns as indicative of a disease state. The best known is alcoholism. While the actual cause is not known, the pathological nature of the behavior is said to indicate the presence of a genuine disease. Similarly, it has been argued that heroin users may have a deficiency in the natural opiate systems of the brain (see Chapter Two). Other drug use could be explained in a similar manner.

Medical treatment involves two main parts. One is the reduction of drug intake. This may be achieved by having the individual undergo withdrawal, possibly with the help of drugs to suppress the symptoms. It may also involve drugs that help reduce further intake. The second involves treatment of associated problems. Primary amongst these are the medical consequences of drug use. They include the various health effects (described in the previous chapter) and underlying psychiatric and social problems. The disease state itself (for example, alcoholism) may be considered one such problem. In the case of alcohol problems, the medical view has been described by Knott, Beard and Fink (1987).

Reduction of Drug Intake

If a person is physically dependent on a drug they may have to undergo withdrawal as a first step. As described in Chapter Two, withdrawal may be a very uncomfortable, even life-threatening process. It is most severe in the case of barbiturate and alcohol use, but also quite pronounced with opiates. Accordingly, drugs may be given to suppress the withdrawal symptoms and ease the transition to a drug-free state.

In the case of benzodiazepine or alcohol use, a long-acting benzodiazepine is usually employed. The person stops taking their normal drug, and substitutes the benzodiazepine instead. Usually, the dose of the substitute is reduced gradually after a few days, and eliminated eventually after several weeks. With barbiturates a long-acting drug from that class (for example phenobarbital) is used in a similar way.

For opiate users methadone serves a similar function. It is a long-acting, orally effective opiate which suppresses heroin withdrawal symptoms. Nevertheless, it is not a cure, but simply transfers dependence from one opiate to another. The alternatives are then to gradually reduce the methadone dose over a period of time or to shift to a methadone maintenance program, described below. In that opiate withdrawal is not a serious medical condition, treatment often involves use of drugs to control symptoms rather than substitution of another opiate. The nonopiate *clonidine* is effective in suppressing a range of opiate withdrawal signs, although the craving is still present.

In recent years another substitute drug has become available. Nicotine in chewing gum form can be prescribed to help alleviate withdrawal in people attempting to give up smoking. Trials suggest that it is effective in suppressing nicotine withdrawal symptoms and this increases the chances of success (Schneider and Jarvik, 1985). However, one problem is the unpleasant taste which prevents many people from using it.

While withdrawal is generally carried out on an outpatient or consulting basis, hospitalization may be necessary in severe cases. Alcohol withdrawal is the most common reason for hospitalization. In such cases the drug therapy may be supported by nutritional supplements and treatment for specific symptoms.

Drug therapy of a different kind may be employed after the withdrawal period. Rather than suppressing symptoms, it is aimed at ensuring that relapse does not occur. For opiate users, maintenance doses of methadone are commonly used. These doses are very large in order to develop a high degree of opiate tolerance in the individual. As a result of this tolerance, any use of street drugs is likely to produce only a very small effect.

The procedure for dispensing methadone varies from country to country, and may also depend on the individual. In many cases the person has to return to a registered clinic or pharmacist on a daily basis. There, he or she is given the methadone tablet(s) or syrup and is required to swallow in the presence of a staff member. In some cases the person may be allowed to take one or more doses home.

Methadone maintenance is probably the most common approach to opiate dependence. In many countries specific clinics have been set up to handle large numbers of opiate dependent individuals. Each person may continue to use methadone for a period of several years. Although not entirely successful, and not without its critics, methadone is a relatively simple and inexpensive way of treating large numbers of heroin users. While it is only substituting one opiate for another, it eliminates most of the dangers associated with use of illegal drugs and allows a person to lead a relatively normal life without having to finance an expensive drug habit (Dole, 1971).

Another type of drug used to prevent relapse of opiate use is the opiate antagonist *naltrexone.* Treatment with the drug usually begins once withdrawal is complete and the person has been abstinent for a period of time. Because of its antagonist properties, any opiate used during the time-course of its action will be ineffective. Naltrexone has the advantages of having both a long duration of action and oral effectiveness, in addition to being a pure antagonist. By taking naltrexone at a regular time (mornings, for example) a person trying to resist further opiate use may be able to exercise the necessary "self-control" at a time when the drug is less available or the temptation not as strong. Any attempt to self-administer an opiate later in the day will not be rewarded with the usual effects.

Several other drugs are being investigated for their potential in preventing opiate relapse. One is LAAM (levo-alpha-acetylmethadol), very similar to methadone but even longer lasting. It would be easier to use simply because fewer clinic visits would be required (approximately three per week). A second is *buprenorphine,* a drug which has some methadone-like properties and some naltrexone-like properties. That is, it produces an opiate effect, but also blocks other opiates the person administers.

Disulfiram (Antabuse) is used extensively in treating alcoholics who are attempting to abstain. It interferes with the normal metabolism of alcohol, causing a build-up of acetaldehyde, one of the by-products of this process. The resultant symptoms are rather unpleasant and include flushing of the skin, difficulty in breathing, a pounding sensation in the head and chest, nausea, vomiting, dizziness, and blurred vision. Note that these only occur when both alcohol and disulfiram are present in the body together. Disulfiram alone does not have these effects.

In order for this reaction to occur the person need only use the disulfiram once a day (usually taken in the morning). Any alcohol taken after that will result in the unpleasant symptoms, the severity of which depends on the amount of alcohol. Disulfiram is not an effective treatment in all cases — some people even drink through the symptoms — but has proven a useful aid for many people. While research is continuing on the effectiveness of oral disulfiram, one recent advance with much promise is the implantation of disulfiram under the skin. Initial studies suggest that this technique may produce significantly greater success rates (Miller and Hester, 1980).

Treatment of Associated Problems

Considerable time and effort spent in medical treatment may be concerned with problems associated with drug use. One group of problems are the adverse health effects resulting from drug use. The types of problems which arise and their treatment were discussed in the previous chapter. Psychiatric problems may also be found to need some attention. As described in Chapter Three, there is evidence that people who develop drug problems have a higher incidence of certain psychiatric disorders, notably anxiety and depression. While some of this may result from drug use, it may also be more common in potential drug users prior to their beginning such use. If this is the case, then treatment of the psychiatric disorder may be essential if the person is to control or eliminate drug use. Otherwise, use may continue or begin again for some of the same reasons it began in the first place. Treatment may involve drugs (for example, an antidepressant or benzodiazepine) or some form of psychotherapy. In such cases a psychiatrist may be involved in treatment. (See, for example, the discussion of alcohol problems and affective disorders in Goodwin and Erickson, 1979).

Additional help may be given in one of two ways. The most common is referral to a self-help group such as Alcoholics Anonymous. This serves to provide some social support and also has an educative function. The person can learn more about their drug problem by discussion with others who have had similar problems. Many medical practitioners see such groups as an essential adjunct to the treatment they provide.

Some hospitals and clinics also arrange sessions in which patients are taught more about the drugs they are taking, the effects produced and the nature of dependence. Other sessions may be chaired by one of the medical personnel but involve general discussion concerning the experiences of the people involved. These serve a similar function to the self-help groups.

PSYCHOTHERAPEUTIC APPROACHES

One model of drug users which had been popular amongst psychoanalysts and other psychotherapists was mentioned briefly in Chapter Three. It suggested that people with drug problems are psychologically immature, dependent individuals who have difficulty forming normal relationships. Maturity may occur relatively late in life, at which stage the person may cease excessive drug use. Psychotherapy can function to hasten this process.

This type of approach has become considerably less popular over time. For one thing, there is little evidence of the type of "addictive personality" on which the approach is based. As described in Chapter Three, the objective evidence indicates otherwise. Secondly, such traditional psychoanalytic approaches do not hold much attraction for many people with drug abuse problems. They simply reject the whole notion and do not wish to participate. Finally, even amongst those who do participate the success rate is not very high. By comparison to many other approaches, psychotherapy is time-consuming and expensive. Such an investment should be rewarded with a high success rate, but unfortunately this is not, conclusively, the case (Blane, 1977).

Another characteristic of older psychotherapeutic approaches is that they tended to regard drug use merely as a symptom. It was said that the real problem was an underlying one and it was this that needed to be resolved. Accordingly, little time was spent in trying to change drug use directly; the focus was on the underlying psychological problems. The danger in this approach is that the person's psychological functioning will improve but their drug use will not change. The notion that drug use is solely symptomatic appears to be incorrect. It has been noted that there are many possible reasons for drug use, including the direct reinforcing effects produced, behavioral and subjective changes, and the avoidance of withdrawal in physically dependent individuals. While underlying psychological disorders may be a factor in certain cases, they are by no means the only factors, and any approach that assumes this is likely to end in failure.

Because of these problems, more recent approaches have tended to focus on both drug use and psychological problems (Blane, 1977). Rather than being used alone, psychotherapy is generally combined with other methods such as drug therapy. The social context of drug use is also acknowledged through the concurrent use of group or family therapy (for example, O'Farrell, 1987). Such innovations are indicative of a more eclectic approach which is much less dependent on psychoanalytic models.

The process of psychotherapy is a long one. While there is a great deal of variation, it is usually considered that a year is required to produce the necessary changes. In the beginning, the person may have to be confronted with their drug use. Denial of excessive use or of adverse effects can be common, particularly amongst alcoholics. Denial may also work in another way, where an individual admits to drug use but refuses to reveal an underlying emotional problem. In such cases the therapist may need to spend time trying to define the problems with the patient.

Having brought the individual to the point of admitting their drug use and other problems which may play a causative role, the next task may be to set stages in the reduction of drug use. These should be agreed to by patient and psychotherapist and may even be written out in a formal manner to prevent later disputes.

The main part of the psychotherapeutic process is concerned with resolving underlying problems revealed in early sessions. In general, the origins of these may be found in the person's early environment, particularly childhood years, or in their present environment. The latter may be aspects of every day life which provoke drug use. For any individual both may be important, but one or the other may seem most deserving of attention by the psychotherapist.

As this process occurs, goals must be set which allow the person to gradually overcome the problem. For example, if the individual has been unable to engage in normal social interaction without use of drugs, they may be given tasks which involve increasing degrees of such interaction. Accordingly, as the psychotherapeutic process reduces the severity of the underlying problem, the individual moves closer to his or her new nondrug using self in everyday life. Once the person can function in a mature, independent manner the psychotherapy sessions become redundant. The person is essentially cured or is in the process of curing himself or herself and no longer needs the therapist.

The psychotherapeutic approach is not without its critics. As mentioned earlier, many have cited the high cost and low success rate of the process. In addition, there are critics of the process itself. For example, Miller (1983) has suggested that the process of denial, said to be characteristic of alcoholics in particular, is instead a product of the initial confrontational approach taken by many psychotherapists. He has shown that an alternative approach may induce the client to tell the therapist about his or her drug use in a straightforward manner. Thus, the common reactions of people undergoing psychotherapy for drug problems may be just as much a product of the therapist's approach as a characteristic of the disorder.

As is the case with other problems, success in psychotherapy is dependent on the actual therapist. If that individual has the ability to be accepting and to develop a strong relationship then the chances of success are relatively high. A psychotherapist without these characteristics is considerably less likely to be successful, no matter what his or her theoretical perspective may be. Unfortunately, these characteristics are not obvious to the patient, at least until they are fairly well into the psychotherapeutic process.

For further information on this approach see Levin (1987).

SOCIAL APPROACHES

From the discussion in Chapter Four it is clear that social factors play a very important role in the development of drug problems. Drug use always occurs in some social context and this context can influence the frequency and amount of drug use. The social factors may relate to both the person's upbringing or the immediate social environment in which drug use occurs. Social factors may also exert an indirect effect. If an individual has difficulty in forming normal social relationships, then they may use drugs as a means of facilitating social interaction or as an alternative source of pleasure in response to the effects of a relatively unhappy environment.

Given all these possible influences, it seems essential to consider an individual's social environment when attempting to deal with a drug problem. Certain approaches are based on the premise that social influences are most important and that any therapy should be designed to alter the individual's social conditions. This may range from modification of current living conditions to attempts at completely changing the way in which the individual interacts with others (Beigel and Ghertner, 1977).

The simplest approach relies on the results of sociological surveys. These may show that people are more likely to have a certain drug problem if they are poor, unemployed, live in certain areas (possibly urban slums), or associate with other drug users, for example. If this is the case then one could try to eliminate, or at least reduce that problem by changing those social conditions. A person may be given job training, be provided with adequate food and shelter, or perhaps given the opportunity to move away from their current living situation and to meet new people. At this point it is up to the individual to use these opportunities rather than return to their old environment and old behavior patterns (although other therapeutic approaches may be employed at this stage).

It should be recognized that this is not a panacea. Changing social conditions does not alter physical dependence, for example. It also fails to address the problem of drug use directly. In this sense it resembles some ineffective psychotherapeutic approaches. Rather than the underlying causes being psychological, however, they are social. Unless other treatment methods are employed, the success rate with this approach is likely to be very low.

There are several types of situations where these methods may be of value. One is where drug use is relatively recent and has been strongly influenced by the social environment. Removal of a person from such an environment may lessen the chances of a major drug problem developing. Secondly, changing the social environment may be particularly useful where drug use has diminished to zero or a nonproblem level, and where the aim is to prevent return to former levels.

Other approaches are concerned more with the person's normal social functioning. One common premise is that many people who develop drug problems have inadequate social relationships and this has played a causative role in the development of their drug problem. Drugs are sometimes seen as a substitute for normal social relationships, particularly the more intense ones. It is suggested that if a person can learn to develop such relationships more easily, then drug use should diminish.

Approaches which share this premise vary considerably. Some use traditional psychotherapeutic methods, but with groups of drug users. Sessions are conducted on a weekly basis, sometimes more frequently. Others are organized on a self-help basis. Alcoholics Anonymous and related groups fall into this category. Almost total involvement is required by the therapeutic communities. Members are physically removed from normal society and immersed in the culture of the community. Each of these will be discussed in turn.

Group Psychotherapy

Group psychotherapy can take several forms (see Levine and Gallogly, 1985, for a detailed exposition). In some cases it is an extension of individual psychotherapy. The patients are carefully selected so as to ensure that they will be responsive to the type of approach taken, and the therapist is highly trained in psychoanalysis or some other psychotherapeutic approach. The group, in addition to enabling the therapist to deal with more than one patient at a time, allows people to share experiences. Certain techniques, not usually used on an individual basis, may also be employed in groups. One such technique is psychodrama. A patient may, for example, role-play prior experiences with other group members.

Groups may be less structured with a leader who is not specifically trained in a particular psychotherapeutic approach. The person may be a counsellor, social worker, psychologist, or other related professional who has had some training in group techniques. Here the role of shared experience, group pressure, and the development of appropriate social interaction are likely to be emphasized more strongly over individual analysis. The success of such groups is hard to judge in that there is little objective evidence. However, it is likely to depend critically on both the leader's skills and the composition of the group. When group "dynamics" are good, opportunities to bring about changes in behavior are likely to be improved considerably.

Alcoholics Anonymous

A.A. was founded in the U.S. in the 1930s. Since then it has expanded to a large worldwide organization. Its members consist of recovering and recovered alcoholics. Indeed, the single qualification for membership is a desire to give up drinking. In addition to the original organization there are now groups for family members of alcoholics and for users of other drugs (for example Narcotics Anonymous). More recently, a number of therapeutic programs have adopted the 'twelve-step' philosophy of A.A. Only A.A. itself will be discussed here, but many of the comments apply to other organizations which have a similar approach.

Most of the ideas that guide A.A. come from its original founders. They, in turn, were heavily influenced by the religious movement known as the Oxford Groups, but also, indirectly, by the psychoanalyst Carl Jung. Ideas on the nature of alcoholism passed on to one of Jung's patients eventually became incorporated into the A.A. philosophy.

A.A. is the sole mode of treatment for many people and is extensively used by many professionals, particularly those who are medically trained. Opinions of its worth vary considerably. There are those who think it the most important element in the recovery of an alcoholic and those who consider it a quasireligious sect with no clear theoretical foundation. The evidence on its effectiveness will be discussed below.

A.A. groups are self-help organizations. They do not employ professionals and there is no clear structure to the group. However, those further down the path to recovery are likely to act in something of a leadership role. The main guides to the activities of the group are the Twelve Steps (a series of steps to be taken in recovery from alcoholism) and the Twelve Traditions (guidelines on the organization of groups and the behavior of individual members). There are also a number of official A.A. books which provide further information. (While these books can be consulted, one useful introduction is Milton, 1984).

On joining A.A. the new member is assigned a sponsor – someone to help them through the recovery process. By volunteering for such responsibility the sponsor believes he or she is helping in their own recovery. It is a central tenet of A.A. philosophy that helping other alcoholics is a way of helping oneself. The relationship between a member and a sponsor can be cancelled by either party at any time – it is not obligatory.

Other relationships are developed through the various A.A. meetings. Certain of these are open to members of the public, while others are closed. It is particularly in the private, small group meetings that the member has the opportunity to develop new interpersonal relationships. These relationships are said to form the basis for recovery. First, they allow normal social interaction in a free and open manner. This may be something which the alcoholic has not experienced for some time, particularly if he or she has been hiding drinking or its effects. Secondly, as is common with other 'social' approaches, social interaction and the relationships that result are considered something of a substitute for alcohol. Thus, if a person has adequate social relationships they should have less need for alcohol (or whatever drug is causing them a problem).

In addition to this social aspect, A.A. also emphasizes the role of spiritual experience. It is suggested that this side of life is almost nonexistent in alcoholics and that recovery requires that it be strengthened. The exact mode is not specified, although recognition of a higher being is usually a prerequisite.

One essential element in the A.A. process is the goal of complete abstinence. Controlled drinking is said to be impossible for an alcoholic. Instead, an alcoholic remains an alcoholic all through life and cannot afford to take even one drink. Doing so may lead to the "loss of control" which characterizes alcoholism. This suggests that there is a virtual biologic inevitability about alcoholism.

In addition to acknowledging that they cannot drink again, new A.A. members must recognize the causal role of alcohol in various personal problems. Essentially, the individual must admit that alcohol has had a devastating effect on their lives, causing them to do things which they would not have done otherwise. In particular, it has caused them to hurt those around them. Having gone through this process, sometimes known as surrender, the person can learn to change their lives with the help of A.A.

The effectiveness of the A.A. approach is very difficult to evaluate. One major problem in such evaluation has been the A.A. insistence on anonymity. A second is that a properly controlled trial is impossible to perform as membership is voluntary and no one can be turned away. Furthermore, it is clear from surveys that A.A. members are far from a random group in the population. For one thing, both lower and upper socioeconomic groups are underrepresented. Members tend to be middle class, socially conservative people who have not been adversely affected psychologically by alcohol. There is some indication that they may be more naturally sociable people whose social activities have been restricted by excessive alcohol use.

Estimates of A.A. success rates vary enormously. The organization claims extremely high rates, but others suggest that it may be considerably below fifty percent (Miller and Hester, 1980). If the latter is true then the A.A. approach may be of limited value, particularly when one considers the self-selected nature of the population. Nevertheless, it remains the sole treatment, or an important component of treatment, for many people.

Therapeutic Communities

The social model is most clearly expressed in the therapeutic community. These began in the 1960s and were largely designed for users of illicit drugs, particularly opiate users. Many share a similar philosophy to A.A. and one, Synanon, used A.A. as a model for many aspects of its program. The general philosophy behind therapeutic communities is described in Kennard (1985), while a range of aspects are considered in De Leon and Ziegenfuss (1986).

Most require that the individual live in the community, although they may be able to go outside for work. The individual's whole social life is centered on the community, which is composed of people in the process of reducing drug use, ex-addicts who serve as counsellors, and in some cases, professionals who guide the process. The structure of communities varies from authoritarian to democratic.

The main activities in the communities are discussions and meetings. Some may be concerned with the organization and day-to-day functioning of the community (particularly where democracy is practiced). However, many are similar to group psychotherapy meetings. The aim is for the individual to gain insight into their own problems and to set about solving them.

Such communities have received a great deal of criticism. Some argue that they substitute a strict social order for drug-taking. It is suggested that the person transfers dependence from the drug to the organization. Another criticism is that they fail to help people to function in the normal world. The community is a very artificial environment, and while a person may be able to exist without drug use in that environment, it is not necessarily the case that they will be able to do so when outside of it. Some have attempted to answer that criticism by incorporating a program of gradual separation from the community and adjustment to the outside world. A final criticism is that a very large proportion of graduates from the communities become professional "ex-addicts." That is, they spend the rest of their lives counseling, either in the community or in a similar facility. In this sense, the community is not helping people cope in their normal living and working environment, but only in an artificial one.

BEHAVIORAL APPROACHES

A relatively new and increasingly popular approach to treatment of drug problems is the behavioral one. The major premise is that drug use is a learned behavior. It is prompted by a variety of antecedent conditions, such as certain social situations, and maintained by a number of possible reinforcers, some of which were discussed in Chapter Three. These include the direct reinforcing effects of the drug, its effects on behavior and subjective experience, and escape from the individual's environment. Which of these are important depends on both the individual and the drug in question, and may not necessarily be the same for each instance of drug taking.

This type of analysis suggests that the potential for reduction of drug intake should be viewed optimistically. As drug use is simply another learned behavior, the various techniques which have been developed to modify other types of behavior can be brought to bear on this particular problem. These techniques have been used in areas such as treatment of psychiatric disorders, education and training of the mentally retarded, general psychological treatment, and so forth.

Given the behavioral analysis of drug-taking briefly described above, what can be done about it? One approach may be to isolate those antecedent conditions which seem to prompt drug-taking and teach the person to avoid them or learn to handle them without drugs (for example, learning to control anxiety without drugs). A second may be to try to alter the reinforcing properties of the drug in question. Alternatively, a therapist may try to arrange other reinforcers contingent on the person not taking the drug. If these are more powerful than the drug, then drug use should diminish.

While some behavioral treatments focus solely on one or other of these aspects, most would include several aspects and would tailor the treatment to the individual. For example, if a person's ability to cope with anxiety is inadequate and they resort to drug-taking in stressful situations, then it is probably of little use to try to alter the reinforcing properties of the drug they are using. This may have a temporary effect, but unless their lifestyle is altered or their coping skills improved, then the change is unlikely to be a permanent one. Each of the various aspects of treatment will be discussed individually below. (More detailed discussions of the behavioral approach can be found in the books edited by Miller, 1980, and Miller and Heather, 1986.)

Measurement

In any area of behavioral work precise measurement of the behavior is essential. This should occur prior to treatment (to obtain a 'baseline'), continue throughout the treatment process and, preferably, for a period following to ensure that the change is a permanent one. In the case of drug-taking, measurement is usually done by the person themselves, but additional evidence may be obtained from others (for example, spouses) in order to ensure accuracy.

Exactly what is measured depends on the drug in question. With an illicit drug it may be the frequency of use and the quantity used on each occasion (although this can only be estimated). Prescription drug use is relatively easy to measure because of the fixed doses in tablets or capsules. Drinking requires that both the size and the type of drink be recorded in order to calculate the amount of alcohol consumed. Smoking is perhaps the most difficult. Usually, it is simply the number of cigarettes smoked, but a more accurate determination would include the number of puffs, the duration of each puff, etc. Unfortunately, there is no easy way to estimate the amount of nicotine that reaches the lungs.

Another type of measurement may be used by the therapist. This involves direct estimation of the concentrations of a drug in the body. For example, a breathalyzer may be used to determine whether an individual has drunk in the last few hours. Portable urinalysis units are now available which allow on-site testing of the presence of drugs such as opiates. Smoking rate can be estimated by measuring carbon monoxide levels in expired air.

Measurement has several important functions. First, it allows ongoing assessment of the success of the treatment. The therapist can determine whether the particular treatment is working or whether it needs to be altered in some way. Only by measuring drug use prior to, and then during treatment is this possible. The second reason for measurement is to provide the client with feedback on his or her progress. This is particularly important if progress is slow but steady. The difference from the pretreatment rate of use may not be noticeable unless meticulous records are kept. Such feedback is often an important source of reinforcement for people trying to reduce drug intake.

The third reason for precise measurement is to permit a functional analysis. To do this, the client needs to keep records not only of how much of the drug was used, but the time of each use, the situation they were in at the time (for example at work, with certain friends), perhaps how they felt before using the drug, and then the changes they noticed after taking the drug (felt more relaxed, had vivid hallucinations, etc.). The most important time to do this is prior to treatment. It allows the therapist to determine the common antecedents and consequences of drug use for that individual. The program can then be tailored to that individual's needs. For example, if social situations such as parties are a common antecedent, then the person may be taught general social skills to help them relax in such situations, and specific skills for refusing drugs offered to them. If alleviation of fatigue is a common consequence of drug use then the therapist may devise ways of altering their lifestyle so as to minimize such fatigue (for instance, improving sleeping habits). Such detailed measurement permits a more carefully designed treatment plan, and, for this reason, may be worth the effort involved.

Negating the Reinforcing Effects of Drugs

One approach to reducing drug intake is to minimize the direct reinforcing effects of the drug. This may be done by using an antagonist, as described earlier, but this works only as long as the antagonist is taken. It would be much more useful to be able to produce a permanent change in the reinforcing properties of the drug. This is done essentially by associating the drug with an unpleasant experience.

In a more primitive form this method dates back a very long time, certainly before the development of modern behavioral techniques. One old method of dealing with children caught stealing alcohol was to force them to drink enough to make them very sick. The association of illness with alcohol had the effect of making the taste and smell of alcohol (or at least that particular form of it) quite aversive. Whether this lasted through their adult lives has not been documented.

This precise method is not used in treating alcohol abusers, in that the amounts they could drink before becoming ill could be highly dangerous. However, it does have a modern parallel in the reduction of cigarette smoking. The technique known as 'rapid smoking' requires that in one or more sessions the person smokes at a high puff rate until they feel ill. The unpleasant effects of nicotine become prominent once the person goes beyond their tolerance level. The feeling is something like that experienced when a novice inhales tobacco smoke for the first time. The association between the smoke and illness should make the smoke less reinforcing following the rapid smoking session.

Controlled trials have shown that rapid smoking is one of the more effective techniques for reducing smoking (Danaher, 1977). Considering its simplicity, the figures are quite impressive. Unfortunately, there are certain associated dangers. In particular, high nicotine levels can cause problems in people who have heart ailments. One approach has simply been to use the technique only with younger people who have no major health problems. A second has been to modify it to reduce the amount which is smoked, but to get the person to concentrate on the effects the smoking is having (increased heart rate, etc.). This has also been found to be effective when used properly.

Other methods have employed artificially-induced illness. Mostly used to reduce alcohol intake, they require the person to take an emetic immediately prior to drinking. The result is severe and unpleasant vomiting associated with drinking. Despite the fact that the person knows that the vomiting was induced by the emetic, an aversion to alcohol develops. One problem with this is that people have to be highly motivated. On the average, a person might have to undergo approximately five sessions. The whole procedure then, can be somewhat unpleasant. Nevertheless, there is evidence that it can be effective. Follow-up results indicate a reasonably high success rate amongst people with severe alcohol dependence (Miller and Hester, 1980; Wilson, 1987). The other means of associating illness with alcohol has been described above — through use of the drug disulfiram.

A somewhat different aversion method involves pairing electric shock with drug intake. Again, this has been done mostly with alcohol. There are a number of variants of this basic procedure. In some cases shock is simply given whenever a person sips a drink (they are instructed to do so in order that they actually receive some shocks), and in others only when they consume excessively. For example, shock may occur when a certain blood alcohol concentration is reached, or if drinks are gulped rather than sipped. In these cases the procedures more closely resemble skills training than aversion therapy in altering the reinforcing effects of alcohol. Initial research had suggested that the treatment was quite promising, with very high success rates. However, more recent research with longer-term follow-up indicates that any effects are relatively short-lived. While it may contribute as part of a treatment package, it is of relatively little value when used alone (Miller and Hester, 1980).

A final technique avoids problems of ethics and compliance. Instead of an aversive event being paired with actual drinking, the patient imagines himself or herself drinking and then the aversive event occurring. In order to do this properly, the patient must first learn to produce vivid images, both of himself drinking and of the unpleasant experience. This is done with the help of the therapist. Over the course of a few sessions the patient then links the two together on a number of occasions. For example, the person may imagine that he or she vomits after drinking in a public place. The vomiting is imagined in a 'larger-than-life' fashion to make the experience as unpleasant as possible. While some success has been reported with this technique, it is not as high as with real emesis. However, it may be of use in certain cases where normal aversive techniques are impossible.

Reinforcing Drug-Free Periods

While the methods just described seek to make the drug a less powerful reinforcer, others have endeavored to make nondrug use more reinforcing. It is argued that drugs are often a major source of reinforcement for users. This is most likely the case if the person has relatively few sources of reinforcement in their lives. One way to counteract the drug is to provide additional reinforcement for not using drugs.

This type of procedure has been used in a variety of settings. Most of the work to date has been in the form of demonstration rather than long-term programs. Nevertheless, the degree of success is quite striking. Drug users of all kinds, from skid-row alcoholics to heroin users are able to modify their drug use when sufficient reinforcement is given for doing so. For example, work with people being treated for alcohol dependence in hospital settings has shown that they will reduce their drinking if this results in access to a preferred hospital environment, a weekend pass from the hospital, or money (see for example Cohen, Liebson and Faillance, 1972). Like the research described in Chapter Three, this shows that alcoholic drinking is not "out of control" or unresponsive to other events in the environment.

A number of studies have been conducted in methadone clinics. Clients who are on methadone maintenance programs sometimes continue use of heroin, albeit at a relatively low rate. In order to reduce this, extra doses of methadone have been made contingent on a urinalysis which revealed no heroin, morphine, or codeine. The person is given their normal methadone dose irrespective of the urinalysis, but can also obtain an additional amount if the urinalysis is negative. When this program was put into practice the frequency of use of other opiates declined substantially. Other drug-taking behavior has also been modified in this manner. For example, use of benzodiazepines by clients in methadone maintenance programs was diminished when extra methadone was contingent on negative urinalysis for those drugs. (See Stitzer, Bigelow and Liebson, 1979 for a review of these studies.)

Many therapists employ these sorts of techniques in trying to reduce other problem drug use. For example, at the beginning of a program a client may be asked to nominate things that they like to do, but do not normally allow themselves. This may be dinner at an expensive restaurant, a night at the theatre or a short holiday, for example. Then, a plan is decided upon so that when certain goals are reached the person can allow themselves the extra privilege. Alternatively, they may be asked to deposit a sum of money in a special bank account. If they successfully complete the program they can spend the money however they want. Otherwise, it is disposed of, perhaps through donation to a least-favored political party.

This type of approach is very promising. For one thing, it is relatively simple to implement as long as one has a reliable measure of drug use. Secondly, there is convincing evidence of its success in a range of drug users. Most importantly, even those drug users considered to have the most serious problems can be influenced by these programs.

Skills Training

Another important aspect of the behavioral approach involves the teaching of skills which will help improve the person's chances of reducing drug intake. Some of these are directly concerned with the actual drug-taking behavior while others involve more general behavioral skills. The latter are taught particularly where specific inadequacies have been identified and need correcting. For example, an individual's poor social skills may be suspected of exacerbating their drug use problem.

The skills directly concerned with drug use are of three main kinds. One is self-monitoring. The person is taught to accurately monitor their drug consumption. For example, early studies showed that people could be taught to discriminate their blood alcohol level with reasonable accuracy (Caddy and Lovibond, 1976). They could then know when they had reached a level which was not to be exceeded and at which they should stop drinking. While people are able to do this, it may be more efficient to simply give them information on the blood alcohol levels produced by different drinks and rates of consumption. With some drugs the manner of use also has to be monitored. For example, smokers need to be informed of the effects of inhaling more deeply. Otherwise they may be inadvertently increasing intake when apparently smoking the same number or even fewer cigarettes.

Once a person is able to monitor their drug use accurately they can then be taught to set limits for it. This is usually part of a gradual process of reduction whereby weekly and even daily targets are set. These may be done in consultation with the therapist, but the individual needs to understand how the limits are determined. This is particularly important in the case of alcohol, where drinks vary in alcohol content, making determination of a limit more complex than simply specifying a number.

Finally, the person may be taught techniques which may help them reduce their intake. For example, heavy alcohol users tend to gulp rather than sip drinks, particularly the early drinks in a bout. Some success has been achieved in teaching them to sip and to space their drinks as a means of moderating consumption. One extreme method has been to get people to drink and to give them electric shocks whenever they drink in an inappropriate manner. In most cases, however, simple instruction and practice is all that is used (see for example, Sobell and Sobell, 1973). Another example is the reduction in cigarette smoke intake through alteration in the topography of smoking behavior, described previously.

A further group of skills helps people handle high risk situations. One example is assertiveness training. Some people have difficulty in refusing drugs which are offered to them, not only because of the attractiveness of the drug, but also because of a desire not to say "no." To counteract this, people may be taught general assertiveness, but also drug refusal skills. Methods for handling specific situations may be devised together with the therapist, practiced, and then used in actual situations the person encounters — for example, refusing an alcoholic drink at a party and asking for a nonalcoholic one instead (Marlatt, 1985).

A second example is relaxation training. If an individual seems to use drugs in response to stressful situations, then it may be appropriate to devise methods for the person to reduce this stress. Ideally, their life should be rearranged to remove as much stress as possible. However, they may also be taught methods for handling the stress when it occurs. For example, they may learn to relax through meditation, yoga, or deep muscle relaxation. While not appropriate for every individual, these methods may be particularly useful in certain cases.

CONCLUSIONS: EFFECTIVE TREATMENT DELIVERY

Quite clearly, there are a variety of ways of dealing with drug problems. The ones described here represent 'mainstream' approaches. There are those who believe that the real key is religion or some kind of 'spiritual awakening,' vitamins, herbal cures, and so forth. They may well be right, but their methods are not well-documented and in most cases there has been no systematic attempt at evaluation.

Given the number of people involved in treatment, particularly of alcohol problems, it is important to ensure that the methods chosen are appropriate and that they work (or at least have a good chance of success). Both choice and success of treatment will be considered below, together with a discussion of relapse, the major problem in drug treatment.

Choice of Treatment

The determination of treatment approach is placed largely in the hands of the individual or organization delivering it. If a medical practitioner is approached, for example, then a medically-oriented approach is likely to be adopted. A psychiatrist may be more likely to use psychotherapeutic methods, while behavioral approaches have been used mainly by psychologists (although they are becoming more widely used by other professionals).

Given the diversity of treatment approaches, how does one choose an optimal strategy for each individual drug user? Naturally, the proponents of many of the approaches would suggest that their methods could be adopted for virtually any individual. However, others involved in treatment have taken a less dogmatic position. They believe that some benefit can be obtained from all, or at least a large number of the various treatment methods described above.

From this view, what is important is that the treatment should be tailored to the individual in question. For example, it was noted in Chapter Three that the frequency of psychiatric disorders such as anxiety and depression was higher than normal amongst people with drug abuse problems. It was also suggested that these may be important etiological factors, in that they frequently existed prior to the onset of drug abuse. Clearly, if such problems are not resolved then the drug abuse may simply recur. Appropriate treatment for such people should then include therapy directed toward alleviating their anxiety or depression. There are many other ways in which client and treatment can be "matched." Unfortunately, there is relatively little study of how this is best done to date (Finney and Moos, 1986).

In the course of therapy an individual may experience a variety of treatment methods. These may be scheduled in such a way that different methods are used at different stages of the recovery process. For example, initial treatment may be concerned with management of withdrawal. Once the worst symptoms have passed, behavioral approaches may be used to help understand and deal with the precipitants of drug use, and psychotherapy aimed at eliminating a psychiatric problem may be commenced. Help may be given to improve the individual's social conditions and he or she may join a self-help group.

The danger of such an eclectic approach is that the person could receive too much information from too many sources. Some of it may even be contradictory. Accordingly, there is often a single therapist (for instance, a drug counselor) who guides the patient through the process, providing the necessary continuity. This type of approach is sometimes known as *multimodal therapy.*

One recent move has been toward simpler forms of therapy. Traditionally, drug treatment has been quite intensive, frequently involving weeks of inpatient care before later follow-up treatment. The expense involved, and the relatively small numbers of people who can be treated, have led to a search for alternatives. In some studies intensive treatment with a therapist has been compared with self-help using therapist-designed manuals. Interestingly, the manuals often turn out to be just as good, and sometimes better (Miller and Taylor, 1980). Naturally, such an approach would not be adopted with someone who had strong physical dependence or health problems resulting from drug use. Nevertheless, it seems that the success of treatment is not necessarily related to the time and effort invested in it.

Treatment Success

Whichever approach is used, the chances of long-term success after treatment for drug problems are not very high. Interestingly, the pattern is much the same whether the drug is heroin, alcohol, or nicotine. With most programs a large proportion of people complete treatment successfully: at the end, their drug use declines to the target level. Unfortunately, however, the proportion whose drug use is still at an acceptable level declines with time from the end of treatment (Hunt, Barnett, and Branch, 1971). While seventy percent may have completed treatment successfully, within six months the number still remaining at the acceptable level may have declined to thirty-five percent and at twelve months it may only be twenty-five percent. This proportion tends to level off, so that most of those successful at twelve months could be counted as long-term successes.

While some treatment programs have better outcomes than others, there is always a limited success rate if people are coming from the general population. Where patients are selected in some way, then greater success may be achieved. For example, people with stable employment and social relationships have a much greater chance of success than those who have lost their jobs, families, and friends. Programs which deal mainly with the former group may report greater success than those concerned mainly with the latter.

Particular programs may also appear to have better-than-average results because only highly motivated individuals are willing to stay in the program, and such people have a greater chance of success. This may be because of demands placed on participants. For example, people in a therapeutic community may be required to join in rigorous sessions of self-examination for a considerable period of time each day. Those few people who are willing to participate over a period of weeks or months may be highly likely to cease drug use. The ones who dropped out may have been less likely to succeed in any program.

Because of these factors it is essential to be careful in evaluating the success of any program. Whether trying to protect their jobs, enhance the profitability of their organization or attract funds, people involved in treatment and rehabilitation frequently have a vested interest in making their figures as attractive as possible. However, proper evaluation is a very difficult process and often requires carefully designed studies with long-term follow-up. Unfortunately, there are very few of these (see Moos and Finney, 1983; Nathan and Skinstad, 1987, for reviews).

Relapse Prevention

It is clear from the figures presented above that the major problem in treatment of drug abuse is preventing relapse once the individual has ceased using the drug for a period of time. While current treatment approaches are not perfect, the best of them have considerable success in decreasing drug use over a short term. What is needed is a means of improving the longer term success.

Some means of doing this have already been mentioned. One is methadone maintenance for opiate users. By arranging a relatively convenient supply of opiate drug it is hoped that the person will not return to illicit sources. Furthermore, when high doses of methadone are used, any other opiate is likely to have a relatively small effect. A second approach adopted with opiate users is naltrexone therapy, also described earlier. It is appropriate only in people who have not used opiates for a period of time, but may be useful in preventing later relapse to opiate use.

Inevitably, however, there are problems associated with these types of therapeutic approaches. Drugs such as methadone have adverse effects that the person has to live with (for example, constipation, impaired sexual functioning, etc.). It may also be argued that these approaches simply postpone the inevitable — sooner or later the person has to try to control their drug use without the aid of methadone, naltrexone or whatever the aid may be.

One alternative is to try to specifically design therapy to teach people to avoid relapses and to cope with relapse if it occurs. The most extensive work in this area has been done by Marlatt and his colleagues (Marlatt and Gordon, 1985). They have developed a model of relapse and a therapeutic approach to relapse prevention based on research with a wide variety of drug users.

According to their model, most relapses occur in a limited number of high risk situations. These can be categorized broadly into three types. One is associated with the pressure of interpersonal conflict (for example, an argument with one's spouse). A second involves social pressure to use the drug, either direct or indirect. (The latter may simply be the presence of other people using it.) In the third type of situation the person experiences a negative emotional state such as depression and this prompts relapse.

One of the main determinants of whether an individual copes with a high risk situation is their expectancy of success. People who have high positive expectancies are much more likely to be successful than those who do not feel they are going to be able to cope. This expectancy is, in turn, influenced by the person's earlier experience. If, in the past, they have been able to handle high-risk situations without drugs, then they are likely to have strong expectancy of further success. Any failure will diminish this expectation.

In addition, any relapse may have several other effects. One is that it will decrease the individual's feelings of self-efficacy. The individual may believe him- or herself to be powerless, unable to control his or her own life. A related problem is that the individual may decide that he or she is fundamentally flawed in some way. For example, after several relapses the individual may decide simply that they have an 'alcoholic' personality. Because of this they believe themselves to have no power to control their urges. Another consequence of relapse is that the person may feel extremely guilty about what they have done. The unpleasantness of this guilt may lead them to drug use as a means of temporary escape.

The model leads naturally on to a therapeutic approach designed to minimize the chances of relapse and to control it once it has begun. The first stage is to identify high risk situations. This can be done in several ways, but the simplest is to use detailed self-monitoring as described above. However, in addition to the high-risk situation itself, it is also necessary that the person learn to recognize the warning signs leading to that high-risk situation. For example, a negative emotional state may be brought on by tiredness and overwork. Rather than deal with this situation (when it is probably too late), the person should learn to recognize when their work output is beginning to become excessive.

For each of these situations the person must decide to avoid the problems completely or learn to cope with them. Naturally, there are only some which can be avoided. It is not possible to go through life without having any negative emotional feelings, for example. However, other situations can be avoided and this may be adopted as the safest strategy. For each situation to be confronted, the person needs to learn specific coping skills to be used in the absence of drug use. It is the therapist's job to design the skills in a way in which the person can learn them.

The client should then practice these skills in actual situations. Ideally, one would start with those high-risk situations which are easiest to cope with. That way the person can get practice when the chances of failure are lowest. As the person gets more and more practice their expectancy of a positive outcome increases. This, in turn, will further improve their chances of success.

If a slip occurs then it is essential that it be contained. In fact, people may be told that a slip is quite likely. Instead of giving up on the idea of controlling his or her drug use after such an event, the person should endeavour to learn from the mistake. This may be done in consultation with the therapist. In some cases the therapist may actually get the client to practice relapse in a controlled setting. That way people can see that they are able to stop after a single drink, cigarette, pill, or injection.

Other aspects of this therapy include education to inform clients of long-term adverse effects of drugs. This, it is hoped, may counteract some of the short-term pleasant effects they produce. In addition, the person may be given more general skills training or helped to alter various 'unhealthy' aspects of their lifestyle.

Marlatt's approach to relapse is not unique, but it illustrates the way in which therapy may be oriented more toward relapse prevention than to short-term reduction of drug use. It is likely that this orientation will become more common in the future. To hasten this process, research needs to progress in a number of directions. Two research samples will be briefly considered here.

The first is further investigation of the phenomenon of conditioned withdrawal described in Chapter Three. Research in this area suggests that the high-risk situations described above may actually induce physiological and subjective effects which resemble certain aspects of the withdrawal syndrome. This occurs because the person has previously used drugs to cope with such situations. The resulting discomfort may, in turn, lead the person to drug use in an effort to alleviate the symptoms. What is needed is a means of reducing or eliminating this conditioned withdrawal reaction.

A second productive line of investigation may be to look more closely at the natural history of drug abuse, discussed in Chapter Four. It is particularly important to note that most people cease drug use without help, despite the obvious difficulties. While they frequently relapse, most will eventually be successful. It may be possible to isolate some of the critical factors determining success and failure from some of those natural experiments.

PREVENTION

In the best of all possible worlds the problems being discussed here would simply not arise. Instead of allowing people to develop patterns of excessive drug use, preventative measures would ensure that everyone used drugs in moderation. This would obviate the need for people to suffer the various adverse effects described earlier. As long as one does not believe that people are born alcoholics or heroin addicts (and there is no evidence to support this for any type of drug problem) then prevention is a very attractive possibility.

Preventive measures can also be designed to reach the whole population. At best, treatment and rehabilitation services help a small proportion of those with drug abuse problems. It is only through prevention, then, that it is possible to produce a major change in drug abuse patterns in society.

Despite this potential, the history of prevention programs does not give great cause for optimism. There are few measures which have had a proven effect, even a very small one. Most measures have been loudly praised by their supporters, but little has been done to evaluate whether they have been successful or not. In other cases the evaluation has been poor, or, even worse, biased.

There are two main types of preventive measures. One is to use the education system to change the behavior of younger people before their patterns of drug use have been established. If, as research suggests, drug problems tend to develop in late teenage years or early twenties, then it is appropriate to try a major preventative effort before that age. The second means is through public health measures. These are directed at the general population rather than at a specific age group.

Education

A variety of approaches to drug education have been, and still are used. One is to provide students with information about drugs. In most cases this comprises factual information about the biological actions of the individual drugs — how they affect the brain and, as a result, how we feel and behave and about their adverse effects. Some programs have emphasized this last aspect, using more of a 'scare tactics' approach rather than an informational one. At the opposite extreme are programs which discuss health and the variety of factors which in turn affect it, but direct little attention specifically to drugs.

The aim of informational programs is to change students' attitudes about drugs and to give them a rational basis on which to make further decisions. Unfortunately, there is no clear evidence that these programs work. Where they have been evaluated, the results have shown a worse result (in other words, more drug use as a result of drug education), no change, or a slight improvement. Assessment also suggests that a key assumption of this approach — if one changes attitudes about drugs then behavior will follow — may be incorrect. The programs may alter attitudes about drugs, but appear to have little effect on actual patterns of drug use (Tobler, 1986; Bangert-Drowns, 1988).

A second type of program aims to increase students' self-esteem. This has its origin in research described in Chapter Three which suggests that, on average, people with drug abuse problems have lower self-esteem than those without such problems. If self-esteem can be raised then there may be less drug abuse. The orientation in such programs is humanistic, and the activities consist mainly of small group discussions led by a teacher or other person with experience of group leadership. They attempt to help the students analyze and decide on their own attitudes and values. By promoting interaction and exchange of ideas it is hoped that all students will develop greater self-confidence and self-esteem. Again, there is little evidence that these programs are at all effective.

A third type of program concentrates on alternatives to drug use. The aim is to find activities which provide the person with similar experiences to those they might obtain by using drugs. For example, an individual who seeks relaxation and relief from anxiety may be given the opportunity to learn yoga or deep muscle relaxation techniques. Stimulation may be obtained from sports which provide a degree of excitement (for example, hang-gliding). "Inner knowledge" may be derived from meditation or religious pursuits. The list could be expanded to include a wide range of activities, depending on the imagination of the person directing the program.

Some success has been reported with such approaches (Tobler, 1986). Where the people learn specific skills there may be a reduction in later drug use. Some have suggested that each type of activity counteracts a specific type of drug problem. For example, excitement is sought by stimulant users and people likely to abuse these drugs need to seek an alternative form of excitement. Such assumptions must be strongly questioned. Certainly, they rest on an oversimplified notion of the effects produced by different drugs.

A different view is that these activities provide an alternative source of pleasure in people's lives. It was noted in Chapter Three that drug use declines when there are other reinforcers available. The 'alternatives training' approach may be one means of teaching people skills that provide them with a source of reinforcement on a relatively permanent basis. In the absence of such opportunities drugs may be a reasonable option.

The final approach is also based on the acquisition of skills, but one more specifically concerned with social interactions. Students are taught drug refusal skills, for example. This may involve discussion on pressures to use drugs and ways in which they can most effectively be thwarted. Students may actually practice the skills (for example, refusing an offer of an alcoholic drink at a party) in the teaching situation before using them in the outside world.

Other social skills may also be taught. Some may be related to refusal (for example supporting friends who do not wish to use a drug), while others may be of a more general nature aimed at improving social competence. Certain programs may also teach more general skills which help people to cope with situations in which they may feel like using drugs (such as coping with feelings of anxiety). In such cases the approach merges with alternatives training.

Evidence indicating reduced drug use as a result of education is strongest for this approach (Tobler, 1986). A number of studies have shown positive outcomes as a result of using skills teaching methods. Nevertheless, further research is necessary to ensure that the effects on drug use are enduring rather than transient.

While these four approaches have been presented separately, many programs combine several of these (Girdano and Dusek, 1980). For example, some information on the different types of drugs and their adverse effects may be given at the beginning of a program concerned mainly with teaching refusal and related skills. Whether there is an ideal combination or not is far from clear at present. However, it does seem that programs which incorporate some form of specific skills training (alternatives, refusal, etc.) may be the most effective.

Public Health

The second type of prevention uses a number of measures which were discussed in Chapter Four. These include controls on availability and price of drugs and educational campaigns through the mass media. While some of these methods have clear value (for example, manipulation of prices), the effect of others are not so clear (mass media campaigns). An ongoing example of efforts in this direction have been the various campaigns against cigarette smoking. While some may have had some success, rates of smoking are still very high.

The difficulties inherent in any major attempt to alter drug use are obvious (see, for example, Nathan, 1983). One such problem is the irrational nature of current drug laws. Drugs with major adverse effects are freely available and are often widely promoted through the most sophisticated advertising campaigns. Many medical practitioners liberally prescribe drugs which may induce physical dependence despite the fact that effective nonpharmacological means of treating problems of anxiety and insomnia are available. At the same time many drugs regarded as benign by users are banned, and strong penalties may be imposed for possession.

The double standard extends farther when world-wide trends are observed. The dominant Western pattern of drug use is being 'exported' around the world and local patterns of drug use obliterated. In particular, practices such as smoking and ingestion of marijuana and opium are being replaced by alcohol consumption. This is occurring even though the former practices are an integral part of the society while the latter may be barely known.

There are obviously good historical, political, and economic reasons for these apparently irrational policies. However, when governments attempt to preach about the evils of certain drugs, the message comes across as simple hypocrisy to many, and perhaps especially to those whom they most want to influence. At best one might argue that people's drug use is channelled to the legal drugs as a result of societal pressure. But, if these are no better than the illegal ones, is this of any value?

A second major problem is that drug use is not easily separable from other aspects of a person's life. The evidence clearly suggests that those who develop severe drug problems are not a random subset of people within a society. Instead, there is a preponderance of people with poor family backgrounds, limited social and educational opportunities, psychiatric problems, and so forth. The various theories attempting to provide a unified explanation for these predisposing factors were discussed in Chapters Three and Four.

If it is acknowledged that drugs are never going to go away no matter what legislation is enacted, what price controls imposed and so forth, and that education (as currently framed) can only have limited utility, then prevention must be oriented around those predisposing factors. If for example, it could be shown that use of drug x was highest amongst those who suffered boredom-induced stress in their work environments, then the appropriate way to alter such use would be by changing their work environments. It is possible to directly attack the drug use dealing with each affected person, but this seems to be grossly inefficient, particularly if the causes remain untouched.

In the end one comes around to the view that drug use is inherent in society as we know it and the type of drug use we observe around us is a reflection of these various societies. Ideally, it may be possible to produce a blueprint for a society in which the frequency of drug use was low and problems of abuse were either minimal or nonexistent. One difficulty is that we might not be accurate in making these predictions — the social sciences are not perfect. A second is that the change to such a society may mean sacrifices in other areas. For example, the rate of economic growth may be slower in a society concerned more with the welfare of its citizens, etc. While the choices may be difficult and changes hard to bring about, these options certainly provide the most realistic approaches to drug problems.

REFERENCES

BANGERT-DROWNS, R.L. (1988).   The effects of school-based substance abuse education—a metaanalysis. *Journal of Drug Education, 18,* 243–264.
BEIGEL, A. & GHERTNER, S. (1977).   Toward a social model: An assessment of social factors which influence problem drinking and its treatment. In B. Kissin & H. Begleiter (Eds.), *Treatment and rehabilitation of the chronic alcoholic.* (pp. 197–233). New York: Plenum Press.
BLANE, H.T. (1977).   Psychotherapeutic approach. In B. Kissin & H. Begleiter (Eds.), *Treatment and rehabilitation of the chronic alcoholic.* (pp. 105–160). New York: Plenum Press.
BYCK, R. (1974).   *Cocaine papers: Sigmund Freud.* New York: Stonehill.
CADDY, G.R. & LOVIBOND, S.D. (1976).   Self-regulation and discriminated aversive conditioning in the modification of alcoholics' drinking behavior. *Behavior Therapy, 7,* 223–230.
COHEN, M., LIEBSON, I., & FAILLANCE, L.A. (1972).   A technique for establishing controlled drinking in chronic alcoholics. *Diseases of the Nervous System, 33,* 46–49.
DANAHER, B.G. (1977).   Research on rapid smoking: Interim summary and recommendations. *Addictive Behaviors, 2,* 151–166.
DE LEON, G. & ZIEGENFUSS, J.T. (1986).   *Therapeutic communities for addiction: Readings in theory, research and practice.* Springfield, Illinois: Charles C. Thomas.
DOLE, V.P. (1971).   Methadone maintenance treatment for 25,000 heroin addicts. *Journal of the American Medical Association, 215,* 1131–1134.
Editorial and Commentaries (1987).   No 'Alcoholism' please, we're British. *British Journal of Addiction, 82,* 1059–1071.
FINNEY, J.W. & MOOS, R.H. (1986).   Matching patients with treatments: Conceptual and methodological issues. *Journal of Studies on Alcohol, 47,* 122–134.
FREDERIKSEN, L.W. (1979).   Controlled smoking. In N.W. Krasnegor (Ed.), *Behavioral analysis and treatment of substance abuse.* (pp. 128–139). Rockville, MD: National Institute on Drug Abuse.
GIRDANO, D.A. & DUSEK, D. (1980).   *Drug education* (3rd ed.). Reading, Mass.: Addison-Wesley.
GOODWIN, D.W. & ERICKSON, C.K. (1979).   *Alcoholism and affective disorders.* New York: Spectrum.
HEATHER, N. & ROBERTSON, I. (1981).   *Controlled drinking.* London: Methuen.
HUNT, W.A., BARNETT, L.W., & BRANCH, L.G. (1971).   Relapse rates in addiction programs. *Journal of Clinical Psychology, 27,* 455–456.
KENNARD, D. (1983).   *An introduction to therapeutic communities.* London: Routledge and Kegan Paul.
KNOTT, D.H., BEARD, J.D., & FINK, R.D. (1987).   Medical aspects of alcoholism. In W.M. Cox (Ed.), *Treatment and prevention of alcohol problems.* (pp. 57–72). Orlando: Academic Press.
LEVIN, J.D. (1987).   *Treatment of alcoholism and other addictions: A self-psychology approach.* Northvale, New Jersey: Jason Aronson.
LEVINE, B. & GALLOGLY, V. (1985).   *Group therapy with alcoholics: Outpatient and inpatient approaches.* California: Sage Publications.
MARLATT, G.A. (1985).   Situational determinants of relapse and skill-training interventions. In G.A. Marlatt & J.R. Gordon (Eds.), *Relapse prevention: Maintenance strategies in the treatment of addictive behaviors.* (pp. 71–127). New York: Guilford.
MARLATT, G.A. & GORDON, J.R. (Eds.) (1985).   *Relapse prevention: Maintenance strategies in the treatment of addictive behaviors.* New York: Guilford.

MENDELSON, J.H. & MELLO, N.K. (1979).   Diagnostic criteria for alcoholism and alcohol abuse. In J.H. Mendelson & N.K. Mello (Eds.), *The diagnosis and treatment of alcoholism.* (pp. 1-18). New York: McGraw-Hill.

MILLER, W.R. (Ed.) (1980).   *The addictive behaviors.* Oxford: Pergamon Press.

MILLER, W.R. (1983).   Motivational interviewing with problem drinkers. *Behavioral Psychotherapy, 11,* 147-172.

MILLER, W.R. & HEATHER, N. (Eds.) (1986).   *Treating addictive behaviors: Process of change.* New York: Plenum Press.

MILLER, W.R. & HESTER, R.K. (1980).   Treating the problem drinker: Modern approaches. In W.R. Miller (Ed.), *The addictive behaviors.* (pp. 11-141). New York: Pergamon Press.

MILLER, W.R., & HESTER, R.K. (1986).   Inpatient alcoholism treatment: Who benefits? *American Psychologist, 41,* 794-805.

MILLER, W.R. & TAYLOR, C.A. (1980).   Relative effectiveness of bibliotherapy, individual and group self-control training in the treatment of problem drinkers. *Addictive Behaviors, 51,* 13-24.

MILTON, M.A. (1984).   *The Alcoholics Anonymous experience: A close-up view for professionals.* New York: McGraw-Hill.

MOOS, R.H. & FINNEY, J.W. (1983).   "The expanding scope of alcoholism treatment evaluation." *American Psychologist, 38,* 1036-44.

MYERS, D.W. (1984).   *Establishing and building employee assistance programs.* Westport, Conn.: Greenwood Press.

NATHAN, P.E. (1983).   Failures in prevention: Why we can't prevent the devastating effect of alcoholism and drug abuse. *American Psychologist, 38,* 459-467.

NATHAN, P.E. & SKINSTAD, A.H. (1987).   Outcomes of treatment for alcohol problems: Current methods, problems and results. *Journal of Consulting and Clinical Psychology, 55,* 332-340.

O'FARRELL, T.J. (1987).   Marital and family therapy for alcohol problems. In W.M. Cox, (Ed.), *Treatment and prevention of alcohol problems: A resource manual.* (pp. 139-155). Orlando: Academic Press.

PATTISON, E.M. (1979).   The selection of treatment modalities for the alcoholic patient. In J.H. Mendelson & N.K. Mello (Eds.), *The diagnosis and treatment of alcoholism.* (pp. 125-227). New York: McGraw-Hill.

SCHNEIDER, N.G. & JARVIK, M.E. (1985).   Nicotine gum vs. placebo gum: Comparisons of withdrawal symptoms and success rates. In J. Grabowski & S.M. Hall (Eds.), *Pharmacological adjuncts in smoking cessation.* (pp. 83-101). Rockville, MD: National Institute on Drug Abuse.

SHAIN, M. & GROENEVELD, J. (1980).   *Employee assistance programs.* Lexington: D.C. Heath.

SIEGEL, S. (1986).   Alcohol and opiate dependence: Reevaluation of the Victorian perspective. In H.D. Cappell, F.B. Glaser, Y. Israel, H. Kalant, W. Schmidt, E.M. Sellers, & R.C. Smart (Eds.), *Research advances in alcohol and drug problems.* (Vol. 9, pp. 279-314). New York: Plenum Press.

SOBELL, L.C. & SOBELL, M.B. (1973).   A self-feedback technique to monitor drinking behavior in alcoholics. *Behavior Research and Therapy, 11,* 237-238.

SOBELL, L.C., SOBELL, M.B., & NIRENBERG, T.D. (1988).   Behavioral assessment and treatment planning with alcohol and drug abusers: A review with an emphasis on clinical application. *Clinical Psychology Review, 81,* 19-54.

STITZER, M.L., BIGELOW, G.E., & LIEBSON, I. (1979).   Reinforcement of drug abstinence: A behavioral approach to drug abuse treatment. In N.A. Krasnegor (Ed.), *Behavioral analysis and treatment of substance abuse.* (pp. 68-90). Rockville, MD: National Institute on Drug Abuse.

TOBLER, M.S. (1986).   Metaanalysis of 143 adolescent drug prevention programs: Quantitative outcome results of program participants compared to a control or comparison group. *Journal of Drug Issues, 16,* 537-567.

WILSON, G.T. (1987).   Chemical aversion conditioning as a treatment for alcoholism, a reanalysis. *Behavior Research and Therapy, 25,* 503-516.

Index